Minimum Wages in China

Li Shi · Carl Lin
Editors

Minimum Wages in China

Evolution, Legislation, and Effects

palgrave
macmillan

Editors
Li Shi
Zhejiang University
Zhejiang, China

Carl Lin
Bucknell University
Lewisburg, PA, USA

ISBN 978-981-15-2420-2 ISBN 978-981-15-2421-9 (eBook)
https://doi.org/10.1007/978-981-15-2421-9

This Palgrave Macmillan imprint is published by the registered company Springer Nature Singapore Pte Ltd.
The registered company address is: 152 Beach Road, #21-01/04 Gateway East, Singapore 189721, Singapore

Contents

List of Contributors

Quheng Deng Institute of Economics, Chinese Academy of Social Sciences, Beijing, China

Yang Du Center for Human Resources Research, Institute of Population and Labor Economics, Chinese Academy of Social Sciences, Beijing, China

Tony Fang Memorial University of Newfoundland, St. John's, NL, Canada

Tim Gindling University of Maryland, Baltimore County, Baltimore, MD, USA

Morley Gunderson Centre for Industrial Relations, University of Toronto, Toronto, Canada

Tobias Haepp Institute for Employment Research (IAB), Nuremberg, Germany

Peng Jia Institute of Population and Labor Economics, Chinese Academy of Social Sciences, Beijing, China

Ravi Kanbur Cornell University, Ithaca, NY, USA

Li Shi Zhejiang University, Zhejiang, China

Yanan Li Beijing Normal University, Beijing, China

Carl Lin Bucknell University, Lewisburg, PA, USA

Xinxin Ma University of Toyama, Toyama, Japan

Hainan Su China Association of Labour Science, Beijing, China

Wenkai Sun Renmin University of China, Beijing, China

Haiyuan Wan Beijing Normal University, Beijing, China

Xia Wang Chinese Academy of Labour and Social Security, Beijing, China

Xianghong Wang Renmin University of China, Beijing, China

Chunbing Xing Beijing Normal University, Beijing, China

Jianwei Xu Beijing Normal University, Beijing, China

Juan Yang Beijing Normal University, Beijing, China

Linxiang Ye Nanjing University of Finance and Economics, Nanjing, China

Myeong-Su Yun Inha University, Incheon, South Korea

Xiaoxi Zhang Renmin University of China, Beijing, China

List of Figures

List of Tables

CHAPTER 1

Minimum Wages in China: Overview and Key Findings

Li Shi and Carl Lin

1.1 Introduction

Since China began its reform and opening-up policies in 1978, the country has been in the midst of a transition from a planned economy to a market economy. As a result, the country faces economic and social problems that have become impediments to its long-term sustainable development. Moreover, social instability resulting from widening income inequality, corruption, and social exclusion has become a major concern for the Chinese government. To respond to these challenges, both the central and local governments are placing a new emphasis on inclusive growth by introducing a number of new policies and regulations. In particular, in recent years, the government has actively intervened in the labor market, including increasing job training opportunities for unskilled workers and migrant workers, more strictly

L. Shi
Zhejiang University, Zhejiang, China
e-mail: lishi9@zju.edu.cn

C. Lin (✉)
Bucknell University, Lewisburg, PA, USA
e-mail: carl.lin@bucknell.edu

L. Shi and C. Lin (eds.), *Minimum Wages in China*,
https://doi.org/10.1007/978-981-15-2421-9_1

implementing new labor contracts, ensuring job stability, and expanding the coverage of social insurance programs.

Raising the minimum wage was one of the Chinese government's most important labor market interventions. Since implementing the "Minimum Wage Regulations" in 2004, the nominal minimum wage has increased significantly, averaging growth of 11% per year nationally. The process is largely driven by political competition between local governments at the city and provincial levels in response to the central government's appeal to raise the wage share of national income, as outlined in the 12th Five-Year Plan.[1] The plan specifies that the mean minimum-to-average wage ratio should reach 0.4 by 2015. As of 2009, the ratio was 0.29.[2]

Because the Chinese political system is highly centralized and hierarchical, the determination of the minimum wage in China can be quite different from that of developed and other developing countries. Local governments are eager to win support from the central government in the form of infrastructure development, fiscal transfers, bank loans, and land use. In particular, the promotions of local officials at the provincial and city levels are determined by the central government.[3] Raising the minimum wage signals their determination to address issues such as income inequality that could otherwise threaten political stability.

In past decades, local governments kept minimum wages low because they worried that high wages would cause jobs to shift to districts with cheaper labor costs, exacerbating already high levels of unemployment. Once China's labor market began to boom, concerns over unemployment diminished, and local governments began substantially and consistently raising wages. Local governments calculated that if any disemployment effect occurred from wage increases, migrant workers would be the ones to lose their jobs. As migrant workers are not eligible for unemployment benefits, any increase in migrant worker unemployment would not drive up fiscal spending. Given this dynamic, the most significant wage hikes have been enacted by local governments in coastal cities, which host the most migrant workers.

Since then, the minimum wage policy has been regarded as the solution by the Chinese government and is extremely welcome among the public, not only to protect workers with a wage floor but also to increase the income of the poor and reduce inequality.[4] Nevertheless, very limited empirical research has studied the consequences of the minimum wage policy in China. This book seeks to answer the following questions:

1. What are the wage and employment effects of China's minimum wage?
2. What are the procedures for minimum wage setting at the city and provincial levels in China, and is there a "race to the top" in minimum wage standards among local governments?
3. What are the impacts of minimum wages on wage distribution, the gender wage gap, and income inequality?
4. What are the impacts of minimum wages on migrant workers in China?
5. Do minimum wages affect Chinese firms' investment in human and fixed capital and profits?

To better understand the important role that the minimum wage policy has played in the Chinese government, we briefly introduce its history and legislative background in the next section.

1.2 A Brief History of Minimum Wage Legislation in China

Prior to 1994, China had no minimum wage law, and the country merely acknowledged the 1928 "Minimum Wage Treaty" of the International Labour Organization (ILO) in 1984. In 1993, China issued the first national minimum wage regulations. In July of 1994, these regulations were written into China's new labor law.

The 1994 legislation required that all employers pay employees wages that were not lower than the local minimum wage. Furthermore, all provincial, autonomous region, and municipal governments were required to set the minimum wage according to six principles: the minimum living expenses of workers, the average number of dependents workers support, local average wages, the level of labor productivity, the level of local employment, and the level of economic development. These conditions provided considerable flexibility for provinces in setting minimum wages, with the economic development principle giving them the flexibility to limit the minimum wage to attract foreign investment (Frost 2004; Wang and Gunderson 2011). High minimum wages would mean higher operational costs, which could reduce China's attractiveness in the eyes of foreign investors in Chinese businesses.

In the early 2000s, sluggish growth in minimum wages and growing concerns for uninsured workers led the government to introduce new minimum wage regulations. The new law, announced in January 2004, extended coverage to employees in state-owned and private enterprises, self-employed businesses, and private nonenterprise (nonprofit) units.[5] In particular, the new law established two types of minimum wages: a monthly minimum wage applied to full-time workers and an hourly minimum wage applied to part-time employees.

Moreover, the minimum wage standards are set and adjusted jointly by the local government, trade union, and enterprise confederation of each province. The draft is then submitted to the Ministry of Labor and Social Security for review, and the ministry asks for opinions from the All-China Federation of Trade Unions (ACFTU) and the China Enterprise Confederation. The ACFTU, however, is a government body, which means that the onus of raising minimum wages is ultimately on the ministry itself.

According to the new regulation, local governments must renew their minimum wage standards at least once every two years, and penalties for violations quintupled—from a range of 100 to 500% of the owed wage. Moreover, employers cannot include extra allowances such as overtime pay or food and traveling subsidies as part of an employee's wage when calculating the minimum wage.

1.3 Major Findings

This book begins by introducing the evolution and effect assessment of China's minimum wage policy in Chapter 2, and then, Chapter 3 looks into the standards for and implications of the minimum wage policy. Chapters 4–14 provide research results from various aspects of the labor market: wages, employment, gender and income inequalities, firm investment and profits, compliance, and regional disparities. In particular, we pay special attention to the 168 million rural–urban migrant workers in China, focusing on the wage and employment impacts they experience as a result of minimum wage policies. Below is a summary of the major findings:

Finding 1: minimum wages helped increase wages but resulted in disemployment for young adults, women, and low-skilled workers

Chapter 4 uses nationally representative survey data from 2002 to 2009 and finds that minimum wage changes in China led to significant negative effects on employment in the eastern and central regions and caused disemployment for young adults and low-skilled workers, which are particularly at-risk groups—i.e., workers who, at the time of a minimum wage increase, are receiving a wage between the old and new minimum wages. On the other hand, minimum wages in the provinces with vigorous enforcement did increase wages while adversely affecting employment. This trade-off between a minimum wage increase and job protection has been extensively noted and commented upon in the literature.

Finding 2: higher minimum wages reduced the gender wage gap

Chapter 5 provides evidence that minimum wages do have an impact on gender wage differentials in urban China based on data from the China Household Income Project Surveys of 1995, 2002, and 2007. The results show that the gender wage gap is the largest in regions with high minimum wage levels and the smallest in regions with middle minimum wage levels.[6] Although the gender wage gap is not obvious at the extremely low-wage distribution, in wage distributions where the quantile is higher than the 6th, the gender wage gap tends to narrow with the rising of wage levels, showing that there is "sticky floor phenomenon"—which is a situation in which there is a wage gap between female workers and their male counterparts, even for jobs that require relatively few skills and little education. Furthermore, using wage decomposition techniques, the study shows that the gender differences in returns to endowments in the minimum wage and the Kaitz index[7] have a larger influence on the gender wage gap compared to the gender wage differences in endowments. Finally, the results show that, from a long-term perspective, the implementation of a minimum wage system contributes to narrowing the gender wage gap (Fig. 1.1). The fourth column in Fig. 1.1 shows that the number decreases from 87% in 1995 to 24% in 2002 and to −17% in 2007, meaning that minimum wages in China significantly help reduce the gender wage gap over time (a positive number means an increase in the gap, and a negative number means a reduction in the gap).

Finding 3: minimum wages had a small negative effect on employment and a positive effect on working hours for migrant workers

The minimum wage in China has received increased attention because of the growing income inequality and the vulnerable position of low-wage migrant workers who are flooding into cities. In China, most low-wage migrant workers are paid by the month, and minimum wage legislation

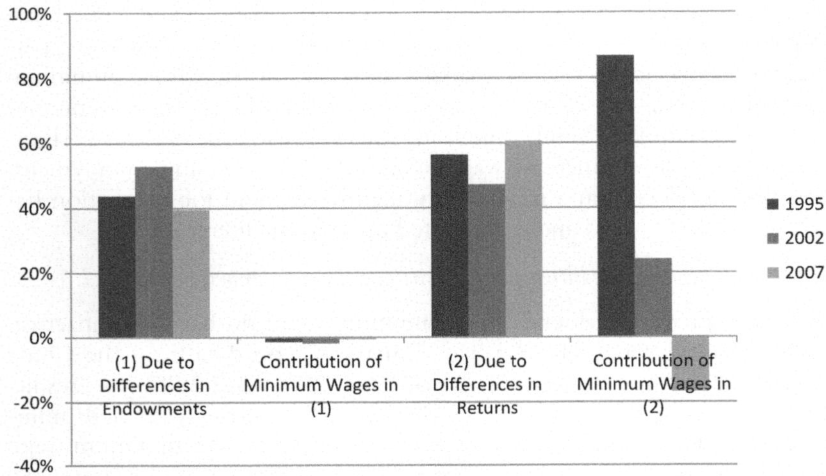

Fig. 1.1 Contribution of the minimum wage to reducing gender wage gaps in China. *Note* The gender wage gap (100%) is decomposed (1) due to differences in endowments and (2) due to differences in returns. The positive number indicates that the factor contributes positively to the gap and vice versa

does not specify the legal working hours. As such, employers may extend the employees' working hours to compensate for the increased costs. Chapter 6 used a large migrant household survey data set and municipal data to investigate the impact of increases in minimum wages on migrant workers' wages, employment, and working hours. The results indicate that the minimum wage has only small negative impacts on migrants' employment, with the largest negative effects impacting rural female workers and workers in East and Central China. The results, however, also indicate that employers increase the hours worked by migrant workers in each month to offset some of the cost increases of higher monthly minimum wages. As such, the hourly wages do not actually increase in response to monthly minimum wage increases. This adjustment may explain some of the lack of adverse employment effects that are commonly found in the minimum wage literature on China. By offsetting the costs of a higher minimum wage by increasing the number of working hours, employers do not see the need to lay off workers, which happens when such adjustments are not possible.

Finding 4: minimum wages helped reduce earnings inequality at the lower end of the earnings distribution

Chapter 7 uses a large set of panel data at the city level that contains relevant information on the minimum wage combined with a longitudinal household survey of 16 representative provinces to estimate the distributional effect of minimum wage changes in China over the period of 2004–2009. Compared with previous studies using provincial-level data and reporting mixed results, the study shows that minimum wage changes significantly help reduce the earnings gap at the bottom end of the earnings distribution. In a placebo test, minimum wage changes had an effect on the earnings gap at the upper end of the distribution. The analysis also suggests that a minimum wage reduces earnings inequality measured, for example, by the Gini index.

The findings are consistent with recent studies for other countries, reporting that the minimum wage plays an essential role in lowering earnings/wage inequality. Both the United States and Mexico, for example, have exhibited a declining minimum wage (both real and effective) and rising inequality, and empirical evidence shows that the declining minimum wage accounts for a substantial part of the growth in inequality in both countries over the past three decades (Lee 1999; Bosch and Manacorda 2010; Autor et al. 2014). In contrast, China has experienced a rapid increase in the minimum wage and rapidly increasing income and earnings inequalities in the past 10 years, which provides an opportunity to study the effect of the minimum wage on inequality in an environment that differs from that in prior research. Table 1.1 shows that minimum wage increases have beneficial effects on the earnings distribution by reducing earnings gaps, particularly at the bottom end of the earnings wage distribution, and both regionally relevant and general implications for the minimum wage literature. For example, the earnings inequality between the median and 10th percentile workers (p50-p10) grows by 0.058 log points from 2004 to 2009. By decomposing this gap, the study finds that labor market characteristics increase the gap by 0.150 log points, whereas the minimum wage significantly decreases the gap (−0.092 log points) during this period.

Finding 5: noncompliance of minimum wages increased, and local governments reacted to each other in the setting and enforcement of minimum wages

Chapter 9 uses survey data from 2007 and 2013 to examine the extent to which minimum wages are complied with in China. The results show

Table 1.1 Decomposition of earnings inequality and contributions of the minimum wage, 2004–2009

Earnings inequality measure	*Total change between 2004 and 2009*	*Due to*	
		(1)	*(2)*
		Changes in the minimum wage	*Changes in labor market characteristics*
p50-p10	.058***	−.092***	.150***
	(.007)	(.012)	(.013)
p50-p25	.031***	−.044***	.076***
	(.006)	(.010)	(.010)
p75-p50	.046***	.043	.003
	(.005)	(.032)	(.012)
p90-p50	.019***	−.003	.022
	(.006)	(.026)	(.025)
p90-p10	.077***	−.095***	.171***
	(.008)	(.033)	(.032)
Gini coefficient	.004***	−.050***	.055***
	(.002)	(.013)	(.012)
Variance of log earnings	.022***	−.069***	.091***
	(.002)	(.013)	(.013)

Note The table is drawn from Lin and Yun (2015). All the numbers are in log points. Bootstrapped standard errors with 100 repetitions are given in parentheses. Earnings gaps, Gini coefficients, and variances are calculated at the individual level

*** statistically significant at the 1% level

that 3.91% of employees in 2007 and 7.32% of employees in 2013 received less than the monthly minimum wage. Overall, there were more workers whose wages were below the monthly minimum wage in 2013 than in 2007. However, when considering weekly working hours and calculating how many workers earned below the hourly minimum wage, the proportion of workers was higher than the proportion earning below the monthly minimum wage (13.64% of employees in 2007 and 12.74% in 2013). The difference between the percent earning below the monthly minimum wage and the hourly minimum wage is explained by the fact that low-wage workers are required to work overtime hours with no additional pay.

On the other hand, the Chinese government has greatly expanded its minimum wage intervention in response to concerns about rising inequality. Chapter 13 shows that there is significant interjurisdictional competition regarding the level of the minimum wage and enforcement among local governments. Such competition could be wasteful and lead to a race to the bottom, undermining the government's objectives. The interactions identified in Chapter 13 thus suggest the need for policy coordination on labor regulation in China. The evidence on jurisdictional interdependence in minimum wage setting within a country also raises a further set of interesting research questions. The results show that Chinese local governments react to each other in setting minimum wages and in the enforcement of minimum wages.

Finding 6: minimum wages had a negative impact on firm profitability in the current year across the whole conditional distribution

Using the firm-level panel data sets and hand-collected data on county-level minimum wage, Chapter 10 estimates the effect of minimum wage on firm profitability. The estimation results suggest that the effect on firm profitability of minimum wages in the current year was negative across the whole conditional distribution of profitability and exhibited an inverted-U shape across conditional quantiles. The effect on the profitability of the lagged minimum wage was positive at the 5th, 10th, and 15th quantiles; negative at the 90th and 95th quantiles; and not significant at other quantiles. Turning to the overall effect on the profitability of the minimum wage, the study finds that the minimum wage exerted a significantly negative effect on profitability at the 5th quantile and quantiles higher than 40th, and the absolute value of the effect of minimum wage increased with these quantiles. For other quantiles, the overall effect of minimum wage on profitability was negligible.

Finding 7: minimum wages had negative effects on firms' human capital investment but no effects on fixed capital investment

Chapter 11 analyzes the impact of Chinese minimum wage regulations on the firm decision to invest in physical and human capital. The study exploited the geographic and intertemporal variations of county-level minimum wages in a panel data set of all state-owned and all above-scale nonstate-owned Chinese firms covering the introduction of the new Chinese minimum wage regulations in 2004. In basic regressions including all Chinese firms, the study finds significant negative effects of the minimum wage on human capital investment rates and no overall effects on fixed capital investment rates. When grouping firms by their ownership structure, these results hold for most firms. Foreign-owned firms are an exception to some extent because the likelihood that they invest in human capital has not decreased in response to the policy.

1.4 Conclusions

Since China enacted its first minimum wage law in 1994, the magnitude and frequency of changes in the minimum wage have been substantial, both over time and across jurisdictions. The growing importance of research on the impacts of the minimum wage and its controversial nature has sparked heated debate in China, highlighting the importance of rigorous research to inform evidence-based policymaking.

The minimum wage has been regarded as an important element of public policy in many countries around the world and in China in particular. Increasing the minimum wage is supposed to raise wages for millions of low-wage workers and therefore enhance their well-being. However, there is no consensus in the existing literature from industrialized countries regarding whether the minimum wage is an effective policy tool. Studying the effects of the minimum wage is even more complicated in developing countries such as China than in industrialized countries owing to the presence of large informal sectors in urban areas, large pools of surplus labor in rural areas, and difficulties in ensuring compliance with minimum wage legislation.

China is a large developing country transitioning to a market economy with an abundance of workers in low-paid occupations who are at risk of being affected by minimum wage changes. Although China's experience with minimum wages is new, our book provides both regionally relevant and general implications for other transitional/developing economies and the minimum wage literature. Most importantly, our findings show that when the minimum wage increases rapidly (11% growth rate per year after 2004 in China), the estimated effects are significant, and the impacts from the minimum wage policy may not be negligible. Our results from China's experience show that the rapidly increasing higher minimum wages have helped increase average wages and reduce the gender wage gap and income inequality. However, the fast-rising minimum wage has resulted in job losses for young adults, women, low-skilled workers, and migrant workers. Additionally, higher minimum wages have a negative impact on firm profitability and adverse effects on firm's human capital investment. In summary, the Chinese minimum wage policy has shown both positive and negative impacts on the affected workers, and our book highlights the importance of rigorous research to inform evidence-based policymaking and provides lessons for other transitional and developing economies.

Notes

1. In the last two decades, the Chinese central government has gradually changed its development goals from more emphasis on economic growth to social development. The government is also less concerned with production incentives and more focused on equitable distribution. This change implies that wage growth and wage equality could become new indicators for the central government to evaluate and monitor the performance of local economic and social developments and the efforts of local officials.
2. According to a nationally representative Urban Household Survey (2004–2009) from the National Bureau of Statistics of China, the mean minimum-to-average wage ratio in China is 0.29.
3. Given the political system in China, the local governments have strong incentives to meet the desires of the central government since the promotion of local officials is decided by the central government (Chen et al. 2005). The relevant studies indicate that the political status of a province is positively correlated with the provincial economic ranking in China (Maskin et al. 2000) when the central government sets up economic growth as a priority. Li and Zhou (2005) present evidence on the link between the political turnover of top provincial leaders and provincial economic performance, which is interpreted as the central government's personnel control over local officials.
4. The political competition among local governments would speed up the rise of the minimum wage. As a matter of fact, this would presumably hasten labor migration to coastal areas, leading to greater imbalances. Moreover, this competition process is hypothesized to be harmful to the economic growth in the western region and leads to widening regional economic disparity in China.
5. Private nonenterprise units are equivalent to NGOs as defined by the Chinese government.
6. According to Table 1 in Ma and Li (2014), middle and high minimum wage levels are 165–175 RMB and over 175 RMB in 1995, 285–330 RMB and over 330 RMB in 2002 and 510–615 RMB and over 615 RMB in 2007.
7. The Kaitz index is the ratio of the minimum wage to the average wage.

References

Autor DH, Manning A, Smith CL (2014). The contribution of the minimum wage to U.S. Wage inequality over three decades: A reassessment, National Bureau of Economic Research Working Paper Series No. 16533.

Bosch M, Manacorda M (2010). Minimum wages and earnings inequality in urban Mexico. *American Economic Journal: Applied Economics* 2, 128–149.

Chen Y, Li H, Zhou L-A (2005). Relative performance evaluation and the turnover of provincial leaders in China. *Economics Letters* 88, 421–425.

Frost S (2004). Chinese outward direct investment in Southeast Asia: How big are the flows and what does it mean for the Region? *The Pacific Review* 17(3), 323–340.

Lee DS (1999). Wage inequality in the United States during the 1980s: Rising dispersion or falling minimum wage? *The Quarterly Journal of Economics* 114, 977–1023.

Li H, Zhou L-A (2005). Political turnover and economic performance: The incentive role of personnel control in China. *Journal of Public Economics* 89, 1743–1762.

Lin C, Yun M-S (2015). The effects of the minimum wage on earnings inequality: Evidence from China, in: Cappellari L, Polachek S, Tatsiramos K (Eds), IZA Workshop on Inequality: Causes and Consequences, Bonn, Germany.

Ma X, Li S (2014). Impact of minimum wage on gender wage differentials in urban China, China Institute for Income Distribution Working Paper No. 16.

Maskin E, Qian Y, Xu C-G (2000). Incentives, scale economies and organizational form. *Review of Economic Studies* 67, 359–378.

Wang J, Gunderson M (2011). Minimum wage impacts in china: Estimates from a prespecified research design, 2000–2007. *Contemporary Economic Policy* 29, 392–406.

CHAPTER 2

Evolution and Effects Assessment of China's Minimum Wage Policy

Xia Wang and Hainan Su

China has formulated and implemented a minimum wage policy for over two decades, and it is of great practical significance to look back on the formulation and evolution of the policy and assess the implementation effects to further improve the minimum wage policy and ensure that fulfills its role.

2.1 Main Contents and Implementation Overview of China's Minimum Wage Policy

2.1.1 Background and Process of Policy Formulation and Its Basic Contents

The production, formulation, and readjustment of China's minimum wage policy have taken place over a period of more than two decades.

X. Wang (✉)
Chinese Academy of Labour and Social Security, Beijing, China
e-mail: wangxia@calss.net.cn

H. Su
China Association of Labour Science, Beijing, China
e-mail: suhainan@vip.sina.com

L. Shi and C. Lin (eds.), *Minimum Wages in China*,
https://doi.org/10.1007/978-981-15-2421-9_2

In 1984, China was approved to participate in the No. 26 *Minimum Wage-Fixing Machinery Convention* of 1930 by the International Labour Organization and promised to formulate and implement the minimum wage policy. However, China continued to implement a planned economy, and all state-owned enterprises implemented the unified wage standard set by the country; the lowest wage standard could completely meet the basic living requirements of laborers and the people supported by them; therefore, China did not implement the minimum wage standard right away.

Later, with the establishment of China's market economy, the contradiction between labor and capital and problems such as decreasing wages and arrears led to a reduction in wages for a few enterprises, especially some nonpublic enterprises, which objectively required governmental intervention. Zhuhai city took the lead to establish the minimum wage system in 1989, and then, Shenzhen City followed to implement the minimum wage system in 1992. The former Ministry of Labor formulated the administrative regulation *Provisions on Minimum Wages* in November 1993 based on the practical experience of Zhuhai and Shenzhen as well as research on beneficial experiences with minimum wage systems in some foreign countries to encourage various provinces and cities to establish a minimum wage system. In July 1994, the 8th session of the 8th National People's Congress adopted and announced the *Labor Law of the People's Republic of China*. Article 48 of this law stipulates that "China implements the minimum wage insurance system," which, for the first time, promotes the minimum wage policy to the national legislation level, strengthening the authoritativeness and coercive effects of the minimum wage policies.

Since entering the twenty-first century, China has established a socialist market economic system with significant changes to various social aspects, and some terms and conditions of the *Provisions on Minimum Wages* became inapplicable to the new situation. Thus, the former Ministry of Labor and Social Security amended and adjusted the previous policies in 2004 and issued the new *Provisions on Minimum Wages*, which came into force in March of the same year and denoted significant progress toward the minimum wage policy.

Changes to the essential contents of the previously mentioned two "*Provisions*" are mainly demonstrated in the following four areas:

First, the concepts and scope of the application are expanded. The minimum wage standard refers to the minimum labor remuneration paid by the employer under the prerequisite that the labourer provides normal work within a legal work period or a work period agreed to in a lawful labor contract; compared with that of 1993, the new *Provisions* extended the allowable time period for normal labor. The extension still adopts the method of exclusion by excluding wages paid due to increased work periods; subsidies for middle shifts, night shifts or special work environments, such as high-temperature, low-temperature, underground, toxic and hazardous environments; benefits for laborers stipulated by national laws and regulations; and social insurance expenditures paid by individuals that were originally incorporated into the list for exclusion, and it is made clear that the form of monthly (for full time employees) and hourly (for non-full time only) minimum wage standards shall be adopted. Additionally, compared with the previous scope, in which the *Provisions* were solely applicable to certain enterprises, the scope has been expanded to certain enterprises, private nonenterprise units, individual businesses with employees with whom labor relations are established, and state organs, public institutions and social organizations with the aforementioned labor units.

Second, adjustments have been made to factor in determining the minimum wage standard. That is, the determination and adjustment of a monthly minimum wage standard shall make reference to six factors, such as the minimum living expenditure of local employees and the people supported by them, urban CPI (Consumer Price Index), all kinds of social insurance contributions and housing funds contributions paid by employee, average wage of employees, economic development growth and employment, and compared with the *Provisions* of 1993, two factors, such as urban CPI and individual social insurance and housing fund contributions, have been added while removing the factor of labor productivity previously included. Additionally, it has been specified that the adjustment to the hourly minimum wage standard shall consider factors such as the basic endowment insurance and medical insurance contributions that are supposed to be paid by relevant employers. Moreover, appropriate consideration shall be given to differences in work stability, working conditions, working intensity, and benefits for part-time and full-time workers; in addition, it is expressly stipulated that the minimum wage standard shall be adjusted at least once every two years, changing the previous provision of "adjustment at most once a year."

Third, the authorities for determination, adjustment and procedures have been reiterated. It has been restated that authorities for adjustments to minimum wage standards include the competent governmental departments of provinces, municipalities and autonomous regions and labor unions and associations of enterprises; the examination of the proposal falls within the authority of the relevant department of the State Council, and the authority to approve the adjustment falls within the authority of the provincial government. The procedures all specify that the aforesaid three authorities shall first conduct research to work out the plan for determining and adjusting the minimum wage standard, which will then be submitted to the competent department of the State Council, and the department can put forward suggestions for revision. If no revisions are put forward within a specified time, it shall be deemed that the State Council approves the plan. Finally, the plan will be submitted to the local provincial people's government for approval, and the plan shall be published in the government bulletin and at least one kind of newspaper circulating throughout the region within 7 days.

Fourth, employers' implementation of minimum wage standards and liability for noncompliance have been tightened. Employers shall announce the standard to all laborers within 10 days of the issuance of the local minimum wage standard, and no matter what kind of form is adopted, the wage paid to laborers shall not be less than the minimum wage standard. The punishment has been made more severe if the remuneration paid by the employer is less than the local minimum wage standard; the relevant administrative department can order the employer to reissue the wage that it owed to laborers and to pay 1–5 times the wage in compensation, and the amount of compensation has been increased.

2.1.2 *Implementation and Evolution of the Minimum Wage Policy Throughout China*

The implementation process of China's minimum wage policy can be divided into the following three stages:

The first stage: explorations of the pilot implementation (1989–1993). Few cities in the Pearl River Delta proactively explored the establishment of the minimum wage system; then, competent departments of the State Council organized in-depth investigations; based on these, the State Council developed the drafts of minimum wage policy at the state level, and through a number of revisions and the solicitation of opinions, the *Provisions on Minimum Wages* was officially promulgated. Relevant follow-up publicity was organized to provide guidance for local governments to gradually establish a local minimum wage system.

The second stage: gradual popularization throughout China (1994–2003). The overwhelming majority of provinces and cities in the coastal areas of East China established a minimum wage system in 1994, and in October of the same year, the competent department of the State Council distributed the "*Notice about Implementing the Minimum Wage Standard*" to instruct local authorities to issue minimum wage rates. Soon after, all provinces and cities in the east, center and northeast of China established the minimum wage system in 1995, and most provinces and cities in the west also subsequently established the minimum wage system. By the end of 2003, all the regions had set up a minimum wage system and promulgated the monthly minimum wage standard except Tibet.

The third stage: widespread establishment and improvement (since 2004). In 2004, the competent department of the State Council revised and promulgated the *Provisions on Minimum Wages* by relying on previous experiences and lessons and analyzing changes to the situation. By the end of 2004, 31 provinces (autonomous regions and municipalities, hereinafter) established, promulgated and implemented a monthly minimum wage standard. In 2007, all provinces and cities promulgated and implemented the hourly minimum wage standard; then, various provinces accelerated the adjustment frequency of the minimum wage standard and increased the adjustment range; moreover, the legal monitoring and supervision on employers with regard to the implementation of the minimum wage standard were strengthened to promote the implementation of the minimum wage system all over China. From 2008 to 2009, in response to the international economic crisis, the competent department of the State Council issued a document to guide various regions to temporarily defer the adjustment to the minimum wage standard. Later, following the growth deceleration of China's economy, the department instructed various regions to prudently and steadily adjust the minimum wage standard. In recent years, the competent department of the State Council has carried out research on how to intensify the guidance and control of the implementation of the national minimum wage policy, and priority has been given to research how to establish a method to assess the minimum wage standards to assist various provinces to scientifically and reasonably adjust the minimum wage standard.

2.1.3 Brief Summary

Looking back on the promulgation and evolution of China's minimum wage policy, we can reach the following conclusions:

(1) The minimum wage policy of China is formulated and promulgated on the basis of guaranteeing basic living standards for laborers and the people supported by him/her, the actual need to safeguard the legal rights and interests of laborers and the fulfillment of obligations as a member country of the International Labour Organization. (2) China's minimum wage policy evolves and is adjusted through the advancement of economic system reform as well as the development and changes of the labor market; coverage of the system has expanded from several cites to various places throughout China, and its scope of application to employers and laborers has also been broadened, while the form of the minimum wage standard has diversified from a single type to many. The adjustment frequency and range has also increased from slow and small to fast and large; additionally, the attitude of employers in implementing the standard has also grown to be serious and careful, as the liability for noncompliance has increased. (3) Since 2004, the department has always attached importance to efforts in adjusting the minimum wage standard, and instituted requirements to speed up the adjustment frequency and strengthen the adjustment range in periods of rapid economic development; moreover, in periods of economic downturn, it has also ordered employers to defer the adjustment or make steady and safe adjustments to properly balance guaranteeing the basic living standard of laborers and the people supported by laborers and the sustainable development of enterprises. (4) The national and local mechanism for assessing the minimum wage standard has not yet been established, which is unfavorable to a comprehensive implementation of the macrocontrol of the competent department of the State Council and the provision of instructions to various regions with regard to scientifically and reasonably adjusting the local minimum wage standards. (5) The connotation and extension of the minimum wage standards of a few provinces are inconsistent with that of the national regulation, which excludes the factor of individual contribution, and fails to uniformly standardize the minimum wage standard throughout China. (6) During the implementation, a small number of employers have not strictly and consistently implemented the minimum wage system according to the policy, undermining the rights and interests of some laborers.

2.2 Adjustments to Minimum Wage Standards in Recent Years

The research has prioritized analyzing adjustments to minimum wage standards in various regions since 2005 based on a brief analysis of adjustments to minimum wage standards over time in China.

2.2.1 *Adjustment Frequency of Minimum Wage Standards in Various Places*

Following the successive establishment of the minimum wage system in various regions until 2013, accumulated adjustments to the minimum wage standard of the 31 provinces reached 326; Beijing saw the most adjustments, totaling 19, and the Tibet Autonomous Region saw the fewest adjustments, totaling 3, and the number of adjustments in the majority of regions was 9. Since 2005, adjustments to the minimum wage standard in 31 provinces occurred 181 times; the highest number of adjustments, 8, occurred in Beijing, Shanghai, and Tianjin, while Tibet had the fewest adjustments, 3; the number of adjustments in most regions was 5. On average, the number of adjustments to the minimum wage standard in various regions was 5.84 since 2005; the annual average of adjustment is 0.65 times, which is notably higher than the average number of adjustments to the standard, 4.68 times before 2004, as well as the annual adjustment average of 0.47 times (see Table 2.1 for details).

2.2.2 *Growth Margin of the Minimum Wage Standard of Various Regions*

For the period from the successive establishment of the minimum wage standard to 2013, we use the highest level of growth in the minimum wage standard for analysis; the summary of 31 provinces is computed to arrive at the arithmetic average (hereinafter the same). The total average growth of the minimum wage standard is 634%, and the annual average growth is 10%; Shandong has the largest growth of 812% with an annual average growth of 11%, and Tibet sees the smallest growth of 270% with an annual growth of 5.1%. According to respective computations before and after the promulgation of the *Provisions on Minimum Wages*, from 1994 to 2004, the total average growth of 31 provinces of China is 222%, with an annual average growth of 7%; Zhejiang attains the highest growth of 310%, with an annual average growth of 10.8%, and Shaanxi

Table 2.1 Adjustment to minimum wage standard by various provinces and cities from 1994 to May 2013

Regions	*Number of adjustments since 1994*	*Number of adjustment after 2005*	*Number of adjustments before 2004*	*Cut-off year*
北京 Beijing	19	8	11	By 2013
天津 Tianjin	16	8	8	By 2013
河北 Hebei	11	6	5	By 2012
山西 Shanxi	11	7	4	By 2013
内蒙古 Inner Mongolia	11	6	5	By 2013
辽宁 Liaoning	7	4	3	By 2013
吉林 Jilin	10	5	5	By 2013
黑龙江 Heilongjiang	7	4	3	By 2012
上海 Shanghai	16	8	8	By 2013
江苏 Jiangsu	15	7	8	By 2013
浙江 Zhejiang	13	7	6	By 2013
安徽 Anhui	10	5	5	By 2013
福建 Fujian	14	7	7	By 2013
江西 Jiangxi	8	5	3	By 2013
山东 Shandong	11	7	4	By 2013
河南 Henan	10	5	5	By 2013
湖北 Hubei	8	6	2	By 2013
湖南 Hubei	14	8	6	By 2013
广东 Guangdong	11	6	5	By 2013
广西 Guangxi	9	5	4	By 2013
海南 Hainan	10	5	5	By 2013
重庆 Chongqing	9	4	5	Not yet published in 2013

(continued)

Table 2.1 (continued)

Regions	*Number of adjustments since 1994*	*Number of adjustment after 2005*	*Number of adjustments before 2004*	*Cut-off year*
四川 Sichuan	10	5	6	By 2013
贵州 Guizhou	9	5	4	By 2013
云南 Yunnan	9	5	4	By 2013
西藏 Tibet	3	3	0	By 2013
陕西 Shaanxi	10	7	3	By 2013
甘肃 Gansu	7	5	2	By 2013
青海 Qinghai	7	6	1	By 2012
宁夏 Ningxia	10	6	4	By 2013
新疆 Xinjiang	11	6	5	By 2013
合 计 Totals	326	181	145	
Average adjustments	10.52	5.84	4.68	
Annual average adjustments	0.7	0.65	0.47	

Note Data from 16 provinces are provided by the competent department of the MOHRSS, and other data are from the Internet without the certification of relevant departments of the Bureau of Human Resources and Social Security in various provinces. The Tibet Autonomous Region did not have the minimum wage standard promulgated until 2004, and other provinces and cities had the minimum wage standard promulgated in approximately 1995. Averages and other computations in the table above are all rounded off

sees the smallest growth of 160%, with an annual average growth of 4.4% (this set of data excludes Tibet, as it did not implement the minimum wage standard until 2004). Since 2005, the total average growth of the minimum wage standard in 31 provinces has been 272%, and the annual average growth is 12%; Jilin attains the greatest growth of 367%, with an annual average growth of 15.5%, and Jiangsu sees the smallest growth of 214%, with an annual average growth of 7.5%. According to the three sets of data about growth, the growth margin since 2005 has been significantly higher than that of the years before 2004 (see Table 2.2 for details).

Table 2.2 Adjustment to minimum wage standards of various provinces from 1994 to 2013[a] Unit: RMB/Month

Provinces and cities	*Minimum wage standard of 1994 (high grade)*	*Minimum wage standard of 2013 (high grade)*	*Total change from 1994 to 2013 (%)*	*Average growth from 1994 to 2013 (%)*	*Minimum wage standard of 2004 (high grade)*	*Total change from 1994 to 2004 (%)*	*Average growth from 1994 to 2004 (%)*	*Minimum wage standard of 2005 (high grade)*	*Total change from 2005 to 2013 (%)*	*Average growth from 2005 to 2013 (%)*
北京 Beijing	210	1400	667	10.0	545	260	9.1	580	241	10.3
天津 Tianjin	210	1500	714	10.3	530	252	8.8	590	254	10.9
河北 Hebei	180	1320	733	10.5	520	289	10.1	520	254	10.9
山西 Shanxi	200	1290	645	9.8	520	260	9.1	520	248	10.6
内蒙古 Inner Mongolia	180	1350	750	10.6	420	233	8.0	420	321	13.9
辽宁 Liaoning	210	1300	619	9.5	450	214	7.2	450	289	12.5
吉林 Jilin	190	1320	695	10.2	360	189	6.0	360	367	15.5
黑龙江 Heilongjiang	200	1160	580	9.2	390	195	6.3	390	297	12.9
上海 Shanghai	270	1620	600	9.4	635	235	8.1	690	235	9.9
江苏 Jiangsu	210	1480	705	10.3	620	295	10.3	690	214	7.5
浙江 Zhejiang	200	1470	735	10.5	620	310	10.8	670	219	9.1

(continued)

Table 2.2 (continued)

Provinces and cities	*Minimum wage standard of 1994 (high grade)*	*Minimum wage standard of 2013 (high grade)*	*Total change from 1994 to 2013 (%)*	*Average growth from 1994 to 2013 (%)*	*Minimum wage standard of 2004 (high grade)*	*Total change from 1994 to 2004 (%)*	*Average growth from 1994 to 2004 (%)*	*Minimum wage standard of 2005 (high grade)*	*Total change from 2005 to 2013 (%)*	*Average growth from 2005 to 2013 (%)*
安徽 Anhui	180	1260	700	10.2	410	228	7.8	410	307	13.3
福建 Fujian	280	1320	471	8.1	480	171	5.0	600	220	9.2
江西 Jiangxi	190	1230	647	9.8	360	189	6.0	360	342	14.6
山东 Shandong	170	1380	812	11.0	410	241	8.3	530	260	11.2
河南 Henan	170	1240	729	10.4	380	224	7.6	480	258	11.1
湖北 Hubei	200	1300	650	9.8	400	200	6.5	460	283	12.2
湖南 Hunan	190	1265	666	9.9	460	242	8.4	480	264	11.4
广东 Guangdong	320	1550	484	8.2	684	214	7.1	684	227	9.5
广西 Guangxi	200	1200	600	9.4	460	230	7.9	460	261	11.2
海南 Hainan	280	1120	400	7.2	500	179	5.4	500	224	9.4
重庆 Chongqing	190	1050	553	8.9	400	211	7.0	400	263	11.3
四川 Sichuan	180	1200	667	10.0	450	250	8.7	450	267	11.5

(continued)

Table 2.2 (continued)

Provinces and cities	*Minimum wage standard of 1994 (high grade)*	*Minimum wage standard of 2013 (high grade)*	*Total change from 1994 to 2013 (%)*	*Average growth from 1994 to 2013 (%)*	*Minimum wage standard of 2004 (high grade)*	*Total change from 1994 to 2004 (%)*	*Average growth from 1994 to 2004 (%)*	*Minimum wage standard of 2005 (high grade)*	*Total change from 2005 to 2013 (%)*	*Average growth from 2005 to 2013 (%)*
贵州 Guizhou	190	1030	542	8.8	400	211	7.0	400	258	11.1
云南 Yunnan	185	1265	684	10.1	470	254	8.8	470	269	11.6
西藏 Tibet	445	1200	270	5.1	445	100	0	445	270	11.7
陕西 Shaanxi	200	1150	575	9.1	320	160	4.4	490	235	9.9
甘肃 Gansu	180	1200	667	10.0	340	189	6.0	340	353	15.0
青海 Qinghai	200	1070	535	8.7	370	185	5.8	370	289	12.5
宁夏 Ningxia	180	1300	722	10.4	380	211	7.0	380	342	14.6
新疆 Xinjiang	180	1520	844	11.3	480	267	9.3	480	317	13.7
平均值 Average	212	1292	634	10	458	222	7	486	272	12.0

[a]The time when the author was drafting the paper

2.2.3 Disparities in the Minimum Wage Standard of Various Regions

In 2006,[1] the highest monthly minimum wage standard of 780 RMB every month was seen in Guangdong, while Jiangxi had the lowest at 360 RMB; the disparity between the two provinces was 420 RMB, and the ratio of the two was 2.2:1. In the same year, the city with the highest hourly minimum wage standard for non-full time laborers was Beijing with 7.9 RMB per hour, and Jiangxi again has the lowest, 3.6 RMB per hour; the disparity and ratio between the two was 4.3 RMB and 2.2:1, respectively. By May 2013, Shanghai became the region with the highest monthly minimum wage standard, 1620 RMB every month. Guizhou had the lowest, 1030 RMB every month, and the disparity between the two cities was 590 RMB; the ratio between the two was 1.57:1. In the same year, Beijing and Xinjiang were the two regions with the highest hourly minimum wage standard, 15.2 RMB/hour, and Hainan had the lowest, 9.9 RMB/hour; the disparity between the two was 5.3 RMB, and the ratio was 1.54:1.

2.2.4 Brief Summary

According to the previous analysis about the adjustment to the minimum wage standard as well as changes to its development in various regions throughout China, the following basic conclusions can be drawn:

Based on the historical evolution, taking 2004 as the boundary, the period could be divided into two parts. The first part was from 1993 to 2003, and the adjustment speed of the minimum wage standard was relatively low, and the number of adjustments was small and had a small range. The second part was from 2004 to 2013, and adjustment to the minimum wage standard accelerated, with the number of adjustments increasing and the range widening. Additionally, the absolute amount of the disparity between the highest and lowest minimum wage standards shows the widening trend, while the ratio of the disparity between the aforementioned two periods has gradually narrowed.

The aforementioned conditions show that, under the guidance of relevant national adjustments to the minimum wage standard, the adjustment frequency and range of the minimum wage standard of various regions throughout China have shown an accelerating and widening trend on the whole. Additionally, the adjustment frequency, range and direction of various regions have generally been consistent.

2.3 Relations of the Minimum Wage Standard and Relevant Economic Indexes

According to the *Provisions on Minimum Wages*, the adjustment to the minimum wage standard shall make reference to six factors: the minimum living expenses, urban CPI, social insurance contributions, housing funds that are individually paid, economic growth and employment. The research focuses on analyzing the proportional relations of various indexes as the minimum wage standard and the *minimum living guarantee standard of urban residents* in various regions, CPI, average wage of all employees and per capita GDP,[2] which will be the basis for analyzing the scientificity and normalization of the adjustment to minimum wage standard.

2.3.1 Minimum Wage Standards and Minimum Living Guarantee Standards for Local Urban Residents

The purpose of the minimum wage policy is to guarantee a basic standard of living for low-income laborers and the people supported by them and to satisfy the requirements of production and the reproduction of labor forces, while the minimum living guarantee system for urban residents is intended to ensure the meeting of the minimum basic life requirements of individuals; hence, there are notable differences between the two with respect to the strength and effects of relief, and the guaranteed standard of the former is supposed to be higher than that of the latter. We can use "the number of people supported by the laborer" as the main basis for determining the disparity between the two; that is, a comparison can be made with regard to the minimum living guarantee standard for local urban residents by multiplying the number of people supported by the laborer, social insurance and housing funds contribution paid by the laborer. According to the measurement, it is appropriate to maintain a proportion of 1.2 times to 1.5 times,[3] and if it is lower than 1.2 times, the minimum wage standard of the region is relatively low, but if it is higher than 1.5 times, the minimum wage standard of the region is relatively high. Moreover, we will choose a proportion, from 2005, 2010 and 2012, of various provincial capitals throughout China for analysis (see Table 2.3 for details).

According to the computation and analysis of the proportional relations between the two in the table, it can be seen that the minimum

Table 2.3 Relations between the minimal living guarantee standard of urban residents and the minimum wage standard in provincial capitals

Regions	*Minimum wage standards of the province in the year (RMB/month)/(local average living guarantee standards of January in the same year (RMB/month) * Number of persons supported by each employee (person))*		
	2005	*2010*	*2012*
北京市 Beijing	1.08	1.16	1.25
天津市 Tianjin	1.11	1.06	1.45
石家庄 Shijiazhuang	1.15	1.26	1.72
太原 Taiyuan	1.41	1.12	1.34
呼和浩特 Hohhot	1.15	1.34	1.44
沈阳 Shenyang	1.01	1.29	1.21
长春 Changchun	1.25	1.27	1.35
哈尔滨 Harbin	0.93	1.14	1.17
上海市 Shanghai	1.23	1.36	1.56
南京 Nanjing	1.38	1.17	1.37
杭州 Hangzhou	1.20	1.17	1.22
合肥 Hefei	1.05	1.44	1.80
福州 Fuzhou	2.03	1.66	1.65
南昌 Nanchang	1.33	1.39	1.23
济南 Jinan	1.33	1.37	1.86
郑州 Zhengzhou	1.10	1.23	1.35
武汉 Wuhan	0.98	1.20	1.19
长沙 Changsha	1.14	1.26	1.44

(continued)

Table 2.3 (continued)

Regions	*Minimum wage standards of the province in the year (RMB/month)/(local average living guarantee standards of January in the same year (RMB/month) * Number of persons supported by each employee (person))*		
	2005	*2010*	*2012*
广州 Guangzhou	1.13	1.47	1.54
南宁 Nanning	1.09	1.55	1.85
海口 Haikou	1.01	1.02	1.21
重庆市 Chongqing	1.07	1.27	1.65
成都 Chengdu	1.04	1.48	1.67
贵阳 Guiyang	1.16	1.44	1.42
昆明 Kunming	1.00	1.41	1.64
拉萨 Lhasa	1.11	1.43	1.52
西安 Xi'an	1.16	1.07	1.30
兰州 Lanzhou	0.98	1.25	1.44
西宁 Xining	0.97	1.46	1.58
银川 Yinchuan	0.98	1.37	1.90
乌鲁木齐 Urumqi	1.83	1.78	2.20

wage standard and minimum living guarantee standard for local urban residents have shown a tendency toward coordinated development on the whole, and the function of guaranteeing has been notably promoted; however, in 2012, the growth in the minimum wage standard was faster than that of the minimum living guarantee standard of local urban residents in 14 cities, and the level was relatively high.

2.3.2 *Growth Rates of the Minimum Wage Standard and the Local CPI*

The CPI is an index applied to measure price fluctuations of residents' daily consumer goods and services. Taking the CPI as the basis for the adjustment of the minimum wage standard over time can eliminate the influences of inflation and keep the actual minimum wage level from decreasing while performing its function of guaranteeing a basic standard of living for laborers and the people supported by them. The analysis of the relations between the two can to some degree determine whether the minimum wage standard is reasonable or not.

The research compares the growth rate of the minimum wage standard and that of the CPI during the same period in various provincial capitals (include municipalities) in 2006 and 2010.[4] If the growth rate of the former is greater than that of the latter, then it indicates that the actual level of the minimum wage standard grows, and the actual lives of low-income laborers are not impacted by the price; on the contrary, the actual living standard of low-income laborers may decrease (see Table 2.4 for details[5]).

According to results of the comparison in the table, it can be preliminarily seen that (1) except Shenyang, the growth rate of the minimum wage standard of 30 cities is higher than that of the local CPI, indicating that the actual living standard of low-income laborers and the people supported by them is guaranteed. (2) The actual growth margin of the minimum wage standard of 20 cities ranges from 20 to 40%, showing that the living standard of low-income laborers and the people supported by them has improved in most cities. (3) The growth margin of the minimum wage standard is over 40% in 7 cities, and the actual growth in Wuhan, Zhengzhou and Lanzhou is 72.79, 55.39, and 51.67%, respectively, manifesting that the lives of low-income laborers and the people supported by them have been greatly improved in the three cities. (4) The actual growth margin of the minimum wage standard of Nanjing and Chongqing is only 11.41 and 4.17%, showing that the living standard of low-income laborers and the people supported by them improved a little. (5) The minimum wage standard of Shenyang has experienced negative growth, and relevant statistical data shows that the CPI growth of the city in 2010 was 102% greater than that in 2009; an in-depth analysis is necessary to determine the reason for this result.

Table 2.4 Comparison of the growth rates of the minimum wage standard and the CPI

City	*Minimum wage standards of 2006*	*Minimum wage standards of 2010*	*Growth of minimum wage standards of 2010 over that of 2006 (nominal) (%)*	*Growth of CPI of 2010 over that of 2006 (%)*	*Growth of minimum wage standards of 2010 over that of 2006 (actual) (%)*	*Nominal growth of minimum wage standards over that of CPI (%)*
北京 Beijing	640	960	50	8.55	38.18	41.45
天津 Tianjin	670	940	40	12.58	24.35	27.42
石家庄 Shijiazhuang	580	900	55	15.02	34.76	39.98
太原 Taiyuan	550	850	55	15.08	34.69	39.92
呼和浩特 Hohhot	560	900	61	11.45	44.46	49.55
沈阳 Shenyang	590	900	53	56.59	−2.29	−3.59
长春 Changchun	510	820	61	11.94	43.83	49.06
哈尔滨 Harbin	620	880	42	13.25	25.38	28.75
上海 Shanghai	750	1120	49	12.12	32.89	36.88
南京 Nanjing	750	960	28	14.89	11.41	13.11
杭州 Hangzhou	750	1100	47	11.23	32.16	35.77

(continued)

Table 2.4 (continued)

City	*Minimum wage standards of 2006*	*Minimum wage standards of 2010*	*Growth of minimum wage standards of 2010 over that of 2006 (nominal) (%)*	*Growth of CPI of 2010 over that of 2006 (%)*	*Growth of minimum wage standards of 2010 over that of 2006 (actual) (%)*	*Nominal growth of minimum wage standards over that of CPI (%)*
合肥 Hefei	520	720	38	14.35	20.69	23.65
福州 Fuzhou	650	900	38	11.89	23.34	26.11
南昌 Nanchang	510	720	41	13.97	23.72	27.03
济南 Jinan	610	920	51	12.47	34.26	38.53
郑州 Zhengzhou	480	860	79	15.19	55.39	63.81
武汉 Wuhan	460	900	96	13.43	72.79	82.57
长沙 Changsha	600	850	42	13.03	25.63	28.97
广州 Guangzhou	780	1030	32	10.18	19.80	21.82
南宁 Nanning	500	820	64	13.91	43.97	50.09
海口 Haikou	580	830	43	15.03	24.31	27.97
重庆 Chongqing	580	680	17	12.31	4.17	4.69

(continued)

Table 2.4 (continued)

City	*Minimum wage standards of 2006*	*Minimum wage standards of 2010*	*Growth of minimum wage standards of 2010 over that of 2006 (nominal) (%)*	*Growth of CPI of 2010 over that of 2006 (%)*	*Growth of minimum wage standards of 2010 over that of 2006 (actual) (%)*	*Nominal growth of minimum wage standards over that of CPI (%)*
成都 Chengdu	580	850	47	13.35	29.68	33.65
贵阳 Guiyang	550	830	51	13.06	33.56	37.94
昆明 Kunming	540	830	54	17.55	31.01	36.45
拉萨 Lhasa	495	850	72	15.52	48.89	56.48
西安 Xi'an	540	760	41	14.57	23.06	26.43
兰州 Lanzhou	430	760	77	16.70	51.67	60.3
西宁 Xining	460	770	67	29.22	29.24	37.78
银川 Yinchuan	450	710	58	17.32	34.67	40.68
乌鲁木齐 Urumqi	670	960	43	15.45	23.87	27.55

2.3.3 *Minimum Wage Standards and Average Wages of Urban Employees*

The minimum wage standard of many countries amounts to 40–60% of the overall average wage, and we can use it as the reference point for this analysis. Currently, China has two statistical datasets of average wages; the first is the average wages for on-job employees of nonprivate enterprises in urban areas, which mainly counts the average wages of employers such as joint-stock companies, limited liability companies, state-owned enterprises, collectively owned enterprises, and foreign-invested enterprises; the second is the average wages of private enterprises in urban areas, solely counting the average wages of private enterprises. From a nationwide perspective, the total number of employees in the latter is almost the same as those in the former. If we add the number of laborers employed by individual businesses, the proportion of on-job employees decreases. Therefore, the average wage of the two types of employees is added together for computation, which meets the statistical range of the average wage of urban employees.

As relevant statistical data of private enterprises started to be issued as late as 2007, only part of cities issued relevant data. Thus, the research collected and analyzed the "average wages of all urban employees" amortized from two data points, the average wage of on-job employees of units (nonprivate enterprises) and that of private enterprises in the urban areas of 7 cities in 2008, 2010 and 2012, and made a comparison with the minimum wage standard of the same year (see details in Table 2.5).

In accordance with the proportional relations between the two for the 7 cities, as shown in Table 2.5, we can see the following: (1) In the three years, the proportional relation of the two was basically in a state of irregular fluctuations. (2) By 2012, the proportion of the two in most cities was rising and that of 5 cities ranged between 30 and 36%; considering that the wages of laborers employed by individual businesses are not included, the actual average wage of employees in those cities may still be overestimated; hence, the proportional relations between the minimum wage standard and average wage of employees may be higher than that reflected in Table 2.5. (3) According to requirements of "Outline of the 12th Five-year Plan" of China, the proportion of the two in most areas shall be up to 40% a by 2015, thus a more rapid growth of minimum wage standard is expected.

Table 2.5 Comparison of the highest grade of minimum wage standards and average wages of urban employees in some cities

City	*Highest grade of the minimum wage standard in 2008*	*Local annual average wages in 2008*	*Ratio of the aforesaid two (%) in 2008 (%)*	*Highest grade of the minimum wage standard in 2010*	*Local annual average wages in 2010*	*Ratio of the aforesaid two (%) in 2010 (%)*	*Highest grade of the minimum wage standard in 2012*	*Local annual average wages in 2012*	*Ratio of the aforesaid two (%) in 2012 (%)*
北京 Beijing	800	44,715	21.47	960	50,415	22.85	1260	62,677	24.12
天津 Tianjin	820	31,200	31.54	920	37,540	29.41	1310	46,464	33.83
长春 Changchun	650	24,142	32.31	820	33,421	29.44	1000	42,620	28.16
石家庄 Shijiazhuang	750	21,470	41.92	900	29,332	36.82	1100	37,126	35.55
广州 Guangzhou	860	37,510	27.51	1030	41,331	29.90	1300	51,438	30.33
上海 Shanghai	960	34,707	33.19	1120	42,789	31.41	1450	51,968	33.48
重庆 Chongqing	680	24,029	33.96	680	29,558	27.61	1050	36,204	34.80

2.3.4 *Growth in the Minimum Wage Standard and Per Capita GDP*

Per capita GDP represents labor productivity and economic development level of one region. The comparison between the per capita GDP of one region and the local minimum wage standard can enable an understanding of the situation regarding the sharing of low-income laborers, which is revealing with regard to local economic and social development achievements. Generally, it is appropriate to choose the per capita GDP of the second and third industries, as the per capita GDP generally amounts to the labor output of laborers from all enterprises, and the GDP and the local minimum wage standard are highly comparable. However, as there exists no authoritative data, the research obtains the per capita GDP by dividing all GDPs of the tertiary industry by the permanent resident population of 31 municipalities and provincial capitals and then compares it with the minimum wage standard of corresponding cities.

Through the analysis, it can be found that (1) the proportional relations of the minimum wage standard of various places and the per capita GDP show a declining trend on the whole. In 2010, the proportional relation between the minimum wage standard and the local GDP in 19 cities dropped compared with that of 2008, and in 2012, the proportion of the two for 17 cities declined compared with that of 2010, and the proportion of the two for 21 cities was even lower than that of 2008. (2) The number of cities with a proportional relation of the two below 20% has decreased from 14 to 15 cities to 10, and during the same period, the number of cities with a proportional relation of 20–30% increased from 8 and 10 to 17, and the number of cities with a proportional relation over 30% decreased from 7 and 8 to 4. (3) The number of cities with a higher proportion tends to decline; that is, the number of cities with a proportion over 35% has decreased from 3 and 2 to 0.

2.3.5 *Brief Summary*

Through a comparison and analysis of the proportional relations between minimum wage standards and the four factors of minimum living guarantee standards of urban residents, the CPI, and average wages of employees and per capita GDP in various provinces, we can get the following basic conclusions: (1) In recent years, the promotion of a minimum wage standard in various provinces across China has been reasonable and capable of playing the role of guaranteeing the basic living conditions of low-income laborers and the people supported by them. (2) In recent years, the growth margin of the minimum wage standard in various places has been relatively large and accelerating, which made up for the small and slow growth before 2004 in particular. (3) Regarding the minimum wage standard, local economic development status and average wages of urban employees, there still is room for improvement. (4) Currently, China's economic development has entered a period of medium-fast growth and an increase in uncertainty; the promotion of a minimum wage standard in some regions is not in line with the six factors of the *Provisions on Minimum Wages* and does not compare unrealistically with that of other regions; the growth margin is controlled at slightly higher than the growth rate of the average wage of urban employees and the growth in per capita GDP.

2.4 Proposals to Improve the Minimum Wage Policy

In summary, currently, due to an insufficiency of policies, China's minimum wage standard still confronts various problems, including poor implementation by employers, the obscurity of national policies, inconsistency in the understanding of the principles of some regions, a lack of an assessment system for macrocontrol, and the problem of a poor understanding or dissimilation of the basic functions of the minimum wage policy of local governments.

Based on the abovementioned analysis, to further advance and promote the minimum wage system to enable it to play a more critical role in safeguarding the legal rights and interests of laborers and advance economic development, we put forward the following proposals for improvement in four areas.

2.4.1 System Promotion and Legislation Improvement

It is suggested to improve and promote the basis for adjustments, calculating method and decision-making procedures of the minimum wage standards, to scientifically and reasonably reflect changes in the basic requirements of low-wage groups. The pace of adjustments to the minimum wage standard should be controlled. Proactive explorations to further standardize the minimum wage system at the legislative level should be made.

2.4.2 Scientific Assessment and Coordinated Guidance

It is suggested to accelerate the establishment of a mechanism to assess the effects of the minimum wage policy and clearly define the requirements about the goal, principle, subject, contents, data source, frequency and results of the assessment and promote the scientificity of adjustments to the minimum wage standard. The construction of the basic database should also be strengthened to ensure sustainable and steady data support and a timely understanding of the influences of adjustments to the minimum wage standard on grassroots employees and the labour costs of labor-intensive enterprises. In addition, research should be conducted to establish a solid theoretical basis as well as feasible and practical nation-wide guidance and assessment system for the minimum wage standard. The competent department of the State Council should examine opinion feedback and provide assistance to various provinces to scientifically and reasonably adjust the minimum wage standard while reducing unrealistic comparisons.

2.4.3 Specified Standards and Consultation-Based Decision-Making

It is suggested to clarify the functional theorizing regarding industries in a district, conduct research on the consultation and decision-making mechanism of the minimum wage standard of various industries, and define the method and procedures for determining the minimum wage standard. Proactive efforts should also be made to establish a dialogue platform for laborers and employers. Negotiations should also be carried out based on equal dialogue, fairness and equity to formulate scientific, reasonable and flexible minimum wage standards for the industry. Once a standard is agreed upon by both parties and reviewed by the government, both parties should be bound by the standard. In addition, proactive guidance should be provided to encourage establishing local tripartite consultation mechanism to determine local minimum wage rates.

2.4.4 Strengthen Efforts in Publicity and Supervision

Efforts shall be strengthened in publicizing the minimum wage system to further promote understanding in various circles in society regarding the minimum wage system and to remove bias and misunderstanding regarding the minimum wage policy. Management of the production quota standard should be promoted and strengthened to prevent some enterprises from randomly increasing their production quotas, reducing the price rate or violating the minimum wage regulation in a disguised form and to promote awareness of and capacity to maintain rights and interests according to the law; moreover, the awareness of employers in implementing the minimum wage standard should be strengthened, and various government agencies should strengthen their efforts to supervise and check employers' implementation of the minimum wage standard and to punish behaviors violating the regulation of the minimum wage standard.

Notes

1. Not all provinces have worked out the minimum wage standard before 2006, and complete data cannot be obtained until after 2006, hence the research takes the year of 2006 as the statistical node.
2. Since the promulgation of the new Provisions in 2004, various regions have started to further standardize the adjustment to minimum wage standards, and the chapter focuses on analysis about relevant data obtained since 2005, moreover, as the adjustment to minimum wage standards in China was deferred in 2008 and 2009 due to financial crisis, data of 2009 was not representative, hence no analysis is made about data of the year.
3. Generally, social insurance and housing costs, which are individually paid, account for 20% of the employee's wage.
4. The existing national statistical data only include data about the CPI in municipalities and provincial capitals from 2006 to 2010; hence, we had to compute based on data from 2006 to 2010. The growth margin of the minimum wage standard since 2011 has been higher than that in 2010 and the previous years, and the growth in the CPI of the same period is not high; hence, we can infer the proportional relations between the minimum wage standard and growth in the local CPI of various regions in 2013 through a comparison of relevant data from 2006 to 2010.
5. The data in the table are based on a computation of relevant data from China Urban Life and Price Yearbook, China Commerce Yearbook and the statistical yearbooks of various provinces.

CHAPTER 3

Minimum Wages in China: Standard and Implementation

Yang Du and Peng Jia

3.1 Introduction

The minimum wage system has been widely accepted in many countries, which makes it one of the fundamental pillars of labor market institutions. The original intention to set up a minimum wage is to intervene in the market wage rate at equilibrium, so the institution per se is regulative. When looking at the compliance of minimum wages, the leakages exist in almost every country, which brings up controversy with the institution regarding its effectiveness and enforcement. Therefore, the policymakers should pay attention to how to design the minimum wage system effectively.

It has been more than two decades since the introduction of minimum wages in China. In the past decade, the minimum wage has been

Y. Du · P. Jia (✉)
Institute of Population and Labor Economics,
Chinese Academy of Social Sciences, Beijing, China
e-mail: jiapeng@cass.org.cn

Y. Du
Center for Human Resources Research,
Chinese Academy of Social Sciences, Beijing, China
e-mail: duyang@cass.org.cn

L. Shi and C. Lin (eds.), *Minimum Wages in China*,
https://doi.org/10.1007/978-981-15-2421-9_3

influencing the labor market outcomes. The existing studies focus on its impacts on employment (Ding 2010; Ma et al. 2012), working time (Jia and Zhang 2013a), spillover (Luo and Cong 2009; Jia and Zhang 2013b), and income distribution (Luo 2011). Concerning the minimum wage per se, however, the policymakers should care about whether the minimum wage is effectively enforced and what affects the compliance of minimum wages.

The first message we need to evaluate the implementation of the minimum wage is to look at the share of workers who earn below the minimum wages. Based on the urban household survey data we use in this chapter, in 2010 there is 13.26% of workers whose monthly wages are less than the local minimum wage. The share is 17.26 and 9.84% in 2005 and 2001, respectively. International comparisons indicate that developed countries tend to have good performance in compliance with minimum wages. According to a report by the Bureau of Labor Statistics (2013), in 2012 only 2.6% of workers are reported to work below the federal minimum wages in the United States. Observation of the UK reveals that 1% of workers earn less than minimum wages (Machin et al. 2003).

In contrast, the situation is much more severe in developing countries where informal employment is ubiquitous. In Brazil, 5–10% of formal employment and 15–30% of informal employment are reported wages below minimum wages (Lemos 2004, 2009). The share is about 30% in Honduras (Gindling and Terrell 2010), 16% in Mexico (Bell 1997), and 24% in Peru (Baanante 2004).

In addition to how many, it is also crucial for labor market regulators to know who are not covered by the minimum wage. To target relevant individuals and improve the implementation of minimum wages, it would be of policy implications to understand the characteristics of those who are not covered by the minimum wage and the job characteristics with minimum wage compliance.

The coverage of minimum wages might be the outcome of implementation, but some other factors also affect coverage. First of all, the level of minimum wages per se is related to how easy to implement the institution. It is evident that a high minimum wage produces large targeting groups of workers, which increases the difficulty of enforcement naturally.

Second, the general trend of labor demand and supply affects how easy it would be to implement the minimum wage. In recent years, driven by demographic change and strong labor demand, the shortage of unskilled labor is more and more frequent and the wage rates have been going up quickly. According to the NBS, the average monthly earnings for migrant workers are RMB 2690 in 2013. It is observed the significant trend of wage convergence between migrant and local workers (Cai and Du 2011). In this context, the spontaneous changes in the labor market would improve the coverage even without further efforts to enforcing the minimum wage.

Third, the dynamics of economic restructuring, industrial organization and other labor market institutions could also affect the compliance of minimum wages. For instance, it is easy for employees in manufacturing to have explicit labor relations with their employers, which makes low costs for enforcement. The improvement in other employment institutions affects the implementation too. For example, a more regulated *Employment Contract Law* would make enforcement in minimum wages easier; the introduction of collective bargaining would facilitate monitoring the minimum wages at the firm level.

To understand the compliance of minimum wages in China, various data sources are applied to evaluate the changes in minimum wages with international comparisons. Using micro-level data, we analyze the coverage of minimum wages and its determinants. The data include the minimum wages at the local labor market, cross-country data, and the China Urban Labor Survey (CULS) conducted by the Institute of Population and Labor Economics in 2001, 2005, and 2010, respectively. The survey was implemented in Shanghai, Wuhan, Fuzhou, Shenyang, and Xi'an. Both local residents and migrants are included in the sample, and the sampling strategy of proportional probability stratification is applied. The sample is representative at the city level. The descriptive statistics and regression are weighted by sampling weights to avoid bias. To meet the purpose of this study, only wage employment is included.

3.2 Minimum Wage Regulations in China

The level of the minimum wage is not only the core element of the minimum wage regulation but also relates to the enforcement and effects of the minimum wage. Although the minimum wage regulation has a history of almost 20 years in China, it is still not very clear at what level should the minimum wage be set, and what factors should be taken into consideration when adjusting minimum wages. These ambiguities have resulted in casualness in setting the minimum wage and increased difficulties in minimum wage enforcement. In this section, we will first review the evolution of minimum wage regulations in China, and then discuss the level and adjustment of minimum wages as well as their relationship with minimum wage enforcement.

3.2.1 Evolution of Minimum Wage Regulations in China

China officially recognized the *Minimum Wage-Fixing Machinery Convention* in 1984.[1] However, from 1984 to 1992, there was no official minimum wage in China. In 1993, the Chinese Government issued its first minimum wage regulation, the *Enterprise Minimum Wage Regulation*. This regulation stipulates that a minimum wage can only be modified after it has been effective for at least one year. This regulation requires that local governments set the minimum wage according to local average wage, productivity, unemployment rate, economic development, and minimum living expenses, and all enterprises should comply with this regulation. These conditions provide considerable flexibility for provinces and cities in setting their minimum wages, with the economic development principle giving them the flexibility to restrain minimum wages to attract foreign investment (Wang and Gunderson 2011). The minimum wage regulation was formally established in 1995 when the *Labor Law of the People's Republic of China* was set into force. As a result, most provinces in China announced their first monthly minimum wages around 1995.

At the end of 2004, temporary labor shortages in some developed areas caught the attention of policymakers. In the same year, a modified minimum wage regulation, the *Minimum Wage Regulation*, was adopted. According to this new regulation, the minimum wage should be adjusted at least once every two years. This is a significant improvement over the 1993 regulation. Employers should not include subsidies, such as overtime pay, as part of the wage, when calculating the minimum wage. Penalties for violation of the regulation were increased from 20–100% of the owed wage to 100–500%. A minimum wage per hour that applies to part-time workers was also stipulated in this updated regulation.

The minimum wage regulation was also part of the *Labor Contract Law* which took effect on May 1, 2008. However, at the end of 2008, the Department of Human Resources and Social Security of China advised local governments against increasing the minimum wage in 2009 in case of possible negative impacts of the international financial crisis. As the influence of the financial crisis waned, there was a new round of minimum wage increases from 2010. In 2010, 30 of 31 provinces increased their minimum wages, with the average increase at 23%.[2] In each of

2011, 2012, and 2013, 24 provinces increased their minimum wages, and the average increase in each year was around 20%.[3] The Chinese Government has also promised to continue this increase in its twelfth five-year plan. In a recent proposal by the National Development and Reform Commission, the Chinese Government has set the goal that by the end of 2015, the minimum wage should reach 40% of the average wage of urban employment persons. It is apparent that China has entered an era of frequent minimum wage adjustments.

3.2.2 The Level of Minimum Wages in China

Unlike many developed economies, China does not set up a universal national minimum wage, while the provincial governments are responsible for minimum wage adjustments in each province. According to the *Minimum Wage Regulation* of 2004, multiple minimum wages are allowed in the same province. Therefore, to obtain a basic understanding of how the minimum wage standard has been set and increased in China, in this section, we use a two-step weighted approach to calculate the national minimum wage in each year. First, we calculate the average minimum wage in each province in each year using the actual enforcement days of each minimum wage as the weight. Second, we calculate the average national minimum wage using urban employment of each province as the weight.

In Fig. 3.1, we present minimum wage changes in China from 1995 to 2013.[4] It is evident that both nominal and real minimum wages have been increasing since 1995. However, if we measure minimum wages by relative minimum wages (the ratio of the minimum wage to the average wage, referred to as relative minimum wages hereafter), we will find that the minimum wage in China has been decreasing in recent years. Compared with OECD countries, minimum wages in China are still at a relatively low level. As of 2012, the relative minimum wage in OECD countries was about 35%, while in China this ratio was only 24%.[5]

Due to the lack of long-term data on average wages from labor force surveys, we used the average wage data published by the National Bureau of Statistics of China (NBS) when calculating the relative minimum wage in Fig. 3.1. However, as pointed out by Du and Wang (2008), the average annual wage published by NBS is based on a labor survey in urban China, and migrant workers and workers in informal sectors, who generally earn less than the average wage, are not adequately represented in the sample. As a result, the official average wage is overestimated, while the relative minimum wage is underestimated.

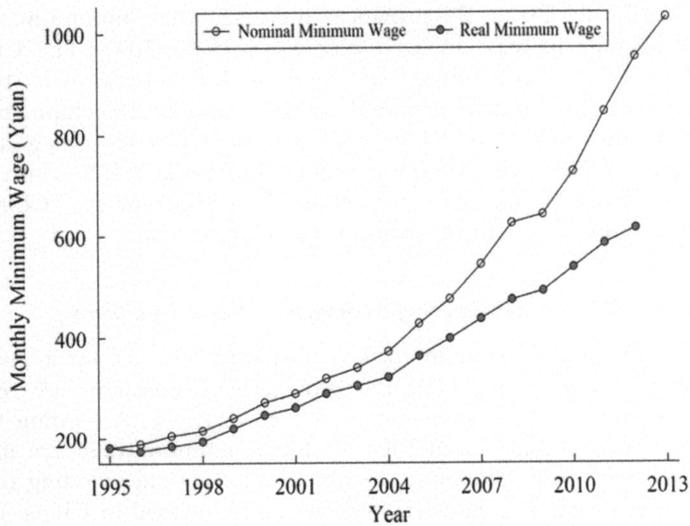

Fig. 3.1 Minimum wage increase in China, 1995–2013 (*Source* China Minimum Wage Database [CMWD], available from https://www.chinaminimumwage.org. *Note* The nominal minimum wage is adjusted by CPI to calculate the real minimum wage, using 1995 as the base year)

In fact, if we calculate the relative minimum wage using the average wage from a well-represented sample, we will find that the minimum wage in China is already at a relatively high level (see Fig. 3.2).[6] The relative minimum wage in China has already reached the target set by the National Development and Reform Commission of China.

For international comparisons, we also collect the latest minimum wage data for 150 countries and calculate the level of minimum wages relative to per capita GDP (see Table 3.1 and Fig. 3.3). From an international perspective, the relative minimum wage and per capita GDP are negatively correlated: High-income countries have a low relative minimum wage, while in low-income countries, the necessary costs of basic living (a proxy for minimum wages) account for a significant proportion of per capita GDP.

As is evident from Fig. 3.3, China is precisely on the fitted curve. If the relationship between the relative minimum wage and per capita GDP is universal, the minimum wage increase in China should not exceed the

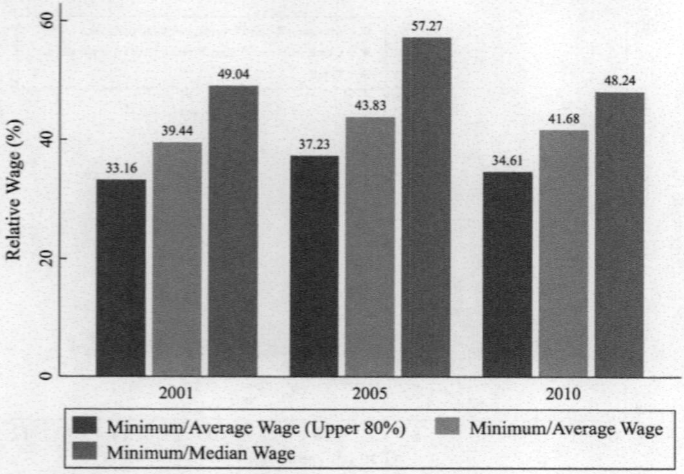

Fig. 3.2 Relative minimum wages: 2001, 2005, and 2010 (*Source* The average and median wages are from the three waves of the China Urban Labor Survey [CULS]. The minimum wage data are from the China Minimum Wage Database [CMWD], available from https://www.chinaminimumwage.org)

Table 3.1 Relative minimum wage and per capita GDP (by the end of 2013)

Income group	*Relative minimum wages (%)*
Low-income countries	104.76
Lower middle-income countries	64.78
China	38.90
Upper middle-income countries	39.83
High-income countries: Non-OECD	28.19
High-income countries: OECD	39.31

Source https://en.wikipedia.org/wiki/List_of_minimum_wages_by_country
Note The relative minimum wage is calculated using the latest available data for each country. China belongs to the upper middle-income countries

increase in per capita GDP over the next few years or even longer term. However, it is evident that, as evidenced by Fig. 3.4, the minimum wage increase in China has greatly exceeded the increase in per capita GDP in recent years.

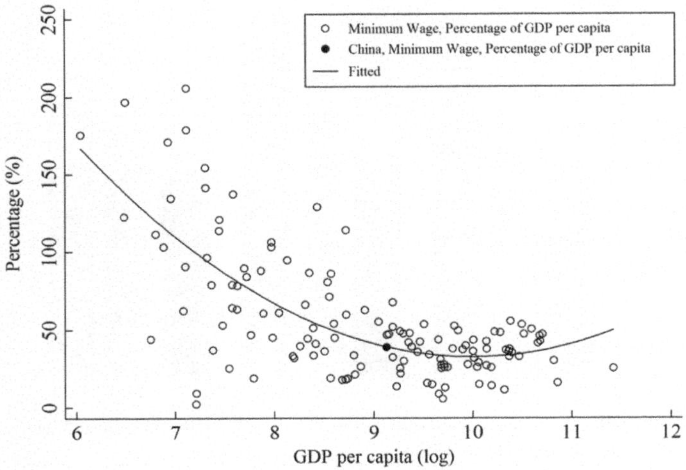

Fig. 3.3 The relationship between minimum wages and per capita GDP (*Source* Per capita GDP is from the World Development Indicator [WDI] database by the World Bank. The 2012 data are used here. The latest available minimum wage is from Wikipedia entry "List of Minimum Wages by Country", available from http://en.wikipedia.org/wiki/List_of_minimum_wages_by_country. *Note* Both minimum wages and per capita GDP have been adjusted by purchasing power parity [PPP], published by the World Bank)

As described above, if we consider the relationship between minimum wages and the stage of economic development, minimum wages in China are already very high, regarding both absolute level and international comparisons. In the current context of economic slowdown, especially when provincial governments tend to use minimum wages as a tool of income redistribution, continued substantial increase of minimum wages may become an essential factor of pushing higher labor cost. If the minimum wage in China continues to increase at 20% in the next few years, it may also generate high pressure on economic growth.

3.2.3 *Monthly or Hourly Minimum Wages?*

From an international perspective, most developed countries, for example, the United States, the UK, and Canada, only adopt hourly minimum wages. In China, according to the *Minimum Wage Regulation* of

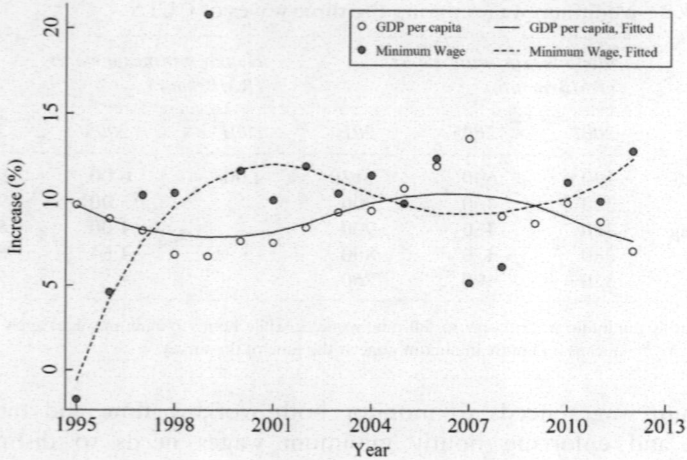

Fig. 3.4 The increase of minimum wages and per capita GDP in China (*Source* Minimum wage data are from the China Minimum Wage Database [CMWD], available from https://www.chinaminimumwage.org; per capita GDP is obtained from the *China Statistical Yearbook* 2013. *Note* All the data have been adjusted by GDP deflator)

2004, there are two kinds of minimum wages: the monthly minimum wage and the hourly minimum wage. The monthly minimum wage applies to full-time workers, while the hourly minimum wage applies to part-time workers. Adopting two types of minimum wages have considered the general tradition of paying wages in China, and the proper protection of part-time workers. However, although there are clear regulations on how monthly minimum wages and hourly minimum wages can be transformed into each other, there are still some problems in actual enforcement of two minimum wages.

First, some provincial governments did not pay much attention to the hourly minimum wage. Taking the five cities in CULS as an example, all cities including Shanghai, Wuhan, Shenyang, Fuzhou, and Xi'an significantly increased monthly minimum wages between 2001 and 2005, and between 2005 and 2010 (see Table 3.2). However, although the *Minimum Wage Regulation* requested local governments to set up an hourly minimum wage in 2004, some cities like Xi'an did not publish hourly minimum wages even in 2005.[7] Besides, enforcing monthly

Table 3.2 Minimum wages during the three waves of CULS

City	*Monthly minimum wages (RMB/month)*			*Hourly minimum wages (RMB/hour)*		
	2001	*2005*	*2010*	*2001*	*2005*	*2010*
Shanghai	490	690	1120	4.00	6.00	9.00
Wuhan	260	460	900	-	5.00	9.00
Shenyang	380	450	900	-	4.00	8.50
Fuzhou	380	470	800	-	4.54	8.50
Xi'an	320	490	760	-	-	7.60

Note Monthly minimum wages apply to full-time workers, while hourly minimum wages apply to part-time workers. "-" means no hourly minimum wage at the time of the survey

minimum wages needs to monitor both working time and monthly wages, and enforcing hourly minimum wages needs to distinguish between part-time and full-time jobs. These can all increase the difficulties and complexities of minimum wage enforcement.

Second, adopting a monthly minimum wage in China will induce firms to take advantage of the current wage system by increasing workings hours when governments do not well monitor maximum working hour regulation. Jia and Zhang (2013a) find that minimum wage adjustment can increase male weekly working hours, although male employment is not affected.

Third, minimum wage workers have less human capital and bargaining power in the labor market, and they need to work longer hours than non-minimum wage workers. The CULS data indicate that there are apparent differences in weekly working hours among different labor forces (see Table 3.3). Migrant workers have to work longer hours than local workers. Workers with low educational attainment have to work longer hours than workers with relatively high educational attainment. If the working hour is not well monitored by governments, enforcing monthly minimum wages will probably sacrifice the interests of migrant and less-educated workers, whom minimum wage regulations need to protect in the first place.

Finally, part-time workers only account for a small proportion of total urban employment. According to the *Labor Contract Law*, "part-time labor" means a form of labor for which the compensation is chiefly calculated by the hour and where the employee averages not more than

Table 3.3 Weekly working hours of different labor forces

Year	*Hukou*		*Education*			
	Migrant	*Local*	*Primary school and below*	*Junior high school*	*Senior high school*	*College and above*
2001	46.69	41.12	46.51	42.43	41.44	40.67
2005	45.02	41.11	43.91	43.14	41.11	40.04
2010	43.21	40.91	44.20	42.49	41.11	40.31

Source Authors' computation based on CULS data

4 hours of work per day and not more than an aggregate 24 hours of work per week for the same employer. According to this definition and CULS data, hourly minimum wages only apply to 2% of total employment.

As can be inferred from the above analysis, to target the minimum wage workers more effectively and decrease the enforcing difficulties, the Chinese Government should try publishing only an hourly minimum wage, which applies to both full-time and part-time workers.

3.3 The Coverage of Minimum Wages

The fundamental information we need to evaluate the enforcement is to look at how many workers are earning below local minimum wages. According to the Minimum *Wage Regulation* enacted in 2004, both monthly and hourly rates are adopted where the former is applied to full-time workers and the latter to part-time jobs. Article 2 of *Employment Contract Law* defines full-time jobs. Based on this definition, we distinguish every job we get from our samples and the application of minimum wages.

3.3.1 Demographics

The demographic determines wages. For the sake of enforcement, the linkages between demographics and wage give an explicit message of who is easy to fall below minimum wage. Based on the three rounds of the household survey, Table 3.4 presents the compliance of minimum wages by gender, education, and age.

Table 3.4 Compliance of minimum wages by demographic

Monthly rate (RMB)				*Hourly rate (RMB)*			*Coverage (%)*		
	2001	*2005*	*2010*	*2001*	*2005*	*2010*	*2001*	*2005*	*2010*
Gender									
Male	1078	1411	2488	6.42	8.39	14.83	93.1	89.1	91.2
	(874)	(1192)	(2049)	(5.83)	(7.74)	(12.8)	(25.4)	(31.1)	(28.3)
Female	844	1109	2012	5.13	6.88	12.29	87.4	81.3	85.1
	(576)	(943)	(1463)	(3.91)	(6.21)	(9.97)	(33.2)	(39.0)	(35.6)
Education									
Primary and below	664	721	1414	3.40	4.02	7.46	75.9	54.9	67.5
	(452)	(344)	(782)	(2.26)	(2.50)	(4.32)	(42.9)	(49.8)	(46.9)
Jr. High	760	900	1620	4.41	5.21	9.12	85.3	74.0	76.2
	(413)	(591)	(920)	(2.71)	(3.94)	(5.46)	(35.4)	(43.9)	(42.6)
Sr. High	943	1184	2000	5.63	7.09	11.99	92.5	88.0	88.0
	(761)	(815)	(1872)	(4.75)	(5.27)	(11.8)	(26.3)	(32.5)	(32.5)
College and above	1404	1875	2954	8.77	11.69	18.21	97.9	96.0	96.9
	(1006)	(1613)	(1984)	(7.14)	(10.4)	(12.9)	(14.2)	(19.5)	(17.3)
Age									
16–20	673	898	1378	3.18	5.09	6.82	83.6	87.0	81.2
	(347)	(369)	(629)	(2.17)	(2.85)	(3.45)	(37.2)	(33.7)	(39.2)
21–30	1080	1484	2401	6.13	8.88	14.61	94.6	93.3	93.9
	(806)	(1181)	(1841)	(5.14)	(7.67)	(12.6)	(22.6)	(25.0)	(24.0)
31–40	957	1175	2525	5.67	6.93	15.11	92.3	83.7	93.2
	(683)	(1104)	(1836)	(4.59)	(7.20)	(11.4)	(26.7)	(36.9)	(25.3)
41–50	910	1203	1967	5.52	7.24	11.63	89.6	82.1	83.2
	(661)	(1060)	(1364)	(4.14)	(6.71)	(8.37)	(30.5)	(38.4)	(37.4)
50+	1070	1389	2304	6.83	8.79	14.18	87.3	87.0	82.8
	(1012)	(1107)	(2394)	(7.23)	(7.49)	(15.1)	(33.3)	(33.7)	(37.7)

Source Authors' computation based on CULS data
Note The standard deviations are in parenthesis

Without controlling for other factors, Table 3.4 indicates that the average wages for females are significantly lower than male. In 2001, average monthly earnings for females are about 78.3% of those of males, and the ratio went up to 80.9% in 2010. Measured by hourly wages, the ratios are 79.9, 82.0, and 82.9% in 2001, 2005, and 2010, respectively. The women are more likely to earn less than the minimum wage since their wages are lower than male workers. In 2001, female workers who earn earnings below the minimum wage are 5.7 percentage points higher than their male counterpart, and the shares are 7.8 and 6.1 percentage points higher in 2005 and 2010, respectively. This significant difference reflects the possible existence of labor market discrimination. More importantly, it provides targeting groups to enforce the minimum wage.

The less-educated workers are always the primary targeting groups for minimum wages. Our sample also indicates a significant difference in coverage among workers with different education. Samples from the three rounds of the survey all indicate the trend of increasing wage with education. When compared to hourly rates, the more educated workers tend to have more advantages. For example, in 2010 the average monthly wage rate for workers with primary education or less is 47.9% of that of workers with college or above. Measured by hourly wages, the former is 41% of the latter. It is evident that less-educated workers are more likely to earn a wage below the minimum wage. Table 3.4 indicates that despite the coverage variations due to adjustment of minimum wages over time, the group of workers with the least education is most likely to fall below the minimum wage. In 2010, 32.5% of workers with primary school or below earned below local minimum wages. For workers with junior high school, the share is 23.8%.

The compliance of minimum wages is also associated with the wage changes over the life cycle. As indicated in Table 3.4, the coverage of the minimum wage shows an inverted U shape with age increase. It is worthwhile to note the coverage for two age groups. The first one is the new labor market entrants whose ages are between 16 and 20. Both their average wage rates and coverage rate are low. In 2010, 18.8 of workers in the group earn a wage rate below the minimum wage. The other interesting group is those aged 50 or above. Although the average wage is not the lowest among groups, they have significant wage variations within groups, as evidenced by high standard deviations in the parenthesis. As a result, we still see a relatively large share of this group of workers earns below the minimum wage.

Table 3.5 Coverage of minimum wages: local workers and migrants

Year	*Local workers*	*Migrant workers*
Monthly wages (RMB)		
2001	986 (775)	934 (745)
2005	1298 (1120)	1086 (844)
2010	2280 (1858)	2304 (1605)
Hourly wages (RMB)		
2001	6.05 (5.17)	4.57 (4.78)
2005	7.91 (7.27)	5.66 (5.26)
2010	13.86 (11.90)	12.61 (10.10)
Coverage (%)		
2001	91.1 (28.5)	87.7 (32.8)
2005	86.3 (34.4)	79.1 (40.7)
2010	88.5 (32.0)	89.4 (30.8)

Source Authors' computation based on CULS data
Note The standard deviations are in parenthesis

3.3.2 *Hukou*

Rural migrant workers have been the indispensable component of labor supply in the urban labor market. According to the NBS, in 2013 the rural migrant workers totaled 166 million, which accounted for 40% of urban employment. With labor market development, *hukou* has disconnected from employment determination and wage formation gradually, even its link with social protection is still apparent.

Table 3.5 presents the same indicators as Table 3.4, but by *hukou* status. In 2001 and 2005, local workers have higher average wages. However, with the increasing labor scarcity, wage rates for migrant workers have been proliferating. In 2010, wages for migrant workers were slightly higher than their local counterpart in our sample. This is consistent with observations from aggregated information. According to the NBS, real wage growth per annum for migrant workers is 12.7% between 2007 and 2013, much faster than urban local workers. It is good to believe that the spontaneous changes in labor demand and supply facilitate the compliance of minimum wages in this case even without additional effort to enforcement.

The results in Table 3.5 indicate that local workers have better compliance in the case of 2001 and 2005. However, the share of local workers falling below the minimum wage in 2010 is one percentage point

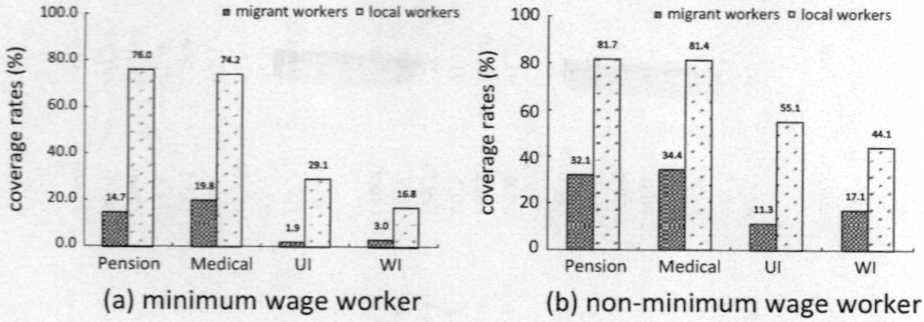

Fig. 3.5 Coverage of minimum wages and social security (*Source* Authors' computation based on CULS data. *Note* "UI" stands for unemployment insurance, while "WI" stands for injury insurance)

higher than migrant workers. It has something to do with the labor market dynamics, which improves the situations of migrant workers. The result is also associated with insufficient social protection of migrant workers. Figure 3.5 depicts the compliance of minimum wages and coverage of social protection for both migrant workers and local workers as well. The left panel reflects the workers working below the minimum wage and the right panel for the above.

Two features of Fig. 3.5 are worth noting. First of all, regardless of compliance with the minimum wage, the coverage of social protection for local workers is much higher than migrant workers. Second, as far as workers working below the minimum wage are concerned, there is an even more significant disparity between migrant workers and their local counterpart.

3.3.3 *Sector, Occupation, and Ownership*

It is of policy relevance to observe the compliance by ownership or sector. The ownership, occupation, and sectors reflect the job characteristics that are associated with how difficult to enforce the minimum wage. Table 3.6 lists the compliance of the minimum wage by the three dimensions respectively.

For simplicity, the sectors are regrouped into four groups of consumer services, business services, manufacturing, and other sectors. The consumer services include wholesale and retail, education, culture, entertainment and sports, and general services. The business services include

Table 3.6 Compliance of minimum wages by sector, occupation, and ownership

Monthly rate (RMB)				*Hourly rate (RMB)*			*Coverage (%)*		
	2001	*2005*	*2010*	*2001*	*2005*	*2010*	*2001*	*2005*	*2010*
Sector									
Consumer service	978	1126	2016	5.68	6.73	12.19	89.3	81.4	81.4
	(688)	(818)	(1518)	(4.86)	(5.31)	(10.6)	(31.0)	(38.9)	(38.9)
Business service	1142	1677	2694	6.85	10.17	16.09	95.9	94.0	95.0
	(1077)	(1509)	(2381)	(7.14)	(9.85)	(14.8)	(19.8)	(23.8)	(21.9)
Manufacture	847	1190	2093	5.16	7.10	12.59	88.9	90.0	91.2
	(617)	(932)	(1321)	(3.92)	(5.91)	(7.94)	(31.4)	(30.0)	(28.4)
Others	987	1312	2458	6.18	8.27	15.01	89.4	80.6	93.9
	(659)	(1249)	(1649)	(4.30)	(8.24)	(9.70)	(31.0)	(39.6)	(24.1)
Ownership									
Public admin.	1066	1454	2693	6.64	9.01	16.96	89.4	89.8	91.2
	(878)	(1133)	(2244)	(6.20)	(7.20)	(14.9)	(30.8)	(30.2)	(28.4)
SOEs	898	1264	2147	5.50	7.65	13.09	91.2	90.2	91.0
	(614)	(972)	(1528)	(3.92)	(6.27)	(9.57)	(28.4)	(29.7)	(28.7)
Private	1058	1178	2167	5.77	6.90	12.44	91.3	78.9	84.8
	(919)	(1176)	(1799)	(6.01)	(7.63)	(11.1)	(28.3)	(40.8)	(36.0)
Occupation									
Person in charge	-	2010	3623	-	12.42	21.52	-	98.1	96.5
	-	(1598)	(3217)	-	(10.2)	(20.3)	-	(13.6)	(18.4)
Professionals	-	1769	2924	-	11.13	18.22	-	97.4	97.0
	-	(1449)	(1864)	-	(9.50)	(12.3)	-	(15.8)	(17.1)
Clerk	-	1251	2688	-	7.92	16.58	-	85.7	94.1
	-	(998)	(2444)	-	(6.85)	(15.3)	-	(35.1)	(23.6)
Attendants	-	1000	1770	-	5.83	10.24	-	73.8	75.9
	-	(888)	(1520)	-	(5.63)	(9.64)	-	(44.0)	(42.8)
Production workers	-	1153	1935	-	6.66	11.46	-	92.3	90.2
	-	(712)	(1093)	-	(4.40)	(6.86)	-	(26.6)	(29.8)

Source Authors' computation based on CULS data
Note The standard deviations are in parenthesis

production and supply of electricity, heat, gas, and water, transportation and logistics, software and IT, finance, construction, real estate, R & D. Both consumer services and manufacturing are characterized by intensively using labor, as evidenced by low hourly wage rates.

Greater variations in the wage distribution are found in the sectors of consumer services. For example, the coefficients of variation in the sector for monthly and hourly rates are 0.75 and 0.87 respectively while the coefficient is 0.63 in manufacturing. So, the disparity in average wage is small, but the compliance with the minimum wage in consumer service is 10 percentage points below. Thus, it can be seen that the performance of minimum wage enforcement has something to do with the industrial organization. In other words, when manufacturing dominates one city and consumer service dominates another, the outcomes could be different even the local governments take the same effort to enforcement.

It seems that the types of ownership make a difference in compliance too. The employers are grouped as public administration, SOEs, and private sectors. Workers in SOEs have similar average wages to those in the private sector; however, the latter has worse compliance in the minimum wage. In 2010, the share of workers earning below the minimum wage was 6.2 percentage point higher in private sectors than in public sectors.

3.3.4 *Informality*

Informal sector is always vital for targeting areas to enforce minimum wages. Informal employee is defined as the employees without employment contract or workers who worked in enterprises with less than seven employees. The findings from the three waves of data are indicated in Table 3.7.

First, it is not surprising that significant disparity in compliance with minimum wages exists between formal and informal sectors. In 2010, the compliance in the formal sector was 17.7 percentage points higher than that in informal sectors. Second, with increasing minimum wages over time, the compliance in informal sectors has been deteriorating. The coverage rate in 2010 has fallen 3.9 percentage points from 2001. Third, more heterogeneity is found within informal sectors over time. For instance, the coefficient of variation for monthly wages in the informal sector was going up from 0.64 in 2001 to 0.82 in 2010. The result is consistent with observations in other countries where the informality

Table 3.7 Compliance of minimum wages by informality

Monthly rate (RMB)				*Hourly rate (RMB)*			*Coverage (%)*		
	2001	*2005*	*2010*	*2001*	*2005*	*2010*	*2001*	*2005*	*2010*
Formal sector	1010	1465	2358	6.09	8.97	14.3	92.1	91.7	90.2
	(790)	(1218)	(1865)	(5.17)	(7.87)	(12.0)	(27.0)	(27.6)	(29.8)
CV	0.78	0.83	0.79	0.85	0.88	0.84	0.29	0.30	0.33
Informal sector	667	885	1526	3.58	5.09	8.06	76.4	72.8	72.5
	(427)	(636)	(1250)	(4.34)	(4.24)	(6.98)	(42.5)	(44.5)	(44.7)
CV	0.64	0.72	0.82	1.21	0.83	0.87	0.56	0.61	0.62

Source Authors' computation based on CULS data
Note The standard deviations are in parenthesis. CV is short for "coefficient of variation"

diversifies with economic development (Andrews et al. 2011). The heterogeneity within informal sectors has been challenging with the enforcement of minimum wages regarding necessity and difficulties. On the one hand, with economic development, some workers might voluntarily choose informal jobs, which brings up the necessity to intervene in the wage through the institution. On the other hand, the heterogeneity of informal employment in job characteristics and job quality makes it more difficult to identify what to enforce in the formal sector, which increases the costs of enforcement.

3.4 Determinants of Minimum Wage Enforcement

In Sect. 3.3, we observe that there are considerable differences in minimum wage coverage among different labor forces. In this section, we will use microdata from the three waves of the CULS to analyze the determinants of minimum wage coverage.

3.4.1 Data

The minimum wage data used in this section are from the China Minimum Wage Database (CMWD), which is available from https://www.chinaminimumwage.org. This database is established by the Institute of Population and Labor Economics, Chinese Academy of Social Sciences. The database contains minimum wages and other labor market indicators of nearly 3000 county-level regions in China from 1993 to the present day.

The micro-level data used in this section are from CULS, which was conducted in 2001, 2005, and 2010 by the Institute of Population and Labor Economics, Chinese Academy of Social Sciences. In the 2001 survey (CULS 1), five cities, Shanghai, Wuhan, Shenyang, Fuzhou, and Xi'an, were sampled. In each city, we interviewed 700 urban households and 600 migrant workers in 70 communities, based on multi-stage random sampling principle. In the 2005 survey (CULS 2), another seven cities, Wuxi, Yichang, Benxi, Zhuhai, Shenzhen, Baoji, and Daqing, were sampled, besides the five cities in CULS 1. We interviewed 500 urban households and 500 migrant households in each city based on the same sampling principle. In 2010 (CULS 3), Guangzhou was added to the survey, besides the five cities in CULS 1. In each city, following the same sampling principle, we interviewed 700 urban households and 600 migrant households.

In this section, to maintain consistency across surveys, we only use data of Shanghai, Wuhan, Shenyang, Fuzhou, and Xi'an, which were sampled in all three rounds. Also, because minimum wage regulations only apply to employees in firms and public institutions, we delete observations whose employment status is employer or self-employment. Besides, according to the definition of "part-time worker" in *Labor Contract Law*, we also distinguish between full-time and part-time workers.

3.4.2 *Model Specifications*

In our model, the explained variable is a dummy variable, i.e., whether one's wage is below the official minimum wage (1 for below or equal to minimum wage, 0 for above the minimum wage). The explained variable is highly related to wage, so the right-hand of the model includes variables that should appear in a typical wage equation. These variables can be classified into three categories: individual demographic and human capital variables, household-level variables, regional and firm-level variables.

Individual demographic and human capital variables include workers' gender (dummy variable, 0 for female), age, age squared, education in years, training (dummy variable, 0 for no training), and health condition (discrete variable, with 1–4 standing for bad, general, good and very good health condition respectively, using "bad" as the base), etc. Household-level variables include workers' marital status (dummy variable, 0 for unmarried), number of household members, whether there are children below 6 in the household (dummy variable, 0 for no children below 6), etc.

Regional and firm-level variables include whether the worker holds a local *hukou* (dummy variable, 0 for non-local *hukou*), city (discrete variable, using Shanghai as the base), industry (discrete variable, using manufacturing as the base; the definitions of production services and consumer services are the same with Sect. 3.3), types of ownership (dummy variable, using the public sector as the base), and the interaction terms of some variables, etc.

A linear probability model is applied in our analysis. As pointed out by Wooldridge (2010), if the purpose of the research is to study the marginal effects of the explanatory variables, and if most of the explanatory variables only take a few unique values, then the use of a linear probability model is much better, and the problem that some predicted value may fall outside the range [0, 1] should not be concerned. Besides, compared with Probit model, it is straightforward to explain the coefficients of a linear probability model. As a result, in this section, we apply a linear probability model in all regressions.

3.4.3 Regression Results

Table 3.8 presents the regression results of the determinants of minimum wage enforcement under three different specifications. In specification (1), the explanatory variables include the city dummies, the industry dummies, and the ownership dummies, but don't include the interaction terms of them. In specification (2), the explanatory variables include the interaction terms of these dummy variables, but don't include the variables separately. In specification (3), the explanatory variables include both the dummy variables and their interaction terms.

After controlling other factors, the minimum wage coverage for females is still worth than male in all three specifications. This may be partially caused by the fact that the average female wage is lower than male. This may also reflect discrimination again female in labor market, and minimum wage protections for females are not enough. In 2005, the coefficients of age and age squared imply an inverse U relationship between minimum wage coverage and age, i.e., younger and older individuals tend to be less likely covered by the minimum wage, which is consistent with our analysis in Sect. 3.3.

Table 3.8 Determinants of the minimum wage coverage

Explanatory variables	*(1)*			*(2)*			*(3)*		
	2001	*2005*	*2010*	*2001*	*2005*	*2010*	*2001*	*2005*	*2010*
Gender	−0.05***	−0.07***	−0.06***	−0.05***	−0.06***	−0.06***	−0.05***	−0.06***	−0.06***
Age	−0.00	0.01**	−0.00	−0.00	0.01**	−0.00	−0.00	0.01**	−0.00
Age squared	0.00	−0.01*	0.01*	0.00	−0.01*	0.01*	0.00	−0.01*	0.01*
Education	−0.02***	−0.03***	−0.02***	−0.02***	−0.03***	−0.02***	−0.02***	−0.03***	−0.02***
Training	−0.01	0.06**	−0.05***	−0.01	0.04	−0.05***	−0.01	0.04	−0.05***
Health: general	−0.11***	−0.27***	−0.17**	−0.11***	−0.27***	−0.16*	−0.11***	−0.27***	−0.16*
Health: good	−0.12***	−0.32***	−0.24***	−0.12***	−0.30***	−0.23***	−0.12***	−0.30***	−0.23***
Health: very good	−0.13***	−0.35***	−0.25***	−0.14***	−0.33***	−0.23***	−0.14***	−0.33***	−0.23***
Marital status	−0.01	−0.02	−0.01	−0.01	−0.01	−0.02	−0.01	−0.01	−0.02
No. of household members	0.01	−0.01	0.01	0.01	−0.01	0.01	0.01	−0.01	0.01
Children below 6 in the family	−0.00	−0.01	−0.00	−0.00	−0.00	−0.00	−0.00	−0.00	−0.00
Local labor	−0.04*	−0.02	0.04***	−0.04**	−0.05*	0.03**	−0.04**	−0.05*	0.03**
City: Wuhan	−0.05***	0.15***	0.06***				−0.04	0.08**	−0.01
City: Shenyang	0.04**	0.12***	0.08***				0.11***	0.17***	0.05
City: Fuzhou	0.00	−0.02	0.01				0.13***	0.16**	−0.02
City: Xi'an	0.03**	0.05***	−0.00				0.02	0.06**	−0.00
Industry: production service	−0.04***	0.00	−0.01				−0.07***	0.04	−0.02
Industry: consumer service	0.00	0.07***	0.09***				0.04	0.08***	0.08**
Industry: other Industries	0.01	0.10***	−0.01				0.02	0.06*	0.03
Private sector	−0.03*	0.07***	0.04***				−0.02	0.04	0.05
Shanghai * Manufacturing * Private sector				−0.02	0.04	0.05			
Shanghai * Production service * Public sector				−0.07***	0.04	−0.02			
Shanghai * Production Service * Private sector				0.03	0.06**	0.01	0.12**	−0.01	−0.01

(continued)

Table 3.8 (continued)

Explanatory variables	*(1)*			*(2)*			*(3)*		
	2001	*2005*	*2010*	*2001*	*2005*	*2010*	*2001*	*2005*	*2010*
Shanghai * Consumer service * Public sector				0.04	0.08***	0.08**			
Shanghai * Consumer service * Private sector				−0.02	0.06*	0.07*	−0.04	−0.06	−0.06
Shanghai * Other industries * Public sector				0.02	0.06*	0.03			
Shanghai * Other industries * Private sector				−0.01	0.25**	−0.13**	−0.00	0.15	−0.21***
Wuhan * Manufacturing * Public sector				−0.04	0.08**	−0.01			
Wuhan * Manufacturing * Private sector				−0.09***	0.28***	0.10	−0.03	0.16*	0.06
Wuhan * Production service * Public sector				−0.06***	0.09*	−0.01	0.04	−0.02	0.02
Wuhan * Production service * Private sector				−0.07***	0.12**	0.08**	0.06	−0.03	0.07
Wuhan * Consumer service * Public sector				−0.03	0.13***	0.12***	−0.03	−0.03	0.04
Wuhan * Consumer service * Private sector				−0.09***	0.38***	0.30***	−0.07	0.18***	0.17**
Wuhan * Other industries * Public sector				−0.04	0.09*	−0.02	−0.02	−0.04	−0.04
Wuhan * Other industries * Private sector				−0.05	0.67***	0.02	−0.01	0.50***	−0.05
Shenyang * Manufacturing * Public sector				0.11***	0.17***	0.05			

(continued)

Table 3.8 (continued)

Explanatory variables	*(1)*			*(2)*			*(3)*		
	2001	*2005*	*2010*	*2001*	*2005*	*2010*	*2001*	*2005*	*2010*
Shenyang * Manufacturing * Private sector				0.10	0.09	0.01	0.02	−0.11	−0.09
Shenyang * Production service * Public sector				−0.03	0.08*	0.05	−0.07	−0.12*	0.02
Shenyang * Production service * Private sector				−0.06*	0.05	0.10**	−0.08	−0.19**	0.03
Shenyang * Consumer service * Public sector				0.06*	0.21***	0.14***	−0.09*	−0.04	0.00
Shenyang * Consumer service * Private sector				−0.05	0.26***	0.21***	−0.17**	−0.03	0.03
Shenyang * Other industries * Public sector				0.04	0.12***	0.12**	−0.09	−0.11*	0.03
Shenyang * Other industries * Private sector				0.21**	0.35***	−0.10	0.10	0.09	−0.23**
Fuzhou * Manufacturing * Public sector				0.13***	0.16**	−0.02			
Fuzhou * Manufacturing * Private sector				−0.07**	0.01	0.04	−0.17***	−0.19**	0.01
Fuzhou * Production service * Public sector				−0.02	0.03	0.04	−0.08*	−0.16**	0.08
Fuzhou * Production service * Private sector				−0.10***	−0.02	0.01	−0.14**	−0.25***	−0.00
Fuzhou * Consumer service * Public sector				−0.01	0.10***	0.05	−0.18***	−0.14**	−0.02
Fuzhou * Consumer service * Private sector				−0.08**	0.08**	0.08**	−0.22***	−0.20**	−0.03

(continued)

Table 3.8 (continued)

Explanatory variables	*(1)*			*(2)*			*(3)*		
	2001	*2005*	*2010*	*2001*	*2005*	*2010*	*2001*	*2005*	*2010*
Fuzhou * Other industries * Public sector				0.03	−0.00	0.04	−0.12**	−0.22***	0.03
Fuzhou * Other industries * Private sector				−0.05	−0.03	−0.02	−0.17**	−0.28**	−0.08
Xi'an * Manufacturing * Public sector				0.02	0.06**	−0.00			
Xi'an * Manufacturing * Private sector				0.11	0.01	0.10	0.11	−0.09*	0.06
Xi'an * Production service * Public sector				0.00	0.07**	0.01	0.04	−0.03	0.04
Xi'an * Production service * Private sector				−0.00	0.08*	−0.01	0.06	−0.06	−0.03
Xi'an * Consumer service * Public sector				0.04	0.15***	0.05	−0.02	−0.00	−0.03
Xi'an * Consumer service * Private sector				0.02	0.15***	0.11***	−0.02	−0.04	−0.01
Xi'an * Other industries * Public sector				0.06*	0.09**	−0.04*	0.01	−0.03	−0.07
Xi'an * Other industries * Private sector				0.14	−0.01	−0.05	0.12	−0.18**	−0.12
Constant	0.47***	0.53***	0.58***	0.47***	0.54***	0.58***	0.47***	0.54***	0.58***
R^2	0.08	0.18	0.14	0.09	0.23	0.16	0.09	0.23	0.16
No. of observations	4602	4324	6445	4602	4324	6445	4602	4324	6445

Note ***, **, and * represent significance level at 1%, 5%, and 10%, respectively

More education tends to decrease the possibility that one's wage will fall below the minimum wage. The contribution of training to wage determination is becoming more and more important in recent years. Better health conditions have a positive impact on wage. Education, training, and health condition are all core elements of human capital, and they all contribute positively to wage, which is consistent with human capital theory.

In all three specifications, household-level variables have little effects on wage. However, married individuals with children have higher responsibilities for their families. As a result, they have to work much harder and hold a more stable job and may be less likely to fall below the minimum wage.

In 2001 and 2005, the average wage of migrant workers was lower than local workers. However, in 2010, migrants' average wage became slightly higher than local workers. As we discussed in Sect. 3.3, the role of market forces is becoming more and more important in wage determinations in recent years, due to the lack of migrant workers. However, if we consider the differences in social protections between local and migrant workers, we will find that the actual income of migrant workers is still lower than local workers. In Table 3.9, we present the differences in social protections between local and migrant workers.

In general, migrant workers are better covered regarding social insurance as time goes on, although the percentage of covered migrant workers is still lower than local workers. Besides, the improvement of social protection for migrant workers is mainly contributed by migrant workers who earn above minimum wages, and the proportion of migrant minimum wage workers covered by social protection is still tiny. In fact, the percentage of migrant minimum wage workers covered by unemployment insurance and working injury insurance declined in 2010 compared with 2005.

Most cities have worth minimum wage coverage than Shanghai. A higher minimum wage coverage implies greater efforts by local labor inspection agencies in enforcing minimum wage regulation. However, as nominal minimum wages are related to the local price level, a seemingly high minimum wage does not necessarily represent strong labor market interventions by local governments. As a result, the enforcing difficulties of minimum wage regulations have no direct connections with nominal minimum wages. In Table 3.2, Shanghai has the highest nominal monthly minimum wages and nominal hourly minimum wages.

Table 3.9 Social protections of local and migrant workers (%)

Social protections	*CULS 1*		*CULS 2*		*CULS 3*	
	Migrant	*Local*	*Migrant*	*Local*	*Migrant*	*Local*
All						
Pension	6.27	37.45	14.03	73.94	30.03	80.75
Medical	6.63	37.34	14.96	65.26	32.66	80.30
Unemployment	-	-	6.84	32.80	10.40	51.82
Working injury	-	-	12.23	28.42	15.62	40.76
Minimum wage worker						
Pension	5.92	21.23	6.33	63.53	14.65	76.04
Medical	5.09	18.03	6.84	45.76	19.75	74.15
Unemployment	-	-	5.94	17.14	1.93	29.12
Working injury	-	-	6.82	9.09	2.97	16.82
Non-minimum wage worker						
Pension	6.28	39.05	16.12	75.85	32.05	81.74
Medical	6.74	39.23	17.25	68.73	34.42	81.39
Unemployment	-	-	7.20	35.60	11.28	55.14
Working injury	-	-	13.87	31.83	17.05	44.14

Note A minimum wage worker refers to a worker whose wage is equal to or below the official minimum wage. A non-minimum wage worker refers to a worker whose wage is above the official minimum wage. In CULS 1, information on unemployment insurance and working injury insurance is not available

However, if we adjust nominal minimum wages by spatial price indices (SPI), which is proposed by Brandt and Holz (2006), to calculate a minimum wage which is comparable among regions, then minimum wages in Shanghai is no longer the highest one (Table 3.10). In 2010, Shenyang and Wuhan have higher minimum wage standards than Shanghai, and as a result, the enforcement is more difficult, and the coverage rate is lower.

3.4.4 Decomposition of Changes in Minimum Wage Enforcement

In this section, we decomposed the changes in minimum wage coverage using the Blinder-Oaxaca method (Blinder 1973; Oaxaca 1973). In Table 3.11, the minimum wage coverage decreased from 2001 to 2005, while the coverage increased from 2005 to 2010. We decompose these changes into three effects: the endowment effect, the return effect, and the interaction effect. The endowment effect represents the changes in the minimum wage coverage because of different sample characteristics in different years. The return effect represents the changes in the minimum wage

Table 3.10 Minimum wage standards during the CULS surveys (SPI adjusted)

City	*Monthly minimum wages (RMB/month)*			*Hourly minimum wages (RMB/hour)*		
	2001	*2005*	*2010*	*2001*	*2005*	*2010*
Shanghai	490	665	952	4.00	5.78	7.65
Wuhan	346	560	959	-	6.09	9.59
Shenyang	501	572	1008	-	5.09	9.52
Fuzhou	466	545	825	-	5.27	8.77
Xi'an	420	626	821	-	-	8.21

Note "Monthly minimum wages" applies to full-time workers, while "hourly minimum wages" applies to part-time workers. "-" indicates that there's no hourly minimum wages during the survey. The data in this table have been adjusted by spatial price indices (SPI) proposed by Brandt and Holz (2006), using Shanghai in 2001 as the base

coverage because of changes in coefficients of sample characteristics in different years. The interaction effect is the changes in the minimum wage coverage because of changes in both sample characteristics and their coefficients.

In Table 3.11, under all three specifications and in all three years, the endowment effects are all positive, while the return effects are all negative and the interaction effects are all minimal. The positive endowment effects imply that better individual, household, regional and firm-level characteristics tend to increase the minimum wage coverage. The adverse return effects indicate that the wage return to the individual, household, regional and firm-level characteristics is declining, and thus can decrease the minimum wage coverage. More specifically, from 2001 to 2005, the return effect was higher than the endowment effect, and as a result, the minimum wage coverage decreased; from 2005 to 2010, the endowment effect was more significant than return effect, and as a result, the minimum wage coverage increased.

In the endowment effect, human capital has the most substantial contribution, while the contribution of household constraints and regional and firm-level characteristics are very small or even negative. In the return effect, although the net effect is negative, the return to human capital is still positive and increasing, and the negative return effect is mainly caused by the decrease of return to regional and firm-level characteristics, which indicates that the differences in wage level and minimum wage coverage caused by household registration, region, industry, and ownership type tend to decrease.

Table 3.11 Decomposition of changes in the minimum wage coverage

Decomposition	*(1)*		*(2)*		*(3)*	
	2001–2005	*2005–2010*	*2001–2005*	*2005–2010*	*2001–2005*	*2005–2010*
Specification						
City	Y	Y	N	N	Y	Y
Industry	Y	Y	N	N	Y	Y
Ownership	Y	Y	N	N	Y	Y
Interaction	N	N	Y	Y	Y	Y
Total						
Group 1	0.0925	0.1422	0.0915	0.1430	0.0925	0.1422
Group 2	0.1422	0.1139	0.1430	0.1144	0.1422	0.1139
Differences	−0.0497	0.0284	−0.0515	0.0287	−0.0497	0.0284
Endowment effect	0.0414	0.0342	0.0250	0.0327	0.0270	0.0326
Return effect	−0.0699	−0.0070	−0.0732	−0.0141	−0.0722	−0.0150
Interaction effect	−0.0211	0.0012	−0.0033	0.0101	−0.0044	0.0108
Endowment effect						
Human capital	0.0469	0.0297	0.0422	0.0292	0.0428	0.0287
Household	0.0023	−0.0008	0.0027	−0.0010	0.0030	−0.0010
Region and firm	−0.0079	0.0053	−0.0199	0.0045	−0.0188	0.0049
Return effect						
Human capital	0.0938	0.0935	0.0795	0.1049	0.0771	0.0829
Household	0.0436	−0.0410	0.0344	−0.0362	0.0356	−0.0407
Region and firm	−0.2073	−0.0595	−0.1870	−0.0827	−0.1849	−0.0573
Interaction effect						
Human capital	−0.0264	−0.0001	−0.0217	−0.0012	−0.0214	−0.0003
Household	−0.0064	0.0007	−0.0067	0.0007	−0.0069	0.0007
Region and firm	0.0117	0.0006	0.0251	0.0105	0.0238	0.0104

As described above, human capital tends to increase the coverage of minimum wage regulations, regarding both endowment effect and return effect. As a result, by promoting education, training and medical services, workers can acquire more return from the labor market, and the pressure of enforcing the minimum wage regulation can also be eased.

3.5 Conclusions

Taking advantage of various sources of data, this chapter describes the evolution of the minimum wage system in China and analyzes its enforcement. In 2010, 13% of workers in our sample earned wages below local minimum wages. This result is worse than most of the developed countries but better than countries with about the same level of economic development as China.

Our analysis indicates that the effect of compliance in minimum wages is not only determined by the effort to enforcement but correlated with many other factors. When the demand for labor is robust, and the demographic transition has more and more constrained labor supply, wages for unskilled workers have been growing rapidly. In this case, the difficulty of enforcement reduces due to the natural forces in the labor market. Also, more regulated labor market institutions, like the *Employment Contract Law*, facilitate to enforcement the minimum wage.

Using urban household survey data, this chapter examines the coverage of minimum wages. Both descriptive statistics and regression analysis indicate that some focused groups of workers ought to be targeted when implementing the minimum wages, including female and less-educated workers. Meanwhile, the significant disparity in returns to human capital implies that in the long run improving job quality is the fundamental means to better enforcement.

The empirical analysis in this chapter also indicates that the variation of enforcement might simply put in a nutshell of different efforts in enforcement among regions. Controlled for individual characteristics, we do find that in the early period the coastal cities had better performance in compliance with minimum wages. However, the most recent data also indicate that the regional disparity would disappear if the ownership and economic structure of the regions are controlled. This implies that the difference in economic structure and development could give rise to compliance among regions.

Notes

1. The Minimum Wage-Fixing Machinery Convention was established in 1928 by the International Labor Organization (ILO).
2. This value is calculated by the author based on the China Minimum Wage Database.
3. This value is calculated by the author based on the China Minimum Wage Database. In 2013, only minimum wage adjustments in the last three quarters were considered.
4. Although minimum wage regulation was first introduced in 1993, most provinces issued their first minimum wages in 1995. That is why we do not report a national minimum wage before 1995 in Fig. 3.1.
5. According to the China Minimum Wage Database, the annual minimum wage in 2012 was 11438 RMB. According to the China Statistical Yearbook 2013, the annual average wage of urban employees in 2012 was 46769 RMB. As a result, the relative minimum wage is 24% for 2012.
6. For Fig. 3.3, the average wage is calculated from the China Urban Labor Survey, which was conducted by the Institute of Population and Labor Economics, Chinese Academy of Social Sciences, in 2001, 2005, and 2010. For more details of the survey, please visit http://iple.cass.cn/cate/1103.htm.
7. Some provinces have been publishing hourly minimum wages since 1995, when the Enterprise Minimum Wage Regulation was first introduced. However, this hourly minimum wage is calculated directly from monthly minimum wage (a typical worker generally works four weeks per month and 20.92 hours per week) and is very different from hourly minimum wage that applies to part-time workers. After the Minimum Wage Regulation of 2004 was set into force, most provinces stopped publishing the calculated hourly minimum wage.

References

Andrews, D., A. C. Sánchez and Å. Johansson (2011), "Towards a Better Understanding of the Informal Economy", *OECD Economics Department Working Papers*, No. 873, OECD Publishing.

Baanante, M. J. (2004), "Minimum Wage Effects Under Endogenous Compliance. Evidence from Peru", *Económica*, Vol. 50, No. 1–2, pp. 85–123.

Bell, L. A. (1997), "The Impact of Minimum Wages in Mexico and Colombia", *Journal of Labor Economics*, Vol. 15, No. S3, pp. S102–S135.

Blinder, A. S. (1973), "Wage Discrimination: Reduced Form and Structural Estimates", *Journal of Human Resources*, Vol. 8, No. 4, pp. 436–455.

Brandt, L. and C. A. Holz (2006), "Spatial Price Differences in China: Estimates and Implications", *Economic Development and Cultural Change*, Vol. 55, No. 1, pp. 43–86.

Bureau of Labor Statistics (2013), "Characteristics of Minimum Wage Workers: 2012", U.S. Department of Labor.

Cai, F. and Y. Du (2011), "Wage Increases, Wage Convergence, and the Lewis Turning Point in China", *China Economic Review*, Vol. 22, No. 4, pp. 601–610.

Ding, Shouhai (2010), "An Analysis of Minimum Wage Effects on the Labor Market: Effect of Interaction with the Law of PRC on Employment Contracts", *Zhongguo Shehui Kexue* (*Social Sciences in China*), Vol. 31, No. 1, pp. 85–102.

Du, Yang and Meiyan Wang (2008), "The Implementation of Minimum Wage System and Its Effects in China", *Zhongguo Shehui Kexueyuan Yanjiushengyuan Xuebao (Journal of Graduate School of Chinese Academy of Social Sciences)*, Vol. 28, No. 6, pp. 56–62.

Gindling, T. H. and K. Terrell (2010), "Minimum Wages, Globalization, and Poverty in Honduras", *World Development*, Vol. 38, No. 6, pp. 908–918.

Jia, Peng and Shiwei Zhang (2013a), "Labor Supply Effects of Minimum Wages Increase: A Natural Experiment Approach", *Nanfang Jingji* (*Southern China Journal of Economics*), Vol. 31, No. 1, pp. 1–13.

Jia, Peng and Shiwei Zhang (2013b), "Spillover Effects of Minimum Wage Increase", *Tongji Yanjiu* (*Statistical Research*), Vol. 30, No. 4, pp. 37–41.

Lemos, S. (2004), "The Effects of the Minimum Wage in the Formal and Informal Sectors in Brazil", *IZA Discussion Paper*, No. 1089.

Lemos, S. (2009), "Minimum Wage Effects in a Developing Country", *Labor Economics*, Vol. 16, No. 2, pp. 224–237.

Luo, Xiaolan (2011), "The Effect of Minimum Wage on Rural Poverty: An Empirical Analysis of Chinese Rural-Workers", *Jingji Kexue* (*Economic Science*), Vol. 31, No. 3, pp. 68–78.

Luo, Xiaolan and Shuhai Cong (2009), "Impact of Chinese Minimum Wage on Other Wages Based on the Effect of Catching Up with Wages", *Tongji Yanjiu* (*Statistical Research*), Vol. 26, No. 6, pp. 60–65.

Ma, Shuang, Jie Zhang and Xi Zhu (2012), "The Effect of Minimum Wage on Average Wage and Employment", *Jingji Yanjiu* (*Economic Research Journal*), Vol. 48, No. 5, pp. 132–146.

Machin, S., A. Manning and L. Rahman (2003), "Where the Minimum Wage Bites Hard: Introduction of Minimum Wages to a Low Wage Sector", *Journal of the European Economic Association*, Vol. 1, No. 1, pp. 154–180.

Oaxaca, R. (1973), "Male-Female Wage Differentials in Urban Labor Markets", *International Economic Review*, Vol. 14, No. 3, pp. 693–709.

Wang, J. and M. Gunderson (2011), "Minimum Wage Impacts in China: Estimates from a Prespecified Research Design, 2000–2007", *Contemporary Economic Policy*, Vol. 29, No. 3, pp. 392–406.

Wooldridge, J. M. (2010), *Econometric Analysis of Cross Section and Panel Data*, 2nd edition, Cambridge, MA: The MIT Press.

CHAPTER 4

Minimum Wages and Employment in China

Tony Fang and Carl Lin

4.1 Introduction

Since China enacted its new minimum wage regulations in 2004, minimum wages have sparked intense debate in the country. In China, supporters of minimum wages advocate them as a way to assist individuals or families to achieve self-sufficiency and to protect workers in low-paid occupations (Zhang and Deng 2005; Sun 2006). Minimum wages can help reduce inequality by providing a wage floor (Zhang 2007; Jia and Zhang 2013). In addition, higher labor cost may promote managerial efficiency and labor productivity, inducing employers to invest in productivity-improving technology (Cooke 2005). Along these lines, many Chinese scholars have argued in favor of the more proactive increase of minimum wages (Du and Wang 2008; Ding 2009; Han and Wei 2011).

T. Fang
Memorial University of Newfoundland, St. John's, NL, Canada
e-mail: tfang@mun.ca

C. Lin (✉)
Bucknell University, Lewisburg, PA, USA
e-mail: carl.lin@bucknell.edu

L. Shi and C. Lin (eds.), *Minimum Wages in China*,
https://doi.org/10.1007/978-981-15-2421-9_4

On the other hand, opponents argue that raising the minimum wage can decrease the employment opportunities of low-wage workers and also lead to a reduction in other components of the compensation package (Xue 2004; Ping 2005; Gong 2009). Such regulations can undermine enterprises' dividend policies and reduce China's comparative advantage in the abundance of low-wage labor (Cheung 2004, 2010). For example, rural–urban migrants (estimated 168 million workers in 2014 by the National Health and Family Planning Commission) usually have very low pay and tend to work in the uncovered sectors (Chan 2001; Ye 2005).[1]

The minimum wage policy is contentious also because its effects on employment cannot be easily estimated. However, in recent years the new policy in China has generated a lot of variation that is useful in identifying the effects of minimum wages. Since January 2004, China promulgated new minimum wage regulations that required local governments to introduce a minimum wage increase at least once every two years, extended coverage to self-employed and part-time workers, and quintupled the penalties for violation or noncompliance. The new regulations were put into effect in March 2004, leading to frequent and substantial increases in minimum wages in the subsequent years. These large variations both across jurisdictions and over time facilitate our estimation of minimum wage effects on employment in China.

Figure 4.1 shows the nominal and real minimum wage (monthly average) in China from 1995 to 2012 as well as those corresponding to the provinces that raised the minimum wages for each year, along with its moving average over the same period.[2] Between 1995 and 2003, the average nominal minimum wage increased steadily from 169 RMB to 301 RMB, amounting to a 78% growth in 9 years. However, since China implemented the new minimum wage regulations in 2004, the nominal minimum wage has increased even more rapidly by over 200%, reaching 944 RMB in 2012.[3] The real minimum wage grew at a slower pace before 2004 and began to rise thereafter. Furthermore, as shown by the moving average curve in Fig. 4.1, there is an apparent rise after 2004 in the number of provinces that raised the minimum wage standards, indicating that minimum wage adjustments had become more frequent after that year.

How did this regulatory environment affect labor market outcomes in China? More specifically, did changes in the minimum wage have any impact on employment in the Chinese labor market? Although there

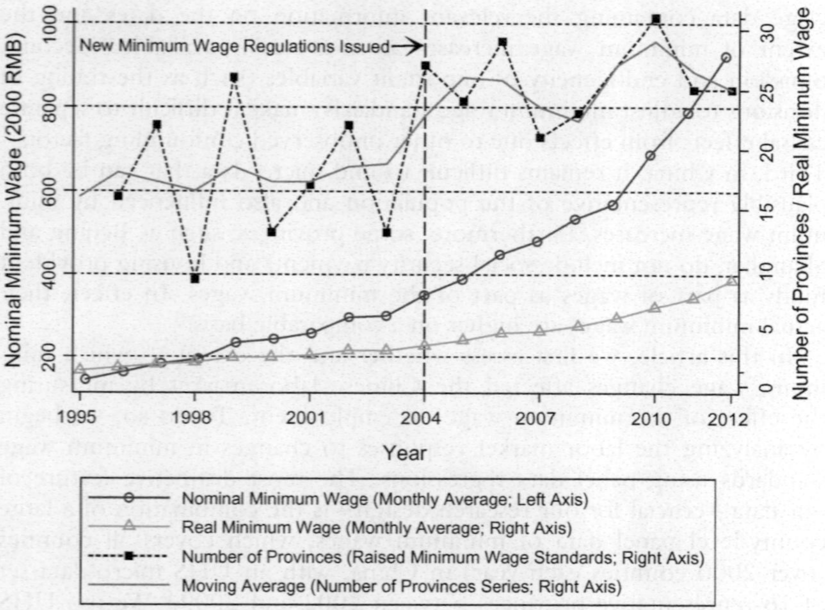

Fig. 4.1 Minimum wages in China, 1995–2012 (*Note* Nominal minimum wages have been adjusted for inflation and expressed in 2000 RMB)

is an enormous literature documenting numerous aspects of minimum wages and their role in the labor market, most studies have been conducted in the high-income economies such as the United States, UK, and Canada; even there, no consensus has been reached on the magnitude of an effect of minimum wages on employment.[4]

This article represents the first paper using county-level minimum wages merged with urban household survey (UHS) micro-data in China. Empirically speaking, there are at least three challenges involved in measuring the employment effects of Chinese minimum wages. First, provinces, municipalities, and autonomous regions[5] in China have considerable autonomy and flexibility in setting their minimum wages according to local conditions. There are often at least 3 or 4 levels of minimum wage standards applicable to various counties in most provinces. The fact that each county is responsible for selecting its own minimum wage standards implies that the county- or city-level minimum wage data containing the relevant information on the dates and the extent of minimum wage increases are not readily available.[6] Second, omission and endogeneity of important variables (such as the timing of decisions to adjust minimum wage standards) make it difficult to separate causal effects from effects due to other unobserved confounding factors.[7] Third, in China, it remains difficult to find micro-data that can be both plausibly representative of the population and also influenced by minimum wage increases. Furthermore, some provinces, such as Beijing and Shanghai, do not include social security payments and housing provident funds as part of wages as part of the minimum wages. In effect, their actual minimum wages are higher on a comparable basis.[8]

In this article, we first assess whether and the extent to which minimum wage changes affected the Chinese labor market by measuring the effect of the minimum wage on employment. To do so, we begin by analyzing the labor market responses to changes in minimum wage standards using panel data regressions. The most distinctive feature of our data—crucial for our research design—is the combination of a large county-level panel data of minimum wages, which covers all counties (over 2000 counties each year) in China, with an UHS micro-data set of 16 representative provinces between 2002 and 2009.[9] We use UHS to construct the county-level variables and then merge the constructed county-level data with the county-level minimum wage data. The use of county-level data rather than provincial-level data allows for a more accurate measurement of the relevant minimum wage and labor market conditions, providing more variation in detecting the effects of minimum wages on employment in China. In particular, we also attempt to evaluate the effects on subgroups of the population, especially those who are at risk of being affected by a minimum wage increase, such as young adults, female, and low-skilled workers.

Our regressions based on county-level panel data reveal significant disemployment effects of minimum wages on young adults (age 15–29) between 2004 and 2009 nationwide—the estimated elasticity of the sum of current and lagged effects is −.259. Please note, for expositional convenience, we refer to the minimum wage relative to the average wage as the minimum wage in all discussion of the empirical results. Our results are reported for such normalized measures. Furthermore, we find that the previous year's minimum wage has the largest adverse effect on the employment of at-risk groups, which as defined as workers whose monthly wages are between the old and new minimum wage standards. We treated it as a simple zero-one dummy variable as the young adult group. As such the wages and employment of this at-risk group are most likely to be affected by the changes in minimum wages. As expected, the sum of the current and lagged effects yields estimated elasticities in the range of −.465 to −.552 over the same period.

Several studies on the employment effects of minimum wages in China found mixed results, and the results for different regions are often opposite to one another. For example, using provincial-level data Ni et al. (2011) focused on all employees and found some negative effects in the more prosperous and rapidly growing Eastern region, and some positive effects in the developing Central region and less developed Western regions over the 2000–2005 period. In contrast, Wang and Gunderson (2011) used 2000–2007 provincial data of rural migrants and found no adverse effects and in fact a positive employment effect in state-owned enterprises in the East and negative effects in the Central and Western regions. The discrepancies between these studies may be explained in part by the fact that the employment effects of minimum wage increases on different target groups tend to differ. By examining the effects on several subgroups, our estimates seem to be consistent with their findings—we find that, similar to Ni et al. (2011), the current minimum wage has a significantly negative effect on all employees in the East and a one-year lagged positive (though statistically insignificant) effect in the Western region in 2004–2009. In contrast, using rural migrants as the target group, we find that the current minimum wage has an adverse and significant effect in the West and a positive (though statistically insignificant) effect in the East over the same period studied in Wang and Gunderson (2011).[10]

Finally, we investigate the impact of the minimum wage on the employment of workers by skill level. In theory, low-skilled workers are relatively vulnerable to job loss when facing minimum wage increases. As anticipated, our county-level panel data analysis shows that the current minimum wage has an adverse, though perhaps mild, effect on the employment of low-skilled workers (defined as those with a high school diploma or below), and the estimated elasticity of the current effect is in the range of −.054 to −.080 for the entire sample, −0.070 for the Eastern region, and −0.070 to −0.077 for the Central region. As a placebo test, we do not find a statistically significant effect for high-skilled workers (defined those with a college diploma or above).

4.2 Minimum Wages in China

Prior to 1994, China had no minimum wage law. In 1984, the country started by acknowledging the 1928 "Minimum Wage Treaty" of the International Labour Organization (ILO) (Su 1993). Due to sluggish wage growth and high inflation in the late 1980s, Zhuhai in Guangdong Province first implemented its local minimum wage regulations, followed by Shenzhen, Guangzhou, and Jiangmen in 1989. It was not until the eruption of private enterprises in 1992 when labor disputes became frequent that the Chinese Central Government began to consider minimum wage legislation (Yang 2006). In 1993, China issued its first national minimum wage regulations, and in July 1994, they were written into China's new version of the labor law.

The 1994 legislation required that all employers pay wages no less than the local minimum wage. All provincial, autonomous region and municipal governments should set their minimum wages according to five principles and report them to the State Council of the Central Government. Specifically, the five principles stipulated that the setting and adjustment of the local minimum wage should synthetically consider the lowest living expenses of workers and the average number of dependents they support, local average wages, labor productivity, local employment, and levels of economic development across regions. These conditions provided considerable flexibility for provinces in setting minimum wage standards, according to economic development principles and the need to attract foreign investment (Frost 2002; Wang and Gunderson 2011). By December 1994, 7 of 31 provinces had set their own minimum wages. By the end of 1995, the number increased to 24.

In the early 2000s, the slow increase of minimum wages along with growing concerns for uncovered/disadvantaged workers prompted the Chinese government to consider new minimum wage regulations. In December 2003, the Ministry of Labour and Social Security passed "The Minimum Wage Regulations" and promulgated the new law in January 2004. The main features of this law involved extending coverage to state-owned, private enterprises, private non-enterprise units, and employees in self-employed businesses. In particular, the new law established two types of minimum wages: a monthly minimum wage applied to full-time workers and an hourly minimum wage applied to non-full-time workers. Importantly, the minimum wage standards were set and adjusted jointly by the local government, trade union, and enterprise confederation of each province. The draft would then be submitted to the Ministry of Labour and Social Security for review. The Ministry would then ask for opinions from the All-China Federation of Trade Unions and the China Enterprise Confederation. The Ministry of Labour and Social Security can request a revision within 14 days after receiving the proposed draft. If no revision request is brought up after the 14-day period, the proposed new minimum wage program is considered to be passed.

In addition, the new regulation required local governments to renew minimum wage standards at least once every two years, and penalties for violation were increased from 20–100% of the owed wages to 100–500% of the owed wages.[11] Employers cannot include subsidies such as overtime pay or canteen allowances, nor travel subsidies, as part of the wage when calculating minimum wages. The new regulations were put into effect on March 1, 2004 and led to substantial increases in minimum wages.

4.3 Data and Research Design

The data collection and research design were motivated by an attempt to estimate the effect of minimum wages on employment and address some of the aforementioned empirical challenges. The purpose of data collection was to obtain information on the minimum wage at the county level over a long time span, with a panel structure allowing for the use of fixed time and county effects to eliminate omitted variable bias arising from unobserved variables that are constant over time and across counties. The wage sample needed to be at the individual level to allow the distribution of minimum wage workers—in each geographic region, age cohort, skill level, and industry—to be estimated. For these reasons, we sought to collect information on counties that were potentially affected over as many years as possible.

4.3.1 Data

Our study uses two primary data sources: the annual UHS from 2002 to 2009 and minimum wage data collected at the county level (6-digit code) between 1994 and 2012. The UHS is a continuous, large-scale social-economic survey conducted by the National Bureau of Statistics of China (NBS) to study the living conditions and standard of urban households, which covers agricultural and non-agricultural residents or non-residents who live in the city for at least six months and migrant households with local residency. Using survey sampling techniques and daily accounting methods, the UHS collects quarterly data from households in all 31 provinces of Mainland China. Starting late December, survey teams in each province and autonomous region are required to verify and then upload the aggregated annual data to the Division of City Socio-economic Survey of NBS via intranet by January 10th of the following year. The UHS contains rich arrays of household information, such as income and consumption expenditure; demographic characteristics; work and employment; housing; other family-related matters; and county identifiers (6-digit code).

Figure 4.2 depicts the 16 provinces (the maximum number of provinces accessible to the researchers) used to study the impact of minimum wages on the Chinese labor market. We divide the 31 jurisdictions into three regions following the NBS: the more prosperous and rapidly growing Eastern region; the developing Central region; and the less developed and more slowly growing Western region. The open-door policy and economic reforms first started in the Eastern coastal regions. It is well documented (see Cai and Wang 2005; Wang and Gunderson 2012) that the labor market in the Eastern region is well developed and mimics a competitive labor market. As such, the external shock of a minimum wage increase with strong enforcement is expected to have significant adverse effects on employment, especially for those who are at risk (youth, females, unskilled, migrants, etc.).

In contrast, the labor market in the Central and Western regions is relatively underdeveloped where there is still plenty of supply of unskilled labor. In a developing country like China, enforcement of the minimum wage could be an important issue that affects the reliability of our results (Khamis 2013). Hence, we first examine the differences in enforcement across 16 provinces from 2002 to 2009 by constructing a measure of enforcement as the ratio of the number of workers earning almost exactly at the ongoing minimum wage (between the exact minimum wage and 1.1 times the minimum wage) divided by number of workers earning less than the minimum wage.[12]

Overall, we find that enforcement increases over time in most provinces, especially after 2004 and particularly in the East part of China (Beijing, Shanghai, Jiangsu, Shandong, Guangdong, and Liaoning). On the other hand, provinces in the West such as Yunnan and Sichuan as

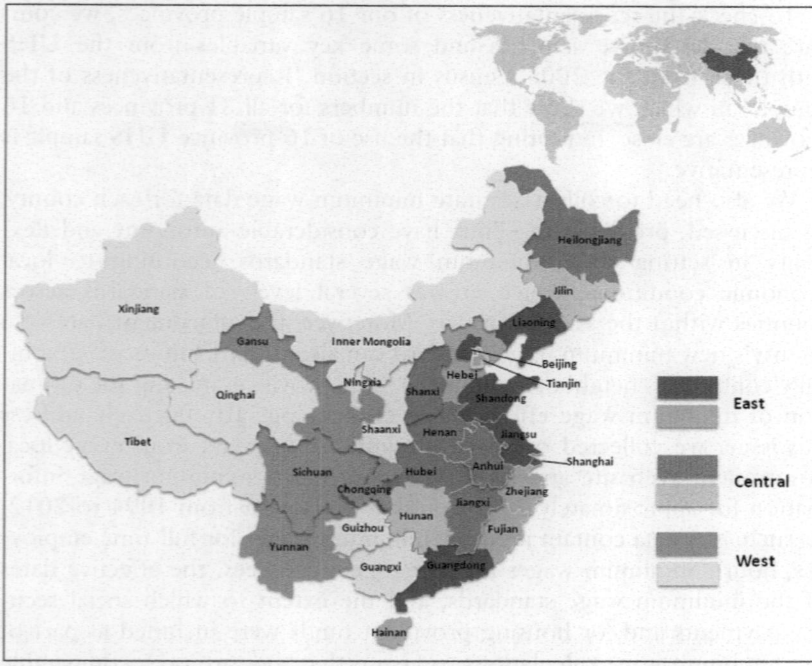

Fig. 4.2 Panel data with minimum wages in Mainland China (*Note* The panel data used in the analysis include 16 provinces [darker areas in the map] covering three regions in Mainland China. The East includes Liaoning, Beijing, Shandong, Jiangsu, Shanghai, and Guangdong; the Central region includes Heilongjiang, Shanxi, Henan, Anhui, Hubei, and Jiangxi; and the West includes Gansu, Chongqing, Sichuan, and Yunnan)

well as Henan in the Central do not show increases in enforcement over the period. Our estimated effects of the minimum wage enforcement on wages and employment show that the enforcement has the largest significant effect on wages and employment in the East, a relatively smaller effect in the Central, and no effect in the West. For example, the estimates of the enforcement on wages for the young adults are .484 and .226 in the East and Central, respectively; for the same group, the estimates of the enforcement on employment are −.313 and −.499 in the East and Central, respectively.

To check the representativeness of our 16 sample provinces, we compare the descriptive statistics and some key variables from the UHS with those from the 2005 Census in section 'Representativeness of the Sample' in which we show that the numbers for all 31 provinces and 16 provinces are close, indicating that the use of 16-province UHS sample is representative.

We also need to collect accurate minimum wage data for each county. As discussed, provinces in China have considerable autonomy and flexibility in setting their minimum wage standards according to local economic conditions, which creates several levels of standards across counties within the same province. Moreover, the adjustment date of a county's new minimum wage standard can also differ from its geographically contiguous neighbors within the same province, making the estimation of minimum wage effects more challenging. To effectively address this issue, we collected our own minimum wage data from every local government Web site and carefully recorded the minimum wage information for approximately 2000 counties every year from 1994 to 2012. As such, our data contain monthly minimum wages for full-time employees, hourly minimum wages for part-time employees, the effective dates of the minimum wage standards, and the extent to which social security payments and/or housing provident funds were included as part of the minimum wage calculations to assure that they are on a comparable basis.

We then merge the minimum wage data into the UHS, a 16-province data set that contains individual/household socioeconomic information over the 2002–2009 period. To calculate average wages, we keep only salaried workers who work for 12 months and then divide their annual wages by 12 to obtain monthly wages for each year.[13] We present a brief summary of the minimum wage data used in our main analysis for the post new minimum wage regulations (2004) period in Table 4.1. Columns (1), (2), and (3) correspond to the mean of the monthly minimum wages, the standard deviation, and the number of counties for the three regions as well as the 16 provinces in 2004, respectively.[14] When calculating the mean minimum wage, we use the time-weighted average method as suggested by Rama (2001).[15] The mean minimum wage has been adjusted for inflation and converted into 2005 RMB using the provincial urban resident CPI. The last row reports the mean of the minimum wages of all provinces, their standard deviations, and the total number of counties that raised minimum wages for each year.

Table 4.1 Means and standard deviations of the minimum wage using county-level information: by region and by province, 2004–2009

Province	*2004*			*2005*			*2006*			*2007*			*2008*			*2009*		
	MW	*S.D.*	*Obs.*	*MW*	*S.D.*	*Obs.*	*MW*	*S.D.*	*Obs.*	*MW*	*S.D.*	*Obs.*	*MW*	*S.D.*	*Obs.*	*MW*	*S.D.*	*Obs.*
East																		
Beijing	509.5	.0	2	562.5	.0	2	611.8	.0	2	665.4	.0	2	735.4	.0	2	820.1	.0	2
Shanghai	590.3	.0	2	662.5	.0	2	712.1	.0	2	757.7	.0	2	894.0	.0	2	984.2	.0	2
Liaoning	282.3	46.0	96	361.9	36.6	96	405.5	41.2	96	465.8	48.7	96	550.1	59.9	97	587.8	63.2	97
Shandong	348.4	35.2	129	440.9	50.0	129	454.6	53.5	129	476.2	66.3	129	571.9	75.6	129	609.9	80.6	129
Jiangsu	416.2	59.9	66	457.6	66.8	66	517.9	70.4	66	591.0	78.0	75	647.8	88.1	75	694.4	94.7	75
Guangdong	361.2	59.9	104	442.1	80.6	104	475.0	84.9	104	516.6	88.5	104	574.3	88.2	104	636.1	98.2	104
All East	349.1	68.5	339	426.7	72.1	399	460.6	76.0	399	507.4	86.5	408	583.6	87.6	409	629.7	95.7	409
Central																		
Heilongjiang	282.0	28.1	30	287.8	28.7	30	384.0	45.7	30	418.0	53.6	30	456.0	58.6	30	486.3	62.5	30
Anhui	304.6	11.7	86	330.7	17.1	86	350.1	19.1	86	400.7	27.1	86	420.4	29.2	86	448.3	31.2	86
Jiangxi	246.7	6.6	99	317.7	8.9	100	328.9	9.4	100	427.5	15.2	100	460.3	21.8	100	490.9	23.3	100
Shanxi	348.2	21.8	119	445.4	22.3	119	454.2	22.4	119	476.3	21.6	119	536.6	22.8	119	642.5	28.6	119
Hubei	271.9	34.9	89	320.6	36.8	89	330.2	37.2	89	402.4	39.1	89	453.4	45.6	89	541.5	58.5	89
Henan	251.5	15.5	127	278.5	17.0	127	345.0	27.9	127	371.1	25.7	127	477.2	42.5	127	509.0	45.3	127
All Central	284.8	43.6	550	337.1	63.8	551	366.2	54.7	551	416.3	46.3	551	473.1	51.7	551	529.1	77.0	551
West																		
Gansu	298.2	8.5	87	304.4	8.7	87	322.1	16.3	87	344.6	35.1	87	471.6	36.3	87	549.4	39.2	87
Chongqing	334.7	21.7	42	365.7	24.6	42	409.0	30.1	42	477.8	39.8	42	554.8	44.5	42	591.7	47.4	42
Sichuan	295.4	32.1	50	352.2	41.9	50	392.2	43.8	50	425.0	42.3	181	477.9	53.0	181	509.7	56.5	181
Yunnan	297.5	18.0	138	365.2	23.4	138	403.6	23.4	138	427.0	22.8	138	527.2	31.5	138	562.3	33.6	138
All West	302.3	23.3	317	346.5	36.1	317	380.1	45.0	317	414.9	51.8	448	499.1	52.3	448	541.3	54.1	448
All Provinces	309.5	56.7	1266	367.7	73.1	1267	399.4	73.3	1267	442.3	74.8	1407	513.5	79.2	1408	562.2	88.3	1408

Note MW represents the mean of time-weighted monthly minimum wages calculated using all counties in a jurisdiction, and it has been adjusted for inflation and converted into 2005 RMB

Table 4.1 reveals several important patterns. First, when calculated at the county level, the mean nominal minimum wage increased by 80% (from 310 RMB to 562 RMB) between 2004 and 2009 for all counties as a whole.[16] Second, the Eastern region has the highest minimum wage, with an average of 522 RMB per month in this period, followed by the West (436 RMB) and the Central region (424 RMB). Interestingly, the minimum wages of the three regions have similar annual growth rates of around 13%.[17] Third, minimum wage hikes sometimes occurred more than once in a year. For example, Beijing increased its minimum wages first in January and then July of 2004, and Jiangsu raised its standards in both April and July of 2008.

We defined employment as working-age population between the ages of 15 and 64 who are employed in the civilian labor force, report positive annual earnings, are not self-employed, and not enrolled in school. Individuals who work in agricultural production or services, farming, forestry, fishing, and ranching industries are also excluded (Neumark and Wascher 1992). Sampling weights are applied in all calculations.

Table 4.2 presents summary statistics for the two key variables, the minimum-to-average wage ratio and the employment-to-population ratio, from 2004 to 2009. Our population is constructed by including all persons in the same demographic group being examined. The second and third rows of the table show that male workers have approximately 10 percentage points lower minimum-to-average wage ratios and 15 percentage points higher employment-to-population ratios than females, suggesting that Chinese female workers are comparatively disadvantaged in the labor market relative to their male counterparts.[18] As anticipated, the more prosperous Eastern region has the lowest minimum-to-average wage ratio (.276) and the highest employment-to-population ratio (.607) among three regions.[19]

A large body of empirical evidence from minimum wage studies has consistently found that minimum wages have a greater impact on young and low-skilled workers, especially teenagers. Compared to older workers, young workers, who are often equipped with less human capital, are more likely to earn the minimum wage. Table 4.2 also shows the two key variables by age cohort and educational attainment over the 2004–2009 period. Indeed, we find that young Chinese workers aged 15–29 have the highest minimum-to-average wage ratio (.392), at least 10 percentage points higher than those of other age cohorts. For workers with different levels of skills, the evidence demonstrates that as the skill

Table 4.2 Summary statistics, 2004–2009

Variable		*Minimum/average wage*		*Employment/population*	
		Mean	*SD*	*Mean*	*SD*
All	100.0	.291	.094	.595	.072
Gender					
Male	55.3	.256	.089	.673	.074
Female	44.7	.354	.115	.520	.087
Region					
East	54.1	.276	.099	.607	.068
Central	32.9	.298	.086	.586	.074
West	13.0	.335	.074	.572	.071
Age cohort					
Age 15–29	13.1	.392	.167	.359	.129
Age 30–39	30.7	.295	.107	.810	.096
Age 40–49	35.8	.283	.096	.802	.094
Age 50–64	20.3	.278	.128	.415	.110
Educational attainment					
Elementary school or below	2.1	.593	.505	.226	.139
Junior high school	20.7	.433	.135	.447	.101
High school	25.2	.355	.107	.566	.098
Vocational school	12.0	.314	.112	.673	.131
Junior college	24.8	.246	.086	.801	.092
College or above	15.2	.183	.085	.797	.120
Industry					
Mining	2.3	.291	.201	–	–
Manufacturing	21.6	.346	.134	–	–
Power production and supply	3.4	.248	.142	–	–
Construction	3.2	.352	.211	–	–
Transportation and postal service	7.6	.288	.132	–	–
Information technology	2.4	.292	.314	–	–
Wholesales and retail sales	9.9	.471	.197	–	–
Hotel and restaurant	2.7	.498	.333	–	–
Banking and finance	2.9	.234	.157	–	–
Real estate	1.9	.355	.353	–	–
Leasing and commercial service	1.6	.371	.313	–	–
Scientific research	2.1	.204	.175	–	–
Environment and public facility	1.3	.311	.212	–	–
Housekeeping	9.6	.509	.213	–	–
Education	7.2	.237	.101	–	–
Health care	4.8	.265	.170	–	–
Sports and entertainment	1.8	.280	.226	–	–
Public service	13.9	.245	.094	–	–
Total observations		620,321			

Note The average wage is calculated as the mean wage in each category. Because age cohort 16–19 and 20–24 only account for .17 and 3.6% of total observations, respectively, we choose the first age cohort to be age 16–29

level increases, the minimum-to-average wage ratio decreases quickly—dropping continuously from .389 for a high school education or below to .183 for college or above education.

Table 4.2 also presents the minimum-to-average wage ratio by industry. The manufacturing sector contains the largest share (21.6%) of workers in our sample; the public service sector is the second largest (13.9%); and the third and the fourth sectors are wholesale and retail sales trade (9.9%) and housekeeping (9.6%), respectively. As to the minimum-to-average wage ratios, unsurprisingly, we find that the housekeeping sector has the highest ratio (.509) among all industries, followed by the hotel and restaurant sector (.498) and wholesale and retail sales trade (.471).

We also provide a summary of the characteristics of workers who earn the minimum wage as well as less/more than the minimum wage over 2004–2009 in Table 4.3. The first row of Table 4.3 shows that approximately 5.62% of all workers earned less than the minimum wage and 3.28% earned just the minimum.[20] Among those who earned the exact minimum wage or less than the minimum wage, 63.84 and 61.52% are females, respectively. Furthermore, the minimum-to-average wage ratio of workers receiving less than the minimum wage is 2.52, suggesting that these disadvantaged workers earn a wage that is only approximately one-quarter of the official standard.

4.3.2 Research Design

Our empirical strategy is to estimate the impact of minimum wages on the employment of potentially affected workers. As noted in Sect. 4.1, nearly all existing studies on minimum wages in China use aggregated data (from the yearbooks) at the provincial level and tend to find mixed results, implying that convincing evidence of the employment effects has not yet been established. Our study takes advantage of household survey data and a more accurate measure of minimum wages at the county level. This, in turn, allows us to calculate the dependent variable—the employment-to-population ratio—at the county level, which contains more variation and information on local conditions. These unique features of our data provide us an opportunity to generate more reliable estimates of the employment effects of minimum wages in China.

First, we estimate the effect of minimum wages on average wages to see whether changes in the minimum wage indeed affect the observed wages of the groups being examined in our analysis. We then estimate a

Table 4.3 Characteristics of workers earning the minimum wage, 2004–2009

Variable	*Less than minimum*	*Minimum*	*Above minimum*
Percent of total (%)	5.62	3.28	91.09
Percent of female (%)	61.52	63.84	42.99
Minimum/average wage	2.52	1.00	.35
	(4.66)	(.06)	(.20)
Region (%)			
East	5.33	3.27	91.40
Central	5.46	2.88	91.66
West	7.26	4.36	88.38
Age			
Age 15–29	9.53	4.30	86.17
Age 30–39	4.73	2.84	92.43
Age 40–49	4.90	3.26	91.83
Age 50–64	5.73	3.33	90.94
Educational attainment			
Elementary school or below	15.75	9.41	74.84
Junior high school	9.43	6.00	84.57
High school	6.60	3.99	89.40
Vocational school	4.89	2.85	92.26
Junior college	3.08	1.50	95.43
College or above	2.17	.82	97.01
Industry			
Mining	3.10	1.88	95.02
Manufacturing	5.50	3.30	91.20
Power production and supply	2.47	1.37	96.16
Construction	5.78	3.04	91.17
Transportation and postal service	4.00	2.10	93.90
Information technology	5.42	2.27	92.31
Wholesales and retail sales	10.46	6.30	83.24
Hotel and restaurant	9.98	6.52	83.50
Banking and finance	2.74	1.21	96.04
Real estate	5.46	3.05	91.49
Leasing and commercial service	6.37	3.16	90.46
Scientific research	2.20	.84	96.96
Environment and public facility	3.89	2.23	93.87
Housekeeping	12.63	7.58	79.79
Education	2.74	1.39	95.87
Health care	3.57	1.74	94.69
Sports and entertainment	4.10	1.77	94.13
Public service	2.41	1.77	95.82

Note Standard deviations are in parentheses. There are 620,321 observations in this period. "Less than the Minimum" are workers earning wages at or below 90% of the minimum wage. Minimum wage workers earn wages above 90% and up to 110% of the minimum wage. Above minimum wage workers earn wages above 110% of the minimum wage

standard set of equations as used in Neumark (2001), Campolieti et al. (2006), and Wang and Gunderson (2011).[21]

Our estimation equations for the wage and employment effects are as follows:

$$W_{i,t} = \eta_0 + \eta_1 MWL_{i,t} + \eta_2 MWL_{i,t-1} + X_{i,t}\theta + Y_t\mu + C_i\tau + \varepsilon_{i,t}, \quad (4.1)$$

$$E_{i,t} = \alpha_0 + \alpha_1 MW_{i,t} + \alpha_2 MW_{i,t-1} + X_{i,t}\beta + Y_t\gamma + C_i\delta + e_{i,t}, \quad (4.2)$$

where $W_{i,t}$ is the log of the average wage variable for county i in year t; $MWL_{i,t}$ and $MWL_{i,t-1}$ are the log of minimum wage variables (in level) for county i in year t and year $t-1$, respectively. $E_{i,t}$ is the log of employment variable (employment-to-population ratio) of the relevant group, e.g., young adult workers employed in urban (county) units divided by the urban working-age population (15–64) for county i in year t; and $MW_{i,t-1}$ are the log of minimum wage index variables (minimum-to-average wage ratio) for county i in year t and year $t-1$, respectively. We include $MW_{i,t-1}$ in the equation to allow a lagged effect of minimum wages to occur as suggested by Burkhauser et al. (2000); X is a set of control variables to capture aggregate business cycle effects; Y_t is a set of fixed year effects; and C_i is a set of fixed county effects. The disturbance terms ε and e are assumed to be serially uncorrelated and orthogonal to the independent variables.

To address the potential bias from misspecification and factors that may affect labor demand, we include several control variables in the estimation equations. First, the county GDP per capita and CPI (at city level) capture aggregate business cycle effects and controls for the Great Recession. Second, county-level foreign direct investment (FDI) is used to control for the possibility that provinces may restrain minimum wage increases to attract foreign investment (Frost 2002) and other factors that may affect the relative labor demand for workers with different skills. We controlled for such local condition variables as they are potential determinants of minimum wage decisions.

4.4 Empirical Results and Discussion

4.4.1 *Minimum Wage Effects Across Regions*

We first present estimates of minimum wage effects on the wages of young adults, at-risk groups, and the entire sample for the East, Central, Western regions, and all regions in Table 4.4. In each region, we estimate

Table 4.4 Estimates of minimum wage effects on wages

Dependent variable: log (wages)	*Young adults (age 15–29)*		*At-risk group*		*Entire sample*	
Independent variables (log)	*(1)*	*(2)*	*(1)*	*(2)*	*(1)*	
A. All regions						
MW level, current year	.782***	.429***	.873***	.883***	.545***	.300***
	(.077)	(.084)	(.034)	(.039)	(.044)	(.050)
MW level, lagged 1 year	.360***	.083*	.100***	.108***	.339***	.171***
	(.076)	(.042)	(.033)	(.036)	(.042)	(.046)
Other controls	No	Yes	No	Yes	No	Yes
R^2	.511	.558	.916	.936	.626	.659
Number of observations	3894	3894	3372	3372	3966	3966
B. East						
MW level, current year	1.434***	.890***	.861***	.905***	.666***	.229***
	(.114)	(.141)	(.097)	(.055)	(.071)	(.075)
MW level, lagged 1 year	.184	.037	.115**	.095*	.449***	.186***
	(.117)	(.124)	(.055)	(.050)	(.060)	(.071)
Other controls	No	Yes	No	Yes	No	Yes
R^2	.676	.700	.933	.934	.698	.718
Number of counties	1716	1716	1518	1518	1734	1734
C. Central						
MW level, current year	.257**	.080*	.874***	.884***	.289***	.256***
	(.118)	(.045)	(.055)	(.061)	(.063)	(.068)
MW level, lagged 1 year	.241**	.205*	.108**	.116*	.078	.009
	(.122)	(.112)	(.055)	(.062)	(.067)	(.069)
Other controls	No	Yes	No	Yes	No	Yes
R^2	.306	.359	.854	.883	.515	.552
Number of counties	1638	1638	1380	1380	1674	1674
D. West						
MW level, current year	.601	.328	1.014	.837	.523	.450
	(.387)	(.517)	(.873)	(.867)	(.377)	(.399)
MW level, lagged 1 year	.233	.477	.022	.102	.087	.040
	(.350)	(.480)	(.091)	(.188)	(.233)	(.348)
Other controls	No	Yes	No	Yes	No	Yes
R^2	.330	.352	.870	.889	.348	.356
Number of counties	540	540	474	474	558	558

Note ***statistically significant at the 1% level; **at the 5% level; *at the 10% level. Cluster-robust standard errors at the county level are in parentheses. All variables in the table are at the county level, except that CPI is at the city level. Young adults are defined as workers who are 15–29 years old. At-risk groups are workers whose monthly wages are between the old and new minimum wage standards. Each estimation has controlled for year and county fixed effects

Eq. (4.1) using a fixed effects model with both fixed year and county effects. All regressions are appropriately weighted by the size of the population in each county and adjust the weight to be the size for the groups such as age and gender.

Our results show that, for each of the three groups, the current year's minimum wage has a statistically significant and positive effect on the average wage for the East, Central, and all regions over 2004–2009. We also find positive but milder effects of the one-year lagged minimum wage variable on the average wage nationwide. However, we do not find any significant wage effect in the Western region. In short, we show that minimum wage changes in the East, Central, and all regions have positively affected the observed wages of young adults, at-risk groups, and the entire sample of workers.[22]

Next, using Eq. (4.2), we estimate the effect of the minimum wage on employment for young adults, at-risk groups, and the entire sample for the East, Central, Western regions, and all regions, respectively, and present the results in Table 4.5. We report the results of two estimation equations for each of the three groups: The first equation uses the minimum wage of the current year t ($MW_{i,t}$) and the previous year $t-1$ ($MW_{i,t-1}$) only, while the second equation further controls for CPI (city level), county GDP per capita, and county FDI (shown as Other controls in the table).

The first and second columns of Table 4.5 report the estimates with cluster-robust standard errors at the county level in parentheses for young adults and at-risk groups across different regions using Eq. (4.2), while in the third column, we report estimates of the entire sample for comparison. The significance of our results is compelling: for the entire country, we find negative effects of the current and lagged minimum wage on employment. For young adults, the estimated elasticities for the current and lagged effects are in the range of −.062 to −.088 and −.136 to −.156, respectively. For the entire sample of individuals, the estimated elasticities for the current and lagged effects are in the range of −.045 to −.055 and −.028 to −.031, respectively.[23]

In the more developed and prosperous East China, covering large urban centers such as Beijing, Shanghai, and Guangzhou, the minimum wage has been an important policy tool as China makes the critical transition into a market economy. Consequently, the magnitude and frequency of minimum wage increases are relatively high and the impact of minimum wages on employment can be evident. Indeed, this is consistent with our results in Table 4.5. Our estimates indicate that minimum

Table 4.5 Estimates of minimum wage effects on the employment-to-population ratio

Dependent variable: log (employment/population)	*Young adults (age 15–29)*		*At-risk group*		*Entire sample*	
Independent variables (log)	*(1)*	*(2)*	*(1)*	*(2)*	*(1)*	*(2)*
A. All regions						
MW, current year	−.088**	−.062	−.213*	−.200	−.055***	−.045**
	(.042)	(.043)	(.128)	(.129)	(.018)	(.018)
MW, lagged 1 year	−.156***	−.136***	−.340***	−.265***	−.031***	−.028**
	(.040)	(.042)	(.102)	(.102)	(.012)	(.011)
MW, sum current and lagged	−.244***	−.198***	−.552***	−.465**	−.086***	−.073***
	(.055)	(.058)	(.192)	(.195)	(.019)	(.019)
Other controls	No	Yes	No	Yes	No	Yes
R^2	.144	.218	.024	.025	.079	.091
Number of counties per year	649	649	562	562	661	661
Average obs. per county per year	270	270	170	170	1658	1658
B. East						
MW, current year	−.234***	−.154**	−.201	−.213	−.068***	−.067**
	(.047)	(.070)	(.219)	(.220)	(.025)	(.027)
MW, lagged 1 year	−.100**	−.046	−.322**	−.310**	−.018	−.015
	(.048)	(.057)	(.128)	(.124)	(.020)	(.020)
MW, sum current and lagged	−.334***	−.201**	−.523*	−.523*	−.086***	−.082***
	(.043)	(.097)	(.307)	(.304)	(.020)	(.025)
Other controls	No	Yes	No	Yes	No	Yes
R^2	.213	.223	.041	.056	.084	.085
Number of counties per year	286	286	253	253	289	289
Average obs. per county per year	329	329	180	180	1917	1917
C. Central						
MW, current year	−.032	−.034	−.297	−.272	−.039	−.039

(continued)

Table 4.5 (continued)

Dependent variable: log (employment/population)	*Young adults (age 15–29)*		*At-risk group*		*Entire sample*	
Independent variables (log)	*(1)*	*(2)*	*(1)*	*(2)*	*(1)*	*(2)*
	(.068)	(.070)	(.181)	(.177)	(.025)	(.026)
MW, lagged 1 year	$-.216^{***}$	$-.216^{***}$	$-.336^{*}$	$-.310^{*}$	$-.041^{***}$	$-.042^{***}$
	(.061)	(.061)	(.174)	(.184)	(.015)	(.014)
MW, sum current and lagged	$-.248^{***}$	$-.250^{***}$	$-.632^{**}$	$-.582^{*}$	$-.080^{***}$	$-.081^{***}$
	(.090)	(.093)	(.297)	(.302)	(.030)	(.031)
Other controls	No	Yes	No	Yes	No	Yes
R^2	.129	.151	.031	.043	.094	.133
Number of counties per year	273	273	230	230	279	279
Average obs. per county per year	214	214	154	154	1385	1385
D. West						
MW, current year	.088	-.037	.018	.022	-.096	-.069
	(.114)	(.106)	(.208)	(.223)	(.063)	(.064)
MW, lagged 1 year	.124	−.153	.000	.124	.055	−.005
	(.107)	(.110)	(.258)	(.276)	(.075)	(.043)
MW, sum current and lagged	.212	−.191	.018	.146	−.041	−.074
	(.191)	(.161)	(.321)	(.384)	(.080)	(.096)
Other controls	No	Yes	No	Yes	No	Yes
R^2	.153	.169	.014	.051	.015	.043
Number of counties per year	90	90	79	79	93	93
Average obs. per county per year	250	250	181	181	1673	1673

Note ***statistically significant at the 1% level; **at the 5% level; and *at the 10% level. Cluster-robust standard errors at the county level are in parentheses. All variables in the table are at the county level, except that CPI is at the city level. At-risk groups are workers whose monthly wages are between the old and new minimum wage standards. Among young adults, less than 3% are at-risk groups in each region; likewise, among at-risk group, less than 3% are young adults in each region. Each estimation has controlled for year and county fixed effects wage increases in the Eastern region have a statistically significant adverse impact on employment with elasticities ranging from −.154 to −.234 and a lagged adverse effect with an elasticity of −.046 to −.100 for young adults. Furthermore, we find a large and negative one-year lagged minimum wage effect on the employment for the at-risk groups—the estimated elasticity for the lagged effect is in the range of −.310 to −.322. The current minimum wage effects are negative but statistically insignificant.

In the developing Central region, we also find that one-year lagged minimum wages have a strong negative employment effect on young adults, at-risk groups, and the entire working population. For the entire working population in the Central region, the elasticity is in the range of −.041 to −.042. The estimated effect of the current minimum wage is negative but statistically insignificant. Finally, in the less developed West, although the estimated coefficients are relatively larger, we do not find a statistically significant effect of the minimum wage on employment. Therefore, we don't report the estimates for the West here and leave the discussion of the result in Sect. 4.4.4.

4.4.2 Gender and Age Cohort

A large number of international studies of minimum wages have reported that young workers are most vulnerable to minimum wage increases, and the disemployment effect seems especially strong for teenagers. Female workers are particularly disadvantaged in the labor market. We therefore separate the sample into four age subgroups: 15–29, 30–39, 40–49, and 50–64.[24] In each age group, we estimate Eq. (4.2) of the fixed effects model separately for males and females and report the results in Table 4.6.

Consistent with most studies in the literature, we find that the minimum wage has strong negative effects on young female workers (age 15–29)—the most disadvantaged and vulnerable groups in the labor market. In contrast, we do not find significant effects on the employment of young male workers (age 15–29) and older workers (age 50–64) in the full sample.

Table 4.6 Estimates of minimum wage effects on employment by age cohort

Dependent variable: log (employment/population)	*Age 15–29*		*Age 30–39*		*Age 40–49*		*Age 50–64*	
Independent variables (log)	*Male*	*Female*	*Male*	*Female*	*Male*	*Female*	*Male*	*Female*
A. All regions								
MW, current year	−.031	−.148***	−.019	−.068***	.017	−.040	.009	.023
	(.047)	(.047)	(.027)	(.025)	(.016)	(.027)	(.053)	(.056)
MW, lagged 1 year	−.027	−.061**	−.031	−.034	−.015	−.040**	−.009	−.023
	(.029)	(.030)	(.019)	(.021)	(.013)	(.017)	(.032)	(.034)
MW, sum current and lagged	−.058	−.210***	−.050	−.102***	−.003	−.080**	−.000	−.000
	(.053)	(.050)	(.039)	(.027)	(.024)	(.025)	(.072)	(.073)
Minimum-to-average wage ratio	.388	.442	.266	.353	.252	.362	.260	.403
MW (level) effects on wages	.433***	.442***	.442***	.356***	.345***	.239***	.498***	.368**
	(.126)	(.117)	(.071)	(.078)	(.071)	(.086)	(.082)	(.156)
R^2	.173	.169	.022	.097	.012	.093	.052	.055
Number of counties per year	632	626	654	653	655	653	653	598
Average obs. per county per year	113	114	253	260	309	272	231	100
B. East								
MW, current year	−.103	−.172**	−.023	−.098***	−.001	−.043	.022	−.057
	(.112)	(.076)	(.022)	(.033)	(.017)	(.032)	(.042)	(.061)
MW, lagged 1 year	−.012	−.040	−.010	.007	−.016	−.021	−.018	−.001
	(.049)	(.046)	(.011)	(.024)	(.013)	(.025)	(.031)	(.041)
MW, sum current and lagged	−.116	−.212***	−.033	−.091***	−.016	−.064**	.004	−.059
	(.136)	(.071)	(.021)	(.033)	(.018)	(.029)	(.042)	(.067)
Minimum-to-average wage ratio	.353	.415	.247	.344	.240	.367	.245	.424
MW (level) effects on wages	.999***	.895***	.664***	.393***	.196	.256	.252	.442
	(.186)	(.194)	(.118)	(.127)	(.125)	(.158)	(.147)	(.324)
R^2	.176	.195	.049	.094	.013	.092	.039	.094
Number of counties per year	280	280	285	287	288	285	286	269
Average obs. per county per year	131	144	299	308	337	302	266	108

(continued)

Table 4.6 (continued)

Dependent variable: log (employment/population)	*Age 15–29*		*Age 30–39*		*Age 40–49*		*Age 50–64*	
Independent variables (log)	*Male*	*Female*	*Male*	*Female*	*Male*	*Female*	*Male*	*Female*
C. Central								
MW, current year	.014	−.155**	−.052**	−.087**	.013	.034	.025	.152**
	(.062)	(.068)	(.020)	(.040)	(.023)	(.062)	(.085)	(.075)
MW, lagged 1 year	−.014	−.066	−.072***	−.071**	−.018	−.013	.021	−.024
	(.068)	(.044)	(.020)	(.036)	(.022)	(.029)	(.052)	(.047)
MW, sum current and lagged	−.001	−.220***	−.123***	−.158***	−.006	.021	.047	.128
	(.082)	(.077)	(.024)	(.051)	(.039)	(.077)	(.124)	(.092)
Minimum-to-average wage ratio	.433	.482	.278	.360	.256	.354	.264	.368
MW (level) effects on wages	.425*	.114*	.295***	.311***	.290***	.260**	.346	.500***
	(.222)	(.068)	(.092)	(.109)	(.096)	(.123)	(.239)	(.125)
R^2	.123	.114	.076	.148	.015	.057	.044	.089
Number of counties per year	265	260	276	273	275	277	276	246
Average obs. per county per year	87	94	211	212	276	235	186	95
D. West								
MW, current year	−.071	−.145	.231*	.078	.093	−.018	−.394**	−.400***
	(.170)	(.109)	(.123)	(.078)	(.080)	(.111)	(.188)	(.120)
MW, lagged 1 year	−.121	−.215*	.117**	−.103**	.004	.066	−.136	−.037
	(.124)	(.110)	(.053)	(.046)	(.053)	(.072)	(.139)	(.093)
MW, sum current and lagged	−.192	−.360*	.348**	−.026	.097	.048	−.530*	−.437**
	(.180)	(.187)	(.166)	(.091)	(.116)	(.156)	(.283)	(.178)
Minimum-to-average wage ratio	.451	.470	.310	.370	.290	.362	.313	.389
MW (level) effects on wages	.610	.511**	.624	.553**	.399	.442	.388***	.217***
	(.893)	(.246)	(.482)	(.269)	(.520)	(.549)	(.133)	(.048)
R^2	.172	.179	.236	.152	.102	.085	.091	.269
Number of counties per year	87	86	93	93	92	91	91	93
Average obs. per county per year	101	107	237	255	316	288	253	107

Note: ***statistically significant at the 1% level; **at the 5% level; and *at the 10% level. Cluster-robust standard errors at the county level are in parentheses. All variables in the table are at the county level, except that CPI is at the city level. Each estimation has controlled for year and county fixed effects as well as other control variables as described in Sect. 4.3.2. In each panel, the estimates of MW effects on wages are taken from Table S1 in Fang and Lin (2015)

4.4.3 *Skill Level*

In the extant literature, the bulk of evidence supports the view that minimum wages reduce the employment of low-wage workers. Moreover, when researchers focus on the least-skilled groups, which are most likely to be directly affected by minimum wage increases, the evidence for disemployment effects seems to be especially strong (Neumark and Wascher 2008). We present the estimation results by three skill groups as measured by educational attainment in Table 4.7. In each group, we report the estimates using the fixed effects model with both fixed year and county effects. Our results show that minimum wages reduce the employment of low-skilled workers, indicating that Chinese workers who have high school education or less, and those who have vocational school degrees were adversely affected by minimum wage increases.[25] In contrast, we do not find an effect of minimum wages on workers with a college degree or above (including junior college).

4.4.4 *Discussion of the Results*

We began with estimating the employment effects of minimum wages by three geographical regions and sought to explain the impact for the 2004–2009 period. The estimates showed that in the more developed East China, the negative employment effects of the current and lagged minimum wages on young adults are statistically significant, with elasticities in the range of −.088 and −.136 to −.156, respectively. Although the numbers are small, they are in the range of those found in the studies of developed and developing countries and are very likely inside of the consensus range of −.1 to −.3 from the earlier literature as noted in Neumark and Wascher (2008).

Moreover, we find that minimum wage changes result in a larger lagged disemployment effect for at-risk groups across the country, with elasticities ranging from −.265 to −.340. In particular, these effects are consistently more pronounced for both young adults and at-risk groups in the Central region. The fact that nearly all the lagged effects are uniformly more pronounced than the current contemporaneous effects for young adults and at-risk groups highlights the importance of the adjustment period through which the disemployment effects would occur. It is worth noting that our finding of a lagged disemployment effect is not

Table 4.7 Estimates of minimum wage effects on employment by educational attainment

Dependent variable: log (Employment/population)	*High school or below*		*Vocational school*		*Junior college*		*College or above*	
Independent variables (log)	*(1)*	*(2)*	*(1)*	*(2)*	*(1)*	*(2)*	*(1)*	*(2)*
A. All regions								
MW, current year	−.080**	−.054**	−.037	−.046*	−.018	−.023	−.006	−.013
	(.040)	(.025)	(.025)	(.025)	(.020)	(.020)	(.013)	(.014)
MW, lagged 1 year	−.019	−.029	−.040**	−.047**	−.002	−.016	−.005	−.019
	(.020)	(.018)	(.020)	(.020)	(.021)	(.021)	(.015)	(.015)
MW, sum current and lagged	−.099***	−.083***	−.077***	−.092***	−.020	−.039	−.011	−.032
	(.030)	(.029)	(.027)	(.027)	(.018)	(.024)	(.015)	(.021)
MW (level) effects on wages	.541***	.326***	.560***	.391***	.056	.053	.157*	.187
	(.056)	(.066)	(.072)	(.078)	(.084)	(.088)	(.095)	(.119)
Other controls	No	Yes	No	Yes	No	Yes	No	Yes
R^2	.046	.076	.036	.068	.044	.079	.003	.032
Number of counties per year	659	659	636	636	653	653	632	632
Average obs. per county per year	744	744	196	196	408	408	277	277
B. East								
MW, current year	−.070*	−.061	−.049	−.054	−.048	−.064	−.031	−.032
	(.038)	(.041)	(.046)	(.047)	(.037)	(.040)	(.020)	(.020)
MW, lagged 1 year	−.025	−.017	−.003	−.006	.028	.018	−.039	−.039
	(.023)	(.024)	(.028)	(.030)	(.027)	(.028)	(.027)	(.027)
MW, sum current and lagged	−.095***	−.079*	−.052	−.060	.020	−.046	−.069	−.072
	(.036)	(.043)	(.054)	(.054)	(.021)	(.035)	(.045)	(.058)
MW (level) effects on wages	.720***	.300***	.619***	.419***	.044	.005	.335	.346
	(.087)	(.110)	(.110)	(.143)	(.186)	(.182)	(.258)	(.254)

(continued)

Table 4.7 (continued)

Dependent variable: log (Employment/population)	*High school or below*		*Vocational school*		*Junior college*		*College or above*	
Independent variables (log)	*(1)*	*(2)*	*(1)*	*(2)*	*(1)*	*(2)*	*(1)*	*(2)*
Other controls	No	Yes	No	Yes	No	Yes	No	Yes
R^2	.056	.062	.028	.036	.053	.091	.011	.032
Number of counties per year	289	289	281	281	286	286	284	284
Average obs. per county per year	819	819	224	224	476	476	355	355
C. Central								
MW, current year	−.071**	−.077**	−.048	−.051	.012	.007	.074	.077
	(.034)	(.035)	(.037)	(.037)	(.023)	(.023)	(.056)	(.057)
MW, lagged 1 year	−.052**	−.047*	−.083***	−.090***	−.030	−.033	.080	.079
	(.025)	(.025)	(.032)	(.033)	(.033)	(.034)	(.038)	(.038)
MW, sum current and lagged	−.123***	−.124***	−.131***	−.141***	−.018	−.026	.155	.157
	(.043)	(.043)	(.040)	(.040)	(.034)	(.035)	(.107)	(.109)
MW (level) effects on wages	.391***	.326***	.434***	.409***	.024	.070	.016	.051
	(.084)	(.091)	(.107)	(.107)	(.105)	(.118)	(.130)	(.143)
Other controls	No	Yes	No	Yes	No	Yes	No	Yes
R^2	.083	.111	.073	.094	.045	.082	.045	.046
Number of counties per year	277	277	263	263	274	274	259	259
Average obs. per county per year	650	650	170	170	341	341	197	197
D. West								
MW, current year	−.184	−.030	−.019	.012	−.068	−.034	.033	.112
	(.163)	(.092)	(.073)	(.086)	(.062)	(.060)	(.084)	(.103)
MW, lagged 1 year	.154	−.037	−.046	−.031	.020	−.021	−.020	−.054
	(.120)	(.092)	(.090)	(.089)	(.078)	(.072)	(.070)	(.062)

(continued)

Table 4.7 (continued)

Dependent variable: log (Employment/population)	*High school or below*		*Vocational school*		*Junior college*		*College or above*	
Independent variables (log)	*(1)*	*(2)*	*(1)*	*(2)*	*(1)*	*(2)*	*(1)*	*(2)*
MW, sum current and lagged	−.031	−.068	−.065	−.019	−.048	−.055	.013	.058
	(.120)	(.092)	(.104)	(.111)	(.081)	(.097)	(.106)	(.138)
MW (level) effects on wages	.365	.060	.436	.605	.424	.232	.498	.343
	(.348)	(.461)	(.398)	(.607)	(.294)	(.411)	(.386)	(.451)
Other controls	No	Yes	No	Yes	No	Yes	No	Yes
R^2	.013	.059	.028	.052	.017	.099	.019	.080
Number of counties per year	93	93	92	92	93	93	89	89
Average obs. per county per year	791	791	183	183	394	394	258	258

Note ***statistically significant at the 1% level; **at the 5% level; *at the 10% level. Cluster-robust standard errors at the county level are in parentheses. All variables in the table are at the county level. All variables in the table are at the county level, except that CPI is at the city level. Each estimation has controlled for year and county fixed effects. In each panel, the estimates of MW effects on wages are taken from Table S2 in Fang and Lin (2015)

an anomaly among the empirical studies in the extant minimum wage literature. Hamermesh (1995) points out that nonlabor inputs such as capital may be costly and slow to adjust in the short run, which will also tend to slow the adjustment of other complementary inputs such as labor. Subsequent empirical studies have tended to find evidence of longer-run disemployment effects of minimum wages: for example, Baker et al. (1999) based on Canadian data, Keil et al. (2001) based on a panel of US state-based data, Burkhauser et al. (2000) based on Current Population Survey data, and Wang and Gunderson (2011) based on a Chinese provincial-level panel data.

Our full sample results (age 15–64) reported in column 3 of Table 4.5 show negative employment effects across the country and in the Eastern region, which is consistent with the findings by Ni et al. (2011), who used general working population (age 15 and above) in their analysis. When focusing on young adults and at-risk groups (which are more likely to be affected by the minimum wage policy), we found stronger disemployment effects in the East, lagged disemployment effects in the Central, and positive while insignificant effects in the Western region. The differential disemployment effects across regions can be explained in part by the fact that in the Central and Western regions, young adults and at-risk groups tend to work in the state-owned enterprises—a sector that is considerably inefficient and less responsive to market pressures (Lin et al. 2001).[26]

Taken together, our results show heterogeneous employment effects of minimum wages by region, skill, and gender.[27] In particular, the effect on young adults and at-risk groups varies highlighting the importance of heterogeneous effects of minimum wages by the characteristics of those affected.[28]

4.4.5 *Robustness Checks*

Normalized Minimum Wages

In their influential works, Neumark and Wascher (1992) and Card et al. (1994) discuss the potential endogeneity issue when normalizing the minimum wage by the average wage which we use in our analysis. The main concern of using a normalized minimum wage variable is that average wages can be related to supply and demand factors (which also affect youth employment) and are affected by minimum wage changes. That is,

Table 4.8 Estimates of minimum wage effects on the employment (non-normalized minimum wage variable)

Dependent variable: log (employment/population)	*Young adults (age 15–29)*		*At-risk group*		*Entire sample*	
Independent variables (log)	*(1)*	*(2)*	*(1)*	*(2)*	*(1)*	*(2)*
A. All regions						
MW level, current year	−.120*	−.005	−.093	−.263*	−.009	−.018**
	(.072)	(.082)	(.084)	(.158)	(.017)	(.010)
MW level, lagged 1 year	−.228***	−.060***	−.047**	−.268***	.016*	−.024**
	(.077)	(.028)	(.024)	(.102)	(.009)	(.013)
MW, sum current and lagged	−.348***	−.065***	−.140*	−.531***	.007	−.039***
	(.075)	(.032)	(.071)	(.121)	(.010)	(.011)
Mean wages[a]	No	Yes	No	Yes	No	Yes
Other controls	No	Yes	No	Yes	No	Yes
R^2	.070	.202	.008	.025	.026	.101
Number of counties per year	649	649	562	562	661	661
Average obs. per county per year	270	270	170	170	1658	1658
B. East						
MW level, current year	−.198***	−.170**	−.050	−.073	−.047*	−.026***
	(.101)	(.090)	(.161)	(.274)	(.028)	(.013)
MW level, lagged 1 year	−.150**	−.171	−.114*	−.206***	−.026	−.025
	(.081)	(.124)	(.068)	(.102)	(.031)	(.031)
MW, sum current and lagged	−.348*	−.341*	−.164**	−.279***	−.073**	−.051***
	(.187)	(.179)	(.079)	(.112)	(.036)	(.021)
Mean wages[a]	No	Yes	No	Yes	No	Yes
Other controls	No	Yes	No	Yes	No	Yes

(continued)

Table 4.8 (continued)

Dependent variable: log (employment/population)	*Young adults (age 15–29)*		*At-risk group*		*Entire sample*	
Independent variables (log)	*(1)*	*(2)*	*(1)*	*(2)*	*(1)*	*(2)*
R^2	.080	.221	.017	.046	.084	.093
Number of counties per year	286	286	253	253	289	289
Average obs. per county per year	329	329	180	180	1917	1917
C. Central						
MW level, current year	−.054	−.056	−.043	−.023	−.038	−.033
	(.125)	(.142)	(.124)	(.173)	(.030)	(.035)
MW level, lagged 1 year	−.126*	−.234*	−.067	−.248***	−.032*	−.046***
	(.075)	(.126)	(.114)	(.119)	(.017)	(.018)
MW, sum current and lagged	−.180*	−.290**	−.110	−.271**	−.070***	−.079***
	(.091)	(.140)	(.109)	(.124)	(.027)	(.025)
Mean wages[a]	No	Yes	No	Yes	No	Yes
Other controls	No	Yes	No	Yes	No	Yes
R^2	.067	.126	.018	.050	.031	.122
Number of counties per year	273	273	230	230	279	279
Average obs. per county per year	214	214	154	154	1385	1385
D. West						
MW level, current year	.021	−.117	.114	.144	−.042	−.166
	(.118)	(.186)	(.599)	(.536)	(.365)	(.244)
MW level, lagged 1 year	.176	.510	−.026	−.178	−.021	−.347
	(.520)	(.662)	(.434)	(.534)	(.183)	(.238)
MW, sum current and lagged	.197	.393	.088	−.034	−.063	−.513
	(.476)	(.581)	(.536)	(.534)	(.270)	(.340)

(continued)

Table 4.8 (continued)

Dependent variable: log (employment/population)	*Young adults (age 15–29)*		*At-risk group*		*Entire sample*	
Independent variables (log)	*(1)*	*(2)*	*(1)*	*(2)*	*(1)*	*(2)*
Mean wages[a]	No	Yes	No	Yes	No	Yes
Other controls	No	Yes	No	Yes	No	Yes
R^2	.058	.168	.030	.076	.059	.160
Number of counties per year	90	90	79	79	93	93
Average obs. per county per year	250	250	181	181	1673	1673

Note [a]The control variables for the mean wage of young adults and at risk groups are mean wages of non-young adults and non-at risk groups, respectively. The control variable for mean wage of the entire sample is the mean wage of the entire sample. Each estimation has controlled for year and county fixed effects

***statistically significant at the 1% level; **at the 5% level; and *at the 10% level. Cluster-robust standard errors at the county level are in parentheses

Table 4.9 Representativeness of the 16-province sample: summary statistics, 2005 Census

Year 2005 variable	*Minimum/average wage*			*Employment/population*		
	All provinces	*16 provinces (in our sample)*	*15 provinces (not in our sample)*	*All provinces*	*16 provinces (in our sample)*	*15 provinces (not in our sample)*
All	.388	.371	.425	.779	.783	.773
	(1.081)	(.087)	(.098)	(.087)	(.082)	(.093)
Gender						
Male	.361	.347	.398	.849	.852	.841
	(.082)	(.074)	(.089)	(.068)	(.058)	(.079)
Female	.432	.421	.470	.711	.719	.696
	(.098)	(.088)	(.102)	(.081)	(.074)	(.092)
Region						
East	.373	380	.461	.824	.841	.799
	(.067)	(.069)	(.100)	(.077)	(.072)	(.087)
Central	.410	.413	.400	.757	.764	.736
	(.083)	(.073)	(.099)	(.079)	(.073)	(.092)
West	.406	.410	.403	.759	.763	.751
	(.103)	(.121)	(.102)	(.093)	(.090)	(.096)
Age cohort						
Age 15–29	.421	.411	.474	.487	.502	.434
Age 30–39	.370	.352	.409	.850	.874	.802
Age 40–49	.377	.363	.403	.867	.887	.832
Age 50–64	.371	.357	.401	.534	.563	.498
Educational attainment						
High school or below	.463	.455	.490	.775	.779	.767
Junior college	.288	.267	.337	.824	.824	.825
College or above	.189	.167	.257	.877	.877	.878
Observations	1,687,919	1,084,190	603,729	1,687,919	1,084,190	603,729

Note Standard deviations are in parentheses. The 16 provinces include Liaoning, Beijing, Shandong, Jiangsu, Shanghai, Guangdong, Heilongjiang, Shanxi, Henan, Anhui, Hubei, Jiangxi, Gansu, Chongqing, Sichuan, and Yunnan

if wages increase more slowly in places where employment grows more slowly, one could possibly find a negative relationship between normalized minimum wages and employment even when the minimum wage does not increase.

To address this concern, we estimate a non-normalized minimum wage model and control for average wages of groups that are not being examined in the regression as an additional covariate (e.g., in the young adults regressions, we use the average wage of non-young adults as an additional control) and show those results in Table 4.8. Overall, we find that our results are robust whether or not the minimum wages are normalized. That is, we still find statistically significant disemployment effects in the East, Central, and all regions for young adults, at-risk groups, and for the entire sample. And we do not find any effect in the Western region.

Representativeness of the Sample

The fact that the NBS only allows limited access to the micro-data up to 16 provinces could cast doubt on the representativeness of the 16-province UHS sample to the entire population. To address this concern, we utilize the 2005 Census data to compare descriptive statistics of the 16 sample provinces with the 15 provinces not in our sample, along with the entire census sample.

We check the representativeness of our 16 sample provinces by comparing the descriptive statistics of the UHS with those of the 2005 Census and report the comparisons in Table 4.9. We also compute the two key variables—minimum wage-to-average wage ratio and employment-to-population ratio—by gender, region, age cohort, and educational attainment for all provinces, 16 provinces in our sample, and 15 provinces not in our sample. The numbers for all provinces and 16 provinces are relatively close to those of 15 provinces not in the sample. In other words, Table 4.9 provides evidence that our 16-province UHS sample is representative of the whole country.

4.5 Conclusions

We use a large county-level panel data set that contains relevant information on minimum wages, combined with UHS micro-data from 16 representative provinces, to estimate the employment effect of minimum wage changes in China over the 2004–2009 period. Compared to previous studies using provincial-level data and reporting mixed results, we find that minimum wage changes in China led to significant negative effects on the employment in the Eastern and Central regions and caused disemployment for young adults and low-skilled workers, particularly at-risk groups.

Our study makes a number of significant contributions to the empirical literature on minimum wages in China, the largest transitional economy in the world. First, the use of detailed county-level data (over 1400 counties) provides greater accuracy and more variations (127 changes) of minimum wages in order to measure their real impact on employment. Second, the unique features of the UHS micro-data allow us to directly evaluate the employment effects of minimum wages on those population groups that are at risk of being affected by minimum wage increases, such as young adults and low-skilled workers. Third, our results are robust to various definitions of minimum wages and the workforce, various subsamples by region, and across a number of population groups. Fourth, minimum wages were strongly enforced after the new minimum wage regulations were enacted in 2004, as such they are expected to have more significant employment effects after 2004. Our results show that minimum wages in the provinces with vigorous enforcement did increase wages of the workers while adversely affecting their employment, especially for young adults and low-skilled workers.

Notes

1. Nevertheless, these two positions are not necessarily in conflict. The minimum wage can have negative impacts but also serve those other goals advocated by its supporters. The existing evidence has shown that the minimum wage poses a trade-off of higher income for some against job losses for others.
2. There is no national minimum wage in China; rather, the minimum wage standards are determined at the provincial level. We discuss how we calculate the mean nominal minimum wages of each year in Sect. 4.3.1.
3. The growth rates of average nominal wage are 155 and 194% for the periods of 1995–2003 and 2004–2012, respectively (National Bureau of Statistics of China 2013).
4. The theoretically expected effect of minimum wages on employment is well established in the literature. For examples, see reviews in Card and Krueger (1995), Brown (1999), Gunderson (2005), Cunningham

(2007), and Neumark and Wascher (2008). However, there is no consensus in the existing empirical studies on the magnitude of disemployment effect associated with minimum wage changes. Please refer to Neumark and Wascher (2007) for the most extensive survey of employment effects; Card (1992), Card and Krueger (1994, 1995, 2000), Neumark and Wascher (1992, 1995), and Williams (1993) for US evidence; Machin and Manning (1994), Dickens et al. (1999), Stewart (2004), and Metcalf (2008) for British evidence; and Campolieti et al. (2005) and Campolieti et al. (2006) for Canadian evidence.

5. For expositional convenience, we refer to "provinces, municipalities, and autonomous regions" as provinces.
6. The implementation date of a new minimum wage standard for a county can also differ across geographically contiguous neighbors within the same province. For example, Liaoning Province has the most complicated minimum wage scheme, in which 14 jurisdictions may enact their own standards on different dates. For instance, in 2007, Shenyang, Benxi, Dandong, and Panjin cities did not increase their minimum wages. In contrast, Dalian and Anshan cities increased their minimum wages from 600 RMB to 700 RMB on December 20th, on which day Jinzhou and Liaoyang cities increased their minimum wages from 480 RMB to 580 RMB and Chaoyang city increased its minimum wage from 350 RMB to 530 RMB. Furthermore, the minimum wages of Fushun and Huludao cities increased from 400 RMB to 480 RMB on January 1st, whereas that of Yingkou city increased from 380 RMB to 480 RMB, that of Fuxin city increased from 350 RMB to 420 RMB, and that of Tieling city increased from 380 RMB to 420 RMB the following year. As such detailed minimum wage data by county are not readily available to the public, we took effort to collect the data by ourselves.
7. We are aware that possible endogeneity of minimum wages may bias our results, especially in China the minimum wage standards are set by provincial governments, labor unions, and employer groups. Neumark and Wascher (2004) argue that the earlier evidence from Wages Councils in the UK (which did not find disemployment effects) is likely not true because a minimum wage is not enacted when the labor market is in trouble, which may lead us to expect fewer adverse effects. But, as will be shown in Sects. 4.4.2 and 4.4.3, we find clear evidence that minimum wages in China have resulted in disemployment for the less skilled workers, women, and young adults; and conversely, we do not find disemployment effects for the more skilled and prime age workers. Such falsification test helps rule out the endogeneity issue unless we believe that Chinese policymakers time their minimum wage increases to coincide with adverse shocks on less skilled labor markets only. In addition, our finding of

strong wage effects for the less skilled worker, women, and young adults also helps dismiss such kind of endogeneity concern. Similarly, our falsification test also helps reduce the concern raised by Dube et al. (2010) and Allegretto et al. (2011) that high-wage industries also experienced lower job growth after minimum wage increases, which is spurious.

8. In other words, depending on whether one accounts for this issue, the difference can be substantial. For instance, the mean monthly minimum wages in Beijing and Shanghai were 651 RMB and 767 RMB in 2004–2009; however, the average expenses of both social security payments and housing provident funds in Beijing and Shanghai are as high as 376 RMB and 452 RMB over the same period, amounting to 58 and 59% of the nominal minimum wages, respectively. We discuss how we address this issue in the data section.
9. There are 31 administrative units at the provincial level in China, including 22 provinces, 5 autonomous regions, and 4 municipalities; as of 2012, there are 2862 county-level administrative units.
10. Although we do not report the results of migrant workers in the article, they are available upon request.
11. This has affected compliance significantly. According to our calculation using 2002–2009 data, nationwide the share of workers who earn less than the minimum wage declined continuously, falling from 7.28 to 5.62% in the pre- and post-2004 periods (2002–2003, 2004–2009), respectively. In particular, the number decreased from 8.08 to 5.33% in the Eastern region between the same periods, whereas in the Central region, the number decreased from 6.19 to 5.46%.
12. We have also calculated three violation indices introduced in Bhorat et al. (2013) which has the form of $V_\alpha = E\{[(mw - w)/mw]^\alpha\}$, where w denotes wage, mw is the relevant minimum wage, α is the index that concerns the depth of violation, and E is the expectation operator. As α increases, there is more weight on greater violations. We use $\alpha = 0$, 1, and 2 to represent the standard, the depth, and the severity measures of violation, respectively. In addition, we also compute the ratio V_1/V_0 as the percentage shortfall of the average wage of violated workers from the minimum wage. Take all regions over the 2004–2009 period for example, the estimates for V_0 and V_1 are .071 and .024, respectively. The V_1/V_0 ratio is .338, indicating that non-complying employers paid wages that were on average 34% short of the legislative minima. Overall, the results are consistent to the descriptive statistics in Table 4.3 and the results using the enforcement variable. We find that all indices show the violation decreases over time in the Eastern and Central regions of China, especially after 2004, while the Western region has relatively higher violation. The results are available upon request.

13. In the original data, we are able to identify how many months a person works and record his/her monthly income and wages in a year. From 2002 to 2009, on average, 91% of the workers have worked for 12 months in a year.
14. Note that there was no minimum wage increase in 2009 because of the Great Recession.
15. For example, if the minimum wage adjustment in a particular county and a particular year took place on September 1, the mean minimum wage for that year and county is an average of the old and the new minimum wages, weighted by three-fourths and one-fourths, respectively. This time-weighted average method is used for our study because the adjustment date varies substantially across county and year in China. It can be in March, May, July, or November (sometimes in January). This method helps reduce the bias from using all the old or the new minimum wage.
16. In fact, the average real minimum wage has also grown at a similar rate. The mean changes in minimum wage are weighted by county worker population.
17. The average annual growth rate of the minimum wage is 12.7% in the Eastern region, 13.2% in the Central region, and 12.5% in the Western region over the 2004–2009 period.
18. Note that the minimum wage standards are the same for men and women.
19. To assure that we are comparing minimum wage standards on a comparable basis, the minimum-to-average wage ratios in Table 4.2 have accounted for the fact that some provinces include social security payments and housing provident funds as part of the wage when calculating minimum wages. For example, the minimum wages in Beijing, Shanghai, and Jiangxi do not include social security payments and housing provident funds, and the minimum wages in Jiangsu began to include only social security payments (but not housing provident funds) on November 1, 2005.
20. Our estimate of few full-time workers in China earn less than the monthly legal minimum wage is similar to Ye et al. (2015) that use a firm-employee matched data of 6 provinces in China and find the number is between 2.1 and 3.4% in 2009. The other estimate is by Sun and Shu (2011) who use a dataset of in 9 cities of Guangdong province in 2006, 2008, 2009, and 2010 and find that the proportion of rural-migrant workers who earn less than the monthly minimum wage in the four years is 9.0, 7.7, 4.0, and 4.2%, respectively.
21. Note that Dube et al. (2010) and Allegretto et al. (2011) have criticized the state/county panel data approach and attempt to construct better counterfactuals for estimating the effects of minimum wages on employment. However, Neumark et al. (2014) provide evidence that the

methods advocated by the above two studies do not isolate more reliable identifying information (or even throw out much useful and potentially valid identifying information), leading to incorrect conclusions. A recent paper by Meer and West (2013) who use three separate state panels of administrative employment data and find that minimum wages reduce net job growth. They show that the disemployment effects are most pronounced for younger workers and in industries with a higher proportion of low-wage workers. Although we don't anticipate the issues raised by Dube et al. (2010) and Allegretto et al. (2011) would undermine our results, further work would be useful and our data permit researchers to explore additional issues.

22. We present the results of the minimum wage effect on wages by age cohort, educational attainment, and the enforcement of minimum wage effects on wages in Additional file 1: Tables S1 to S3 of Fang and Lin (2015), respectively.
23. We also show results for a high skill group (defined as workers with a college degree or above) as a placebo test in Sect. 4.4.3.
24. Because the number of workers aged 15–19 is relatively small in our sample, we use the group of workers aged 15–29 to represent young workers.
25. The working population defined in our analysis so far excludes the self-employed. That is, we focus on wage employees only. However, there are some concerns that by excluding the self-employed, the estimations may actually capture the effect of minimum wages on the structure of employment (wage versus self-employed) rather than on the share of people actually working. In response to the concerns, we re-examine the effects based on a broader definition of workforce by including the self-employed. Overall, our results are similar to Table 4.5 in that minimum wage changes result in statistically significant disemployment effects for young adults, at-risk groups, and the entire sample in the East, Central, and all regions over the same period of analysis. Likewise, we do not find any effect in the West. The results are available upon request.
26. Over 2004–2009, 42% of young adults work in the state-owned enterprises in the Eastern region; 59 and 61% of young adults work in the state-owned enterprises in the Central and Western regions, respectively. For at-risk groups, 24% of them work in the state-owned enterprises in the Eastern region, while 43 and 47% work in the state-owned enterprises in the Central and Western regions, respectively.
27. It is important to recognize that the UHS is designed to be representative at the provincial level, not at the county level. Due to random sampling errors, our samples for some specific counties may be noisy. To address this concern, we re-examine our main results in Table 4.5 at the provincial level. Similar to the results at the county level in Table 4.5, the

provincial level estimations do not alter our findings. Minimum wage increases continue to have significant disemployment effects on the three groups in the East, Central, and all regions, but no effect in the West.

28. Indeed, our sample shows that the three groups are different in terms of employment type, skill, and wage distribution. Over the period of 2004–2009, less than 3% of young adults are in at-risk groups in each region. Likewise, less than 3% of at-risk groups are young adults in each region.

References

Allegretto SA, Dube A, Reich M (2011). Do minimum wages really reduce teen employment? Accounting for heterogeneity and selectivity in state panel data. *Industrial Relations: A Journal of Economy and Society* 50, 205–240.

Baker M, Benjamin D, Stanger S (1999). The highs and lows of the minimum wage effect: A time-series cross-section study of the Canadian law. *Journal of Labor Economics* 17, 318–350.

Bhorat H, Kanbur R, Mayet N (2013). A note on measuring the depth of minimum wage violation. *LABOUR* 27, 192–197.

Brown C (1999). Chapter 32 minimum wages, employment, and the distribution of income, in: Ashenfelter OC, Card D (Eds), *Handbook of labor economics*, vol. Volume 3, Part B. Elsevier, New York; pp. 2101–2163.

Burkhauser RV, Couch KA, Wittenburg DC (2000). A reassessment of the new economics of the minimum wage literature with monthly data from the current population survey. *Journal of Labor Economics* 18, 653–680.

Cai, F, Wang, M (2005) The economic analysis of labor shortage: Evidence from the Pearl River area. *Guangdong Social Sciences* 2, 5–10 (in Chinese).

Campolieti M, Fang T, Gunderson M (2005). How minimum wages affect schooling-employment outcomes in Canada, 1993–1999. *Journal of Labor Research* 26, 533–545.

Campolieti M, Gunderson M, Riddell C (2006). Minimum wage impacts from a prespecified research design: Canada 1981–1997. *Industrial Relations: A Journal of Economy and Society* 45, 195–216.

Card D (1992). Do minimum wages reduce employment? A case study of California, 1987–89. *Industrial and Labor Relations Review* 46, 38–54.

Card, D, Katz, LF, Krueger, AB (1994) Comment on David Neumark and William Wascher, "Employment effects of minimum and subminimum wages: Panel data on state minimum wage laws". *Industrial and Labor Relations Review* 47, 487–497.

Card D, Krueger AB (1994). Minimum wage and employment: A case study of the fast-food industry in New Jersey and Pennsylvania. *American Economic Review* 84, 772–793.

Card D, Krueger AB (1995) *Myth and measurement: The new economics of the minimum wage*. Princeton University Press: Princeton.

Card D, Krueger AB (2000). Minimum wages and employment: A case study of the fast-food industry in New Jersey and Pennsylvania: Reply. *American Economic Review* 90, 1397–1420.

Chan A (2001). *China's workers under assault: The exploitation of labor in a globalizing economy*. Armonk: ME Sharpe.

Cheung SNS (2004). Another eye on minimum wages, *Southern Weekly*, June 17 (in Chinese).

Cheung SNS (2010). The lethality of minimum wages, *Economic Information Daily*, February 24 (in Chinese).

Cooke FL (2005). *Hrm, work and employment in china*. London: Routledge.

Cunningham W (2007). *Minimum wages and social policy: Lessons from developing countries*. Washington, DC: World Bank.

Dickens R, Machin S, Manning A (1999). The effects of minimum wages on employment: Theory and evidence from Britain. *Journal of Labor Economics* 17, 1–12.

Ding S (2009). An analysis of minimum wage effects on the employment of rural-urban migrant-evidence from the survey of 827 rural-urban migrants in Beijing. *China Rural Survey* 4, 26–36 (in Chinese).

Du Y, Wang M (2008). The implementation of minimum wage system and its effects in china. *Journal of Graduate School of Chinese Academy of Social Sciences* 6, 56–62 (in Chinese).

Dube A, Lester TW, Reich M (2010). Minimum wage effects across state borders: Estimates using contiguous counties. *The Review of Economics and Statistics* 92, 945–964.

Fang T, Lin C (2015). Minimum wages and employment in China. *IZA Journal of Labor Policy* 4, 22.

Frost S (2002). *Labour standards in china: The business and investment challenge*. Association for Sustainable and Responsible Investment in Asia.

Gong Q (2009). The impact of minimum wages on welfare of firm and labor in china. *Journal of Nanjing University* 2, 61–68 (in Chinese).

Gunderson M (2005). *Minimum wages in Canada: Theory, evidence and policy*, in: Commission FLSR (Ed). Fair Labour Standards Review Commission: Ottawa.

Hamermesh DS (1995). Myth and measurement: The new economics of the minimum wage: Comment. *Industrial and Labor Relations Review* 48, 835–838.

Han Z, Wei Z (2011). Minimum wage standards: Questions and policies. *Guangdong Social Sciences* 1, 192–200 (in Chinese).

Jia P, Zhang S (2013). Spillover effects of minimum wages increase. *Statistical Research* 30, 37–41 (in Chinese).

Keil MW, Robertson D, Symons J (2001). Minimum wages and employment. Claremont Colleges.

Khamis M (2013). Does the minimum wage have a higher impact on the informal than on the formal labour market? Evidence from quasi-experiments. *Applied Economics* 45, 477–495.

Lin JY, Cai F, Li Z (2001). *State-owned enterprise reform in china.* The Chinese University of Hong Kong: Hong Kong.

Machin S, Manning A (1994). The effects of minimum wages on wage dispersion and employment: Evidence from the U.K. wages councils. *Industrial and Labor Relations Review* 47, 319–329.

Meer J, West J (2013). Effects of the minimum wage on employment dynamics. NBER Working Paper No. 19262.

Metcalf D (2008). Why has the British national minimum wage had little or no impact on employment? *Journal of Industrial Relations* 50, 489–512.

National Bureau of Statistics of China (2013). China labour statistical year book.

Neumark D (2001). The employment effects of minimum ages: Evidence from a pre-specified research design. *Industrial Relations: A Journal of Economy and Society* 40, 121–144.

Neumark D, Salas JMI, Wascher W (2014). Revisiting the minimum wage—Employment debate: Throwing out the baby with the bathwater? *ILR Review* 67(3_suppl), 608–648.

Neumark D, Wascher W (1992). Employment effects of minimum and subminimum wages: Panel data on state minimum wage laws. *Industrial and Labor Relations Review* 46, 55–81.

Neumark D, Wascher W (1995). Minimum-wage effects on school and work transitions of teenagers. *American Economic Review* 85, 244–249.

Neumark D, Wascher W (2004) Minimum wages, labor market institutions, and youth employment: A cross-national analysis. *ILR Review* 57(2), 223–248.

Neumark, D, Wascher W (2007) Minimum wages and employment. *Foundations and Trends in Microeconomics* 3, 1–182.

Neumark D, Wascher W (2008) *Minimum wages.* Cambridge: The MIT Press.

Ni J, Wang G, Yao X (2011). Impact of minimum wages on employment: Evidence from china. *The Chinese Economy* 44, 18–38.

Ping X (2005). On the industrial relations of private companies. *China Reform* 4, 61–62 (in Chinese).

Rama M (2001). The consequences of doubling the minimum wage: The case of Indonesia. *Industrial and Labor Relations Review* 54, 864–881.

Stewart MB (2004). The employment effects of the national minimum wage. *The Economic Journal* 114, C110–C116.

Su H (1993). Research on the legislation of minimum wage law of china. *Review of Economic Research* Z1, 26–36 (in Chinese).

Sun S (2006). The economic analysis for the Chinese employment influence to the adjusting the lowest wage policy. *Journal of Hubei College of Finance and Economics* 18, 13–15 (in Chinese).

Sun Z, Shu B (2011). The standard of the minimum wage, and the wages of peasant workers—a case study based on Zhujiang Delta. *Management World* 8, 45–56 (in Chinese).

Wang J, Gunderson M (2011). Minimum wage impacts in china: Estimates from a prespecified research design, 2000–2007. *Contemporary Economic Policy* 29, 392–406.

Wang, J Gunderson, M (2012) Minimum wage effects on employment and wages: Dif-in-dif estimates from eastern China. *International Journal of Manpower* 33, 860–876.

Williams N (1993). Regional effects of the minimum wage on teenage employment. *Applied Economics* 25, 1517–1528.

Xue Z (2004). The undesirable minimum wage law, 21st Century Business Herald, November 18 (in Chinese); pp. 11–18.

Yang T (2006). What is the social background when China implemented its minimum wage law? *People's Daily.*

Ye M (2005). Discussions on the effects of minimum wages on rural-urban migrant workers and the youth. *Theory and Modernization* 7, 86–87.

Ye L, Gindling T, & Li S (2015). Compliance with legal minimum wages and overtime pay regulations in China. *IZA J Labor Develop* 4, 16.

Zhang Z (2007). Will minimum wage decrease immigrant peasant workers' employment? *Finance and Economics* 10, 103–110 (in Chinese).

Zhang J, Deng J (2005). On minimum wage system of peasant laborers. *Journal of Beijing Agricultural Vocation College* 19, 46–49 (in Chinese).

CHAPTER 5

Impacts of Minimum Wages on Gender Wage Gaps in Urban China

Li Shi and Xinxin Ma

5.1 Introduction

Does the minimum wage (MW) policy that has been implemented since 1993 affect gender wage differentials in China? In this article, we provide evidence on this issue. The significant points of the study are the following.

First, as is well known, along with the progress of economic reform, an increase in income inequality has become a serious social problem that should concern the government. In fact, there have been many studies on the issue, such as those of Zhao et al. (1996), Li and Gustafsson (2008), Li, Sato et al. (2013), and Li, Sicular et al. (2013). Because wages represent the largest share of the incomes of urban residents, a study on wage gaps is undoubtedly of great significance to investigate

L. Shi
Zhejiang University, Zhejiang, China
e-mail: lishi9@zju.edu.cn

X. Ma (✉)
University of Toyama, Toyama, Japan
e-mail: xxma@eco.u-toyama.ac.jp

L. Shi and C. Lin (eds.), *Minimum Wages in China*,
https://doi.org/10.1007/978-981-15-2421-9_5

the causes of income inequality. Currently, there is a variety of forms of wage gaps in China. From among them, the gender wage gap has risen to prominence along with the institutional transition.

The gender wage gap has become an issue primarily for two reasons: The widening gender wage gap is a factor contributing to the widening income gap and the reverse phenomenon arising with institutional reform and economic development. Specifically, the gender wage gap was small during the period of the planned economy because the government focused more on gender equality and positively carried out a number of policies to promote female employment and gender equality; thus, the wage distribution was relatively equal (Gustafsson and Li 2000; Li and Ma 2006; Li and Song 2013). Conversely, the economic transition has had an indirect effect on the expansion of the gender wage gap. For example, during the employment adjustment of state-owned enterprises (SOEs), the probability of becoming unemployed is greater for females than for males, and there is a gender wage gap among re-employed workers, primarily because of the discrimination against females (Li and Gustafsson 2008; Ma 2008). In addition, because the gender wage gap of the non-state-owned sector is larger than that of SOEs (Ma 2009), the ownership reform promoted the rapid development of the non-state-owned sector but also resulted in an increased gender wage gap. Furthermore, unlike in Europe, Japan, and other developed countries, the changing trend of the gender wage gap, which is from small to large, is a reversal phenomenon accompanying economic development. Actually, it can be considered a quasi-natural experimental model for a study on changes in policy and the gender wage gap. Thus, from both social policy and academic perspectives, the gender wage gap in urban China is an important issue.

Second, to improve the efficiency of the implementation of public policies in various economic fields, policy evaluation has become a very important practice in recent decades. During the economic transition period, the Chinese government introduced a number of new policies and regulations addressing the gender gap in employment and wages. Gender equality may be explicitly stipulated in such new regulations. Nevertheless, there is no empirical study to prove whether those policies have narrowed the gender wage gap. This article aims at discussing the effects of the MW policy on the gender wage gap.

We focus on the MW policy for the following two reasons. First, the implementation of the MW, in theory, may increase the income of low-wage workers and is beneficial to reduce poverty. Therefore, the

MW is enacted as an important labor policy. To examine the policy effect, many empirical analyses have been conducted in other countries. In contrast, although the MW has been in effect since 1993 in China, empirical analysis of it using micro-data is rare. Second, the effects of the MW on the gender wage gap depend on many factors. Some of these factors include, for example, the gender gap in the proportion of workers whose wages are below the regional MW level and the gender gap between actual wages and the MW level before the implementation of the MW (Robinson 2002, 2005). Therefore, although the implementation of the MW does not imply a reduction of the gender wage gap, in theory, we need to verify its effects through an empirical analysis.

This article attempts to answer the following questions through an empirical analysis using micro-data from CHIP1995, CHIP2002, and CHIP2007. First, is the proportion of the population with wages below the MW level greater for males than for females? Is the gap between actual wages and the MW level greater for females than for males? Second, would different MW levels adopted in various regions lead to a regional difference in the gender wage gap? Third, does the MW system affect the gender wage gap? What are the effects of endowment differentials? What are the effects of endowment return differentials? Fourth, has the MW system, which was implemented in 1993, affected the gender wage gap? If it has, is there a difference in short-term and long-term effects? Because we use the cross-sectional micro survey data from three periods, a repeated cross-sectional analysis should also investigate the changes (if any) in the abovementioned issues along with policy changes. Considering that the MW primarily affects low-income groups, we employ different models to conduct the analysis on average wages and wage distribution.

5.2 The Implementation of the MW in China

In China, since the 1980s, there has been increasing migration from rural to urban areas, which has been accompanied by an increase in the low wages of migrants and a rise in income inequality. To deal with these social problems, the MW policy was first promulgated as a law in 1993. The MW is applicable to two kinds of wages, the monthly wage and the hourly wage. Minimum monthly wage standards are applied to regular workers, while the minimum hourly wage is applied to non-regular workers. Wage, which is defined by the MW policy, is the basic wage with the exception of overtime work payment and some allowances.

As per policy, the MW level is determined by the regional government, the union, and the representatives of companies. However, in reality, MW levels are determined primarily by the regional governments. The MW level is adjusted once every two years, according to many factors such as the regional lowest living cost, consumer price index of urban residents, social insurance, the housing fund that individual workers are paid, the regional average wage level, the status of economic development, and employment status. The adjustment of the MW level is carried out by the local government (province or city governments); as a result, there are regional disparities. For example, the MW level is higher in the eastern regions as compared to the western and central regions, and the increase within these bands of the MW levels is also different across regions (see Fig. 5.1). These regional disparities allow us to use a quasi-natural experiment model to prove the effects of MW. We will provide detailed explanations about this in the following paragraphs.

Although the government enforced the implementation of the MW, there are no penalties for violations; hence, there are several compliance

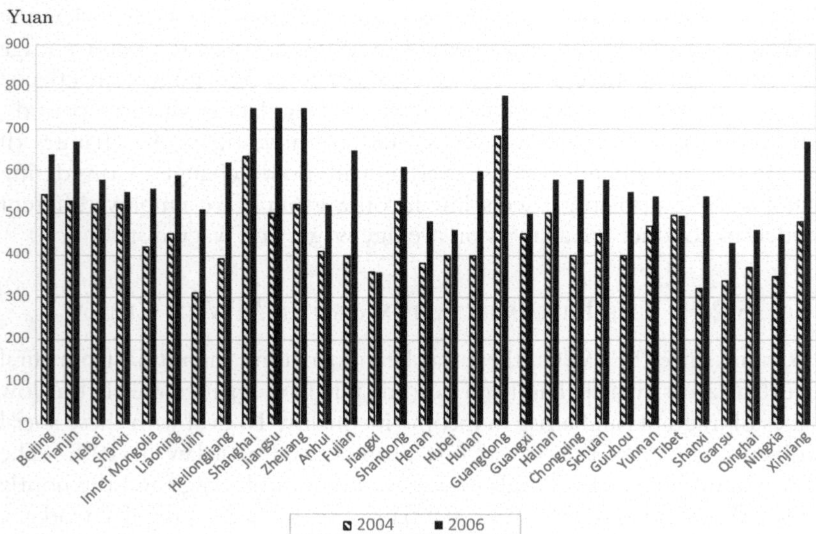

Fig. 5.1 Regional disparities of the MW levels (2004 and 2006) (*Source* Published information by each regional governments)

problems and MW is not thoroughly implemented in the private sector. These compliance problems account for the phenomenon of workers with wages below the prescribed level, although the MW has been in existence since 1993.

5.3 Literature Review

There are a large number of empirical studies on the effects of the MW on employment[1] and wage distribution for other countries. The studies related to the empirical analyses in this article are reviewed in the following.

Dinardo et al. (1996) conducted studies on the effects of the MW on wage gaps. In particular, they assumed other things equal to evaluate the wage distribution in 1988 based on the fixed MW level in 1979 and then compared the 1979 level with the actual level in 1988 to reveal the effects of the MW system on a wage gap. The analysis shows that there is an increase in the wage gap in 1988 compared with 1979; the decrease of the MW level results in an increased wage gap (17% for male, 24% for female). Card and Krueger (1995) conducted a study on the effects of changes in the MW level from 1989 to 1992 on changes in wage gaps in the United States. Using a natural experiment model based on the MW system change, in which the MW level was increased in some states in 1990 and 1991, they indicated that the Minimum Wage Act pulled up the incomes of low-wage workers and narrowed the regional wage gap.

In addition, to investigate the effects of the MW on the gender wage gap, Robinson (2002, 2005) uses the British Labor Force Survey data from 1997 to 2000 to study the effects of the MW implemented throughout the country in April 1999 on the gender wage gap. The analysis, based on a quasi-DID model (using London, whose gender wage gap is the smallest before the implementation of the MW, as a control group and other regions as treatment groups), shows that the effects of the MW on gender wage gap vary in different regions. Shannon (1996) utilized the Canadian Labor Force Survey data in 1986 and the Oaxaca-Blinder decomposition method to conduct a relevant study that shows that the MW narrowed the gender wage gap among the population aged 16–24 but had little effect on those aged 25–64. Currently, there is no empirical analysis of the effects of the MW on the gender wage gap in urban China. Our study may address this lack to a certain extent.

5.4 Methodology and Data

5.4.1 Model

Robinson Model for the Effects of the MW on the Gender Wage Gap
Robinson (2002, 2005) established a model to analyze the effects of the MW system on the gender wage gap in the UK. This model is primarily used to show that there are two reasons for the effects of the MW on the gender wage gap. First, the MW level has various effects on wage distribution:

$$\begin{aligned} W_i &= W_i \text{ if } W_i > MW \\ W_i &= MW \text{ if } W_i^* \leq MW \end{aligned} \tag{5.1}$$

Equation (5.1) shows that for groups with a wage greater than the MW level ($W_i > MW$) before the implementation of the MW, the wage remains the same after such implementation, whereas, for those with a wage lower than the MW level ($W_i^* \leq MW$) before the implementation, the wage increases to the MW level after such implementation. As a result, the average wage after the implementation of the MW should be a composite value affected by these two weights and expressed as follows:

$$\begin{aligned} \ln \bar{W}_{\text{after}} &= \left[\sum_{mw} \frac{(MW)}{N_{mw}}\right] * \left(\frac{N_{mw}}{N}\right) + \left[\sum_{N-N_{mw}} \frac{(W_i)}{N - N_{mw}}\right]\left(\frac{N - N_{mw}}{N}\right) \\ &= \sum_{mw} (MW) * \frac{1}{N} + \sum_{N-N_{mw}} (W_i) * \frac{1}{N} \end{aligned} \tag{5.2}$$

The changes in the average wage before and after such implementation can be expressed as follows:

$$\Delta \bar{W} = \frac{1}{N}\left[\sum_{mw} (MW - W_i)\right] \tag{5.3}$$

Equation (5.3) indicates that there are two reasons for the changes in average wage before and after the implementation of the MW: the number of workers with wages lower than the MW level and the gap between the actual wage and the MW level. Consequently, the gender wage gap before the implementation of the MW can be expressed as Eqs. (5.4) and (5.5):

$$\left(\frac{\bar{W}_f}{\bar{W}_m}\right)^{\text{before}} = \frac{\sum\limits_{W_f \leq MW} (W_f) * \frac{1}{N_f} + \sum\limits_{W_f > MW} (W_f) * \frac{1}{N_f}}{\sum\limits_{W_m \leq MW} (W_m) * \frac{1}{N_m} + \sum\limits_{W_m > MW} (W_m) * \frac{1}{N_m}} \tag{5.4}$$

$$\left(\frac{\bar{W}_f}{\bar{W}_m}\right)^{\text{after}} = \frac{\sum\limits_{W_f \leq MW} (W_f) * \frac{1}{N_f} + \sum\limits_{W_f > MW} (W_f) * \frac{1}{N_f}}{\sum\limits_{W_m \leq MW} (W_m) * \frac{1}{N_m} + \sum\limits_{W_m > MW} (W_m) * \frac{1}{N_m}} \tag{5.5}$$

The following assumptions are drawn based on a comparison between Eqs. (5.4) and (5.5). (i) When the number of females is greater than that of males among workers having wages lower than the MW level before the implementation of the MW, and (ii) When the gap between actual wages and the MW level for females is greater than that for males before the implementation of the MW, such an implementation may contribute to narrowing the gender wage gap at the low-wage distribution.

Because (i) and (ii) stated above are only assumptions, the implementation of the MW does not imply a certain reduction of the gender wage gap in theory. Further investigations must be conducted with the following models.

Estimates of the Gender Wage Gap of Regions by the MW Level

Based on the MW level, we classified the samples into high MW regions, medium MW regions, and low MW regions[2] to estimate the wage function. The wage function is represented with Eq. (5.6).

$$\ln W_{ijt} = a_{ijt} + \beta_{ijt} + \varepsilon_{ijt} \tag{5.6}$$

In Eq. (5.6), i represents individual workers, t represents periods, and j represents three categories of regions (high MW regions, middle WM regions, and low MW regions). X is other variables affecting wages (such as education and work experience as a proxy for human capital, or male dummy variable), a is a constant, ε is an error term, and β represents the coefficient estimates of variables. Using coefficients of the male dummy estimated by regional subgroups, we compare the regional differentials of gender wage gaps.[3]

To see the different effects by the wage distribution, we adopt the quantile regression model (Koenker and Bassett 1978), which can be expressed as:

$$\min_{X(\theta)}\left[\sum_{h:\ln W_i \geq \beta(\theta)X_i} \theta|\ln W_i - \beta(\theta)X_i| + \sum_{h:\ln W_i < \beta(\theta)X_i} (1-\theta)|\ln W_i - \beta(\theta)X_i|\right] \tag{5.7}$$

$$\rho_\theta \in (0, 1)$$

In Eq. (5.7), i represents individual workers, and θ represents quantile of wages (1% quantile is expressed as 1th). The equation's other variables are the same as those of Eq. (5.6). $\rho_\theta \in (.)$ is a check (or indicator) function. The QR model is designed for estimation using the optimal method, which minimizes the two error terms in Eq. (5.7).

Decomposition Model for the Effects of the MW Level on Gender Wage Gaps
To decompose the effect on gender wage gaps, the Oaxaca–Blinder decomposition method[4] (Oaxaca 1973; Blinder 1973) is commonly used. However, Cotton (1988), Neumark (1988), and Oaxaca and Ransom (1994) note that the Oaxaca–Blinder decomposition method using estimated coefficient and average values of males or females may lead to an index number problem. To address this problem, this article adopts the Oaxaca–Ransom decomposition model (Oaxaca and Ransom 1994).

$$\ln \bar{W}_m - \ln \bar{W}_f = (\bar{X}_m - \bar{X}_f)\beta^* + \bar{X}_f(\beta^* - \beta_f) + \bar{X}_m(\beta_m - \beta^*) \tag{5.8}$$

In Eq. (5.8), m represents males, f represents females, $\ln \bar{W}$ is the logarithm of the average wage, $\bar{X}$ is the average of variables, and β_m and β_f represent the estimated coefficients resulting from the wage function of males and females, respectively. Note the β^* (no-discrimination wage structure) therein, which is a gender-neutral coefficient estimated based on wage functions using the entire sample. Concerning the Oaxaca and Ransom model, $(\bar{X}_m - \bar{X}_f)\beta^*$ represents the gender wage gap resulting from a difference in endowment including, for example, human capital, $\bar{X}_f(\beta^* - \beta_f)$ represents the gap caused by too-low endowment return of females (known as "female loss") and $\bar{X}_m(\beta_m - \beta^*)$ represents the gap generated by too-high endowment return of males (known as "male gain"). The sum of these two decomposition values stands for the gender wage gap resulting from differences in endowment return, including discrimination.[5] We add the variable of the MW levels and Kaitz index[6] in this model to decompose these MW factors' effects on the gender wage gap.

DID Analysis for the Effects of the MW on the Gender Wage Gap
Although the effect of the MW on gender wage gap can be decomposed by the endowment difference and endowment returns difference as described above, it is necessary to provide evidence on whether the MW has affected gender wage differentials. Here, we apply the DID model, which is frequently used for policy evaluation. DID analysis[7] can be represented as follows:

$$\begin{aligned}\ln W_{ijt} = & a + \gamma_x X_{ijt} + \gamma_{ye} Year_{ij} + \gamma_{tr} Treat_{ijt} + \gamma_m Male_{ijt} + \gamma_{yetr} Year * Treat_{ijt} \\ & + \gamma_{yem} Year * Male_{ijt} + \gamma_{trm} Treat * Male_{ijt} + \gamma_{did} DID_{ijt} + v_{ijt}\end{aligned} \tag{5.9}$$

In Eq. (5.9), i stands for the individual, t for years, j represents categories of regions, *Year* for policy implementation years (1995, 2002, and 2007 in this article), *Treat* for the treatment group, *Male* for the male dummy variable, a is the constant term, and v is the error term. γ represents the estimated coefficient for each variable.

We used the retrospective data of CHIP1995 to gain wages information for the previous five years and generated several treatment groups and control groups.[8] Specifically, we use the years before the implementation of the MW (1990, 1991, 1992, 1993, and 1994) as the initial years and the years of 1995, 2002, and 2007 as the policy implantation years. We distinguish the treatment group and the control group.

We sampled districts with relatively large gender wage gaps in the initial years before the implementation of the MW and relatively high MW levels (where the value of Kaitz index is higher) during the implementation years as the simulation treatment groups. It is thought that the MW should provide the largest effect to this group. For example, using the 1990–1995 data, we defined Henan province as a treatment group because the gender wage gap is largest in 1990, as the ratio of female and male wage is 0.78, while in other districts it is 0.80–0.86; accordingly, the Kaitz index is highest (Henan is 0.44, the other districts are 0.25–0.38). On the other hand, we sampled districts with relatively small gender wage gaps during the initial years and a MW level lower than that of the treatment group in the policy implementation years as a control group. In this case, the MW should have the smallest effect on these groups. Since 1993, MW was implemented across all districts in China; therefore, we cannot treat a non-implementation district as a treatment group (this is the strict definition). Accordingly, we defined the treatment groups as the district most impacted by the MW implementation.[9]

Here, the *DID* item is the cross term of the three items used—male, the policy implementation years, and treatment group (*Male*Year*Treat*). If the estimated coefficient of *DID* is statistically significant, it indicates that the implementation of the MW has an effect on the gender wage gap. If the estimated coefficient is a negative value, it shows that the MW system has some effect on reducing the gender wage gap, and vice versa.

5.4.2 *Data*

CHIP1995, 2002, and 2007 are used for the analysis. These data are gained from the three surveys of the CHIP conducted by NBS, Economic Institute of CASS, and Beijing Normal University, including respective information about employment and wages of urban residents. Using retrospective survey data of income in CHIP1995, we can differentiate the years before and after the MW implementation to analyze the treatment group and control group.

Because there are design similarities of the data in the questionnaire, we can use the same information for analysis for all three periods. To make comparisons in three periods, we selected the regions (provinces) covered in all three surveys, including Beijing, Shanxi, Liaoning, Jiangsu, Anhui, Guangdong, Henan, Hubei, Sichuan, Yunnan, and Gansu.[10]

The wage[11] is defined as the total earnings from work (called "the total wage"). Here, it comprises the basic wage, bonus, cash subsidy, and no cash subsidy.[12] We use the CPI in 1995 as the standard and adjust the nominal wage in 2002 and 2007.

The analytic objects of this article are employees, excluding the self-employed and the unemployed. Considering the retirement system of the state-owned sector, to reduce the effect of that system on the analysis result, the analytic objects are limited in the groups between the ages of 16 and 60.

In the wage function, the explained variable is the logarithm of the monthly wage,[13] and the explaining variables are the variables likely to affect the wage, such as education (primary school or below, junior high school, senior high school/vocational school, college, university,[14] and above), experience years,[15] ownership (state-owned enterprises, collectively owned enterprises, foreign/private enterprises), occupation (manager, technician, clerk, manual worker), industry (agriculture, fishing and forestry, manufacturing, mining, construction, transportation/communication, wholesale, retail, and catering, real estate, health and social welfare, education, culture, and arts, financial industry, public management and social organizations, and other industries).

We apply the Chinese National Minimum Wage Databases to classify the regions by the MW level, as shown in Table 5.1. Table 5.2 shows sample statistical descriptions by gender groups.

Table 5.1 Regional classification by the MW levels

		Low-MW region	*Mid-MW region*	*High-MW region*
1995	level	160–165 Yuan	165–175 Yuan	over 175 Yuan
	regions	Shanxi, Anhui, Shichuan, Yunnan, Gansu	Jiangsu, Hernan, Hubei	Beijing, Liaoning
2002	level	225–285 Yuan	285–330 Yuan	over 330 Yuan
	regions	Shanxi, Hernan, Shichuan, Gansu	Liaonin, Anhui, Hubei, Yunnan	Beijing, Jiangsu, Guangdong
2007	level	375–510 Yuan	510–615 Yuan	over 615 Yuan
	regions	Anhui, Hubei, Yunnan, Gansu	Shanxi, Liaonin, Hernan, Guangdong, Shicuan	Beijing, Jiangsu

Note Chinese national minimum wage database

Table 5.2 Statistical descriptions

	1995			*2002*			*2007*		
	Male	*Female*	*F-M*	*Male*	*Female*	*F-M*	*Male*	*Female*	*F-M*
Monthly wage	536	462	86.2%	1045	852	81.5%	1722	1271	73.8%
Education									
Elementary school or less	3.6%	5.6%	1.9%	2.2%	2.5%	0.4%	2.2%	2.2%	0.0%
Junior high school	28.1%	32.7%	4.6%	24.3%	21.7%	−2.7%	20.4%	17.0%	−3.4%
Senior high school	38.9%	44.2%	5.3%	37.7%	45.1%	7.4%	35.3%	40.4%	5.1%
College	18.7%	12.5%	−6.2%	23.0%	23.0%	0.0%	24.5%	27.7%	3.2%
University	10.7%	5.1%	−5.6%	12.8%	7.7%	−5.1%	17.6%	12.7%	−5.0%
Years of experience	28	27	−2	30	27	−3	31	28	−3
Han	95.4%	95.3%	0.0	96.0%	95.9%	−0.1%	97.4%	96.9%	−0.5%
Married	87.1%	87.9%	0.8%	89.1%	86.6%	−2.5%	88.4%	86.4%	−2.0%
Ownership									
SOE	86.2%	76.9%	−9.3%	70.0%	64.5%	−5.5%	59.4%	49.7%	−9.7%
COE	12.0%	20.7%	8.7%	5.5%	9.0%	3.5%	5.1%	7.0%	1.9%
Foreign/private firm	1.5%	1.7%	0.2%	23.4%	23.9%	0.5%	29.3%	30.3%	1.0%
Others	0.2%	0.7%	0.5%	1.2%	2.6%	1.4%	6.2%	13.1%	6.8%
Occupation									
Manager	17.3%	6.3%	−11.0%	19.8%	9.3%	−10.5%	6.7%	2.8%	−4.0%
Engineer	19.5%	22.2%	2.6%	17.8%	23.8%	6.0%	33.3%	37.5%	4.2%
Clerical staff	22.5%	23.4%	0.9%	20.4%	22.8%	2.4%	20.5%	19.1%	−1.4%
Manufacturing worker	37.7%	41.4%	3.7%	32.6%	23.1%	−9.4%	23.9%	11.7%	−12.2%
Others	2.9%	6.7%	3.8%	9.4%	21.0%	11.5%	15.6%	28.9%	13.3%

(continued)

Table 5.2 (continued)

	1995			*2002*			*2007*		
	Male	*Female*	*F-M*	*Male*	*Female*	*F-M*	*Male*	*Female*	*F-M*
Industry									
Agriculture, forestry, fisheries	2.1%	1.3%	−0.8%	1.3%	1.3%	0.0%	1.0%	0.7%	−0.3%
Manufacturing	43.3%	41.7%	−1.6%	26.4%	23.3%	−3.1%	22.5%	15.1%	−7.4%
Mining	1.2%	0.9%	−0.3%	2.1%	0.8%	−1.3%	1.5%	0.6%	−1.0%
Construction	3.3%	2.7%	−0.6%	4.2%	2.2%	−2.0%	4.1%	1.8%	−2.3%
Transportation/communication	5.9%	4.3%	−1.6%	10.2%	5.1%	−5.1%	13.6%	6.5%	−7.1%
Wholesale, retail and catering	12.1%	17.3%	5.2%	9.9%	15.4%	5.5%	11.1%	18.6%	7.5%
Real estate	3.3%	4.0%	0.7%	6.0%	4.4%	−1.6%	7.7%	5.3%	−2.4%
Health and social welfare	3.6%	5.8%	2.3%	4.0%	6.7%	2.7%	3.2%	5.6%	2.4%
Education arts and culture	6.4%	8.0%	1.6%	8.4%	9.8%	1.3%	8.4%	10.8%	2.4%
Technical services	2.7%	2.1%	−0.6%	9.3%	15.6%	6.4%	2.6%	1.6%	−1.0%
Financial industry	1.8%	2.1%	0.3%	2.4%	3.0%	0.6%	2.9%	4.0%	1.1%
Public administration and social organizations	13.6%	9.1%	−4.5%	13.6%	10.2%	−3.4%	15.1%	15.9%	0.8%
Others	0.7%	0.5%	−0.1%	2.1%	2.2%	0.1%	6.4%	13.5%	7.1%
Samples	5002	4629		5473	4398		8272	6703	

Notes 1. The gender wage gaps = female wage mean values/male wage mean values
2. The gender gaps of another variables = female variable mean values-male variable mean values
Source Calculated using CHIP1995, 2002 and 2007

5.5 Descriptive Statistics Results

5.5.1 Proportions of Male and Female with Wages Below the MW Level

The gender gaps of proportions of workers with wages below the MW level are shown in Fig. 5.2. The proportion of workers with wages below the MW level all are greater for females than for males in 1995 (3.2 percentage points), 2002 (1.4 percentage points), and 2007 (2.1 percentage points).

The Gender Gap of the Difference Between Wage and the MW Level
We subtracted the MW level from the wage as an index to show how serious the gap is between the wage and the MW level. A greater numerical value is associated with a larger gap between the wage and the MW level; that is, the more serious is the amount by which the wage is lower than the MW level. We provide the results calculated by year, gender, and groups in Fig. 5.3.

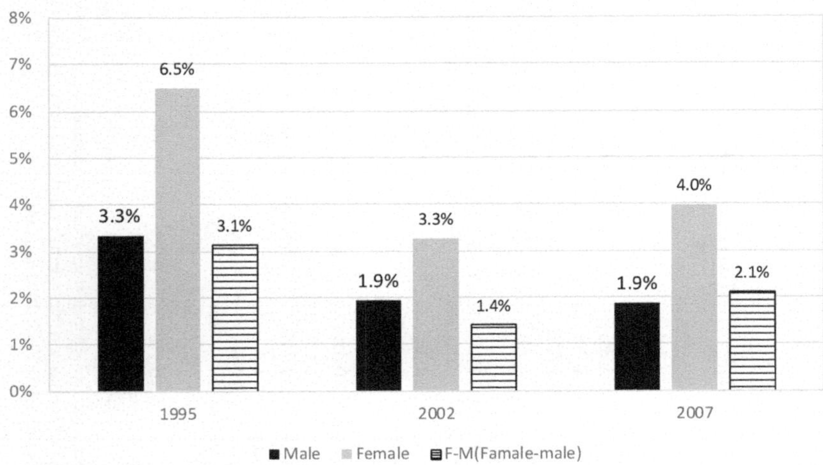

Fig. 5.2 Proportions of males and females with wages below MW levels (*Note* Calculated results shown in Fig. 5.1 are the ratios of the workers whose monthly wage is below the MW level to the total workers in each group. *Source* Calculated using CHIP1995, CHIP2002, CHIP2007)

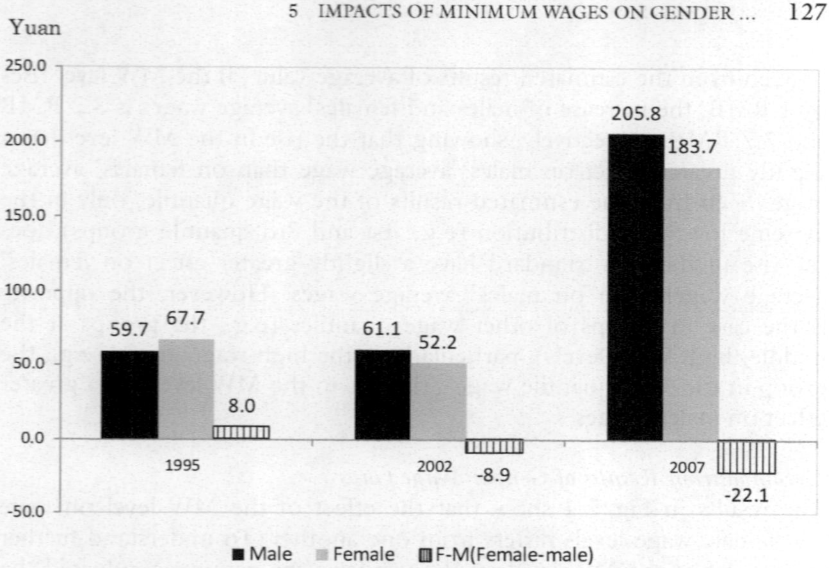

Fig. 5.3 Gender gap and the difference between wage and MW levels (*Notes* 1. Calculated results shown in Fig. 5.2 are the gaps of wage level and the MW in each group. 2. Wages in three periods are adjusted by CPI [based on 1995 national level]. *Source* Calculated using CHIP1995, CHIP2002, CHIP2007)

In 1995, the gender gap between the wage and the MW level was 8.0 RMB. In 2002 and 2007, however, the gaps between male and female are −8.9 RMB (2002) and −22.1 RMB (2007), respectively. These calculations show that in 1995, females' wages were considerably lower than the MW level compared with those of males; in 2002 and 2007, in contrast, males' wages were considerably lower than the MW level compared with those of females.

5.6 Econometric Analysis Results

5.6.1 Impacts of MW Levels on Males and Females' Wages

To compare the effects of MW level and Kaitz index on males and females' wage, we made the estimation by Model 1 (MW level model) and Model 2 (Kaitz index model). The analysis results were obtained with OLS and the quantile regression model. The simulation results are shown in Fig. 5.3.

Seen from the estimated results of average value, if the MW level rises by 1 RMB, the increase of males and females' average wages is 3.2 RMB and 2.7 RMB, respectively, showing that the rise in the MW level has a slightly greater effect on males' average wage than on females' average wage. Seen from the estimated results of the wage quantile, only in the extreme low-wage distribution (e.g., 1st and 3rd quantile groups) does the rise in the MW standard have a slightly greater effect on females' average wages than on males' average wages. However, the opposite is the case in groups of other wage quantiles (e.g., the groups at the middle/high-wage levels); particularly in the high-wage group (e.g., the group in the 90th quantile wage), the rise in the MW level has a greater effect on males' wages.

Decomposition Results of Gender Wage Gaps

The results in Fig. 5.4 show that the effect of the MW level on male and female wage levels differs from one another. To understand further the impact of the MW level on the gender wage gap, we conducted the decomposition analysis for the gender wage gap by using the Oaxaca–Ransom decomposition model. Considering that the Kaitz index may affect the gender wage gap, we also provide the decomposition result based on Kaitz index. See the decomposition results in Table 5.3.

Above all, seen from the overall decomposition result, the effect of a difference in endowment return on the gender wage gap is greater than that of endowment differentials. For example, in 1995, the difference

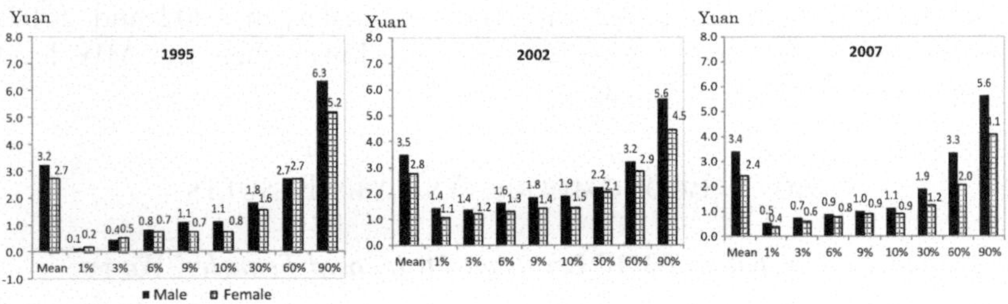

Fig. 5.4 Impacts of MW levels on males and females' wages (*Notes* 1. These are the simulation results showing wage rise level if the MW rises 100 Yuan. 2. OLS based on means, the results of 1–90 percentile are estimated using quantile regression models. *Source* Calculated using CHIP1995, CHIP2002, CHIP2007)

Table 5.3 Decomposition results of the gender wage gaps

	Decomposition (1)-The MW model				*Decomposition (2)-Kaitz index model*			
	Endowment differences (%)	*Return gaps*			*Endowment differences (%)*	*Return gaps*		
		Female loss (a) (%)	*Male gain (b) (%)*	*Total (a+b) (%)*		*Female loss (a) (%)*	*Male gain (b) (%)*	*Total (a+b) (%)*
1995								
100%	**43.0**	29.9	27.1	**57.0**	**43.7**	29.5	26.8	**56.3**
Decomposition results of each factor								
The MW	**0.7**	**−5.4**	**−7.1**	**−12.5**				
Kaitz index					**−1.3**	**45.9**	**40.7**	**86.6**
Education	13.1	−3.0	−0.1	−3.1	14.7	−0.6	1.3	0.7
Experience years	8.5	−125.2	−79.5	−204.7	9.0	−131.0	−86.6	**−217.6**
Race	0.0	−16.9	−12.4	−29.3	0.0	−17.3	−13.3	−30.6
Married	−0.4	39.3	43.1	82.4	−0.3	44.0	47.1	91.1
Ownership	9.2	−2.0	1.9	−0.1	10.2	−2.1	1.8	−0.3
Occupation	9.3	11.0	6.9	17.9	9.0	7.2	4.3	11.5
Industry	2.6	−3.8	1.0	−2.8	2.4	−5.1	0.0	−5.1
Constant term	0.0	135.8	73.3	209.1	0.0	88.5	31.5	120.0
2002								
100%	**48.8**	28.6	22.6	**51.2**	**52.9**	26.2	20.9	**47.1**
Decomposition results of each factor								
The MW	**−3.0**	**2.4**	**6.3**	**8.7**				

(continued)

Table 5.3 (continued)

	Decomposition (1)-The MW model				*Decomposition (2)-Kaitz index model*			
	Endowment differences (%)	*Return gaps*			*Endowment differences (%)*	*Return gaps*		
		Female loss (a) (%)	*Male gain (b) (%)*	*Total (a+b) (%)*		*Female loss (a) (%)*	*Male gain (b) (%)*	*Total (a+b) (%)*
Kaitz index					**−1.8**	**18.3**	**5.7**	**24.0**
Education	6.3	2.1	−1.2	0.9	7.0	2.4	−0.2	2.2
Experience years	15.6	−13.9	−4.8	−18.7	20.8	−20.0	−14.0	−34.0
Race	0.0	23.2	20.8	44.0	0.0	25.9	21.3	47.2
Married	1.3	20.4	27.6	48.0	0.5	19.0	27.6	46.6
Ownership	6.6	−1.3	−0.4	−1.7	6.2	−1.7	−0.6	−2.3
Occupation	17.9	6.8	−1.8	5.0	14.4	6.9	0.2	7.1
Industry	4.1	6.9	1.1	8.0	5.8	5.0	−0.6	4.4
Constant term	0.0	−18.1	−25.0	−43.1	0.0	−29.6	−18.5	−48.1
2007								
100%	**36.5**	35.2	28.3	**63.5**	**39.5**	33.4	27.1	**60.5**
Decomposition results of each factor								
The MW	**1.2**	**1.7**	**6.4**	**8.1**				
Kaitz index					**−0.5**	**−12.5**	**−4.3**	**−16.8**
Education	3.3	2.7	−6.0	−3.3	3.6	2.7	−5.0	−2.3
Experience years	4.1	−21.1	−0.9	−22.0	7.4	−13.8	7.9	−5.9
Race	0.2	−2.4	−4.7	−7.1	0.1	−4.3	−6.0	−10.3

(continued)

Table 5.3 (continued)

	Decomposition (1)-The MW model				Decomposition (2)-Kaitz index model			
	Endowment differences (%)	*Return gaps*			*Endowment differences (%)*	*Return gaps*		
		Female loss (a) (%)	*Male gain (b) (%)*	*Total (a+b) (%)*		*Female loss (a) (%)*	*Male gain (b) (%)*	*Total (a+b) (%)*
Married	0.8	23.0	24.7	47.7	0.5	18.1	19.4	37.5
Ownership	14.3	−6.7	0.4	−6.3	14.1	−7.5	−0.5	−8.0
Occupation	4.4	4.0	−3.5	0.5	4.8	5.3	−1.9	3.4
Industry	8.2	−2.2	1.5	−0.7	9.5	−5.1	−1.3	−6.4
Constant term	0.0	36.2	10.5	46.7	0.0	50.5	18.7	69.2

Source Calculated using CHIP1995, CHIP2002, CHIP2007

in endowment return is 57.0% and the endowment difference is 43.0%; in 2007, the former is 36.5% and the latter is 63.5%. The analysis result based on the Kaitz index also shows that, in both 1995 and 2007, the differences in endowment return are greater than endowment differentials. In 1995, the former is 56.3% and the latter is 43.7%; in 2007, the former is 60.5% and the latter is 39.5%. Both composition results indicate that, from 1995 to 2007, the effect of differences in endowment return has increased. The increase in the impact of differences in endowment return on gender wage gap shall be brought to the forefront because one of its causes lies in the increase in terms of the effect of gender discrimination.

Now, we discuss the effect of MW level on gender wage gaps. In 1995, the endowment difference of the MW was 0.7%, and the difference in endowment return of the MW was −12.5%, showing that the gender wage gap is caused by that proportion of males in the regions whose relatively high MW level is greater than those of females. The reason that the impact of the MW level on wage is greater for females than for males comes from the narrowing of the gender wage gap. Compared with the situation in 1995, the status is reversed in 2002. In 2002, the endowment difference of the MW level is −3.0%, and its difference in endowment return is 8.7%. These numbers show that the reason that the proportion of workers in the regions with relatively high MW level is greater for females than for males is the narrowing of the gender wage gap, and the gender wage gap is caused by the MW level having a relatively greater impact on wages for males than for females. In 2007, both the endowment difference and difference in endowment return of the MW level are positive values, i.e., 1.2% (endowment difference) and 8.1% (difference in endowment return). These differences reveal that for both factors, the proportion of workers in the regions with relatively high MW level is greater for males than for females and that the MW level has a greater impact on wages for males than for females, affecting the gender wage gap. The decomposition results of all three periods show that the gender difference in terms of the effect of the MW level on the wage (difference in endowment return) has a greater effect than the gender difference of the distribution in the regions with different MW levels (endowment difference).

Finally, we discuss the effect of the Kaitz index on the gender wage gap. In 1995, the endowment difference of the Kaitz index is −1.3% and the difference in endowment return of the Kaitz index is 86.6%.

These results reveal that the reason that the proportion of workers in the regions with a relatively high Kaitz index is greater for males than females is the narrowing gender wage gap, and the gender wage gap is caused by the Kaitz index having a greater effect on wages for males than for females. In 2002, the direction of the Kaitz index has an effect on gender wage gap similar to that in 1995; for example, the endowment difference of the Kaitz index is −1.8% and the difference in endowment return of the Kaitz index is 24.0%. Note that, compared with 1995, the reason that the Kaitz index has a greater effect on wages for males than for females is that its effect decreased. In 2007, both the endowment difference and difference in endowment return of the Kaitz index are negative values, i.e., −0.5% (endowment difference) and −16.8% (difference in endowment return). These changes have two causes: The proportion of females in the regions with relatively higher MW level is greater than that of males, and the Kaitz index has a greater effect on females' wage level, thus having an effect on narrowing the gender wage gap. The decomposition results of all three periods show that the gender difference in terms of the effect of the Kaitz index on the wage (difference in endowment return) has a greater effect than does the gender difference of distribution in regions with different Kaitz indexes (endowment difference).

DID Analysis Results of Gender Wage Gaps

To further examine the effects of the MW implementation on the gender wage gap, we also conducted DID analysis. See Table 5.4 (OLS) and Table 5.5 (QR) for these results. First, the effects of the MW on the gender wage gap varied by period (Table 5.5). For example, the results in 1990–2007, 1991–2007, and 1992–2007 all showed that the MW implementation contributed to narrowing the gender wage gap. However, in other periods (such as 1990–1995 and 1990–2002), the effects of the MW on the gender wage gap are statistically insignificant. These results indicate that the MW implementation contributes to narrowing the gender wage gap in the long term, but the effect is not obvious in the short term.

Second, the MW has a more noticeable effect on narrowing gender wage gap in low-wage and mid-wage groups (Table 5.5) in comparison with high-wage groups. However, the MW has a more significant effect on narrowing gender wage gap in the low-wage group, which is possible because that increase of MW level has the largest influence on

Table 5.4 DID analysis results—based on OLS estimations

The initial years: 1990	*1990 vs. 1995*		*1990 vs. 2002*		*1990 vs. 2007*	
	Coeff.	*SE.*	*Coeff.*	*SE.*	*Coeff.*	*SE.*
Male	0.1327***	0.0123	0.1552***	0.0135	0.1404***	0.0086
year	0.0062	0.0140	0.4767***	0.0194	0.7921***	0.0146
The treatment group	−0.2598***	0.0233	−0.0947***	0.0183	−0.2110***	0.0198
Male × year	0.0319*	0.0181	0.0420*	0.0253	0.1616***	0.0185
Male × The treatment group	0.0649**	0.0309	−0.1097***	0.0247	0.1361***	0.0254
year × The treatment	−0.0817**	0.0385	−0.0144	0.0344	0.1712***	0.0409
DIDterm	−0.0077	0.0503	0.0572	0.0468	−0.1125**	0.0508
The initial years: 1991	*1991 vs. 1995*		*1991 vs. 2002*		*1991 vs. 2007*	
	Coeff.	*SE.*	*Coeff.*	*SE.*	*Coeff.*	*SE.*
Male	0.1249***	0.0133	0.1603***	0.0185	0.1194***	0.0112
year	0.0207	0.0142	0.4845***	0.0214	0.8015***	0.0155
The treatment group	−0.2753***	0.0230	−0.1201***	0.0223	−0.1263***	0.0206
Male × year	0.0106	0.0191	0.0332	0.0284	0.1800***	0.0199
Male × The treatment group	0.0252	0.0312	−0.1335***	0.0313	0.1060***	0.0306
year × The treatment	−0.0819**	0.0383	0.0107	0.0367	0.0866**	0.0412
DIDterm	−0.0568	0.0504	0.0809	0.0506	−0.0803 +	0.0536
The initial years: 1992	*1992 vs. 1995*		*1992 vs. 2002*		*1992 vs. 2007*	
	Coeff.	*SE.*	*Coeff.*	*SE.*	*Coeff.*	*SE.*
Male	0.1232***	0.0133	0.1429***	0.0187	0.1209***	0.0110
year	−0.0525***	0.0141	0.4128***	0.0214	0.7325***	0.0153
The treatment group	−0.2555***	0.0217	−0.1353***	0.0229	−0.1432***	0.0210
Male × year	0.0150	0.0191	0.0529*	0.0285	0.1809***	0.0198

(continued)

Table 5.4 (continued)

The initial years: 1992	*1992 vs. 1995*		*1992 vs. 2002*		*1992 vs. 2007*	
	Coeff.	*SE.*	*Coeff.*	*SE.*	*Coeff.*	*SE.*
Male × The treatment group	0.1262***	0.0303	−0.1127***	0.0325	0.1174***	0.0298
year × The treatment	−0.1364***	0.0383	0.0256	0.0370	0.1028**	0.0413
DIDterm	−0.0548	0.0496	0.0593	0.0513	−0.0922*	0.0531

Notes 1. Estimations using Kaitz index in models. Treatment group: the region where the gender wage gap is lowest before the MW implementation, and the Kaitz index is higher after the MW implementation

2. The other variables such as education, experience years, han race, married are also estimated

3. *, **, *** statistically significant in 10%, 5%, 1% levels

Source Calculated using CHIP1995, CHIP2002, CHIP2007

wages of people in a low-wage group (i.e., at slightly higher or lower than MW level). Therefore, if there are more female than male workers at approximately the MW level, the increase of the MW level can narrow a gender wage gap. Figure 5.1 shows that, in three periods, the proportion of workers having wages lower than the MW level is greater for females than males. The related figures are 3.1 (1995), 1.4 (2002), and 2.1 (2007) percentage points. Why does the MW contribute to narrowing the gender wage gap of mid-wage groups? It may be due to the spread effect brought by a wage increase for low-wage groups (this effect is called "the spillover effect" of the MW); in other words, the wage of mid-wage groups will go up when that of low-wage groups goes up. The analysis results indicate that, in China's urban labor market, the increased MW level has influenced not only the lower-wage workers whose wage approaches the MW level but also wage levels to a significant extent.

Table 5.5 DID analysis results-based on quantile regression estimations

	1%	*3%*	*6%*	*10%*	*30%*	*60%*	*90%*
Estimation 1: 1990–2007							
Male	0.4422***	0.2035***	0.2128***	0.1682***	0.1222***	0.1111***	0.1051***
	(0.11)	(0.05)	(0.02)	(0.02)	(0.01)	(0.01)	(0.01)
2002	0.5500***	0.4569***	0.5691***	0.5613***	0.6611***	0.8523***	1.0342***
	(0.17)	(0.05)	(0.04)	(0.03)	(0.02)	(0.01)	(0.02)
The treatment group	−0.7978***	0.0713	−0.1811***	−0.1427***	−0.1868***	−0.2071***	−0.2191***
	(0.23)	(0.10)	(0.05)	(0.04)	(0.02)	(0.02)	(0.02)
Male*2002	0.0314	0.1528**	0.1699***	0.2398***	0.2270***	0.1502***	0.1279***
	(0.22)	(0.07)	(0.05)	(0.03)	(0.02)	(0.02)	(0.02)
Male*The treatment group	0.9070***	−0.0695	0.1269*	0.0933*	0.1007***	0.1074***	0.1466***
	(0.32)	(0.14)	(0.07)	(0.05)	(0.03)	(0.03)	(0.03)
2002*The treatment group	1.2952***	−0.0884	0.1387	0.1859**	0.2392***	0.1778***	0.0311
	(0.49)	(0.16)	(0.11)	(0.08)	(0.05)	(0.04)	(0.05)
DIDterm	−1.0092+	0.3830*	0.0767	−0.0594	−0.1357**	−0.1329***	−0.1074*
	(0.64)	(0.21)	(0.14)	(0.10)	(0.06)	(0.05)	(0.06)
Estimation 2: 1991–2007							
Male	0.3238**	0.1477***	0.1267***	0.0947***	0.1058***	0.1084***	0.1221***
	(0.16)	(0.04)	(0.03)	(0.02)	(0.02)	(0.01)	(0.02)
2007	0.3839**	0.4934***	0.5300***	0.5603***	0.6992***	0.8726***	1.0636***

(continued)

Table 5.5 (continued)

	1%	*3%*	*6%*	*10%*	*30%*	*60%*	*90%*
	(0.19)	(0.05)	(0.04)	(0.03)	(0.02)	(0.02)	(0.02)
The treatment group	0.4178	0.0951	0.0212	−0.0655	−0.1340***	−0.1794***	−0.1497***
	(0.35)	(0.09)	(0.06)	(0.05)	(0.03)	(0.03)	(0.04)
Male*2007	0.1083	0.1845***	0.2462***	0.3133***	0.2370***	0.1620***	0.0891***
	(0.25)	(0.06)	(0.05)	(0.03)	(0.02)	(0.02)	(0.03)
Male*The treatment group	−0.2488	−0.0211	0.0474	0.0868	0.0848*	0.1194***	0.1394**
	(0.47)	(0.12)	(0.09)	(0.06)	(0.05)	(0.04)	(0.06)
2007*The treatment group	−0.0204	−0.1441	−0.0441	0.1129	0.1796***	0.1606***	−0.0536
	(0.56)	(0.14)	(0.10)	(0.07)	(0.06)	(0.05)	(0.07)
DIDterm	0.2135	0.3710**	0.1540	−0.0571	−0.1155	−0.1542**	−0.0654
	(0.74)	(0.19)	(0.14)	(0.10)	(0.07)	(0.06)	(0.09)
Estimation 3: 1992–2007							
Male	0.2417	0.2588***	0.1727***	0.1212***	0.1189***	0.1166***	0.1169***
	(0.16)	(0.04)	(0.03)	(0.02)	(0.01)	(0.01)	(0.02)
2007	0.2376	0.5811***	0.4781***	0.4874***	0.6212***	0.8106***	1.0110***
	(0.19)	(0.05)	(0.04)	(0.02)	(0.02)	(0.01)	(0.02)

(continued)

Table 5.5 (continued)

	1%	*3%*	*6%*	*10%*	*30%*	*60%*	*90%*
The treatment group	0.2146	−0.3440***	−0.0263	−0.0801*	−0.1489***	−0.1802***	−0.1702***
	(0.34)	(0.08)	(0.06)	(0.04)	(0.03)	(0.03)	(0.04)
Male*2007	0.2195	0.0831	0.2087***	0.2808***	0.2264***	0.1512***	0.1060***
	(0.24)	(0.07)	(0.05)	(0.03)	(0.02)	(0.02)	(0.03)
Male*The treatment group	−0.0364	0.3459***	0.0672	0.0678	0.0782*	0.1153***	0.1342***
	(0.45)	(0.11)	(0.09)	(0.06)	(0.04)	(0.04)	(0.05)
2007*The treatment group	0.1879	0.2933*	−0.0157	0.1319*	0.2049***	0.1544***	−0.0319
	(0.55)	(0.16)	(0.10)	(0.07)	(0.05)	(0.04)	(0.06)
DIDterm	0.0100	−0.0103	0.1452	−0.0351	−0.1187*	−0.1429**	−0.0684
	(0.72)	(0.21)	(0.14)	(0.09)	(0.07)	(0.06)	(0.08)

Notes 1. The other variables such as education, experience years, han race, married are also estimated
2. SE values are showed in ( )
3. +,*,**,***: statistically significant in 15%, 10%, 5%, 1% levels
Source Calculated using CHIP1995, CHIP2002, CHIP2007

5.7 Conclusions

In urban China, the gender wage gap was small during the period of the planned economy; however, during the economic transition period, particularly after the 1990s, when SOEs were further reformed, the gender wage gap gradually increased. Conversely, the Chinese government has been officially implementing the MW system since 1993. The implementation of the MW policy contributes to increasing incomes of low-wage groups. Therefore, if the proportion of workers with wages lower than the MW level is greater for females than for males, the MW may narrow the gender wage gap. This article provides evidence on whether the MW has had an effect on gender wage gaps in urban China using CHIP1995, 2002, and 2007. Several major conclusions emerge.

First, by the descriptive statistical analysis, we had the following two findings. (1) In 1995, 2002, and 2007, the proportion of workers with wages lower than the MW level was greater for females than for males. (2) The gaps between wages and the MW level for males and females are different during the three periods. In addition, the local MW levels in different regions influence males and females' wages differently. Second, the gender wage gap is largest in regions with high MW levels and smallest in regions with middle MW levels. Although the gender wage gap is not obvious at the extremely low-wage distribution (e.g., in the 1st quantile), in wage distributions in which quantile is higher than 6th, the gender wage gap tends to narrow with increasing wage levels, showing that there is a sticky floor phenomenon. Furthermore, the decomposition results using the Oaxaca–Ransom model show that gender differences in returns on endowments in the MW levels and Kaitz index have a greater influence on the gender wage gap, in comparison with gender differences in endowments. Finally, the results obtained by DID analysis model show that, in the long term, implementation of a MW system contributes to narrowing gender wage gap and that such an effect in a low-wage group is more significant than that in a high-wage group. However, that effect is not obvious in the short term.

According to the empirical analysis, we can conclude that the MW implementation contributes to narrowing gender wage gap in the long term; however, there are three points worthy of attention. First, the analysis results show that MW started to contribute to narrowing the gender wage gap after the MW system had been implemented for 15–17 years (1990, 1991, 1992–2007) and that the gender wage gap had hardly been influenced during a shorter period of implementation of this system. Why does the long-term effect differ from the short-term effect? It is necessary to extend the analysis in the future. This may be because we could only use the quasi-DID model instead of the real DID analysis model. Second, the MW system has a greater influence on the gender wage gap at an extremely low-wage distribution, which may be related to a greater proportion of females at the low-wage distribution. To further analyze the causes of the gender wage gap at the low-wage distribution is a promising area of issues for discussion, such as an in-depth investigation of females' poverty. Third, although this article only discusses the MW effect on gender wage gaps, there may be gender gap effects of unemployment and informality (Hunt 2002; Muravyev and Oshchepkov 2013).[16] There are many factors influencing female labor participation such as household structure, macroeconomic environment, firm recruitment, and employment system, so detailed empirical studies on this issue should be done in the future.

Notes

1. Regarding the debate on the MW employment effect in the 1980s, it is indicated that there is a negative significant but modest −1 to −3% employment effect (Brown et al. 1982). After the 1990s, using cross-sectional data, Neumark and Wascher (1992, 2000), Deere et al. (1995), Currie and Fallick (1996), and Burkhauser et al. (2000) also found results consistent with the standard model prediction of a negative employment effect. On the other hand, using panel data to conduct quasi-natural experiment studies, Card (1992a, b), Katz and Krueger (1992), and Card and Krueger (1995) pointed out that there are no unemployment effects. Similarly, there is no consensus on the effect of MW on employment.
2. We apply Chinese National Minimum Wage Databases to classify the regions by the MW Level; the regions are shown in Table 5.1.
3. Another approach to investigating regional differences in the gender wage gap is to use the cross term of males and regions. However, such an approach compares based on the assumption that there is the same endowment of human capital in each region, which allows for variables with assumptions but is not very realistic. We, therefore, relax the limiting conditions to estimate by region groups. Anyone who is interested in the results of using the cross term may contact the author directly.

4. The Oaxaca–Blinder composition method can be expressed with the following two equations. Please note that the coefficient estimates and average of variables used in the following equations are different.

$$\ln \bar{W}_m - \ln \bar{W}_f = \beta_m(\bar{X}_m - \bar{X}_f) + (\beta_m - \beta_f)\bar{X}_f$$
$$\ln \bar{W}_m - \ln \bar{W}_f = \beta_f(\bar{X}_f - \bar{X}_m) + (\beta_f - \beta_m)\bar{X}_m$$

5. Strictly speaking, the decomposition value here does not represent discrimination as a whole because it also contains a part of the gap resulting from some interpreted variables that cannot be observed, for example, working attitude and abilities.
6. The Kaitz index is defined as the ratio of the MW to the average wage of the working population.
7. Please note that we can use only the quasi-DID model rather than the real DID model. The main reason is that the Chinese government published the *Minimum Wage Regulations for Enterprises* in 1993, and the MW policy was carried out in all regions (provinces) covered by the CHIP survey. In other words, we cannot find the real control group (the province in which the MW is not implemented during two compared periods). Therefore, we applied this alternative method.
8. Meyer (1995, pp. 157–158) noted that to improve the robustness of the quasi-natural experiment model, the use of multiple treatment groups and multiple comparison groups is the development direction of future quasi-natural experiments. Based on that statement, this article has made full use of the characteristics of CHIP data and selected multiple treatment groups and control groups when applying the DID method.
9. Based on the definition proposed in this article, we use Hernan (1990 vs. 1995), Hubei (1990 vs. 2002), Shanxi (1990 vs. 2007), Shanxi (1991 vs. 1995), Hubei (1991 vs. 1992), Shanxi (1991 vs. 2007), Shanxi (1992 vs. 1995), Hubei (1992 vs. 2002), and Shanxi (1992 vs. 2007) as treatment groups.
10. There may be representative errors when making the master sample by consolidating the data in each region. Therefore, the weight can be used for adjustment. However, it is not applied in this article, first, because CHIP is applied by the NBS according to a national survey sample. It is a stratified multiple-stage sample in which the master sample consolidating error arising from the difference in sample number in regions can be forecast to be very small. Second, according to the calculation of Li and Song (2013), the population census data in 2000 and 1% population census data against CHIP2002 and CHIP2007 are used as the weight. The adjusted results are the same as the results without being adjusted.

Moreover, no relevant data against CHIP1995 can be used to correct it. For more details regarding this point, see Li and Song (2013, Note 1).

11. According to the MW Article published in 1993, the main content of the MW consists of total earnings from work (except the overtime hours subsidy), any risk job subsidy and social security subsidy. We cannot distinguish the detail subsidy items from CHIP data. We also made an analysis using the basic wage. The results are similar to the results using the total wage. Therefore, we show the results using total wage in this article. The earnings data do not include unofficial payments, and if such payments are more likely to be made to men, the gender wage gap will be underestimated.
12. We calculated the total values of the material objects and added them to wage accounts.
13. There are two reasons for using the logarithm of monthly wage as the explained variable.
    First, there is only monthly wage information in the CHIP2007; therefore, we calculated monthly wage using CHIP1995 and CHIP2002. Second, the MW standard for a regular worker in each region is defined based on a monthly wage. The data of the urban worker in the CHIP we use are dominated by regular worker data, so we perform the analysis by taking the regular worker as the object according to the MW standard based on monthly wage. Therefore, we use the corresponding logarithm of the monthly wage as the explained variable in the wage function.
14. In China, college courses are for three years, whereas university courses are over four years.
15. Experience years = age − years of education.
16. Hunt (2002) shows that with a fall in the gender wage gaps, the unemployment of low-skilled women increased in Germany. Muravyev and Oshchepkov (2013) further indicate the effects of MW on the informality and unemployment in Russian regions.

References

Blinder A (1973) Wage Discrimination: Reduced Form and Structural Estimates. *Journal of Human Resources* 8(4):436–455.

Brown C, Curtis G, Andrew K (1982) The Effect of the Minimum Wage on Employment and Unemployment. *Journal of Economic Literature* 20(2): 487–528.

Burkhauser RV, Kenneth A, Wittenburg DC (2000) A Reassessment of the New Economics of the Minimum Wage. *Journal of Labor Economics* 18(4):653–681.

Card D (1992a) Using Regional Variation in Wages to Measure the Effects of the Federal Minimum Wage. *Industrial and Labor Relations Review* 46(1):22–37.

Card D (1992b) Do Minimum Wages Reduce Employment? A Case Study of California, 1987–89. *Industrial and Labor Relations Review* 46(1):38–54.

Card D, Krueger A (1995) *Myth and Measurement: The New Economics of the Minimum Wage*. Princeton: Princeton University Press.

Cotton J (1988) On the Decomposition of Wage Differentials. *Review of Economics and Statistics* 70(2):236–243.

Currie J, Fallick B (1996) The Minimum Wage and the Employment of Youth: Evidence from the NLSY. *Journal of Human Resources* 31(2):404–428.

Deere D, Murphy K, Welch F (1995) Employment and Minimum Wage Hike. *America Economic Review, Papers and Proceedings* 85:232–237.

Dinardo J, Fortin NM, Lemieux T (1996) Labor Market Institutions and the Distribution of Wages, 1973–1992: A Semiparametric Approach. *Econometrica* 65(4):1001–1044.

Gustafsson B, Li S (2000) Economic Transformation and the Gender Earnings Gap in Urban China. *Journal of Population Economics* 13(2):305–329.

Hunt J (2002) The Transition in East Germany: When Is a Ten-Point Fall in the Gender Wage Gap Bad News? *Journal of Labor Economics* 20(1):148–169.

Katz LF, Krueger AB (1992) The Effect of the Minimum Wage on the Fast Food Industry. *Industrial and Labor Relations Review* 46(1):6–21.

Koenker RW, Bassett GJ (1978) Regression Quantile. *Econometrica* 46(1):33–50.

Li S, Ma X (2006) The Gender wage Gaps and Gender Occupational Segmentation in Urban China. *Chinese Population Science* 2006(5):1–14 (in Chinese).

Li S, Gustafsson B (2008) Unemployment, Earlier Retirement, and Changes in the Gender Income Gap in Urban China, 1995–2002. In Gustafsson B, Li S, Sicular T (eds.) *Income Inequality and Public Policy in China*, Cambridge: Cambridge University Press.

Li S, Sato H, Sicular T (2013) *The Analysis of the Changes of Income Distribution in China*, Beijing: The People's Press (in Chinese).

Li S, Sicular T, Gustafsson B (2013) *Income Distribution in China III*, Beijing Normal University Press (in Chinese).

Li S, Song J (2013) The Change of Gender Wage Gaps in Urban China. In Li S, Sato H, Sicular T, *The Analysis of the Changes of Income Distribution in China*, Beijing: The People's Press (in Chinese).

Ma X (2008) Gender Gaps in Wages of Re-employment Workers and Employment Restructuring in China. *The Japanese Journal of Labor Studies* 571:104–119 (in Japanese).

Ma X (2009) A Comparison of the Wage Differentials in Regular and Irregular Sectors Between Japan and China. *The Journal Ohara Institute for Social Research* 601:17–28; 602:86–98 (in Japanese).

Meyer BD (1995) Natural and Quasi-Experiments in Economics. *Journal of Business & Economic Statistics* 13(2):151–161.

Muravyev A, Oshchepkov AY (2013) *Minimum Wages, Unemployment and Informality: Evidence form Panel Data on Russian Regions.* IZA Discussion Paper No. 7878.

Neumark D (1988) Employer's Discriminatory Behavior and the Estimation of Wage Discrimination. *Journal of Human Resources* 23(3):279–295.

Neumark D, Wascher W (1992) Employment Effects of Minimum and Subminimum Wages: Panel Data on State Minimum Wage Laws. *Industrial and Labor Relations Review* 46(1):55–81.

Neumark D, Wascher W (2000) The Effect of New Jersey. Minimum Wage Increase on Fast-Food Employment: A Re-evaluation Using Payroll Records. *The America Economic Review* 90(5):1362–1396.

Oaxaca RL (1973) Male–Female Wage Differentials in Urban Labor Markets. *International Economic Review* 14(3):693–709.

Oaxaca RL, Ransom MR (1994) On Discrimination and the Decomposition of Wage Differentials. *Journal of Econometrics* 61(1):5–21.

Robinson H (2002) Wrong Side of the Track? The Impact of the Minimum Wage on Gender Pay Gaps in Britain. *Oxford Bulletin of Economics and Statistics* 64(5):417–448.

Robinson H (2005) Regional Evidence on the Effect of the National Minimum Wage on the Gender Pay Gap. *Regional Studies* 39(7):855–875.

Shannon MT (1996) Minimum Wages and the Gender Wage Gap. *Applied Economics* 28(12):1567–1576.

Zhao R, Li S, Riskin C (1996) *Re-research of Income Distribution in China: During the Economy Reform and Development*, Beijing: Chinese Financial and Economic Press (in Chinese).

CHAPTER 6

The Impact of Minimum Wages on Migrant Workers' Wages

Juan Yang, Morley Gunderson and Li Shi

6.1 Introduction

Minimum wages have attracted increased interest in China for a variety of reasons. The increase in income inequality in China has created pressure to enhance the earnings of low-wage earners. The increased role of market forces places an emphasis on ensuring that the benefits are widely distributed, including to those at the bottom of the wage distribution through minimum wages. There is a concern that the benefits of growth will not filter down to those at the bottom of the wage distribution, given that the abundance of surplus labor from the countryside puts

J. Yang (✉)
Beijing Normal University, Beijing, China
e-mail: yangjuan@bnu.edu.cn

M. Gunderson
Centre for Industrial Relations, University of Toronto, Toronto, Canada
e-mail: morley.gunderson@utoronto.ca

L. Shi
Zhejiang University, Zhejiang, China
e-mail: lishi9@zju.edu.cn

L. Shi and C. Lin (eds.), *Minimum Wages in China*,
https://doi.org/10.1007/978-981-15-2421-9_6

downward pressure on those wages. Broadly distributing the benefits of economic growth can reduce resistance to the adjustment consequences of market forces (Laliberté 2012). Increased emphasis is being placed on providing a degree of protection to the most vulnerable through labor standards such as minimum wages (ILO 2014, pp. 9, 10). China is also sensitive to its image on the world stage, with adherence to providing labor standards, including minimum wages, being an important component of that image. There is also a view that higher minimum wages may encourage investment in productivity-improving technology to foster the restructuring away from low-wage low value-added sectors toward higher value-added sectors that can sustain the higher wages (Cooke 2005).

There is also a concern, however, that minimum wages can lead to adverse employment effects for the individuals that are to be helped by minimum wages. Such adverse employment effects can foster political instability, especially when it comes at a time when the economy may be slowing and dramatic restructuring is occurring in the move away from state-owned enterprises. Rising minimum wages can foster what Li et al. (2012) termed "the end of cheap labor" whereby China loses its comparative advantage of being a low-wage labor-intensive economy with an industrious workforce. Higher labor costs induced by minimum wage increases can deter competitiveness and the growth that has been so crucial in lifting many out of poverty in China, potentially "killing the goose that lays the golden egg."

Issues associated with migrant workers are also attracting increased attention in China. Such migration has been described as "the largest domestic migration flow in human history" (Qu and Zhao 2011, p. 1), with 11.6% of the total population having moved into cities and towns in 2000 (Lu and Song 2006, p. 338). Such migration is generally regarded as crucial for filling labor shortages that can otherwise lead to production bottlenecks that can hurt competitiveness and lead to shifting production offshore to lower-wage countries in Asia and even Africa. While migrant labor is regarded as crucial in China's development, increased attention has also been drawn to the plight of migrant workers (Cooke 2005; Cooke and Rubery 2002; Zhang 2007). The extensive supply of these workers from the countryside has made them vulnerable, enabling employers to provide low wages and benefits and limited health and safety and other protections. As well, most migrant workers do not have *hukou* status that provides rights to education, medical care, and other social services to which urban residents are entitled. As China's presence in the world stage increases, so does its image in terms of how it treats vulnerable migrant workers.

Clearly, *each* of the issues of minimum wages or migrant workers is attracting increased attention. The intersection of *both* issues—minimum wages *and* migrant workers—compounds that importance. That intersection is the focus of this analysis. Such migrant workers are especially likely to be affected by minimum wages given their generally low skills and educational qualifications.

The main contributions of the article are: (1) It utilizes survey evidence where the individual worker is the unit of analysis, which is the level where decisions with respect to wages, employment, and hours of work are made and which enables distinguishing effects by such factors as gender and region; (2) it enables incorporating individual control variables as well as controls at the level of the prefecture (municipality); (3) it is based on recent data for 2011 and 2012 which is after the important 2004 revisions in minimum wages; (4) it enables estimating causal effects through the methodology of difference-in-differences (DID) which facilitates controlling for unobservable factors that can otherwise affect outcomes; (5) it provides Propensity Score Matching estimates as a robustness check to deal with the potential non-random assignment of minimum wage increases; and (6) it estimates the effect on three outcomes (employment, wages, and hours) with the effect on hours seeing if hours are increased to offset some of the costs for those paid by the month.

6.2 Literature on Minimum Wage Impacts

There is an extensive literature on minimum wage impacts in *developed* countries and especially the USA. There is no consensus in that literature, with some reviews and studies documenting no adverse employment effects (e.g., Card and Krueger 1995; Metcalf 2008) and other reviews and studies documenting that minimum wage increases lead to reductions in employment, especially of teens and youths who are most affected by minimum wage increases (e.g., Neumark and Wascher 2008). The same lack of consensus prevails for *developing* countries (e.g., reviews in Cunningham 2007; Khamis 2013; Kristensen and Cunningham 2006; and the World Bank 2006).

A similar lack of consensus prevails for China, in part reflecting different datasets, data aggregations, methodologies, time periods, and regions. Negative effects on the employment of rural migrant workers are found in Ding (2010), Ma et al. (2012) in the Western and especially Central region, and in Luo (2007b) for the Central region. In contrast, positive effects on employment for rural migrant workers are found in Li and He (2010) for the Yangtze River Delta as well as in Luo (2007a) for Shanghai and Luo (2007b) in the Eastern and Western region, Wang and Gunderson's (2012) analysis is restricted to the Eastern Region. They find no substantial adverse employment effect in that region overall, although there is a small adverse effect in the more market-driven sectors, in the low-wage sector of retail and wholesale trade and restaurants, and for women. For the country as a whole, Wang and Gunderson (2011) also find no adverse employment effect in the prosperous and rapidly growing Eastern region. However, they find adverse employment effects in the slower growing and less prosperous Central and Western regions, especially in the non-state-owned organizations that tend to be more responsive to market pressures and that disproportionately employ rural migrant workers. Fang and Lin (2015) find negative effects on employment in the Eastern and Central regions, especially for females, young adults, and low-skilled workers. Over the period 2000–2005, Ni et al. (2011) find little effect on employment for all workers overall, but some negative effects on employment in the Eastern regions and some positive effects in the Central and Western regions.

6.3 Minimum Wage Policy in China

Since China implemented its minimum wage (MW) policy in 1994, minimum wages have continuously increased but remain at a very low level relative to the general increase in wages that has occurred. The "Regulations on Company Minimum Wages" in 1993 did not specify the adjustment of MWs in detail but proposed an adjustment when there have been substantial changes in the local employees' living expenses or relevant prices. The regulated frequency of adjustment was to be at most once a year and to not limit the bottom line for organizations. Therefore, the MW standards in many regions have remained the same for many years, particularly those in undeveloped areas. For example, the MWs in Gansu and Qinghai province have been adjusted once in 10 years. Because the MWs stagnated for many years, the MW standard has lagged behind the general increase in wages. Specifically, the ratio of MWs to average wages dropped from 46 to 24% from 1995 to 2009 and recovered somewhat to 30% by 2011. In contrast, over that same period the ratio increased from 35 to 38% for OECD countries.[1]

This situation, however, changed substantially in 2004 when the Ministry of Labor and Social Security revised the Regulations on Company MWs. This new regulation notes that there are two types of MWs: monthly MWs and hourly MWs. The monthly MW is applicable to full-time employees who are paid by the month, and the hourly MW is applicable to part-time employees who are paid by the hour. The MW standard is based on the average living expenses of local people in poverty, also taking into account social insurance, housing funds, average wages in the community, social assistance funds, and unemployment insurance. However, the revised standard did not specify the exact working hours per week (or month) for the monthly MW, simply noting "within legal working hours or legal contract regulated working hours." As such, for workers on a monthly minimum wage, firms may extend working hours for those who remain employed so as to offset some of the costs due to the increase in the MW. Testing for the possibility of this cost offset is an important component of this article.[2]

6.4 Estimating Equations

We take advantage of the substantial variation in minimum wages across prefectures (municipalities) and overtime after the 2004 reforms to estimate the impact of increases in MW on migrant workers' employment, wages, and working hours. Specifically, we use conventional difference-in-difference (DID) equations:

$$Y_i = \alpha + \beta_1 \text{Group}_\text{i} + \beta_2 \text{Time}_\text{i} + \beta_3 (\text{Group} * \text{Time})_i + \gamma X_i + \tau \text{Z}_\text{i} + \in_i \quad (6.1)$$

Group_i is a dummy variable coded 1 for the group that ultimately receives the treatment, in this case being in a jurisdiction that increased their minimum wage in 2012; otherwise, it is coded 0 for the comparison group that was in a jurisdiction that did not adjust their minimum wage in 2012. Time_i is a dummy variable coded 1 for the post-treatment period (i.e., year 2012) and 0 for the pre-treatment period (i.e., year 2011). The coefficient β_3 on the interaction term $(\text{Group*Time})_\text{i}$ is the difference-in-difference estimate of the treatment effect of the treatment group being in a jurisdiction with a minimum wage increase after controlling for the effect of the Group and Time differences. The constant term is α. Individuals' characteristics and municipal variables are denoted by X_i and Z_i, respectively. Individual characteristics include age, education, marital status, and gender. Municipal characteristics include GDP per capita, population, and average wages so as to control for certain external labor market influences.

We estimate the impact of MW changes on three outcome measures: employment, monthly earnings, and hours worked. The employment dependent variable (emp), is dichotomous coded 1 if the person is employed and 0 if not employed.[3] Both the monthly earnings dependent variable (ln)earnings[4] and the hours of work dependent variable (hours) can be estimated only for those still employed after the minimum wage increase. To deal with any potential sample selection bias we use the Heckman 2SLS method, adding the inverse Mills ratio to the second-step estimation of the equivalent of Eq. (6.1). Again, the coefficient on the Group*Time interaction term, β_3 is the coefficient of interest, giving the DID estimate of the impact of minimum wage changes on migrant workers monthly earnings and hours, respectively. As illustrated subsequently, our selection correction turns out not to matter substantially, yielding results that are similar to those without the correction.

6.5 Data

We estimate our equations by combining microdata at the individual level, macro data at the municipal level and MW data at the county level. The microdata originates from the household survey on migrant workers by the National Population and Family Planning Commission (NPFPC) collected in 2011 and 2012. The macro data regarding municipalities' population, GDP and employment information originates from the China Economic Information Network database. To account for the lagged effect of the macro data on individuals, the macro data were based on 2010 and 2011, which is one year earlier than the individuals' data. We restricted our analysis to those with a non-local household registration, between the ages of 16–65, and having lived in the local area for more than one month. The survey questionnaire includes information on the individuals' age, education, gender, marital status, household registration, employment, earnings, and covers all of the 31 provinces. There are 234 municipalities and 128 thousand observations in 2011 and 239 municipalities and 158 thousand observations in 2012. Since we are analyzing the effect of MW increases we solely retain the individuals participating in both surveys.

The migrant workers' survey data were collected between July and October in 2011 and between May and August in 2012; therefore, we treat provinces that did not adjust their MWs between July 2011 and August 2012 as comparison groups and those that adjusted their MWs between November 2011 and April 2012 as treatment groups. The 16 provinces in the treatment group were Beijing, Tianjin, Shanghai, Shanxi, Inner Mongolia, Jiangxi, Shandong, Hubei, Guangxi, Chongqing, Sichuan, Yunnan, Shaanxi, Gansu, Qinghai, and Ningxia. The 10 provinces in the comparison group were Hebei, Liaoning, Jilin, Heilongjiang, Zhejiang, Anhui, Fujian, Henan, Guangdong, and Hainan. The MWs of four provinces (Jiangsu, Hunan, Guizhou, and Xinjiang) were adjusted during the migrant workers survey period and are excluded from the analysis because it is difficult for us to define their group. The autonomous region of Tibet is also excluded from the sample due to its non-market operations. Because the macro data does not include certain minority autonomous prefectures and construction regions, the observations belonging to these areas are also exempted from the analysis. Ultimately, the research sample size is 91,871, and more than 80% are rural migrant workers. The summary statistics of the data are reported in Table 6.1.

Table 6.1 indicates that approximately half (46.4%) of individuals were employed in the sample. The average earnings are 7932 RMB per month, and the migrants work an average of 50 hours per week.

Table 6.1 Summary statistics for research sample

Variable	*Obs.*	*Mean*	*Std.*	*Min*	*Max*
Employment rate (%)	91,871	0.464	0.500	0	1
Ln monthly wages (RMB)	49,203	7.932	0.577	7.09	10.134
Working hours per week	49,203	50.186	14.822	30	84
Age (years)	49,203	34.529	7.615	19	62
Years of education	49,203	9.910	2.603	3	19
Married	49,203	0.699	0.423	0	1
Male	91,871	0.481	0.500	0	1
ln prefecture GDP per capital (10,000)	49,203	2.210	0.667	0.842	3.76
Prefecture pop (million)	49,203	5.261	4.811	0.384	17.706
Employment pop (million)	49,203	3.324	3.170	0.037	10.44
Ln prefecture average wage (10,000 RMB/year)	49,203	1.576	0.266	0.414	2.043

Their average age is approximately 34 years, highlighting their young age, and their average education is 9.9 years highlighting their low levels of education. Most (70%) of the migrants are married and 48% are male.

6.6 The Impact of MWs on Migrant Workers' Employment, Earnings and Hours

In this section, we analyze the impact of MWs on migrant workers' employment, earnings, and working hours after controlling for the effect of characteristics of individuals and their prefectures (municipalities).

6.6.1 Employment Effects

Our Linear Probability Estimates of the effect of minimum wages on migrant workers' employment based on the DID model are shown in Table 6.2. The first column reports the effect of minimum wages when there are no controls; the second column after controlling for the individuals' age, education, and marital status; and the third column also controlling for prefecture characteristics. The effect of minimum wage increases is estimated by the coefficients on the Group*Time interaction term of the third row, highlighted in bold hereafter.

Table 6.2 Effect of MW increase on migrant worker employment probability (clustered at prefecture level)

Variable	*Both sexes*			*Male*	*Female*
	(1)	*(2)*	*(3)*	*(4)*	*(5)*
Group	0.018	−0.273***	−0.265***	−0.116***	−0.345***
	(0.083)	(0.012)	(0.013)	(0.027)	(0.017)
Time	0.0388	0.035***	0.028**	−0.064**	0.069***
	(0.085)	(0.012)	(0.014)	(0.027)	(0.018)
Group*Time	**0.117**	**−0.143***	**−0.137***	**−0.145**	**−0.143***
	(0.252)	(0.081)	(0.078)	(0.156)	(0.079)
Observations	91,871	91,871	91,871	44,098	47,773
Individual controls	No	Yes	Yes	Yes	Yes
Prefecture controls	No	No	Yes	Yes	Yes

Notes Standard errors are in parentheses. *$p < 0.05$, **$p < 0.01$, ***$p < 0.001$

When there are no controls (column 1) minimum wage increases have no statistically significant effect on employment. However, when individual control variables are added (column 2) MWs have a statistically significant and large negative effect on employment. Specifically migrants in jurisdictions that have increased their minimum wages have a probability of being employed that is 14.3 percentage points lower than migrants in jurisdictions that did not increase their minimum wage, after controlling for the effect of individual characteristics in those regions. Adding controls for prefecture characteristics did not alter the picture. With full controls, migrants in jurisdictions that have increased their minimum wages have a probability of being employed that is essentially 14 percentage points lower than migrants in jurisdictions that did not increase their minimum wage. Hereafter we will base our discussion on the models with full controls.

This large negative effect on employment reflects the fungible nature of migrant workers in the employment decisions of firms. This is especially the case for female migrant workers as outlined subsequently. They are a group that is hired to absorb demand fluctuations, but if their cost is increased because of minimum wage increases employers find substitutes including perhaps non-migrant workers or shifting production to areas of lower labor cost.

As indicated in columns 4 and 5 of Table 6.2, this negative employment effect for both sexes is completely due to the statistically significant negative effect of −0.14 for females. Males have the same point estimate of −0.14, but it is statistically insignificant ($t < 1$).

Table 6.3 repeats the analysis based on the full controls, separately for each of the three regions of China. For comparison purposes, the first column repeats the column 3 estimates of Table 6.2 for the regions combined. As indicated by the coefficient for the Group*Time interaction in the third row in the top panel, the negative employment effect of −0.137 for all regions combined is due entirely to the statistically significant negative employment effect of −0.132 in the Central region. For both the East and the West, the effects are statistically insignificant.

As indicated by the coefficient on the Group*Time interaction in the third row of the middle panel, none of the effects across the regions are statistically significant for males. However, as indicated in the third row of the bottom panel, the negative effect of −0.132 for both sexes in the Central region is due entirely to the negative effect of −0.131 for females. For females, the effect in the West is negative and significant at −0.336.

Table 6.3 Effect of MW increase on migrant worker employment by region

Variable	*All regions*	*East*	*Central*	*West*
	(1)	*(2)*	*(3)*	*(4)*
Both sexes				
Group	−0.265***	−0.261***	−0.138***	0.652***
	(0.0127)	(0.022)	(0.027)	(0.106)
Time	0.028**	0.001	−0.005	−0.100*
	(0.0136)	(0.018)	(0.027)	(0.059)
Group*Time	**−0.137***	**0.036**	**−0.132***	**−0.342**
	(0.078)	(0.062)	(0.007)	(0.311)
Observations	91,871	56,960	14,699	20,212
Males				
Group	−0.116***	−0.112**	0.021	0.897***
	(0.027)	(0.051)	(0.059)	(0.316)
Time	−0.064**	0.018	−0.230***	−0.463***
	(0.027)	(0.038)	(0.055)	(0.152)
Group*Time	**−0.145**	**0.038**	**−0.141**	**−0.313**
	(0.156)	(0.065)	(0.103)	(0.307)
Observations	44,098	27,340	7344	9414
Females				
Group	−0.345***	−0.256***	−0.178***	0.905***
	(0.017)	(0.028)	(0.037)	(0.127)
Time	0.069***	−0.029	0.163***	0.012
	(0.018)	(0.024)	(0.037)	(0.073)
Group*Time	**−0.143***	**0.032**	**−0.131***	**−0.336***
	(0.079)	(0.029)	(0.038)	(0.099)
Observations	47,773	29,619	7357	10,797

Notes Standard errors are in parentheses. *$p < 0.05$, **$p < 0.01$, ***$p < 0.001$
Includes controls for individual and prefecture characteristics

In summary, the overall adverse employment effect of −0.14 (Table 6.2) is due entirely to the adverse employment effect of −0.14 for females (Table 6.2), particularly females in the Central and Western regions. Males experienced no significant adverse employment effects as was the case for females in the Eastern region. These results are consistent with the notion that minimum wage increases will have their greatest adverse employment effect among lower-wage workers, such as females, for whom minimum wages will be a binding constraint. The same can apply to the regional pattern of adverse employment effects. There is no adverse effect in the higher wage and growing East, a moderate adverse employment effect for females in the middle wage and moderately growing Central region, and a large adverse employment effect in the lowest wage and slower growing West. Males and females in the higher wage and growing East region do not seem to be affected by minimum wage increases.

6.6.2 *Effects on Earnings for Those Who Remain Employed*

The coefficient on the Group*Time interaction term in the third row of Table 6.4 gives the effect of minimum wage increases on the monthly earnings of those who remain employed. For both sexes combined (top panel) there is little difference in the earnings effects depending upon the inclusion of control variables, with individual migrant workers experiencing about a 5% earnings increase if they are in a jurisdiction that increased its minimum wage relative to one that did not increase its minimum wage. That effect increases to about 6% after controlling for possible sample selection bias (column 4). The effects on earnings are slightly higher for males at 6.1% (column 5) compared to females at 4.8% (column 6) based on full controls including controlling for possible selection bias.

Table 6.4 Effect of MW increase on migrant workers' (ln)monthly earnings

Variable	*Both sexes*				*Male*	*Female*
	(1)	*(2)*	*(3)*	*(4)*	*(5)*	*(6)*
Group	3.022***	1.021***	1.077***	−1.039**	−1.083***	−1.169***
	(0.004)	(0.004)	(0.004)	(0.017)	(0.028)	(0.009)
Time	3.111***	3.102***	3.067***	3.071***	3.039	3.094***
	(0.104)	(0.104)	(0.104)	(0.117)	(0.126)	(0.106)
Group*Time	**5.141*** **	**4.849*** **	**4.841*** **	**6.038*** **	**6.146*** **	**4.839*** **
	(0.619)	(0.617)	(0.616)	(0.614)	(0.612)	(0.617)
Observations	49,203	49,203	49,203	49,203	23,618	25,585
Individual controls	No	Yes	Yes	Yes	Yes	Yes
Prefecture controls	No	No	Yes	Yes	Yes	Yes
2SLS Selection control	No	No	No	Yes	Yes	Yes

Notes Standard errors are in parentheses. $*p < 0.05$, $**p < 0.01$, $***p < 0.001$

Table 6.5 repeats the analysis based on the full controls including controls for sample selection bias, separately for each of the three regions of China.[5] For comparison purposes, the first column repeats Table 6.4 estimate for the regions combined. As indicated by the coefficient on the Group*Time interaction term in the third row in the top panel, the positive earnings effect of 6.04% for all regions combined is due to the statistically significant positive earnings effect of approximately that amount in the Central and Western regions, with the earnings effect being statistically insignificant in the Eastern region.

The positive earnings effects in the Central and Western regions are fairly similar for males (bolded third row, middle panel) and females (bolded third row, bottom panel). The positive earnings effect of 4% for females in the Central region is statistically insignificant, albeit with a *t*-value of 1.4.

In summary, the overall positive earnings effect of 6.04% (Table 6.4) for all regions combined is due to the statistically significant positive earnings effect of approximately that amount in the Central and Western regions, with fairly similar effects for males and females. The earnings effects for both sexes and males and females separately are statistically insignificant in the Eastern region. The lack of any earnings effect in the Eastern region is consistent with there being no adverse employment effect in that region. It appears that minimum wages are not a binding constraint in the more prosperous and growing higher wage Eastern region—not affecting either employment or earnings.

Table 6.5 The impact of MWs on migrant workers' employment in each area

	East		*Central*		*West*	
Variable	*Urban*	*Rural*	*Urban*	*Rural*	*Urban*	*Rural*
Group	−0.272***	−0.171***	0.080	−0.175***	0.421	0.559***
	(0.061)	(0.024)	(0.067)	(0.030)	(0.261)	(0.119)
Time	−0.036	−0.003	0.041	−0.010	−0.021	−0.144**
	(0.051)	(0.020)	(0.062)	(0.030)	(0.127)	(0.068)
Inter	0.008	−0.061	−0.313	−0.859***	0.081	0.023
	(0.160)	(0.084)	(0.284)	(0.125)	(0.200)	(0.089)
Observations	12,576	61,536	4201	17,788	5782	24,529
Adj-R2	0.0835	0.0987	0.0908	0.0776	0.0946	0.111

Note In addition to the regressing variables in Table 6.4, we control the gender as well. Standard deviations are reported in parentheses. ***$p < 0.01$, **$p < 0.05$, *$p < 0.1$

6.6.3 *Effects on Hours for Those Who Remain Employed*

Table 6.6 illustrates the effect of minimum wage increases on the monthly hours of work for those who remain employed. The theoretically expected effect is for an increase in their hours of work as a mechanism for employers to offset some of the cost increase for those who receive a monthly minimum wage increase and remain employed.

As expected, for both sexes combined (bolded third row) migrant workers who remain employed in jurisdictions that increased their minimum wage experienced an increase in their hours of work compared to migrant workers in jurisdiction where there was no minimum wage increase, although the effect was statistically significant only in the regressions where there were full controls (column 3) as well as also correcting for possible sample selection bias (column 4). Based on the 2SLS estimates that corrected for selection bias, those migrant workers experienced a 2.7 hours increase in their hours of work. This is entirely driven by the increased hours for male workers (column 5). For female workers (column 6) the change in hours of work is statistically insignificant across all specifications.

Table 6.6 Effect of MW increase on migrant workers' monthly working hours

Variable	*Both sexes*				*Male*	*Female*
	(1)	*(2)*	*(3)*	*(4)*	*(5)*	*(6)*
Group	−2.729***	−1.497	−0.837	−1.426	−1.010	−1.482
	(1.127)	(1.122)	(1.130)	(1.135)	(1.380)	(1.209)
Time	−0.391***	−0.248**	0.109	0.153	0.224	1.110***
	(0.123)	(0.118)	(0.130)	(0.130)	(0.370)	(0.197)
Group*Time	**2.304**	**2.256**	**2.232****	**2.671***	**2.884*****	**−2.477**
	(1.691)	(1.546)	(1.297)	(1.505)	(0.778)	(1.987)
Observations	49,203	49,203	49,203	49,203	23,618	25,585
Individual controls	No	Yes	Yes	Yes	Yes	Yes
Prefecture controls	No	No	Yes	Yes	Yes	Yes
2SLS Selection control	No	No	No	Yes	Yes	Yes

Notes Standard errors are in parentheses. *$p<0.05$, **$p<0.01$, ***$p<0.001$

Table 6.7 repeats the analysis based on the full controls including controls for sample selection bias, separately for each of the three regions of China. As indicated in the bolded third row of the top panel, the offsetting increase in hours work across all regions is driven entirely by the large increase of 7.2 hours in the Central region (column 3). For the Eastern and Western region, the changes in hours were statistically insignificant. The increased hours of work in the Central region in turn were driven entirely by the increased hours for males (column 3, third row, middle panel).

Table 6.7 Effect of MW increase on migrant workers' monthly working hours by region and sex

Variable	*All regions*	*East*	*Central*	*West*
	(1)	*(2)*	*(3)*	*(4)*
Both sexes				
Group	−0.426***	−0.381*	−3.283***	3.505***
	(0.135)	(0.212)	(0.337)	(0.933)
Time	0.153	0.982***	−1.710***	0.331
	(0.130)	(0.159)	(0.325)	(0.526)
Group*Time	**2.671***	**1.088**	**7.226*****	**−0.783**
	(1.505)	(0.954)	(2.431)	(1.026)
Observations	49,203	28,832	8556	11,815
Males				
Group	−0.010	1.090	−3.946***	−2.164
	(0.380)	(0.977)	(0.425)	(4.850)
Time	−0.224	0.216	−2.229***	2.097
	(0.370)	(0.687)	(0.496)	(2.437)
Group*Time	**2.884*****	**1.333***	**5.267*****	**1.554**
	(0.778)	(0.718)	(2.215)	(1.023)
Observations	23,618	14,704	4363	5434
Females				
Group	−0.482**	−0.795**	−2.222***	2.257*
	(0.209)	(0.310)	(0.545)	(1.277)
Time	1.110***	1.820***	−0.779	1.423*
	(0.197)	(0.243)	(0.526)	(0.741)
Group*Time	**−2.477**	**1.103**	**3.192**	**−2.102****
	(1.987)	(0.811)	(2.244)	(1.035)
Observations	25,585	14,704	4363	5434

Notes Standard errors are in parentheses. *$p<0.05$, **$p<0.01$, ***$p<0.001$
Includes controls for individual and prefecture characteristics and 2SLS sample selection

The cost offset from employers increasing their hours of work can explain in part why males in the Central region did not experience any significant adverse employment effect (Table 6.3, column 3, middle panel) in spite of receiving a large wage increase from the minimum wage increase (Table 6.5, column 3, middle panel). In essence, employers offset much of the cost increase of the higher wages for males by increasing their hours of work—a feasible mechanism when minimum wages are based on monthly earnings rather than hourly wages. This also explains, in part, why females in the Western region experienced the largest adverse employment effect of −0.336 (Table 6.3, column 4, bottom panel). Those who remained employed had the largest wage increase of 5% (Table 6.5, column 4, bottom panel) the cost of which was not offset by any increase in their hours of work after their wage increase. In fact, their hours of work were also reduced by 2.1 hours (Table 6.7, column 4, bottom panel). What is a puzzle, however, is why employers chose to offset some of the cost of the wage increase for males by increasing their hours of work rather than reducing their employment, while for females they did the opposite by reducing their employment and not increasing their hours of work—in fact, they also reduced their hours of work.

In summary, employers in jurisdictions that increased their monthly minimum wage offset part of that cost increase by increasing the monthly hours of work of those who remained employed. This occurred only for males and not females, and only for males in the Central region. This can explain in part why males in the Central region did not experience any significant adverse employment effect in spite of receiving a large wage increase from the minimum wage increase. In contrast, employers in the Western region did not offset part of the cost increase from their large wage increases for females by increasing their hours of work (in fact they decreased) and as such those females experienced large adverse employment effects.

6.7 Propensity Score Matching as a Robustness Check

As a robustness check, we also use Propensity Score Matching procedures to deal with the possibility that increases in minimum wages are not random across the various jurisdictions. This method estimates the average treatment effect on the treated (ATT) by matching individuals in the treatment group with individuals in the comparison group who

Table 6.8 Propensity score estimates of the effect of MW increases on migrant workers' employment, wages, and working hours

Dependent variable	*Propensity score estimates (ATT)*				*DID*
	ATTN	*ATTR*	*ATTK*	*ATTS*	
	(1)	*(2)*	*(3)*	*(4)*	*(5)*
Employment	−0.142*	−0.129**	−0.117**	−0.115**	−0.137*
	(0.060)	(0.050)	(0.045)	(0.042)	(0.078)
Wages	5.487***	5.385***	5.209***	5.119***	6.038***
	(0.692)	(0.677)	(0.668)	(0.655)	(0.614)
Working hours	4.581***	4.056***	3.883***	3.193***	2.671*
	(1.148)	(1.274)	(1.211)	(1.159)	(1.505)

Notes Standard errors are in parentheses. $*p < 0.05$, $**p < 0.01$, $***p < 0.001$
Columns (1)–(4) are the propensity score estimates of the Average Treatment on the Treated (ATT). The letter at the end of each heading denotes the type of propensity score estimate: Nearest-Neighbor Matching (ATTN), Radius Matching (ATTR), Kernel Matching (ATTK), and the Stratification Method (ATTS). The DID estimates in column 5 are the difference-in-difference estimates from the previous regressions with full controls: Table 6.3 column 1 for employment; Table 6.4 column 4 for wages; and Table 6.6 column 4 for hours. They are included for comparison purposes

are as similar as possible in that they have the same or similar probabilities of being treated but are not treated. Rosenbaum and Rubin (1983), Dehejia (2005), and Glazerman et al. (2003) show that using the method of Propensity Score Matching can reduce the bias in the estimation of treatment effects with observational datasets, particularly when combined with a natural experimental method such as DID.

There are different methods to match the subjects between the control and treatment groups, including Nearest-Neighbor Matching (ATTN), Radius Matching (ATTR), Kernel Matching (ATTK), and the Stratification Method (ATTS) (see Becker and Ichino 2002). We report the results using all four matching methods in our analysis.

As indicated in Table 6.8, the results are very similar across the four alternative propensity score estimation procedures. Importantly, they are also similar to our general results based on our DID procedures as reproduced in the last column. This suggests that our DID results are not subject to the concern that minimum wage increases are not random across the different jurisdictions.

6.8 Concluding Observations

The various results of the effect on minimum wage increases on employment, wages, and hours of work highlight the importance of drilling deeper and disaggregating results by such factors as gender and region. They also highlight the importance of examining effects by such factors as employment, earnings, and hours of work to delineate the differential impacts, cost offsets, and tradeoffs that can be involved. When minimum wages are based on monthly earnings, for example, employers may offset the cost of wage increases by increasing the monthly hours of work of those who receive the wage increases, and this may negate any adverse employment effects. If such cost offsets do not occur, then reductions in employment will ensue.

The adverse employment effects tend to fall on females and especially those in the lower wage and slower growing Central and Western regions. Females who remain employed tend to have higher wages as a result of the minimum wage increases but those higher wages lead to reductions in employment since the cost increase is not offset in part by increasing the monthly hours of work for those on a monthly minimum wage. In contrast, males tend not to experience an adverse employment effect even though they tend to have higher wages as a result of the minimum wage increases, because at least part of the cost increase is offset by employers increasing their monthly hours of work for those who remain employed. Reasons for this differential response for males and females are not obvious and remain a subject for further research.

The analysis highlights a policy trade-off that is so common in economics. In this situation, increases in minimum wages can increase the wages of those who remain employed, but at the cost of reducing their probability of being employed, unless some of the cost increased can be offset by increasing the hours of work for those who remain employed at the higher wage. There appears to be no such thing as a free lunch.

Notes

1. The data were obtained from the statistics year book and the official website of human resources and social security department in each province.
2. Wang and Gunderson (2015) document cost offsets in the form of reduced fringe benefits and changes in working conditions in response to minimum wage increases in China.

3. For the binary-coded employment dependent variable, we use the Linear Probability Model (LPM) since the mean of the dependent variable of 0.464 lies between 0.3 and 0.7 which is considered a range where it is appropriate for using the LPM. Our estimates are close to the marginal effects from a logit model.
4. In log earnings equations, the true proportional change is $\exp(\beta)-1$, where β is the estimated coefficient. For low values of β, the approximation is very close, underestimating the true value by less than 0.005 for values of $\beta < 0.10$, which is the case for our main variables of interest; hence, we report the β coefficients.
5. These results are very similar to those that do not control for possible selection bias, but control only for individual and prefecture characteristics (available on request).

References

Becker, S.O., and A. Ichino. 2002. "Estimation of Average Treatment Effects Based on Propensity Score", *Stata Journal*, 2(4): 358–377.

Card, David, and Alan B. Krueger. 1995. *Myth and Management: The New Economics of the Minimum Wage*. Princeton: Princeton University Press.

Cooke, F. Lee. 2005. *HRM, Work and Employment in China*. London: Routledge.

Cooke, F. Lee., and J. Rubery. 2002. *Minimum Wage and Social Equality in China*. Geneva: International Labour Organization.

Cunningham, Wendy. 2007. *Minimum Wages and Social Policy: Lessons from Developing Countries*. Washington: World Bank.

Dehejia, R. 2005. "Practical Propensity Score Matching: A Reply to Smith and Todd", *Journal of Econometrics*, 125: 355–364.

Ding, Shouhai. 2010. "Employment Effects of Minimum Wage Regulation and Cross Effect of the Employment Contracts Law", *Social Science in China*, 31: 146–167.

Fang, T., and C. Lin. 2015. "Minimum Wages and Employment in China", *IZA Journal of Labor Policy*, 4(22): 1–30. https://doi.org/10.1186/s40173-015-0050-9.

Glazerman, S., D. Levy, and D. Myers. 2003. *Nonexperimental Replications of Social Experiments: A Systematic Review*. Princeton, NJ: Mathmatica Policy Research, Inc.

ILO. 2014. *Minimum Wage Systems*. Geneva, Switzerland: International Labour Organization.

Khamis, M. 2013. "Does the Minimum Wage Have a Higher Impact on the Informal Than on the Formal Labour Market? Evidence from Quasi-Experiments", *Applied Economics*, 45: 477–495.

Kristensen, Nicolai, and Wendy Cunningham. 2006. "Do Minimum Wages in Latin America and the Caribbean Matter? Evidence from 19 Countries", World Bank Policy Research Working Paper 3870.

Laliberté, Pierre (ed). 2012. "Social Justice and Growth: The Role of the Minimum Wage", *International Journal of Labour Research*, 4(1): 5–127.

Li, H., L. Lei, B. Wu, and Y. Xiong. 2012. "The End of Cheap Chinese Labor", *Journal of Economic Perspectives*, 26(4): 57–74.

Li, Xisochun, and Ping He. 2010. "Effects of the Minimum Wage on the Employment of Rural Migrant Workers—A Case Study of the Yangtze River Delta", *Jiangsu Social Science*, 4: 59–66 (in Chinese).

Lu, Z., and S. Song. 2006. "Rural-Urban Migration and Wage Determination: The Case of Tianjin, China", *China Economic Review*, 17: 337–345.

Luo, Xiaolan. 2007a. "Analysis of the Employment Effect of Minimum Wages in China's Monopsony Labor Market", *Finance and Trade Research*, 4: 1–5 (in Chinese).

Luo, Xiaolan. 2007b. "An Analysis on the Minimum Wage's Employment Effect Over the Rural-Workers in China", *Journal of Finance and Economics*, 33: 114–123 (in Chinese).

Ma, Shuang, J. Zhang, and X. Zhu. 2012. "The Effect of Minimum Wage on Average Wage and Employment", *Economic Research*, No. 5: 133–147 (in Chinese).

Metcalf, David. 2008. "Why Has the British National Minimum Wage Had Little or No Impact on Employment?" *Journal of Industrial Relations*, 50: 489–512.

Neumark, David, and William L. Wascher. 2008. *Minimum Wages*. Cambridge, MA: MIT Press.

Ni, J., G. Wang, and X. Yao. 2011. "Impact of Minimum Wages on Employment: Evidence from China", *The Chinese Economy*, 44: 18–38.

Qu, Z., and Z. Zhao. 2011. "Evolution of the Chinese Rural-Urban Migrant Labour Market from 2002 to 2007", IZA Discussion Paper 5421.

Rosenbaum, P., and D. Rubin. 1983. "The Central Role of Propensity Score Matching in Observational Studies for Causal Effects", *Biometrika*, 70: 41–55.

Wang, Jing, and Morley Gunderson. 2011. "Minimum Wage Impacts from a Pre-specified Research Design: China 2000–2007", *Contemporary Economic Policy*, 29(3): 392–406.

Wang, Jing, and Morley Gunderson. 2012. "Minimum Wage Effects on Employment and Wages: Diff-in-Diff Estimates from Eastern China", *International Journal of Manpower*, 33(8): 860–876.

Wang, Jing, and Morley Gunderson. 2015. "Adjustments to Minimum Wages in China: Cost-Neutral Offsets", *Relations industrielles/Industrial Relations*, 70(3): 510–531.
World Bank. 2006. *Minimum Wages in Latin America and the Caribbean: The Impact on Employment, Inequality and Poverty*. Washington, DC: Human Development Management Unit, LAC Region.
Zhang, Z. 2007. "Will Minimum Wage Decrease Immigrant Peasant Workers' Employment?" *Finance and Economics*, 10: 103–110 (in Chinese).

CHAPTER 7

The Effects of the Minimum Wage on Earnings Inequality: Evidence from China

Carl Lin and Myeong-Su Yun

7.1 Introduction

Since the reform and opening-up policy in 1978, China's economy has been growing remarkably at a rate of at least 9.5% per year. As the economy has grown, Chinese workers' earnings have also increased rapidly over the same period. According to the latest figures from the National Bureau of Statistics of China (NBS), disposable earnings per capita have risen substantially—more than 70-fold—over the past few decades in urban China, rising from 343 RMB in 1978 to 24,565 RMB in 2012, while net earnings per capita in rural China have grown 60-fold, increasing from 134 RMB in 1978 to 7917 RMB in 2012 (National Bureau of Statistics of China 2013).

C. Lin (✉)
Bucknell University, Lewisburg, PA, USA
e-mail: carl.lin@bucknell.edu

M.-S. Yun
Inha University, Incheon, South Korea
e-mail: msyun@inha.ac.kr

L. Shi and C. Lin (eds.), *Minimum Wages in China*,
https://doi.org/10.1007/978-981-15-2421-9_7

As the Chinese economy has rapidly grown, the earnings distribution has deteriorated. For example, the urban-to-rural earnings per capita ratio increased from 2.57 in 1978 to 2.90 in 2001 and further to 3.10 in 2012. The Gini coefficient, a commonly used measure of inequality, was at a very low level in 1978, at .16 and .22 for urban and rural areas, respectively (Li and Zhao 1999). However, as shown in Fig. 7.1, China's overall Gini coefficient began to rise from .376 in 1988 to .439 in 1995 (Wang 2007) and increased further to .454 and .490 in 2002 and 2007, respectively (Li and Luo 2011).[1] In contrast, high inequality countries such as Brazil and Mexico had shown declined Gini coefficients over a similar time period, whereas for the US it was relatively stable.[2]

The deterioration of the earnings distribution and growing gap between the rich and the poor has engendered challenges to economic development and social stability in China. As shown by the experience of developed countries, public policies, such as tax reforms, can play an essential role in countering rising inequality. Since the early 2000s, the Chinese government has intensively promulgated a series of policies,

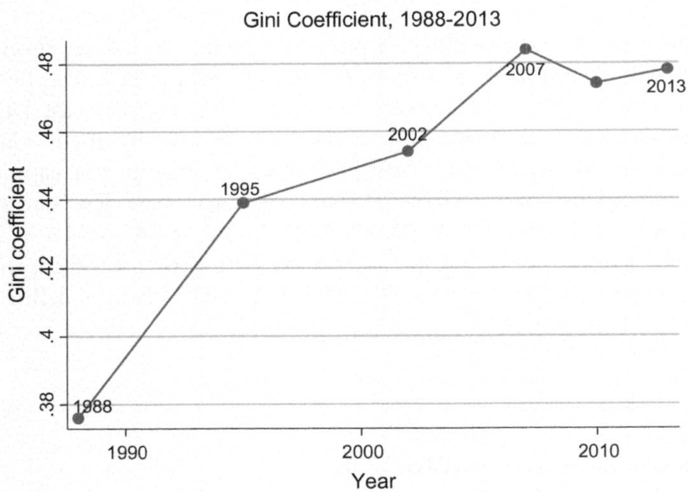

Fig. 7.1 Growing Inequality in China. The NBS of China publishes the official Gini coefficients in 2013 for the first time. The numbers of 2007, 2010, and 2013 are from the NBS Web site, whereas those of 1988 and 1995 are from Wang (2007), and the number of 2002 is from Li and Luo (2011)

such as aid to the poor, rural minimal social security, and the minimum wage policy. Among these policy initiatives, the minimum wage policy is the most controversial.[3]

The contentiousness of the debate on the minimum wage policy in China arises from the difficulty of measuring its effects on employment, wages, and the earnings distribution, among others. However, the initial evidence suggests that the magnitude and frequency of changes to the minimum wage have been substantial both over time and across different jurisdictions, particularly since 2004. These large variations both across jurisdictions and over time facilitate our estimation of minimum wage effects on inequality in China. For example, in January 2004, China promulgated new minimum wage regulations that required local governments to introduce a minimum wage increase at least once every two years, that extended coverage to self-employed and part-time workers, and that quintupled the penalties for violations or noncompliance. The new regulations entered into force in March 2004, engendering frequent and substantial increases in the minimum wage in the years that followed.[4]

Although the literature widely documents numerous aspects of the minimum wage and its role in the labor market, there is no consensus regarding whether the minimum wage can reduce inequality (Neumark and Wascher 2008). Moreover, research on the effect of the minimum wage on inequality in developing countries is scant. This study contributes to the literature by examining the effect of the minimum wage on inequality in China. China provides a particularly interesting context for such a study since it has experienced both rising inequality and a rising minimum wage (nominal and real), whereas countries such as the US (Lee 1999) and Mexico (Bosch and Manacorda 2010) have experienced rising wage inequality with a declining minimum wage (real).

Using OLS and IV panel regressions at the aggregated city level, we first examine the effect of minimum wage changes on the earnings gaps at the bottom and upper end of the earnings distribution as well as the extent of such an effect. Our analysis shows that minimum wage increases significantly help reduce earnings gaps, particularly at the bottom end of the distribution. Next, to measure the contribution of minimum wage changes to the change in earnings inequality, we construct a counterfactual scenario to capture how China's earnings distribution would have evolved without the rise in the minimum wage. The difference between the observed and the counterfactual scenario is the real effect of the minimum wage. Indeed, we find that the contribution of minimum wage changes in reducing inequality is substantial, particularly at the bottom end of the earnings distribution. That is, had it not been for the increase in the minimum wage, the earnings gap at the bottom end of the earnings distribution would have been larger.[5]

7.2 Literature on the Distributional Effect of the Minimum Wage

Most evidence on the distributional effect of the minimum wage comes from the US. In early studies using simulation methods, Johnson and Browning (1983) and Burkhauser and Finegan (1989) show that a moderate reduction of the minimum wage could reduce income inequality. Since the 1990s, studies have commonly used regression methods. Neumark et al. (2005), who apply a nonparametric method to estimate the minimum wage effect on income inequality, analyze several inequality measures (e.g., Gini coefficient, coefficient of variation, standard deviation, and Atkinson index) and find that a rise in the minimum wage can increase inequality. However, using data from 1979 to 1991 at the state level, Lee (1999) finds that the falling real minimum wage can explain from 70 to 100% of the growth in wage inequality in the lower tail of the female wage distribution and argues the declining minimum wage accounts for a substantial part of the growth in inequality in the US from 1979 to 1991. Autor et al. (2016) find that the minimum wage reduces wage inequality in the lower tail of the wage distribution (the 50/10 wage ratio), but the effects are typically less than half as large as those reported in Lee (1999) and are almost negligible for males. Taken together, most findings from the US show that if the target group for the study of distributional effects is at the bottom end of the income/wage distribution, the minimum wage can help reduce inequality.

Evidence outside the US is also limited, focusing primarily on Central and South American countries. The World Bank (2006) finds that the distributional effects of the minimum wage are ambiguous in Central and Southern America. Both positive and negative effects are found; however, the results show that the minimum wage has no effect on poverty and that the effect on inequality varies from country to country. Neumark (2006) use a before-and-after method to study whether the minimum wage can help improve income inequality in Brazil and find that although the minimum wage has a positive effect on the income distribution at the 20th percentile, there is no effect at the 10th and 30th percentiles. Moreover, when a lagged minimum wage is added, the results show a significant negative effect. They also find that the results are not robust in different model specifications, and they ultimately conclude that the evidence from Brazil shows that the minimum wage does not reduce inequality. Gindling and Terrell (2007) use industry-level data from 2001 to 2004 in Honduras to study the effect of the minimum wage on the income distribution and find that the minimum wage has an effect on reducing inequality. Bosch and Manacorda (2010) study the effect of the minimum wage on earnings inequality in Mexico from the late 1980s to the early 2000s. They find that the Mexican minimum wage can explain a large part of earnings inequality in Mexico, and they show that at the bottom end of the earnings distribution, most of the growing inequality can be attributed to the rapid decline in the real value of the minimum wage.

Research on the effect of the minimum wage on inequality in China is limited. In the first empirical study, Wen (2007) uses pooled cross-sectional data from 2004 to 2006 at the provincial level to estimate the effect of the minimum wage on the employment and income distribution of rural migrant workers. He finds that the minimum wage has a positive effect on the employment and income distribution of rural migrants over the period of analysis. Wang (2011) discusses the effect of the minimum wage on patterns in income distribution and economic development, and he argues that the minimum wage could have possibly reduced the income gap in China. Using the time-series data from Chongqing City for the period between 1997 and 2010, Chen (2012) finds that increasing the minimum wage could help mitigate the growing income gap between urban and rural areas.

Wang (2013) uses a simulation method and shows that increases in the minimum wage can reduce earnings inequality and that the effect of minimum wage policy increases with the strength of its enforcement. Jia (2013) uses microdata sets from three different surveys conducted between 1995 and 2008 to study the effect of the minimum wage on wage inequality, and he finds that increasing the effective minimum wage can help reduce wage differentials in the lower tail of the wage distribution. In the only study to offer a different view of the minimum wage effect, Quan and Li (2011) test the growing income gap between urban and rural regions in Shanghai and show that the distributional effect of the minimum wage is limited.

In sum, almost all the limited studies on the minimum wage effect from China use aggregated data (published statistics), such as cross-sectional or time-series data. In contrast, information on the minimum wage (all at the provincial level) for calculating the mean minimum wage is insufficient. More important, the representativeness of the sample in previous studies is questionable. This study aims to address these concerns and to fill this research gap by providing a better data set, richer models, and more complex estimation methods.

7.3 Minimum Wage Policy in China

Prior to 1994, China had no minimum wage law. In 1984, the country simply acknowledged the 1928 "Minimum Wage-Fixing Machinery Convention" of the International Labour Organization (Su 1993). Because of sluggish wage growth and high inflation in the late 1980s, Zhuhai of Guangdong Province implemented the first local minimum wage regulations in 1989, and similar regulations followed in Shenzhen, Guangzhou, and Jiangmen in the same year. It was not until the eruption of private enterprises in 1992, when labor disputes became frequent, that the Chinese Central Government began to consider minimum wage legislation (Yang 2006). In 1993, China issued the first national minimum wage regulations, and in July 1994, these regulations were written into China's new version of the Labor Law.

The 1994 legislation required that all employers pay wages no less than the local minimum wage to employees. Further, all provincial, autonomous region and municipal governments were required to set the minimum wage according to five principles and report them to the State Council of the Central Government. Specifically, the five principles indicated that the setting and adjustment of the local minimum wage should synthetically consider the lowest living expenses of workers, the average number of dependents that workers support, local average wages, the level of labor productivity, the level of local employment, and the level of economic development among regions. These conditions provided considerable flexibility for provinces in setting minimum wage standards, with the economic development principle giving them the flexibility to limit the minimum wage to attract foreign investment (Wang and Gunderson 2011; Frost 2002). By December 1994, 7 of 31 provinces had set their own minimum wage, and by the end of 1995, that number had increased to 24.

In the early 2000s, the slowly increasing minimum wage, along with growing concerns for uncovered/disadvantaged workers, began to increase the government's focus on new minimum wage regulations. In December 2003, the Ministry of Labor and Social Security passed "The Minimum Wage Regulations" and promulgated the new law in January 2004. Regarding its main features, this law extends coverage to employees in state-owned and private enterprises, self-employed businesses, and private non-enterprise units. In particular, the new law establishes two types of minimum wages: a monthly minimum wage applied to full-time workers and an hourly minimum wage applied to non-full-time employees. Moreover, the minimum wage standards are set and adjusted jointly by the local government, trade union, and enterprise confederation of each province. A draft for the minimum wage standards is submitted to the Ministry of Labor and Social Security for review, and the Ministry then asks for opinions from the All-China Federation of Trade Unions and the China Enterprise Confederation. The Ministry of Labor and Social Security can request a revision within 14 days of receiving the proposed draft. If no revision is brought up after the 14-day period, the proposed new minimum wage scheme is considered to be passed.

In addition, the new regulation requires that local governments renew their minimum wage standards at least once every two years, and penalties for violations increased from 20 to 100% of the owed wage to 100–500% of the owed wage.[6] Moreover, employers cannot include subsidies such as overtime pay or canteen and traveling supplements as part of employees' wages when calculating the minimum wage. The new regulations were entered into force on March 1, 2004, and they have led to substantial increases in the minimum wage across China.

7.4 Data and Research Design

Although there is considerable interest in studying the effect of the minimum wage on inequality in China, research on this topic has been hampered by difficulties in collecting data. First, because provinces, municipalities, and autonomous regions in China have considerable flexibility in setting their minimum wage according to local conditions, at least 3 or 4 levels of minimum wage standards are often applicable to various cities in most provinces.[7] Each city is responsible for documenting its own minimum wage standards; hence, city-level minimum wage data containing relevant information on the dates and extent of minimum wage increases are not readily available.[8] Second, in China, it is difficult to obtain microdata that can reasonably be considered representative of the population and that may be influenced by minimum wage increases. Furthermore, some provinces, such as Beijing and Shanghai, do not include social security payments and housing provident funds as part of wages when calculating the minimum wage, rendering their "official" minimum wage higher than the real minimum wage.[9] The data and research design were chosen to estimate the effect of the minimum wage on earnings inequality and to attempt to address some of the aforementioned challenges in research on the effect of the minimum wage on inequality. Hence, our study uses two data sources: (1) the annual Urban Household Survey (UHS) collected by NBS of China from 2002 to 2009 (more details in Sect. 7.4.1) and (2) minimum wage data collected by authors at the city level (4-digit area code) between 1994 and 2012.[10]

7.4.1 Data

The UHS is a continuous, large-scale, socioeconomic survey conducted by the NBS to study the conditions and standard of living of urban households, which include agricultural residents, nonagricultural residents, nonresidents who have lived in a city for at least six months, and some migrant households with local residency. By using sampling techniques and daily accounting methods, the survey collects data from households in different cities and counties in all 31 provinces in Mainland China for each quarter. In late December, survey teams from all provinces are required to verify and then upload the aggregated annual data to the Division of City Socio-economic Survey of the NBS through Intranet by January 10 of the following year. The UHS data contain information on households, such as income, earnings, and consumption expenditures; demographic characteristics; work and employment; housing; and other family-related matters.

Our primary objective is to thoroughly and accurately acquire relevant information on the minimum wage for each city. In China, provinces have considerable flexibility in setting their minimum wage standards according to local economic conditions; thus, there are several levels of standards across cities within the same province. Moreover, the adjustment date of a city's new minimum wage standards can also differ from its geographically contiguous neighbors within the same province, rendering the estimation of minimum wage effects more challenging.

To effectively address this issue, we collected our minimum wage data from every local government Web site and carefully recorded the minimum wage information for every year from 1994 to 2012. As such, our data contain the monthly minimum wage for full-time employees, the hourly minimum wage for part-time employees, the effective dates of the minimum wage standards, and the extent to which social security payments and/or housing provident funds were included as part of the minimum wage calculations. We then merge the minimum wage data with the UHS data, a 16-province data set containing individual/household socioeconomic information for the period 2002–2009.

In Table 7.1, we present a brief summary of the minimum wage data used in our main analysis for the period following the implementation of new minimum wage regulations (2004). Columns (1), (2), and (3) correspond to the mean of the monthly minimum wage, the standard deviation, and the number of counties for the three regions and the 16 provinces in 2004, respectively.[11] When calculating the mean minimum wage, we use a time-weighted method, as suggested in Rama (2001), to address the issue of different adjustment dates among cities in a province within a year. The mean minimum wage is adjusted for inflation and converted into 2005 RMB by using the urban resident CPI for comparison over time. In addition, to account for the differing living costs among provinces, we apply the PPP-adjusted deflator developed by Brandt and Holz (2006).[12] The last row reports the mean of the minimum wage for all provinces, its standard deviation, and the total number of counties for each year.

Table 7.1 reveals several important patterns. First, the mean nominal minimum wage increased by 80% (from 310 RMB to 562 RMB) between 2004 and 2009 throughout China.[13] Second, the Eastern region has the highest minimum wage during this period, with an average of 522 RMB per month, and the Western (436 RMB) and Central regions (424 RMB) follow. Surprisingly, the minimum wage shows a similar annual growth rate of 13% for the three regions.[14] Third, the minimum wage was sometimes raised more than once in a year. For example, Beijing increased its minimum wage in January and July of 2004, and Jiangsu raised its minimum wage in April and July of 2008.

We restrict the analysis to salaried workers between the ages of 16 and 59 who are employed in the civilian labor force, report positive annual earnings, are not self-employed, and are not enrolled in school. To reduce the effect from outliers, we winsorize the top two percentiles of the earnings distribution in each city-year group by assigning the value of

Table 7.1 Minimum wages across various jurisdictions in China, 2004–2009

Province	*2004*			*2005*			*2006*			*2007*			*2008*			*2009*		
	MW	*S.D.*	*Obs.*	*MW*	*S.D.*	*Obs.*	*MW*	*S.D.*	*Obs.*	*MW*	*S.D.*	*Obs.*	*MW*	*S.D.*	*Obs.*	*MW*	*S.D.*	*Obs.*
East																		
Beijing	509.5	.0	2	562.5	.0	2	611.8	.0	2	665.4	.0	2	735.4	.0	2	820.1	.0	2
Shanghai	590.3	.0	2	662.5	.0	2	712.1	.0	2	757.7	.0	2	894.0	.0	2	984.2	.0	2
Liaoning	282.3	46.0	96	361.9	36.6	96	405.5	41.2	96	465.8	48.7	96	550.1	59.9	97	587.8	63.2	97
Shandong	348.4	35.2	129	440.9	50.0	129	454.6	53.5	129	476.2	66.3	129	571.9	75.6	129	609.9	80.6	129
Jiangsu	416.2	59.9	66	457.6	66.8	66	517.9	70.4	66	591.0	78.0	75	647.8	88.1	75	694.4	94.7	75
Guangdong	361.2	59.9	104	442.1	80.6	104	475.0	84.9	104	516.6	88.5	104	574.3	88.2	104	636.1	98.2	104
All East	349.1	68.5	339	426.7	72.1	399	460.6	76.0	399	507.4	86.5	408	583.6	87.6	409	629.7	95.7	409
Central																		
Heilongjiang	282.0	28.1	30	287.8	28.7	30	384.0	45.7	30	418.0	53.6	30	456.0	58.6	30	486.3	62.5	30
Anhui	304.6	11.7	86	330.7	17.1	86	350.1	19.1	86	400.7	27.1	86	420.4	29.2	86	448.3	31.2	86
Jiangxi	246.7	6.6	99	317.7	8.9	100	328.9	9.4	100	427.5	15.2	100	460.3	21.8	100	490.9	23.3	100
Shanxi	348.2	21.8	119	445.4	22.3	119	454.2	22.4	119	476.3	21.6	119	536.6	22.8	119	642.5	28.6	119
Hubei	271.9	34.9	89	320.6	36.8	89	330.2	37.2	89	402.4	39.1	89	453.4	45.6	89	541.5	58.5	89
Henan	251.5	15.5	127	278.5	17.0	127	345.0	27.9	127	371.1	25.7	127	477.2	42.5	127	509.0	45.3	127
All Central	284.8	43.6	550	337.1	63.8	551	366.2	54.7	551	416.3	46.3	551	473.1	51.7	551	529.1	77.0	551
West																		
Gansu	298.2	8.5	87	304.4	8.7	87	322.1	16.3	87	344.6	35.1	87	471.6	36.3	87	549.4	39.2	87
Chongqing	334.7	21.7	42	365.7	24.6	42	409.0	30.1	42	477.8	39.8	42	554.8	44.5	42	591.7	47.4	42
Sichuan	295.4	32.1	50	352.2	41.9	50	392.2	43.8	50	425.0	42.3	181	477.9	53.0	181	509.7	56.5	181
Yunnan	297.5	18.0	138	365.2	23.4	138	403.6	23.4	138	427.0	22.8	138	527.2	31.5	138	562.3	33.6	138
All West	302.3	23.3	317	346.5	36.1	317	380.1	45.0	317	414.9	51.8	448	499.1	52.3	448	541.3	54.1	448
All Provinces	309.5	56.7	1266	367.7	73.1	1267	399.4	73.3	1267	442.3	74.8	1407	513.5	79.2	1408	562.2	88.3	1408

Note MW represents the mean of time-weighted monthly minimum wages calculated using all counties in a jurisdiction, and it has been adjusted for inflation and converted into 2005 RMB

the 97th percentile to the 98th and 99th percentiles.[15] Sampling weights are used in all calculations.

In Table 7.2, we provide summary statistics for the workers in our sample for the period 2004–2009. The total number of observations is 289,009. The mean age is approximately 41 years, and men comprise 55% of the sample. Furthermore, the workers earn 237,716 RMB on average annually, the average number of years of schooling is 12.87, and approximately 97% of the workers are of Han ethnicity. Regarding marital status, 88% of the workers are married with a spouse present. Because of the nature of the UHS, not surprisingly, 97% of the workers have local hukou (legal household registration in a city), and the average length of residence in a city is 31 years. Finally, the average work experience is approximately 22 years.

In Table 7.3, we summarize the characteristics of the minimum wage standards in China. The first row of Table 7.3 shows that approximately 6.81% of all workers earn less than the minimum wage and that 1.88% earn the minimum wage, indicating that 8.69% of Chinese employees are minimum wage workers during the period 2004–2009.[16] Among those who earned the minimum wage or less than the minimum wage, 63.81% and 62.38% are females, respectively. Furthermore, the minimum-to-average-wage ratio of workers receiving less than the minimum wage is 2.35, indicating that these disadvantaged workers earn a wage that is only approximately one-quarter of the official standard. Regarding regional differences, in the Eastern and Central regions, approximately

Table 7.2 Summary statistics of salaried worker aged 16–59, 2004–2009

Variable	*Mean*	*Standard deviation*
Age	40.71	9.09
Men	0.55	0.50
Earnings (annual, rmb)	23,716	18,811
Years of schooling	12.87	2.74
Han ethnicity	0.97	0.17
Married with spouse present	0.88	0.32
Local hukou (household registration)	0.97	0.16
Work experience (year)	21.81	10.07
Years of residence	31.19	14.60

Note The number of observations is 289,002. Standard deviations are in parentheses. Earnings have been adjusted for inflation and accounted for the differing living costs among provinces by applying the PPP-adjusted deflator developed by Brandt and Holz (2006)

Table 7.3 Characteristics of minimum wage standards in China, 2004–2009

Variable	*Less than the minimum*	*The minimum*	*Above the minimum*
Percent of total (%)	6.81	1.88	91.31
Percent of female (%)	62.38	63.81	43.36
Minimum-to-average wage ratio	2.35	1.00	0.36
	(4.34)	(0.03)	(0.21)
Region (%)			
East	6.43	1.84	91.73
Central	6.64	1.79	91.57
West	8.61	2.23	89.17
Age cohort (%)			
Age 16–19	41.48	5.34	53.18
Age 20–29	10.77	2.30	86.93
Age 30–39	5.77	1.62	92.61
Age 40–49	6.14	1.95	91.91
Age 50–59	6.74	1.86	91.41
Educational attainment (%)			
Elementary school or below	19.71	4.71	75.58
Junior high school	11.61	3.34	85.04
High school	8.12	2.35	89.53
Vocational school	5.84	1.58	92.57
Junior college	3.52	0.96	95.52
Occupation (%)			
Administrative persons of enterprises, state organs and party organizations	2.54	0.55	96.91
Professional and technical staff	2.49	0.61	96.90
Clerical and related staff	4.19	1.21	94.60
Commercial service worker	14.57	4.24	81.19
Agricultural worker	14.85	3.89	81.26
Production, transport equipment operator or related worker	7.34	2.30	90.37
Other	17.78	4.76	77.46
Industry (%)			
Mining	3.71	1.05	95.24
Manufacturing	6.73	1.84	91.44
Power production and supply	2.99	0.82	96.19
Construction	6.88	1.77	91.34

(continued)

Table 7.3 (continued)

Variable	*Less than the minimum*	*The minimum*	*Above the minimum*
Transportation and postal service	4.74	1.23	94.03
Information technology	6.14	1.38	92.48
Wholesales and retail sales	12.81	3.55	83.64
Hotel and restaurant	12.43	3.55	84.03
Banking and finance	3.12	0.73	96.15
Real estate	6.80	1.65	91.55
Leasing and commercial service	8.01	1.84	90.15
Scientific Research	2.49	0.47	97.04
Environment and public facility	4.72	1.40	93.88
Housekeeping	15.37	4.45	80.17
Education	3.29	0.78	95.94
Health care	4.11	1.02	94.88
Sports and entertainment	4.83	0.99	94.17
Public service	2.87	1.06	96.07

Note Standard deviations are in parentheses. There are 289,002 salaried workers aged 16–59 in this period. "Less than the Minimum" are workers earning wages at or below 95% of the minimum wage. Minimum wage workers earn wages above 95% and up to 105% of the minimum wage. Above minimum wage workers earn wages above 105% of the minimum wage. The East includes Liaoning, Beijing, Shandong, Jiangsu, and Guangdong; the Central region includes Heilongjiang, Shanxi, Henan, Anhui, Hubei, and Jiangxi; and the West includes Gansu, Chongqing, Sichuan, and Yunnan

92% of the workers earn a wage above the minimum wage, whereas the corresponding figure for the Western region is 89%.

Regarding the different age cohorts, Table 7.3 shows that teenagers (aged 16–19) are very likely to be minimum wage workers, as approximately 47% of teenagers in our sample are minimum wage workers. The percentage of minimum wage workers decreases substantially as workers' age increases. A similar decreasing pattern is observed with respect to skill, as measured by educational attainment. Regarding the characteristics of workers by occupation and industry, Table 7.3 shows that 19% of workers in clerical and related occupations and commercial service occupations combined earn less than the minimum wage. The housekeeping industry has the largest share of minimum wage workers, with approximately 20% of housekeepers earning the minimum wage or less. In both the wholesale and retail sector and the hotel and restaurant sector, approximately 16% of workers earn the minimum wage or less.

7.4.2 Research Design

Our objective is to assess the effect of the minimum wage on the earnings distribution in China. As noted in Sect. 7.2, nearly all existing studies on the minimum wage in China use pooled time-series/cross-sectional data at the provincial level and report mixed results, implying that a "consensus" regarding distributional effects of the minimum wage remains to be established. Our study attempts to reconcile existing findings by using detailed/complete minimum wage data, which allow us to employ a panel structure analysis of minimum wage effects, to exploit the greater variation in the relative minimum wage at the city level and to avoid the measurement error caused by using a uniform provincial minimum wage. Moreover, unlike previous studies that use aggregate published statistics, our study uses household survey microdata, which allow us to calculate the dependent variable—earnings differentials—at the city level. Thus, the dependent variable contains more variation and information on local conditions. Ideally, this feature should facilitate more reliable estimates of the distributional effects of the minimum wage in China.[17]

Following Lee (1999) and Autor et al. (2016), we parameterize the minimum wage effect as a quadratic function of the difference between the log minimum wage and the p-th percentile of the actual log earnings distribution by expressing the q to p percentile differential $w_{ct}^{q} - w_{ct}^{p}$ as a function of the latent wage differential plus a minimum wage effect. That is, our estimation equation is

$$w_{ct}^{q} - w_{ct}^{p} = \beta_1^q \left(MW_{ct} - w_{ct}^{p}\right) + \beta_2^q \left(MW_{ct} - w_{ct}^{p}\right)^2 + X_{ct}^{'}\gamma^q + \alpha_c^q + \alpha_t^q + u_{cqt}, \quad (7.1)$$

where $MW_{ct} - w_{ct}^{p}$ is the "effective" minimum wage variable of city c in year t, denoting the minimum wage relative to some level of local earnings that is unaffected by the minimum wage and that proxies for local living standards. We include a quadratic term "$(MW_{ct} - w_{ct}^{p})^2$" in the equation to capture the property that $w_{ct}^{q} - w_{ct}^{p}$ exhibits "flatten[ing] to the left," as proposed by Lee (1999) and shown in Fig. 7.2; for example, the quadratic term for 2008 is statistically significant at the 5% level. In estimating Eq. (7.1), w_{ct}^{p} is defined as the median wage. Further, X is a set of control variables used to capture aggregate business cycle effects; α_t^q is a set of year fixed effects; and α_c^q is a set of city fixed effects. The disturbance term u is assumed to be independent of city and year effects.[18]

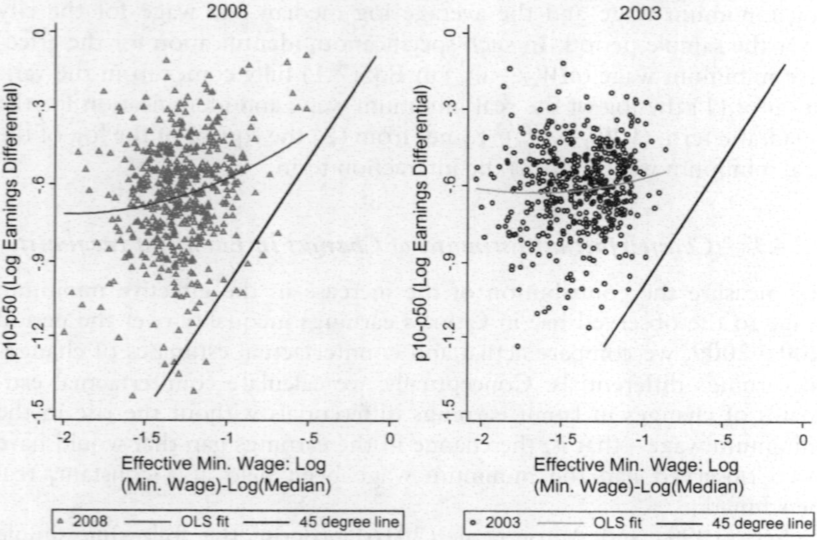

Fig. 7.2 Log Earnings Differential (p10/p50) and the Effective Minimum Wage across cities in 2003 and 2008. The estimated coefficient on the quadratic term for 2008 is statistically different from zero at the 0.05 level, while it is insignificant for 2003

Lee (1999) assumes the errors are orthogonal to the independent variables (the effective minimum wage and its square) in his estimation. However, Autor et al. (2016) point out the problem with the OLS estimation of Eq. (7.1) is that potential measurement errors will lead to upward-biased estimates of the effect of the minimum wage on inequality in both the lower and upper tail of the earnings/wage distribution. Hence, Autor et al. (2016) follow the approach in Durbin (1954) by applying IVs to address the bias caused by such a measurement error problem. Likewise, Bosch and Manacorda (2010) apply the IV approach to address this issue in their study on Mexico. Since we use Lee's methodology, we need instruments to deal with the problem of measurement error. In the 2SLS regressions, we instrument the observed effective minimum wage and its square by using three instruments as in Autor et al. (2016): (1) the log of the real minimum wage, (2) the square of the log of the real minimum wage, and (3) the interaction between the log minimum wage and the average log median real wage for the city over the sample period. In such specification, identification for the effective minimum wage ($MW_{ct} - w_{ct}^{p}$) in Eq. (7.1) fully comes from the variation of (1) the log of the real minimum wage and identification for the quadratic term $(MW_{ct} - w_{ct}^{p})^2$ comes from (2) the square of the log of the real minimum wage and (3) the interaction term.

7.4.3 Counterfactual Estimates of Changes in Earnings Inequality

To measure the contribution of the increase in the effective minimum wage to the observed rise in China's earnings inequality over the period 2004–2009, we compare actual and counterfactual estimates of changes in earnings differentials. Conceptually, we calculate counterfactual estimates of changes in latent earnings differentials without the rise in the minimum wage—that is, the change in the earnings gap that would have been observed had the minimum wage been held at a constant, real benchmark.

Lee (1999) and Autor et al. (2016) propose the following simple procedure to estimate changes in latent earnings differentials. For each observation in the data set, we calculate its rank in its respective city-year earnings distribution. Then, to simulate the earnings of the qth percentile worker in city c in t_1 (such as 2009) with the minimum wage at its t_0 (such as 2004) relative level, we adjust each worker's actual log earnings by the quantity:

$$\Delta w_{ct}^{q} = \hat{\beta}_1^{q}(\widetilde{MW}_{c,t_0} - \widetilde{MW}_{c,t_1}) + \hat{\beta}_2^{q}(\widetilde{MW}_{c,t_0} - \widetilde{MW}_{c,t_1}), \quad (7.2)$$

where $\widetilde{MW}_{c,t_1}$ is the observed end-of-period effective minimum wage in city c in t_1, $\widetilde{MW}_{c,t_0}$ is the corresponding beginning-of-period effective minimum in t_0, $\hat{\beta}_1^{q}$ and $\hat{\beta}_2^{q}$ are estimated coefficients from Appendix Tables 7.6 and 7.7. Take $t_0 = 2004$ and $t_1 = 2009$ example, adding Δw_{ct}^{q} to each observed earnings in 2009 would adjust the 2009 earnings distribution to its counterfactual under the realized effective minimum wage in 2004. Next, we pool these adjusted earnings distribution to get a counterfactual national earnings distribution, and then compare changes in earnings inequality between the observed earnings distribution and the simulated distribution obtained from the above method.[19] Finally, standard errors are calculated by bootstrapping the estimates within the city-year panel.[20]

7.5 Empirical Results and Discussion

7.5.1 Minimum Wage Effects on Earnings Differentials

We first present the estimation results of minimum wage effects on earnings differentials in Table 7.4. In each column, we estimate Eq. (7.1) by using a fixed-effects model with four different specifications. All regressions are weighted by the size of the city's population, and standard errors (in parentheses) are clustered at the city level. Entries in the tables refer to the estimated first derivative (marginal effect) of each dependent variable with respect to the effective minimum wage evaluated at the population-weighted average across cities and years.[21] In addition to OLS, we use 2SLS regression to address potential endogeneity issues as suggested in Autor et al. (2016). To check the validity of our instruments, the weak identification test and overidentification test (Hansen J statistics) show that our instruments are valid.[22]

We report the OLS and 2SLS results in terms of the marginal effects of four specifications for each percentile gap. Each entry refers to a separate regression, where each row refers to the differential between the 10th, 25th, 75th, and 90th percentiles of the earnings distribution and the median. The first column of Table 7.4 reports the estimates with cluster-robust standard errors at the city level presented in parentheses for the specification using fixed year and city effects. In the second column, we report the estimates of the specification with fixed year and city effects and the interaction of the province and year dummies. This specification allows us to abstract from the differential changes in the minimum wage and latent wages across cities. The estimation of the third column further contains city trends, whereas in the fourth column, we additionally include city covariates to control for the local economic conditions and business cycle effects.

The significance of our results is compelling: Overall, we find that the minimum wage can reduce the earnings differentials at the bottom end of the earnings distribution (i.e., p50-p10 and p50-p25); in contrast, as a placebo test, we do not find a statistically significant effect at the upper end of the earnings distribution (e.g., p75-p50 and p90-p50). For example, the OLS estimates of −.118 and −.094 in column (1) show that a 10% increase in the effective minimum wage leads to statistically significant 1.18% and .94% reductions in the p50-p10 and p50-p25 earnings differentials, and the corresponding reductions according to the marginal effects

Table 7.4 Marginal effects of the minimum wage on earnings differentials, 2004–2009

Earnings differential	*(1)*		*(2)*		*(3)*		*(4)*	
	OLS	*2SLS*	*OLS*	*2SLS*	*OLS*	*2SLS*	*OLS*	*2SLS*
p50-p10	−.118**	−.277*	−.113**	−.237*	−.137***	−.206**	−.094**	−.117*
	(.047)	(.154)	(.048)	(.143)	(.051)	(.091)	(.049)	(.064)
p50-p25	−.094***	−.163**	−.101***	−.146**	−.107***	−.146***	−.116***	−.131***
	(.028)	(.070)	(.028)	(.063)	(.034)	(.056)	(.036)	(.047)
p75-p50	.025	.027	.025	.024	.026	.024	.025	.024
	(.028)	(.068)	(.030)	(.081)	(.026)	(.064)	(.028)	(.050)
p90-p50	.037	.040	.036	.034	.037	.036	.038	.036
	(.040)	(.101)	(.043)	(.124)	(.037)	(.089)	(.039)	(.073)
Observation	989		989		989		989	
City fixed effects	Yes		Yes		Yes		Yes	
Province × Year (interactions)			Yes		Yes		Yes	
City trends					Yes		Yes	
City controls							Yes	
Weak identification test	Reject		Reject		Reject		Reject	
Overidentification test	Not reject[a]		Not reject		Not reject		Not reject	

Note ***statistically significant at the 1% level; **at the 5% level; *at the 10% level. Cluster-robust standard errors at the city level are in parentheses. Entries in the tables refer to the estimated first derivative of each dependent variable with respect to the effective minimum wage evaluated at the sample mean which is $\beta_1^q + 2\beta_2^q(MW - w^p)$, where variables without the *ct* subscript refer to sample means over all cities and all periods. The statistics of weak identification and overidentification tests for each earnings differential are in the Appendix Tables 7.6 and 7.7

[a]Note that except specification (1) for the p75-p50 and p90-p50 earnings differentials which reject the exogeneity of the instruments, all other test results do not reject the null hypothesis that the instruments are exogenous

of the 2SLS results are 2.77% and 1.63%, which are also statistically significant. As expected, the point estimates tend to be smaller for the p50-p25 earnings differential than for the p50-p10 earnings differential, implying some spillover, but the effect is attenuated as we move up the earnings distribution ladder.[23] Note that the OLS and 2SLS results at the upper end (p75-p50 and p90-p50) are not statistically significant, suggesting the minimum wage does not have an effect on earnings above the median.

In column (2) of Table 7.4, we additionally control for the interaction of the year dummies with the province dummies. By including province–year interaction fixed effects, we control for province-specific factors that have been shown to be important predictors of changes in the earnings structure. These regressions effectively identify the effect of the minimum wage based on its differential variation across cities. Compared with the results in column (1), the 2SLS results in column (2) show weaker effects of the minimum wage on the earnings distribution by reducing the earnings gaps at the bottom end of the distribution.

Column (3) of Table 7.4 additionally controls for city-specific linear time trends. As shown, the marginal effects decrease in absolute value for the p50-p10 and p50-p25 earnings differentials in the 2SLS estimates. The marginal effects are statistically significant up to the median and are not significant afterward, implying pronounced spillover effects of the minimum wage that propagate to higher percentiles of the earnings distribution at the bottom but not the upper end of the earnings distribution. For example, the 2SLS result in column (3) for the period 2004–2009 suggests that a 10% increase in the effective minimum wage reduces the p50-p10 earnings differential by almost .206 log points and the p50-p25 earnings differential by .146 log points.

Potential concerns regarding the results in the previous columns are that the correlation between earnings inequality and the minimum wage might be contaminated by the opening of the Chinese economy after China became an official member of the WTO in December of 2001 and that soaring FDI might have contributed to shaping the trends in earnings inequality, as others have claimed. To address these possible issues, we additionally control for factors that might be correlated with the trend in the effective minimum wage. The marginal effects that include these additional controls are presented in column (4) of Table 7.4, and they are smaller than those in columns (1), (2), and (3). In short, we find that minimum wage changes have reduced earnings inequality in China by essentially decreasing earnings gaps at the bottom end of the earnings distribution.[24]

Note that our results are based on the assumption that minimum wages have effects on employment or hours. However, recent studies that use firm level or household surveys to examine the employment effect of minimum wages in China have found either negative or no effects (Huang et al. 2014; Fang and Lin 2015; Mayneris et al. 2018). In particular, Ye et al. (2015) use 2009 matched firm-employee data which contain detailed wage information (basic monthly wages, bonus, supplements, and hours) and find evidence that Chinese firms adjust to the higher minimum wage by increasing hours worked of those low-skilled workers in the most labor-intensive firms. If we were to consider these findings that employment and hours go down in response to a minimum wage change, our estimates could overstate the effect of minimum wages on reducing earnings inequality in China and should be interpreted with caution.

7.5.2 *Results of Counterfactual Estimates of Changes in Earnings Inequality*

Table 7.5 presents the results of the counterfactual estimates of changes in the p50-p10 and p50-p25 earnings differentials. The calculations are done at the city level by using the estimated coefficients from Appendix Tables 7.6 and 7.7 and the method illustrated in Sect. 7.3. The third column reports the earnings differentials in log points for 2004 and 2009. The fourth column presents the observed actual change, which equals the difference in the log gaps of 2004 and 2009 100 times, whereas the fifth and the sixth columns provide the counterfactual estimates of the latent change (100 times the log change) based on the OLS and 2SLS results from the four model specifications.

Because the minimum wage policy particularly aims to help low-earning workers, we are interested in how the minimum wage affects inequality at the bottom half of the earnings distribution. Take the p50-p10 earnings differential as an example: The actual log earnings gap is .892 in 2004 and .922 in 2009. Hence, the actual change is −.0296 log points between the two years, indicating that the earnings inequality deteriorates. Had there been no minimum wage increase between 2004 and 2009, what would the p50-p10 earnings gap be in 2009? We answer this counterfactual question by reporting the latent changes: The numbers are larger for both the OLS and the 2SLS models and for all

Table 7.5 Actual and latent changes in earnings differentials, 2004–2009

Earnings differential	*Year*	*Log gap*	*Actual change*	*Latent change (OLS)*				*Latent change (2SLS)*			
				(1)	*(2)*	*(3)*	*(4)*	*(1)*	*(2)*	*(3)*	*(4)*
p50-p10	2004	.892	−.0296	−.0415	−.0396	−.0375	−.0335	−.0495	−.0436	−.0395	−.0360
	2009	.922		(.010)	(.011)	(.015)	(.015)	(.009)	(.012)	(.015)	(.015)
p50-p25	2004	.463	−.0047	−.0059	−.0053	−.0052	−.0051	−.0055	−.0051	−.0050	−.0049
	2009	.468		(.001)	(.001)	(.002)	(.002)	(.001)	(.001)	(.002)	(.002)

Note Actual and latent changes are in log points calculated at city level. Actual change = [log gap(2004)–log gap(2009)]. Marginal effects are bootstrapped and standard deviations associated with the estimates are in parentheses

specifications. For example, the latent change in 2SLS specifications (1) and (4) is −.0495 and −.0360 log points, respectively, which indicates that the p50-p10 earnings gap in 2009 would have been 67 to 22% higher if the minimum wage had not increased (Appendix Table 7.6). Note that the numbers are lower than those in Lee (1999) but close to those in Autor et al. (2016). The results for the p50-p25 earnings differential tell a similar story, i.e., that the inequality would have been higher if there were no minimum wage increase in China between 2004 and 2009.

7.6 Conclusions

We use a large set of panel data at the city level that contains relevant information on the minimum wage, combined with a longitudinal household survey of 16 representative provinces, to estimate the distributional effect of minimum wage changes in China over the period 2004–2009. Compared with previous studies using provincial-level data and reporting mixed results, our study shows that minimum wage changes significantly help reduce the earnings gap at the bottom end of the earnings distribution. In a placebo test, we do not find that minimum wage changes have an effect on the earnings gap at the upper end of the distribution.

To gauge the contribution of minimum wage increases to reducing earnings inequality, we calculate the counterfactual changes in earnings differentials and decompose the total change in China's earnings distribution. Indeed, we find that minimum wage changes substantially contribute to reducing the earnings gap at the bottom end of the distribution. Likewise, the results for the Gini coefficients and variance in our analysis suggest that the minimum wage helps reduce earnings inequality.

In sum, our findings are consistent with recent studies reporting that the minimum wage plays an essential role in earnings/wage inequality. Both the US and Mexico have exhibited a declining minimum wage (both real and effective) and rising inequality, and empirical evidence shows that the declining minimum wage accounts for a substantial part of the growth in inequality in both countries over the past three decades (Autor et al. 2016; Bosch and Manacorda 2010; Lee 1999). In contrast, China has experienced a rapid increase in the minimum wage and rapidly increasing inequality in the past 10 years, which provides an opportunity to study the effect of the minimum wage on inequality in an environment that differs from that in prior research (e.g., US and Mexico).

Our finding that minimum wage increases have reduced inequality—by reducing earnings gaps particularly at the bottom end of the earnings distribution—has both regional relevance and general implications in the context of the minimum wage literature.

Notes

1. These numbers are consistent with the official statistics published by the NBS in 2013, which also reports high inequality (e.g., .484 in 2007 and .474 in 2012). The publication of these official statistics marks the first time that the Chinese government released information on the Gini coefficient.
2. According to the 2015 World Development Indicators, the Gini coefficients of Brazil were .614 in 1988, .596 in 1995, .586 in 2002, then decreased to .552 and .527 in 2007 and 2012, respectively. For Mexico, the numbers decreased from .519 in 2000 to .481 in 2012. The Gini coefficient of the U.S. was .402 in 2000, increased to .416 in 2007, and slightly decreased to .411 in 2010.
3. Supporters of the minimum wage in China argue that the minimum wage assists individuals or families in achieving self-sufficiency and protects workers in low-paid occupations. The minimum wage can help reduce inequality and serve as an important safety net by providing a wage floor. In addition, rising labor costs due to the minimum wage increases may promote managerial efficiency and labor productivity, inducing employers to invest in productivity-improving technology (Cooke 2005). Along these lines, many Chinese scholars have argued in favor of a more proactive increase in the minimum wage. In contrast, opponents argue that raising the minimum wage can decrease the employment opportunities of low-wage workers and lead to a reduction in other components of workers' compensation packages. Such regulations can further undermine enterprises' dividend policies to shareholders and reduce China's comparative advantage given the abundance of low-wage labor (Cheung 2004, 2010). Moreover, rural-urban migrant workers tend to have very low pay, and they may accept jobs that pay less than the current minimum wage; thus, the minimum wage may exist in name only (Chan 2001).
4. According to our calculation, the average growth rate of the minimum wage is 10 to 20% per year throughout the country since 2004.
5. It is important to note that, like many studies do, our analysis assumes that minimum wage increases do not have an impact on employment or hours worked. Therefore, our results should be interpreted cautiously since the estimates could overstate the effect of minimum wage on reducing inequality.

6. The increase in penalties for violations has significantly affected compliance. According to our calculation using 2002–2009 data, throughout the country, the share of workers who earn less than the minimum wage continuously declined, decreasing from 7.28 to 5.62% in the pre- and post-2004 periods (2002–2003, 2004–2009), respectively. In particular, the number decreased from 8.08 to 5.33% in the Eastern region between the same periods, whereas the number decreased from 6.19 to 5.46% in the Central region.
7. For expositional convenience, we refer to "provinces, municipalities, and autonomous regions" as provinces.
8. The implementation date of a new minimum wage standard of a city can also differ across geographically contiguous neighbors within the same province. For example, Liaoning Province has the most complicated minimum wage scheme, in which 14 jurisdictions may enact their own standards on different dates. For instance, in 2007, the cities of Shenyang, Benxi, Dandong, and Panjin did not increase their minimum wage. In contrast, on December 20, the cities of Dalian and Anshan increased their minimum wage from 600 RMB to 700 RMB, the cities of Jinzhou and Liaoyang increased their minimum wage from 480 RMB to 580 RMB, and the city of Chaoyang increased its minimum wage from 350 RMB to 530 RMB. Furthermore, the cities of Fushun and Huludao increased their minimum wage from 400 RMB to 480 RMB on January 1, whereas the city of Yingkou increased its minimum wage from 380 RMB to 480 RMB, the city of Fuxin increased its minimum wage from 350 RMB to 420 RMB, and the city of Tieling increased its minimum wage from 380 RMB to 420 RMB the following year.
9. The housing provident fund is a long-term, compulsory, indemnificatory, and mutual aid housing fund program that is open to employees of government agencies, state enterprises, universities, hospitals, and some semi-state companies. It was founded as a form of involuntary savings to assist home financing. Workers who join the program agree to have their salary (between 4 and 10%) deposited into a special account in a state-owned bank and the participants' employer provides a one-for-one match for the amount that the employee deposits into the account. Designated banks would further supplement the fund with individual housing loans through a mortgage system. In other words, the difference between accounting for and not accounting for this issue can be substantial. For instance, the mean monthly minimum wage was 651 RMB and 767 RMB in Beijing and Shanghai between 2004 and 2009; however, the average expenses of both social security payments and housing provident funds in Beijing and Shanghai were as high as 376 RMB and 452 RMB over the same period, amounting to 58 and 59% of the nominal minimum wage, respectively. We discuss how we address this issue in the Data section.

10. Because such detailed minimum wage data by city are not readily available to the public, we collected the data together with a team at Beijing Normal University.
11. Note that there was no minimum wage increase in 2009 because of the global financial crisis.
12. The updated version, which is extended to 2010, is available at http://ihome.ust.hk/~socholz/SpatialDeflators.html.
13. In fact, the average real minimum wage has also grown at a similar rate.
14. The average annual growth rate of the minimum wage is 12.7% in the Eastern region, 13.2% in the Central region, and 12.5% in the Western region over the period 2004–2009.
15. Alternatively, we also drop the top 99th percentile and the bottom 1st percentile, and the results are not affected.
16. Our number of the average 93.2% compliance rate (16 representative provinces) over 2004–2009 is close to Ye et al. (2015) who use a matched Chinese firm-employee data from 6 provinces in 2009 and find that compliance rates are as high as 96.5% for full-time workers. Although the 2004 regulation raised the penalties for violations substantially (see Sect. 7.3), penalties for violating the minimum wage are still small. In practice, almost all firms that are found to be violating the regulations correct the violation after receiving warnings from the government labor authorities (no fines). Very few firms are required to pay fines and almost none are referred to the judicial authorities (Ye et al. 2015), resulting in some workers still being paid below the minimum wage despite the high overall compliance rate. Nevertheless, bindingness of the minimum wage can affect our analysis. Due to data limitation, we are not able to investigate this issue so our results should be interpreted with caution. Several studies have attempted to deal with the issues of enforcement and compliance such as Gindling et al. (2015) for Costa Rica, Bhorat et al. (2012) for South Africa, Ronconi (2010) for Argentina, and Ye et al. (2015) for China.
17. As stated in Sect. 7.1, our analysis assumes minimum wages have no effects on employment or hours. We discuss how this assumption affects the interpretation of our results in the last paragraph of Sect. 7.5.1.
18. We also include several control variables in the equation to try to reduce the concern of endogeneity. First, the city's GDP per capita and CPI (city level) capture aggregate business cycle effects and control for the global financial crisis. Second, the city's level of foreign direct investment (FDI) is used to control for provinces that may restrain the minimum wage to attract foreign investors (Frost 2002).
19. $\widetilde{MW}$ is calculated by correcting the estimation for changes in the minimum wage and changes in the city's median earnings, while Lee (1999) and Autor et al. (2016) use national and state median wages when calculating $\widetilde{MW}$.

20. As in Autor et al. (2016), we start by drawing cities with replacement in our sample and then estimate Eq. (7.1) and apply the coefficients to compute the counterfactual in Eq. (2). We report the standard deviation using 200 replications in Table 7.5.
21. That is, each entry mean is, $\beta_1^q + 2\beta_2^q\,(MW - w^p)$ where variables without the *ct* subscript refer to the sample mean values over all cities and all periods.
22. For all 2SLS models, the weak identification test shows that the instruments are highly significant and able to pass standard diagnostic tests for weak instruments, as suggested in Stock et al. (2002).
23. The spillover effects of the minimum wage are quite evident from our results. However, Autor et al. (2016) provide a mundane but plausible explanation for their findings of spillover effects using US data, which is that it is a measurement error. Since we are using household survey data, and survey data on sensitive questions such as earnings often have considerable measurement error, it is possible that the spillover effects we find may be due to measurement error. On the other hand, Jia and Zhang (2013) find spillover effects of minimum wages in China using longitudinal data at the individual level from the China Health and Nutrition Survey. Their results indicate that spillover effects of the minimum wage increase can reach to 1.50 and 1.25 times of minimum wages on male and female wage distribution, respectively. Although we cannot rule out the possibility of measurement error, our use of IV regression can substantially reduce this concern as shown in Autor et al. (2016).
24. Note that if the endogeneity problem we try to instrument for mainly comes from measurement error, we would expect the 2SLS estimates in Table 7.4. to be smaller (in absolute value) than the OLS estimates. As expected, the upper end of the earnings distribution (p75-p50 and p90-p50) shows that the 2SLS estimates are smaller than the OLS estimates (except specification 1). However, for the lower end (p50-p10 and p50-p25) shows the opposite. There can be two possible reasons. First, it could be possible that the measurement error problem is not the major endogeneity issue (not as severe as we expect in the lower end of the earnings distribution in the data). Second, our instruments marginally pass the Stock and Yogo's weak instrument test, signaling we might have weak instrument issues. Due to lack of data, we are not able to pursue further. Although we cannot rule out these concerns, our conclusions do not change and should be interpreted with caution.

Appendix

See Appendix Tables 7.6 and 7.7.

Table 7.6 OLS and 2SLS estimates of minimum wages on p50-p10 earnings differential: 2004–2009

Dependent variable: p50-p10	*Model*							
	(1)		*(2)*		*(3)*		*(4)*	
Independent variable	*OLS*	*2SLS*	*OLS*	*2SLS*	*OLS*	*2SLS*	*OLS*	*2SLS*
Effective MW	−.173	−.386	−.124	−.351	−.108	−.215	−.053	−.142
	(.306)	(.225)	(.299)	(.232)	(.290)	(.121)	(.297)	(.091)
(Effective MW)^2	−.024	−.154	−.005	−.140	.012	−.083	.018	−.056
	(.125)	(.091)	(.120)	(.094)	(.121)	(.049)	(.125)	(.038)
Observations	989		989		989		989	
City fixed effects	Yes		Yes		Yes		Yes	
Province × Year (interactions)			Yes		Yes		Yes	
City controls					Yes		Yes	
City trends							Yes	
Weak identification test	12.861		10.410		13.657		21.208	
Overidentification test	0.120		0.746		0.797		0.833	
(*p*-value)	(0.73)		(0.39)		(0.31)		(0.27)	

Note The instruments are (1) the log of the real minimum wage, (2) the square of the log of the real minimum wage, and (3) the interaction between the log minimum wage and the average log median real wage for the city over the sample period

Table 7.7 OLS and 2SLS estimates of minimum wages on p50-p25 earnings differential: 2004–2009

Dependent variable: p50-p25	*Model*							
	(1)		*(2)*		*(3)*		*(4)*	
Independent variable	*OLS*	2SLS	*OLS*	*2SLS*	*OLS*	*2SLS*	*OLS*	*2SLS*
Effective MW	−.327	−.194	−.305	−.156	−.226	−.137	−.309	−.120
	(.182)	(.103)	(.180)	(.101)	(.193)	(.077)	(.218)	(.062)
(Effective MW)^2	−.100	−.076	−.088	−.061	−.051	−.053	−.083	−.046
	(.077)	(.042)	(.075)	(.041)	(.080)	(.031)	(.091)	(.025)
Observations	989		989		989		989	
City fixed effects	Yes		Yes		Yes		Yes	
Province × Year (interactions)			Yes		Yes		Yes	
City controls					Yes		Yes	
City trends							Yes	
Weak identification test	12.861		10.410		13.657		21.208	
Overidentification test	0.387		0.908		0.997		1.189	
(*p*-value)	(0.53)		(0.34)		(0.30)		(0.24)	

Note The instruments are (1) the log of the real minimum wage, (2) the square of the log of the real minimum wage, and (3) the interaction between the log minimum wage and the average log median real wage for the city over the sample period

References

Autor D. H., Manning A., Smith C. L. (2016). The contribution of the minimum wage to us wage inequality over three decades: A reassessment. *American Economic Journal: Applied Economics*, 8 (1), 58–99.

Bhorat H., Kanbur R., Mayet N. (2012). Estimating the causal effect of enforcement on minimum wage compliance: The case of South Africa. *Review of Development Economics*, 16, 608–623.

Bosch M., Manacorda M. (2010). Minimum wages and earnings inequality in urban Mexico. *American Economic Journal: Applied Economics*, 2 (4), 128–149.

Brandt L., Holz Carsten A. (2006). Spatial price differences in china: Estimates and implications. *Economic Development and Cultural Change*, 55 (1), 43–86.

Burkhauser R. V., Finegan T. A. (1989). The minimum wage and the poor: The end of a relationship. *Journal of Policy Analysis and Management*, 8 (1), 53–71.

Chan A. (2001). *China's workers under assault: The exploitation of labor in a globalizing economy*. Armonk, NY and London, UK.

Chen, J. (2012). *The employment effect and income distribution effect from the minimum wage standard: Evidence of Chongqing*. Chongqing Normal University (in Chinese).

Cheung S. N. S. (2004). Another eye on minimum wages. *Southern Weekly*.

Cheung S. N. S. (2010). The lethality of minimum wages. *Economic Information Daily*.

Cooke F. L. (2005). *HRM, work and employment in china*. Routledge, London.

Durbin J. (1954). Errors in variables. *Revue de l'Institut International de Statistique / Review of the International Statistical Institute*, 22 (1/3), 23–32.

Fang T., Lin C. (2015). Minimum wages and employment in China. *IZA J Labor Policy*, 4, 22.

Frost S. (2002). Labour standards in China: The business and investment challenge. Association for Sustainable and Responsible Investment in Asia.

Gindling T. H., Mossaad N., Trejos J. D. (2015). The consequences of increased enforcement of legal minimum wages in a developing country: An evaluation of the impact of the campaña nacional de salarios mínimos in Costa Rica. *ILR Review*, 68 (3), 666–707.

Gindling T. H., Terrell K. (2007). The effects of multiple minimum wages throughout the labor market: The case of Costa Rica. *Labour Economics*, 14 (3), 485–511.

Huang Y., Loungani P., Wang G. (2014). *Improving or disappearing: Firm-level adjustments to minimum wages in China*. IMF Working Paper WP/14/184. Retrieved from https://www.imf.org/external/pubs/ft/wp/2014/wp14184.pdf.

Jia P. (2013). Minimum wage effects on employment and income distribution. Jilin University (in Chinese).

Jia P., Zhang S. (2013). Spillover effects of minimum wages increase. *Statistical Research*, 30 (4), 37–41 (in Chinese).

Johnson W. R., Browning E. K. (1983). The distributional and efficiency effects of increasing the minimum wage: A simulation. *American Economic Review*, 73, 204–211.

Lee D. S. (1999). Wage inequality in the United States during the 1980s: Rising dispersion or falling minimum wage? *The Quarterly Journal of Economics*, 114 (3), 977–1023.

Li S., Luo C. (2011). How unequal is China? *Economic Research Journal*, 4, 68–78 (in Chinese).

Li S., Zhao R. (1999). Re-examining the income distribution in China. *Economic Research Journal*, 4 (in Chinese).

Mayneris F., Poncet S., Zhang Y. (2018). Improving or disappearing: Firm-level adjustments to minimum wages in China. *Journal of Development Economics*, 135, 20–42.

National Bureau of Statistics of China. (2013). China labour statistical year book.

Neumark D., Cunningham W., Siga L. (2006). The effects of the minimum wage in Brazil on the distribution of family incomes: 1996–2001. *Journal of Development Economics*, 80 (1), 136–159.

Neumark D., Schweitzer M., Wascher W. (2005). The effects of minimum wages on the distribution of family incomes: A nonparametric analysis. *Journal of Human Resources*, 40 (4), 867–894.

Neumark D., Wascher W. L. (2008). *Minimum wages*. MIT Press, Cambridge, MA.

Quan H., Li L. (2011). The income distribution effect of minimum wage in Shanghai: evidence and simulation. *Shanghai Economic Research*, 4, 96–109.

Rama M. (2001). The consequences of doubling the minimum wage: The case of Indonesia. *Industrial and Labor Relations Review*, 54 (4), 864–881.

Ronconi L. (2010). Enforcement and compliance with labor regulations in Argentina. *Industrial & Labor Relations Review*, 63 (4), 719–736.

Stock J. H., Wright J. H., Yogo M. (2002). A survey of weak instruments and weak identification in generalized method of moments. *Journal of Business & Economic Statistics*, 20 (4), 518–529.

Su H. (1993). Research on the legislation of minimum wage law of China. *Review of Economic Research*, Z1, 26–36 (in Chinese).

Wang D. (2011). On the minimum wage system of china: Probable effects on income distribution and economic development. *Zhejiang Social Sciences*, 2, 11–17 (in Chinese).

Wang D. (2013). Minimum wage effects on income distribution. Jilin University (in Chinese).

Wang H. (2007). *Income distribution and income liquidity of residents in China*. Sun Yat-Sen University (in Chinese).

Wang J., Gunderson M. (2011). Minimum wage impacts in China: Estimates from a prespecified research design, 2000–2007. *Contemporary Economic Policy*, 29 (3), 392–406.

Wen Q. (2007). Research on the effect of minimum wages on rural migrants' employment and income distribution. University of Electronic Science and Technology of China (in Chinese),

World Bank. (2006). Minimum wages in Latin America and the Caribbean: The impact on employment, inequality, and poverty. Office of the Chief Economist, Washington, DC.

Yang T. (2006). What is the social background when China implemented its minimum wage law? *People's Daily*.

Ye L., Gindling T. H., Li S. (2015). Compliance with legal minimum wages and overtime pay regulations in China. *IZA Journal of Labor & Development*, 4 (16), 1–35.

CHAPTER 8

Effects of Minimum Wage Regulations on Wage Growth and Distribution in China

Li Shi and Haiyuan Wan

8.1 Introduction

Since the mid-1980s, overall income inequality in China has shown a stable, increasing trend (Khan and Riskin 2005). Drawing on an analysis based on the household survey data and aggregate data from official sources, many economists attributed the increasing inequality in China to different kinds of policies and regulations (Ravallion and Chen 2007). Furthermore, Chaudhuri and Ravallion (2008) showed that gains from growth had been spread too unevenly because of labor market policies, such as employment protection regulations, labor contract laws, and minimum wage policies, so disadvantaged individuals benefitted little from rapid economic growth in recent years.

L. Shi
Zhejiang University, Zhejiang, China
e-mail: lishi9@zju.edu.cn

H. Wan (✉)
Beijing Normal University, Beijing, China
e-mail: why@bnu.edu.cn

L. Shi and C. Lin (eds.), *Minimum Wages in China*,
https://doi.org/10.1007/978-981-15-2421-9_8

The minimum wage regulation in the labor market in China was further updated in 2004, which aimed to establish fixed, stable minimum wage growth for disadvantaged workers and increase the wage level for low-wage workers. Moreover, the minimum wage regulation has been somewhat more strictly implemented than previous versions, and the level of the minimum wage standard has steadily increased annually since 2005. Many debates related to the updated minimum wage regulation have arisen, particularly with regard to its adverse effect on issues in the labor market, which have presented interesting topics for researchers over the past few decades.

On the one hand, pioneers in the literature, including Stigler (1946) and others, have analyzed the effect of minimum wage policies on wage distribution in the USA and Europe. Their analysis suggested that labor regulations could increase the labor cost and then reduce the labor demand for enterprises. This conclusion was confirmed by the research of Brown (1982), Neumark and Wascher (1995), as the wage level for low-skilled workers would decrease by 1–3% because of a 10% increase in the minimum wage. However, on the other hand, many economists such as Card and Krueger (1994) highlighted the positive effect of labor regulations on wage distribution for low-paid workers; they believed that enterprises could reduce the inspection cost and signal screen cost based on the efficiency wage. Therefore, from the perspective of the theoretical and empirical results above, we argue that the effect of the minimum wage policy on wage distribution is mixed in the USA and European countries.

Regarding the minimum wage in China, its effect on wage distribution is still little documented in China, while the existing literature presents entirely conflicting results. Zhang and Gao (2009) showed that the wage distribution improved as low-skilled workers' wages increased substantially. However, Ding (2010) demonstrated that low-wage enterprises suffered a much larger negative impact from the new minimum wage policy in the short turn, so the labor demand and then the wage level for low-paid workers decreased. The existing literature agrees with the argument that the minimum wage policy affects individuals' wages, but the question of who benefits more remains unclear. In other words, the impact of the minimum wage policy on wage distribution is still ambiguous (Ma et al. 2012). Therefore, evidence-based research is critical for determining the effect of minimum wages to fix a more appropriate minimum wage to ensure the achievement of policy goals without compromising the labor market and economic outcomes.

Therefore, in this article, we empirically investigate the contribution of the minimum wage policy to wage growth and wage distribution in China. Compared to other empirical studies related to the minimum wage policy in China, we have many advantages. First, few papers have empirically analyzed the impact of minimum wages on wage growth and wage distribution, although rising income inequality has become one of the most important issues for China. Second, most of the papers, such as Zhang and Gao (2009), used macro or aggregate dataset to investigate the effect of minimum wages on labor market issues. However, this article uses a microeconomic dataset to incorporate individuals' reactions to the increased minimum pay during the analysis.

8.2 Literature Review

Generally, with regard to papers connecting minimum wages and wage distribution in the literature, most highlight the heterogeneous effect of the minimum wage on different subgroups in the labor market, especially in terms of gender, age, and education groups across different industries and ownership types. However, the results are mixed.

For example, Fajnzylber (2001) in Brazil simply divides the overall market into labor and capital-intensive industries; the wage level in capital-intensive industries is higher than that in labor-intensive industries as there are fewer low-skilled workers in those markets. Based on the empirical evidence, the author finds that the wage level in labor-intensive industries decreases because of the minimum payment so that the wage distribution is worsened as a result of the minimum wage. Other papers also concern the increasing labor cost for enterprises because of the increased minimum wage, which causes less demand for low-paid workers. Research by Neumark and Wascher (2000) in the USA demonstrates that a 10% increase in the minimum wage can cause a 1–3% decrease in wages for low-skilled workers. Moreover, as seen from the Gindling and Terrell (2005) in Costa Rica, the increasing minimum wage increases unemployment in the covered sectors according to the labor demand curve, which makes those low-wage earners become non-wage earners. Additionally, Vedder and Gallaway (2002) find that the minimum wage policy has an adverse effect on eliminating poverty, as the minimum wage policy increases the 2% poverty rate for low-paid workers. With the division of covered and uncovered sectors, Gindling and Terrell (2004) also find that the increased labor supply in the uncovered sectors decreases the market wage, which also reduces the wage level for low-paid workers. As a result, the minimum wage regulation worsens the wage distribution.

However, other papers highlight the positive effect of the policy on improving the wage distribution. Card and Krueger (1994) in the USA distinguish the different impacts of the minimum wage policy for high-skilled and low-skilled workers. As the wage level for skilled is much higher than the minimum wage standard, their wage level is not affected and remains the same in the short turn. However, for low-skilled workers, their wage level increases substantially as a result of the increased minimum wage standard, so the minimum wage can raise the wage share for low-wage families, which could effectively improve the wage distribution. Therefore, the authors find that the rapidly increasing minimum wage has a significantly decreased effect on overall inequality using both secondary and household survey data in the USA since the 1980s.

Lemos (2004) also proposes a channel by which minimum wages lower wage inequality and increased minimum pay could improve the consumption ability of laborers, which increases the number of jobs in the tertiary industry. As the majority of low-wage workers gather within the tertiary or service sectors, the increasing minimum wage could boost the labor demand for low-paid workers. Therefore, the induced demand could overtake the decreased effect to raise low-skilled workers' wages and improve the wage distribution. Additionally, other empirical analyses also find that the minimum wage could improve the wage level for the poor from the perspective of the efficiency wage. Using a model with time series data set from 1983 to 1996, Addison and Blackburn (1999) analyze the relationship between poverty rate and the minimum wage, and they find that the minimum wage has efficiently improved the working efficiency and reduced poverty for young, low-educated workers.

Moreover, regarding empirical research in China, Luo (2007) presents the first paper devoted to connecting the minimum pay and wage distributions. Using the 2005 provincial, cross-sectional dataset, the paper analyzes the effect of a minimum wage on wage inequality while taking the urban-rural wage rate as the dependent variable and the minimum wage as the independent variable. The result is that improvement in the minimum wage reduces wage inequality. Moreover, Ni et al. (2011) analyze the impact of minimum wages on the wage distribution. With the 2000–2005 panel datasets, the authors find that the minimum wage has an insignificant effect on wage distribution, as the regression coefficient is not significant at all. Moreover, Ding (2010) also confirms that the minimum wage is too low to be useful, so the effect of minimum payments on the wage distribution is not significant in China.

As seen from the results above, we conclude that the effect of the minimum wage regulation on wage growth or wage inequality is ambiguous in China, so evidence-based research is critical for obtaining its effect for specific groups. This question is particularly relevant in light of the recent global crisis, which requires a better understanding of how the wage distribution fared during the crisis and what new policy responses can be sought.

8.3 Minimum Wage Policy in China

At present, 80% of the countries in the world implement the "minimum wage regulations" launched by the International Labour Organization (ILO); China first committed to it in 1984. Afterward, China formally launched the "Labour Contract Law of China" in June 1994 to confirm the minimum wage regulation by legislation. From 1995 on, some of the cities in China began to implement the minimum wage policy.

However, as a result of imbalanced employer-employee power and imperfect collective bargaining systems, enterprises have been trying to escape the implementation of the regulation since 1995. As a result, workers' real wages are usually lower than the minimum wage, and laborers' rights cannot be effectively protected. At the same time, some enterprises usually extend the work time and increase the intensity of the labor while still paying the same minimum wage. For those reasons, it is believed that there is a high proportion of low-skilled laborers in China, so their wages are usually lower than the minimum wage, especially in labor-intensive industries (Ding 2010). Additionally, low-educated workers know very little about the minimum wage regulation and cannot use the regulation to protect their labor rights themselves. Most important of all, in practice, the minimum wage regulation in China is not detailed enough to implement when enterprises do not abide by the law, and there are few mandatory measures to punish enterprises if they violate the minimum wage regulation.

Once it became aware of those problems, the Chinese government began to pay special attention to the implementation of the minimum wage policy in practice. To protect workers' benefits, a revised minimum wage regulation was launched in 2004 to better guarantee the implementation of the minimum wage policy. From then on, the regulation began to be strictly implemented. Additionally, the minimum wage level has also steadily increased year after year from 2004. Currently, the minimum wage is nationally widely settled and sets the lowest hourly, daily or monthly remuneration that employers can legally pay to workers. The definition of the minimum wage excludes overtime pay, special subsidies for odious working conditions, and all kinds of nonmonetary income, including social insurance, welfare, and so on. Moreover, when adjusting the minimum wage according to the law, inflation, cost of living, average wage, unemployment, and economic development should be taken into consideration.

By calculating the minimum wage changes from the aggregate data released by the Ministry of Human Resources and Social Security, we obtain the result that, since 1994, the monthly minimum wage standard rose almost 606% by 2013 in nominal terms and approximately 364% in real terms. Meanwhile, the increasing annual rate from 1994 to 2013 was approximately 9% in nominal terms. Moreover, as can be seen in Fig. 8.1, the minimum wage dynamics in China are marked by two periods of development that strongly depended on government policy. A restrictive minimum wage policy was implemented throughout the first period (1994–2004) to achieve economic stabilization and growth. The nominal minimum wage experienced a very strong increase during that period. However, as seen from Fig. 8.2, a striking fact is that the rapid increase has played a crucial role for almost all cities since 2005 to a much more significant extent than that their did in the previous ten years

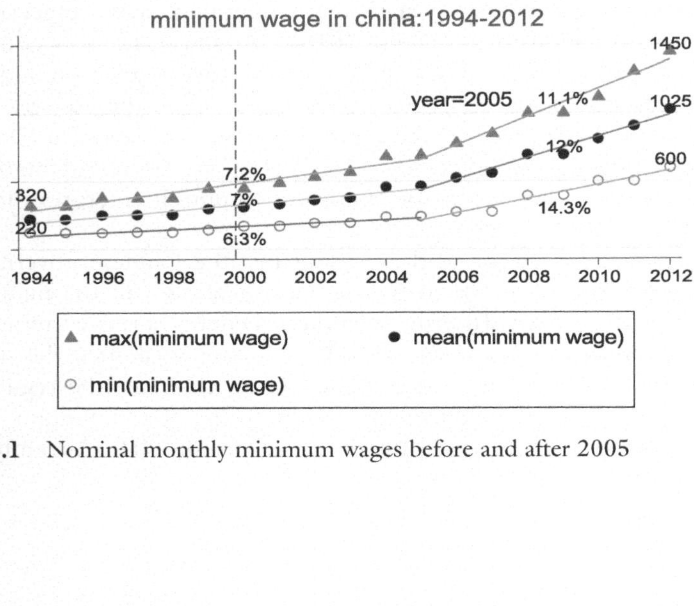

Fig. 8.1 Nominal monthly minimum wages before and after 2005

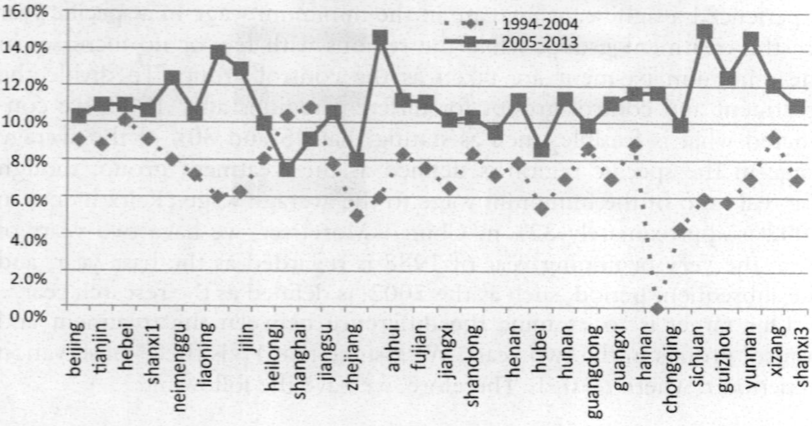

Fig. 8.2 Annual growth rate of the nominal minimum wage during two periods (*Note* As the definitions of the minimum wage in different provinces are not the same, we adjust some cites' minimum wage standards into a unified frame, which is similar to the definitions in Beijing, Shanghai, and Jiangxi)

(1994–2004). On average, the annual growth rate of the minimum wage from 1994 to 2004 was 7%, while the annual growth rate from 2005 to 2013 was approximately 11%. Furthermore, from the perspective of regional minimum wage growth (see Fig. 8.2) from 2005 to 2013, we find that the adjustment of the nominal minimum wage level was larger than its counterpart during the period of 1994–2004.

8.4 Methodology

As a preliminary stage, a simple way to measure the effect of minimum wages on wage growth is to use the OLS approach. However, the causality relationship between minimum pay and wage distribution could be confused by other factors, including average social wages and social security. Therefore, to obtain the effects of minimum wages on wage distribution, we adopt a more sophisticated analysis, typically relying on difference-in-difference (DID) regression analysis.

Regarding the DID method in this article, the fundamental objective is to test whether the wage difference between the treatment and control groups is significant. To be specific, we assume that the regions that experienced a significant increase in the minimum wage in a specific year are the treatment group, while the regions with few or no increases in the minimum payment are taken as the control group. To divide the treatment and control groups for different regions after 1988, we considered what is feasible, such as stating that 25 and 30% of the average wage in the specific region is defined as the treatment group, though the real ratio of the minimum wage to the average wage (Kaitz index) in 2002 is approximately 32% in China.[1] Moreover, we have two years of data; the very beginning year of 1988 is regarded as the base year, and the subsequent period, such as the 2002, is defined as the research year.

Our target is to examine the difference between the treatment and control groups in the two years. We assume that Y_1^T is the ith observation in period t, where $t=0, 1$. Therefore, we have the following:

$$DID = E(Y_1^T - Y_0^T \mid T_1 = 1) - E(Y_1^c - Y_0^c \mid T_1 = 0) = E(G_1 \mid T_1 = 1)$$

where Y_I^T is the outcome of interest (monthly wage in our case) for individual i at time t (with $t=0, 1$). The first term eliminates separate change trends for both groups. Moreover, the second term not only controls the time series trend and some other time-varying factors but also obtains the minimum wage regulation's net impacts on wage level (Bertrand et al. 2004). Moreover, to exclude the compounding effect from other factors, we have to move on to a more sophisticated analysis, typically relying on more explainable variables. Thus, a simple regression specification of the difference-in-differences method would be:

$$Y = \beta_1 + \beta_2\, decision * year + \beta_3\, year + \beta_4\, decision + \beta_5 X + \varepsilon,$$

where Y is wage level, X is the vector of control variables, such as age, gender, and so on, and β_2 is the net effect of minimum wage on wage level.

8.5 Data and Statistical Analysis

8.5.1 Data Description

The microdata used in this article come from the China Household Income Project (CHIPs) in 1988, 2002, 2007, and 2009, which was conducted by the Chinese Academy of Social Science, Beijing Normal

University and National Bureau of Statistics (NBS).[2] The purpose of this survey is to estimate the wage, income, and related economic issues overall in China. The database is selected from significantly larger samples (approximately 65,000 rural households and 35,000 urban households) drawn by the NBS. The purpose of this survey is to examine the social, population, and economic status of residents in China through the collection of information on wages, employment, income, consumption, and so on.

A stratified random sampling method is used to collect the data, and the survey investigates the information at the household and individual levels. Enumerators come to the household and ask about the related wage, income and expenditure information. As we know, the database is a national representative dataset[3] that can be used to investigate the effects of minimum wage policy on wage distribution that covers an extended period across all sectors, industries, and regions in China. Furthermore, the broad cross-sectional data from 1988 to 2009 could effectively solve the problem of time invariance and improve the reliability of causal inferences. Based on the conventional procedures in the wage literature, we also confine our sample to individuals whose age ranges from 15 to 64. After merging and clearing the dataset, we finally obtain 54,185 individuals in 23,604 households.

8.5.2 *Minimum Wages and Wage Definition*

Regarding minimum pay, we only use the monthly minimum wage standard of the traditional minimum wage literature, while the hourly standard is excluded from our article. Moreover, we only keep the highest minimum wage standard, as some cities have implemented two or three standards for different districts. Additionally, the last minimum wage adjustment was used as our final standard as some cities adjust the minimum standard twice within the same year. Moreover, some provinces in specific years do not adjust the minimum wage level, so the minimum wage level in the year before is regarded as the current standard.

Furthermore, regarding the wage level, one point we should keep in mind is that our interest in this paper is to estimate the wage distribution effect coming from the minimum wage policy. Therefore, we only include the wage in this paper, while the real housing subsidy, real health insurance, real unemployment insurance, catering subsidies for meals, or accommodation subsidies are excluded. Moreover, we use the monthly but not hourly wage income as the basic unit because the minimum wage standard is in the form of monthly wages according to the regulation, so the annual wage in our dataset will be transformed into monthly wages in this paper.

The first adjustment in the variables comes from the weighting in our survey. In the microdataset, the observations are not proportional to their share in the national population; therefore, weighting is needed to make the samples nationally representative. Therefore, in this paper, we used the three-level weights based on the population shares of each group within each province and region to adjust the variables.[4] Another adjustment is derived from the price level difference when comparing variables between two years. For comparison over time, it is necessary to deflate the wages using the consumer price indexes published by the NBS to obtain values in constant 2002 prices.

8.5.3 *Wage Growth and Wage Distribution*

By using a comparable wage in different years that eliminates the inflation factor in different periods in our data, we can easily obtain the kernel density distribution of the logarithm of monthly wages from the dataset, which can be seen in Figs. 8.3 and 8.4.

As can be seen in Figs. 8.3 and 8.4, we find that the adjustment of the wage distribution is apparent. Compared to the logarithmic form of the wage distribution in the previous year, the curve in subsequent years substantially moves to the right side. In Fig. 8.3, for example, we distinguish the wage growth and wage distribution effect between 2007 and 2009. After excluding the static wage growth effect, the wage curve in 2007 (*wage_2007_original*) moves directly to the right side (*wage_2007_moved*). Moreover, we can then compare the new moved curve with the curve for 2009 (*wage_2009*).

Therefore, in Fig. 8.3, we find that there is a universal wage increase from the curve of *wage_2007_original* to *wage_2007_moved*. In other words, increasing the minimum wage standard leads to universally higher wages. These "spillovers" or "ripple effects" exist so that skilled workers can also share in the benefits because of the higher demand in response to an increase in the wage floor. Moreover, skilled workers even get slightly higher benefits compared to unskilled workers according to the figure above. Therefore, the potential for such ripple effects is often cited by opponents of the minimum wage. Moreover, when comparing the

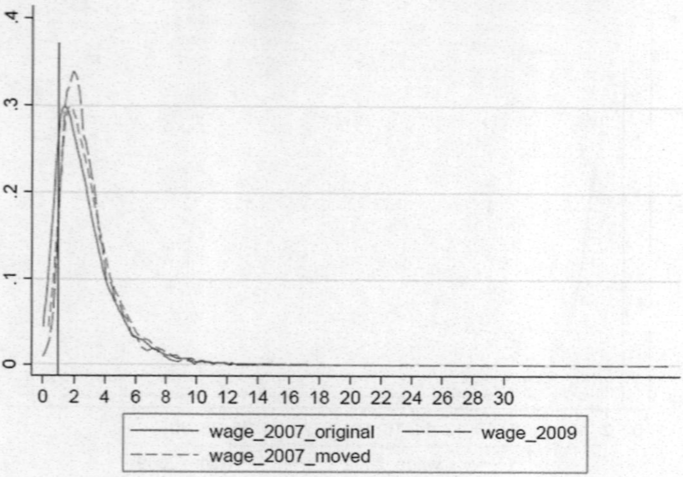

Fig. 8.3 Kernel density of log-monthly wages (*Note* The figure in the horizontal axis is the proportion of the monthly wage to the city-level minimum wage, so the amount of 1 in the horizontal axis is a key threshold to measure the extent of the minimum wage)

new moved curve of ***wage_2007_moved*** and the curve in 2009, it is clear that the curve for 2009 is very left tailed, so there are fewer low-paid workers in 2009 compared to 2007.

While it is not too clear if we list three curves in the same graph of Fig. 8.3, we have also provided the same graph with the years 2002 and 2009, while only the curve that excluded the wage growth effect is listed in Fig. 8.4. An even more apparent distribution effect between two years is found, which probably comes from the minimum wage regulation.

Therefore, from the two figures above, we find that the real effect of the minimum wage on reducing the amount of low-paid workers is significant, as it truncates the lower tail of the wage distribution (below the minimum), and the proportion of low-paid workers decreases dramatically compared with the effects of the previous minimum pay regulation. Moreover, the proportion of workers who earned slightly more than the minimum wage before also receive a positive increase because of the minimum payment. Therefore, overall wage inequality might fall after 2009. However, the above descriptive analysis only provides us with an intuition about the minimum wage's effect, while the causal relationship

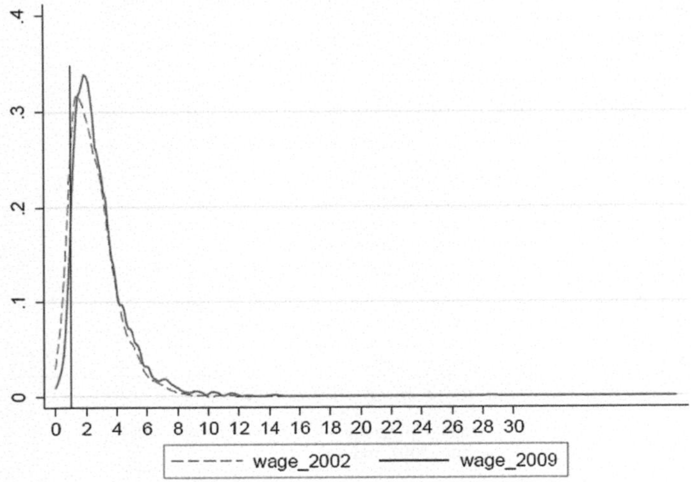

Fig. 8.4 Kernel density of log-monthly wages (*Note* The figure in the horizontal axis is the proportion of the monthly wage to the city-level minimum wage, so the amount of 1 in the horizontal axis is a key threshold to measure the extent of the minimum wage)

between minimum pay and wage distribution is hard to judge without substantial evidence.

8.5.4 *The Effect of the Minimum Wage on Wage Growth*

To obtain the exact impact of the minimum wage on wage growth and its distribution, it is necessary to employ a more sophisticated econometric tool to exclude the disturbing effect from other factors; typically, we rely on DID regression analysis in this section. Notably, by the simple DID, we also take the individual characteristics and other controlled variables into consideration.

Moreover, we use 1988 as a benchmark because no individual is affected by the minimum pay regulation, as it started in 1994 in China. However, for the treatment group in 2002, we have tried to define it many different ways, such as 25 and 30% of the average wage in 2002.[5] Using the DID with the controlled variables method, we obtained the regression results, which can be found in .1 (Table 8.1).

Table 8.1 The effect of minimum wages on wage levels (DID)

	Model 1 (*25% of minimum pay to average wage*)		*Model 2* (*30% of minimum pay to average wage*)		*Model 3* (*30% of minimum pay to average wage*)		*Model 4* (*30% of minimum pay to average wage*)	
	1988–2002		*1988–2002*		*1988–2007*		*1988–2009*	
	Coefficient	*se*	*Coefficient*	*se*	*Coefficient*	*se*	*Coefficient*	*se*
rmw_agg	1.552***	(0.160)	2.089***	(0.092)	3.762***	(0.186)	5.603***	(0.547)
rpgdp	0.043***	(0.006)	0.008***	(0.002)	0.010**	(0.004)	0.004	(0.015)
rwage_agg	0.941***	(0.057)	0.285***	(0.032)	1.165***	(0.089)	0.798***	(0.114)
lowedu_agg	−4.695***	(0.882)	1.422	(0.890)	−4.432***	(1.506)	−16.377**	(7.101)
emp_agg	8.533***	(2.470)	−2.055	(1.345)	27.574***	(3.025)	55.847***	(10.408)
Age2	−0.398***	(0.070)	−0.944***	(0.077)	−1.346***	(0.120)	−0.782***	(0.216)
Age	37.411***	(5.804)	78.038***	(6.626)	111.822***	(10.425)	51.254***	(18.489)
Gender	171.428***	(11.831)	374.411***	(13.675)	514.507***	(20.941)	391.943***	(40.964)
Ethty	9.372	(28.819)	24.983	(36.496)	−1.153	(60.512)	38.079	(112.686)
Marry	66.692***	(23.805)	142.148***	(26.765)	171.284***	(40.696)	70.160	(81.476)
Manual worker	−368.35***	(18.941)	−666.388***	(26.110)	−1,057.51***	(47.675)	−164.733**	(71.356)
Office worker	−288.80***	(19.311)	−530.278***	(25.224)	−824.801***	(44.645)	−257.966***	(57.843)
Professional	27.425	(20.186)	−40.451	(26.983)	231.997***	(47.857)	218.479***	(64.515)
Constant	−928.77***	(131.629)	−1752.0***	(143.631)	−3863.45***	(261.27)	−3381.0***	(538.775)
Observations	9402		9402		15,270		6156	
R-squared	0.238		0.288		0.247		0.151	

Note (1) Standard errors are in parentheses, $^{***}p<0.01$, $^{**}p<0.05$, $^{*}p<0.1$; (2) The basement group of the occupation is managers, officials, and others; (3) Variable definitions can be found in Table 8.5

In model 1, 25% of the minimum wage to the average wage is defined as the treatment group, while the others are the control group. Additionally, 30% of the minimum wage to the average wage in model 2 is regarded as the treatment group. However, regardless of how the treatment and control groups are defined, the impact coefficient of the minimum wage on wage growth is significantly positive. Moreover, the stricter the treatment group is defined, the larger the policy effect is on wage growth in models 1 and 2. On average, there is a 2.1% increase in the wage level triggered by the minimum wage, even if we control for many factors in model 2.

Moreover, since the minimum wage before 2002 could reasonably affect wage growth, we also consider that the impact could appear more substantial after 2004, as the minimum pay is dramatically increased and the law is also significantly enhanced in practice in 2004. The result in model 3 during the period of 1988–2007 is indeed larger, as there is a 3.8% increase in wage level because of the policy. Moreover, the result in model 4 also provided evidence, with the data from 1988 to 2009, that 5.6% of the positive increase in the wage level comes from the minimum wage regulation.

In total, from the perspective of the positive coefficients of minimum payments on the average wage level, the overall effect of a minimum wage in the three models is to boost the wage level, as the effect of a minimum wage is significantly positive, and the effect is even larger in 2007 and 2009 than in 2002. We argue that this change might be the reason for the new minimum wage regulation in 2005, as it is much more strictly implemented, and the minimum pay standard is dramatically increased.

8.6 Robustness Checks

8.6.1 Control Group Redefinition

Apart from the results in Sect. 8.6, we are still worried about the stability of the regressions in the different models, so in this section, we change the definition of the control group and treatment group again to test the regression robustness. In general, we propose a new solution that is based on a redefinition of the control group. Instead of defining controls as those that never participate, we define controls as those that did not participate until a certain period. Hence, the corresponding parameter of

Table 8.2 The effect of a minimum wage on wage levels (DID)

	Variable redefinition		*Sample adjustment*					
	Model 1 1988–2002		*Model 2* 2002–2007		*Model 3* 2007–2009		*Model 4* 2002–2009	
	Coefficient	*se*	*Coefficient*	*se*	*Coefficient*	*se*	*Coefficient*	*se*
rmw_agg	2.064***	(0.160)	2.092***	(0.092)	2.306***	(0.149)	3.372***	(0.140)
rpgdp	0.044***	(0.006)	0.008***	(0.002)	0.011***	(0.004)	0.024***	(0.004)
rwage_agg	0.944***	(0.057)	0.283***	(0.032)	0.210***	(0.046)	0.443***	(0.038)
lowedu_agg	−4.745***	(0.882)	1.383	(0.889)	2.129	(1.490)	−4.526***	(1.074)
emp_agg	8.675***	(2.469)	−2.137	(1.346)	4.824**	(2.281)	5.790***	(1.807)
Age2	−0.375***	(0.071)	−0.936***	(0.079)	−1.179***	(0.106)	−0.639***	(0.086)
Age	35.600***	(5.877)	77.411***	(6.718)	94.513***	(9.138)	50.435***	(7.221)
Gender	170.757***	(11.830)	374.485***	(13.669)	499.520***	(18.863)	252.067***	(15.211)
Ethty	7.829	(28.838)	22.699	(36.515)	21.357	(53.768)	1.517	(38.465)
Marry	69.044***	(23.846)	141.907***	(26.800)	185.838***	(36.739)	63.836**	(30.506)
Manual worker	−369.138***	(18.942)	−666.659***	(26.085)	−682.508***	(38.341)	−323.478***	(24.450)
Office worker	−289.278***	(19.317)	−530.659***	(25.202)	−483.859***	(34.534)	−266.720***	(23.422)
Professional	25.516	(20.185)	−42.291	(26.967)	67.624*	(37.557)	101.382***	(25.095)
Constant	−898.686***	(132.555)	−1,735.18***	(144.867)	−2,196.25***	(215.832)	−1,066.08***	(155.823)
Observations	9402		11,340		6156		6156	
R-squared	0.238		0.288		0.208		0.318	

Note (1) All the regressions are the same as those in Table 8.1, except the methodology and sample changes; (2) the definition of the control variables can be found in Appendix; (3) standard errors are presented in parentheses, ***$p<0.01$, **$p<0.05$, *$p<0.1$

interest in this setting is then defined as the effect of joining a program now rather than waiting longer.[6]

As seen from Table 8.2, the effect of a minimum wage on wage growth is almost the same as the results before. On average, a 1% increase in the minimum wage leads to a 2.1% increase in wage level. Moreover, it is sufficient to obtain consistent estimates from the 1% significance level.

8.6.2 Sample Adjustments

Moreover, apart from changing the control group definition, we also test the regression stability using different samples. While using the year 2002 or 2007 as the base year, we present the regression results in Table 8.2.

As seen from Table 8.2, in all the sub-samples of 2002–2007, 2007–2009, and 2002–2009, the coefficient of the minimum wage on wage growth is significantly positive. Moreover, the extent of impact increases with the maintenance of the minimum wage regulation. On average, a 1% increase in the minimum wage creates a 2.1% increase in wage growth from 2002 to 2007, while the increase is 2.3 and 3.4% for the period of 2007–2009 and 2002–2009, respectively.

8.7 Heterogeneous Effect of a Minimum Wage on Wage Distribution

8.7.1 Heterogeneous Effects Across Industries

Furthermore, considering the heterogeneous wage structure and wage decision mechanisms in different industries, it is necessary to distinguish the heterogeneous effects across different industries and ownership types.

In Table 8.3, we compared the minimum wage's impact on different ownership types. Moreover, the results demonstrate that the minimum wage creates a positive wage growth effect for private owned/holding enterprises and public service units. However, the effect of the minimum wage on government agencies, party agencies, and other ownership enterprises is not significant.

Furthermore, from the perspective of the effect on different industries, in the wholesale and retail trade, electricity, gas and water supply and service, information transmission, computer services and software

Table 8.3 Robustness check across ownership types and industries (DID)

	Ownership				*Industry*					
	①	②	③	④	①	②	③	④	⑤	⑥
mw_agg	3.934***	1.436***	1.160	0.364	0.338	−3.046	2.187	4.227***	3.656***	−6.594***
	(1.352)	(0.339)	(2.944)	(0.379)	(0.570)	(2.067)	(2.124)	(1.266)	(0.520)	(0.570)
Aggregate variables	yes	yes	yes	yes	yes	yes	yes	yes	yes	yes
Individual variables	yes	yes	yes	yes	yes	yes	yes	yes	yes	yes
Observations	3282	8077	1073	4085	2957	516	1541	2801	7042	360
R-squared	0.461	0.599	0.149	0.233	0.537	0.870	0.548	0.145	0.472	0.605

Note (1) We categorize the different ownership types as ①private owned/holding enterprises, ②public service unit, ③government agencies and party agencies, and ④other enterprises. (2) We classify industries as ①manufacturing; ②construction; ③transportation, storage and post industry; ④wholesale and retail trade, electricity, gas and water supply and service, information transmission, computer services and software industry, financial intermediation, real estate industry; ⑤public service, education, health, social security and social welfare, culture, sport and entertainment, public management and social organization, international organizations; ⑥agriculture, forestry, animal husbandry, fisheries, mining, hotel and catering services and others. (3) All the control variables are the same as those in Table 1, while the definitions are presented in the Appendix. Standard errors are presented in parentheses, ***$p<0.01$, **$p<0.05$, *$p<0.1$. (4) As all the combinations are between two different years, the basic results are almost the same, so in this table, we only keep the results for 1988 and 2002

industry, financial intermediation, real estate industry, the impact coefficient of the minimum wage is shown to be significantly positive at the 1% level. This finding demonstrates that the minimum wage helps to boost wage growth in those industries. Additionally, the positive effect of the minimum wage is found in public service et al. industries as well. Moreover, both industry categories are regarded as skilled-intensive industries, as there are many skilled workers in those industries. However, apart from the positive effect on the industries above, the increase in the minimum wage induces negative wage growth in the agriculture, forestry, animal husbandry, fisheries, mining, hotel and catering services, and other industries (generally, those are regarded as low-skilled-intensive industries by Ni et al. [2011]); thus, the minimum wage produces more low-paid workers in those industries. Therefore, the minimum wage in those industries does not truncate or thin out the lower tail of the wage distribution (below the minimum), as predicted by the Card and Krueger (1994), but creates a substitute effect for the unskilled workers in those industries.

As shown in Table 8.3, an increase in the minimum wage leads to more wages for the group that is higher up in the wage distribution. These spillovers or ripple effects increase as skilled workers substitute away from the lowest-skilled workers in some industries and toward workers with somewhat higher skills in response to an increase in the wage floor. Thus, the wages of workers earning above the minimum wage are pushed up by the increase in the demand for their services.

8.7.2 Heterogeneous Effects Across Population Groups

However, getting the overall effect is not enough for us to examine the heterogeneous effect of minimum wages on different population groups, so in this section, we go further to conduct a sensitivity analysis regarding the heterogeneous impacts on wage distribution.

In Table 8.4, we specifically introduced the interaction term of minimum wage variables and different dummy variables into the regression, so the comparison of the results obtained by a further check in the different groups yields additional insights.

As model 1 in Table 8.4 shows, the coefficients of the interaction term for college and above are significantly larger at the 1% level compared to that of other education groups. All else being equal, a 1% increase in the minimum wage leads to a wage increase of 1.519% more for the college

Table 8.4 Heterogeneous effect of minimum wages on wage distribution (DID)

	(1)	*(2)*	*(3)*	*(4)*	*(5)*	*(6)*	*(7)*	*(8)*
MW*college and above	1.519*** (0.482)							
MW*technical school		0.477 (0.765)						
MW*upper middle school			−1.154** (0.519)					
MW*lower middle school				−1.220** (0.567)				
MW* primary and below					−1.321** (0.571)			
MW*with labor contract						1.101* (0.650)		
MW*gender							1.378*** (0.468)	
MW* *hukou*								1.326 (1.204)
Individual variables	yes	yes	yes	yes		yes	yes	yes
Aggregate variables	yes	yes	yes	yes		yes	yes	yes
Observations	16,496	16,496	16,496	16,496	16,496	1173	16,518	1180
R-squared	0.387	0.387	0.387	0.388	0.387	0.510	0.388	0.373

Note (1) In model 5, the control group is the group of working without a labor contract, and the basement group, for models 6 and 7, is the female and rural *hukou* group. (2) The individual and aggregate variables in this table are the same as those in model 3 of Table 8.1. (3) Standard errors are in parentheses, ***$p<0.01$, **$p<0.05$, *$p<0.1$. (4) As all the combinations are between the two different years, the basic results are almost the same, so in this table, we only keep the results for 1988 and 2002

educated and above than for the other education groups. In sum, the minimum wage not only exerts an impact on the low-educated group but also has a larger positive effect on the educated population.

Additionally, we also estimate the impact of the minimum wage policy on the actual wage distribution for groups with and without a labor contract. As seen from model 6, the impact of the minimum wage is mainly concentrated on the population with stable labor contracts. Our estimates suggest that if the minimum wage grows by 1%, there will be a 1.101% greater increase in wages for the population with labor contracts than its counterpart. Therefore, the increase in the minimum wage leads to more of a positive impact on the population in the covered sector, as most of the workers with labor contracts are gathered in the formal work sector. Similarly, the positive effect of minimum wages on wage growth for the male group is more significant than that for the female group according to model 7.

Overall, the evidence presented in this table indicates that a minimum wage has a heterogeneous effect on different population groups, especially on skilled and unskilled workers and formal and informal workers. According to the evidence from China, a minimum wage creates a spike in the wage distribution and appears to provide a positive ripple effect to wages for skilled workers. However, the amount of the impact coming from the minimum wage is rather small.

8.8 Conclusions

At the beginning of the new millennium, the increasing minimum wage level attracted the attention of the public in China, and many opposing voices from the media were also raised. In particular, from 2005, increases in the nominal minimum wage standard accelerated, so the increasing minimum wage was partly blamed by economists for triggering extra labor costs and decreases in the labor force demand resulting in a decreased employment rate and weakened economic competitiveness. Therefore, analyzing the effect of minimum wages on the labor market, especially on wage growth and wage distribution, has been particularly important in recent years.

The target of this paper is to examine how minimum wage changes affect wage growth, both for low-wage workers and for workers higher up in the wage distribution. Additionally, the paper also explains the reason, based on the minimum wage, for the wage growth differences in recent years among different groups and assesses the effects of the minimum wage that are closely related to the development of the labor market.

With the microdataset for 1988, 2002, 2007, and 2009, we found that the minimum wage helps boost wage growth for workers on average. Moreover, we have also obtained the heterogeneous impact of the minimum wage policy on subgroups and found that workers that earn slightly more than the minimum wage receive higher benefits, though the low-paid population also experience a slight wage increase.

Therefore, we conclude that it is necessary to be more prudent in raising the minimum wage standard because of the ripple or leak effects on high-paid workers, although the original objective of the minimum wage is kindly intended to improve the conditions for low-paid workers. A minimum wage forbids workers from selling their labor below a certain price and therefore is expected to create unemployment for low-productivity workers in a competitive labor market. Therefore, by combining the weak effect of minimum wages on earnings for unskilled workers in China in our paper, our evidence also empirically supports the view that the low-wage labor market can be reasonably approximated by the competitive framework; thus, the minimum wage increase creates a substitute effect for unskilled workers, which finally induces lower wage growth for low-paid workers. Moreover, the wages of workers earning more than the minimum wage before are pushed up by the increase in demand because of the ripple effect, so the wage level for workers earning more than the minimum wage is even higher than it was before.

Considering the weak effect of minimum wages on the wage distribution for low-paid populations, we argue that using a minimum wage as a direct tool for social security policy and substantially raising the minimum wage level is not currently a sensible choice for China. Despite the increasing income inequality in the past years and the hard living conditions of low-paid workers, we should consider other policy options to improve their wage level, decrease poverty and alleviate income inequality, but we should not do so though the minimum wage increases.

Appendix

See Appendix Table 8.5

Table 8.5 Definition of variables

	Variable definition
Dependent variable	
wage_m	Monthly wages for each worker (unit: *yuan*)
Aggregate variables	
mw_agg	Monthly minimum wages in the prefecture level (unit: *yuan*)
low_wage	We define low-wage workers as the population below the minimum wage standard in each city (%)
pgdp	The yearly GDP per capita in the prefecture level (unit: *yuan*)
wage_agg	The yearly average wage per capita in the prefecture level (unit: *yuan*)
lowedu_agg	Proportion of low education (literacy group) to the overall population (ranges from 0 to 1)
emp_agg	Employment rates for the workers in the provincial level (unit: %)
Individual level variables	
Gender	Dummy variable: male = 1
Age	Individuals' age, while only keeps the obs whose age ranges from 15 to 64
Age2	Age square
Marriage status	Dummy variable: being married = 1, others = 0
Ethnicity	Han ethnicity is defined as 1, others to be 0
Education level	Five levels of education (college and above = 5, technical school = 4, upper-middle school = 3, lower middle school = 2, primary and below = 1)
Occupation	Four occupation categories (manual worker = 1, office worker = 2, professional = 3, managers and officials, others = 4)
Other variables	
Regional effects	Dummy variables for the provinces (16 dummies)
Other effects	Dummy variables for the year of 1988, 2002, 2007, and 2009

Notes

1. According to the calculation by authors, the Kaitz index ranges from 20 to 60% in China during 1994–2013, while the mean ratio of the minimum wage to the average wage is around 32%. Moreover, the Kaitz index in most of provinces is around 20–30%. Therefore, the way to define the treatment group in our paper is using the Kaitz index; we will take 25 and 30% as the threshold to define the treatment group step by step and test the regression stabilization for different possibilities.
2. As for the data in the year of 2007 and 2009, it mainly comes from RUMIC (Rural to urban migration in China) dataset. And it was conducted by Beijing Normal University and National University of Australia.
3. In the microdataset, the observations are not proportional to their shares in the national population; therefore, weights are needed in order to make the samples nationally representative. Specifically, we used the three-level weights based on the population shares of each group (urban, rural) within each province and region.
4. The details about the weighting using the data provided by the NBS from the 2000 census and the 1% population sample survey in 2005 can be found in Song et al. (2011).
5. We only use 25 and 30% to define the treatment group in Table 8.1, as 40 and 55% yield the same results.
6. Fredriksson (2004) formalize their approach and argue that the standard way of defining a control group might lead to biased results because the unconfoundedness assumption might be violated. The reason for this is that, in the standard approach, the treatment indicator itself is defined as conditional on future outcomes.

References

Addison, John T., and McKinley L. Blackburn. (1999). "Minimum Wages and Poverty." *Industrial and Labor Relations Review*, 52(3): 393–409.

Bertrand, M., E. Duflo, and S. Mullainathan. (2004). "How Much Should We Trust Differences-in-Differences Estimates?" *Quarterly Journal of Economics*, 119(1): 249–275.

Brown C., C. Gilroy, and A. Kohen. (1982). "The Effect of the Minimum Wage on Employment and Unemployment." *Journal of Economic Literature*, 20(2, June): 487–528.

Card, David, and Alan Krueger. (1994). "Minimum Wages and Employment: A Case Study of the Fast Food Industry in New Jersey and Pennsylvania." *American Economic Review* 84(September): 772–793.

Chaudhuri, Shubham, and Martin Ravallion. (2008). "Uneven Growth in China and India." *Economic Research*, 1: 4–20.

Fajnzylber, Pablo. (2001). *Minimum Wage Effects Throughout the Wage Distribution: Evidence from Brazil's Formal and Informal Sectors*. Belo Horizonte: Cedeplar, Universidade Federal de Minas Gerais.

Fredriksson, Johansson P. (2004). "Dynamic Treatment Assignment-The Consequences for Evaluations Using Observational Data." Discussion Paper Nr. 1062, IZA Bonn.

Gindling, Thomas, and Katherine Terrell. (2004, May). "The Effects of Multiple Minimum Wages Throughout the Labor Market." IZA Discussion Paper No. 1159.

Gindling, T.H., and Katherine Terrell. (2005). "The Effect of Minimum Wages on Actual Wages in the Formal and Informal Sectors in Costa Rica." *World Development*, 33(11): 1905–1921.

Khan, Aziz, and Riskin Carl. (2005). "Household Income and Its Distribution in China, 1995 and 2002." *China Quarterly*, June, 1.

Lemos, Sara. (2004). *The Effects of the Minimum Wage on Wages and Employment in Brazil: A Menu of Minimum Wage Variables*. London: University College London, unpublished.

Luo, Xiaolan. (2007). "An Analysis on the Minimum Wage's Employment Effect Over the Rural Workers in China." *Journal of Finance and Economics*, 133(111): 114–123 (in Chinese).

Ma, S., J. Zhang, and X. Zhu. (2012). "The Effect of Minimum Wage on Average Wage and Employment." *Economic Research Journal*, 2012(5): 132–146 (in Chinese).

Neumark, David, and William Wascher. (1995). "Minimum-Wage Effects on School and Work Transitions of Teenagers." *American Economic Review*, 85(2): 244–249.

Neumark, David, and William Wascher. (2000). "Minimum Wages and Employment: A Case Study of the Fast-Food Industry in New Jersey and Pennsylvania: Comment." *American Economic Review*, 90(5, December): 1362–1396.

Ni, J., G. Wang, and X. Yao. (2011). "Impact of Minimum Wages on Employment: Evidence from China." *Chinese Economy*, 44: 18–38.

Ravallion, Martin, and Chen Shaohua. (2007). "China's Uneven Progress Against Poverty." *Journal of Development Economics*, 82(1): 1–42.

Shouhai, Ding. (2010). "An Analysis of Minimum Wage Effects on the Labour Market—Effect of Interaction with the Law of the PRC on Employment Contracts." *Social Science in China*, 2010(1): 85–102 (in Chinese).

Song, Jin, Terry Sicular, and Ximing Yue. (2011). "Appendix II: The 2002 and 2007 CHIP Surveys: Sampling, Weights, and Combining the Urban, Rural and Migrant Samples." University of Western, Ontario, CIBC Working Paper, October.

Stigler, G.J. (1946). "The Economics of Minimum Wage Legislation." *American Economic Review*, 36(3, June): 358–365.
Vedder, R., and L. Gallaway. (2002). "The Minimum Wage and Poverty Among Full-Time Workers." *Journal of Labor Research*, XXIII(1): 41–49.
Zhang, J.W., and S.M. Gao. (2009). "An Analysis on the Impact of Labor Contract Law on Labor Markets." *Chinese Journal of Population Science*, 2009(2): 26–33.

CHAPTER 9

Compliance with Legal Minimum Wages and Overtime Pay in China, Effects Across the Distribution of Wages

Linxiang Ye, Tim Gindling and Li Shi

9.1 Introduction

Although most developing countries have extensive labor regulations, compliance is generally low (i.e., Maloney and Mendez 2004; Ronconi 2010; Strobl and Walsh 2003). There is a growing theoretical and empirical literature on the problem of non-compliance with minimum wage laws in developing countries (i.e., Gindling et al. 2015; Andalon and Pages 2008; Basu et al. 2010). Compliance with minimum wages has also generated research in China (Fang and Lin 2013; Yang et al. 2014;

L. Ye
Nanjing University of Finance and Economics, Nanjing, China
e-mail: dashuihe@sina.com

T. Gindling (✉)
University of Maryland, Baltimore County, Baltimore, MD, USA
e-mail: tgindlin@umbc.edu

L. Shi
Zhejiang University, Zhejiang, China
e-mail: lishi9@zju.edu.cn

L. Shi and C. Lin (eds.), *Minimum Wages in China*,
https://doi.org/10.1007/978-981-15-2421-9_9

Xie 2010; Sun and Shu 2011; Du and Wang 2008; Ye et al. 2015; Ye and Yang 2015). Almost all of these papers use data from before 2010. However, unlike from 1995 to 2010, minimum wage increases tend to be higher than increases in average wages after 2010, so that the minimum wage/average wage ratio has been increasing gradually from 2010 to 2014. What is more important, a new Labor Contract Law of the People's Republic of China took effect on May 1, 2008.

The Labor Contract Law led to important changes in the way minimum wages and overtime pay are enforced. The 2008 Law makes it clear that on the date an employer recruits an employee a written labor contract shall be signed to establish a formal labor relationship. So we could expect that after 2008 employees could more easily claim their rights, including (as made explicit in the new labor law) minimum wages and restrictions on the maximum number of hours an employee can work in one week. To focus on the impact of the new Labor Contract Law, in this article we use data from before 2008 and after 2008 to examine changes in compliance with minimum wage and overtime laws. Specifically, we examine changes between 2007 and 2013. One reason for using these two years is that the minimum wage to average wage ratio (the "bite" of the minimum wage) is similar in 2007 and 2013, so that any changes that we see are likely not due to changes in the level of minimum wages in the labor market.

Minimum wages in China are set as monthly wages for full-time workers, so we begin by measuring the fraction of workers whose monthly earnings are below the monthly minimum wage. We find that the proportion of employees earning less than the monthly minimum wage increased from 3.91% in 2007 to 7.32% in 2013. However, when we consider overtime hours and calculate an implicit hourly wage, the proportion of workers earning less than the hourly minimum wage is much higher than the proportion earning less than the monthly minimum wage (13.64% in 2007). This is because low-wage workers are more likely to work overtime hours and yet not be paid for additional work. In a previous paper (Ye et al. 2015), we showed that while employers in China mostly pay above the monthly minimum wage, a large proportion of low-wage employees work overtime hours but that employers do not comply with overtime pay laws and either do not pay workers for these overtime hours, or pay less than required.

What is also interesting is that the proportion of workers earning below the hourly minimum wage declined from 2007 to 2013 (from 13.64 to 12.74%), at the same time that the proportion of workers earning below the monthly minimum wage increased. Why did the proportion of workers earning less than the monthly minimum wage increase while the proportion of workers earning below the hourly minimum wage decrease? We present evidence in this article that between 2007 and 2013 the overtime hours worked by low-wage workers in China declined, while their monthly wages did not (or at least declined more slowly). Thus, average hourly wages of low-wage workers increased. We argue that the decline in unpaid overtime hours was related to the increased compliance with overtime pay regulations after the 2008 Labor Contract Law.

Finally, we use a newly developed empirical technique to measure not only the number of workers earning less than the minimum wage, but also the degree to which sub-minimum wage workers are earning less than the minimum wage (Bhorat et al. 2013). In the empirical literature, a standard way of measuring non-compliance is as the fraction of all covered workers whose wages are below the minimum. However, this measure does not distinguish between different degrees of violation. For example, a wage just below the minimum is counted the same as a wage at one-third of the minimum, surely an inexact way to measure a violation of the regulation. In this article, we present a family of violation indices that can emphasize the depth of violation to different degrees.

While we find that while the fraction of workers earning below the hourly minimum wage fell between 2007 and 2013, we also find that the average wage shortfall of workers earning below the minimum wage increased. This is because although there was a decrease in the number of workers earning just below the minimum wage, there was also an increase in the number of workers earning well below the minimum wage. This is consistent with the hypothesis put forward in Bhorat et al. (2015) that increased enforcement could lead to partial compliance with minimum wage laws, where employers increase the earnings of those just below the minimum wage to the minimum wage (for whom compliance with minimum wage laws is relatively inexpensive), but continue to pay those with very low human capital below the minimum wage.

9.2 Legal Minimum Wages and Overtime Pay Regulations in China

Prior to 1994, China had no minimum wage regulations. In 1993, the first regulations on minimum wages were issued by the Labor Ministry of China (the "Enterprise Minimum Wage Regulations"). In July 1994, a minimum wage was written into China's new version of the labor law. Clause 48 of that law states that all types of enterprises in China should comply with paying local minimum wages.

In 2004, the Enterprises Minimum Wage Regulations were replaced by more general Minimum Wages Regulations issued by the Department of Labor and Social Security. In these regulations, the adjustment frequency of minimum wages was set to be no less than once every two years and coverage was extended to town-village enterprises, to employees in micro-enterprises, and to part-time workers. Penalties for violations were increased substantially from an earlier range of 20–100% of the wage that was owed to a new range of 100–500% of the wage that was owed. Restrictions were also placed on what employers could include as part of the wage when comparing to the minimum wage (Wang and Gunderson 2012). In determining if the wage is above the legal minimum, employers must not include overtime pay and legally mandated supplements to the wage such as those for night shifts and dangerous environmental conditions such as high temperature, low temperature, underground working conditions, and working in poisonous or noxious conditions.

Minimum wages are set relative to monthly earnings. The monthly minimum wage is based on a 40-hour workweek. According to labor regulations passed in 1994, laborers shall work no more than eight hours per day, five days per week. After consultation with trade unions and workers, a firm can extend the workday. If workers work more than the legal maximum of 40 hours per week, they must be paid at least 150% the wage they receive for regular hours, at least 200% of the regular wage if the overtime is on a "day of rest" (weekend), and at least 300% the regular wage if the overtime is on a statutory holiday. Fines for violating overtime pay regulations include back pay plus an additional 50 to 100% of the wage owed.[1]

On May 1, 2008, the Labor Contract Law of the People's Republic of China took effect. Article 7 of the Labor Contract Law of the People's Republic of China states that an employer's labor relations with an employee shall be established on the date it recruits the employee. The employer shall keep the records of its employees for references. Article 10 of the Labor Contract Law of the People's Republic of China states that a written labor contract shall be concluded in establishing a labor relationship. So we expect an employee will be able to more easily claim their rights after the Labor Contract Law of the People's Republic of China took effect.

Minimum wages and overtime regulations were also part of the Labor Contract Law. Article 20 states that the wage of the employee shall not be less than the minimum wage rate in the place where the employer is located. Article 31 states that the employers shall strictly implement the work quota standards and shall not force or in a disguised manner force the employees to work overtime. Where the employers arrange for employees to work overtime, overtime payment shall be paid to the employees in accordance with relevant state regulations. Article 85 states that if a violation is found, the labor administration authority shall order the employer to pay labor remuneration, overtime pay or economic compensation within a prescribed period of time; where the standard of the labor remuneration is lower than the local minimum wage rate the employer shall make up the balance. Where the due payment is not made within the time limit, the employer shall be ordered to pay additional damages to the employee ranging from 50 to 100% of the amount payable. In effect, minimum wage and overtime pay regulations become more strict after the Labor Contract Law of the People's Republic of China took effect on May 1, 2008.

There is no unified minimum wage level for the entire nation. Instead, the task of setting minimum wages is delegated to the local governments. Clause 48 of the 1994 labor law requires that local governments set the minimum wage according to five principles: local minimum living expenses; the average wage level; local productivity; unemployment; and local economic development. In practice, each province-level government determines several possible minimum wage levels that could be adopted by local governments, generally three to five levels, according to local economic conditions and living standards. Then each prefectural city-level government within the province-level administrative area chooses the appropriate minimum wage levels from this published list, also based on local economic conditions and living standards. The law provides considerable flexibility for provinces and prefectural cities in setting their minimum wages. Typically, urban and suburban counties within a prefectural city have different minimum wage

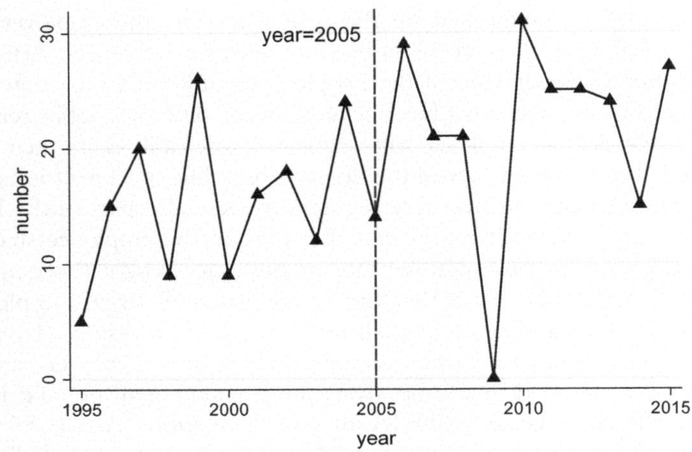

Fig. 9.1 The number of provinces which adjusted minimum wages

levels. Consequently, not only each province-level administrative area but also each prefectural city-level administrative area may have multiple county-level minimum wages.

Figure 9.1 gives a demonstration of the number of provinces which adjusted minimum wages in each year. We can see from Fig. 9.1 that there is an apparent shift in the number of provinces that raised the minimum wage standards in 2004, indicating that the minimum wage adjustment had become more frequent since that year. We can also see that there are no provinces which adjusted minimum wages in 2009. The reason is that at the end of 2008 the Department of Human Resources and Social Security instructed local governments to restrain from increasing minimum wages in 2009 as a way to ease the negative influence of international financial crisis. However, as the influence of financial crisis faded, there was a new round of minimum wages increase since 2010. In 2010, 30 of the 31 provinces increased minimum wages and the average increase was around 20%.

In order to measure the minimum wage standard at a national level, we first calculate average minimum wages in each province according to minimum wages applied in different regions in that province. We then calculate weighted average minimum wages with the weight being the actual days of implementation of each minimum wage.

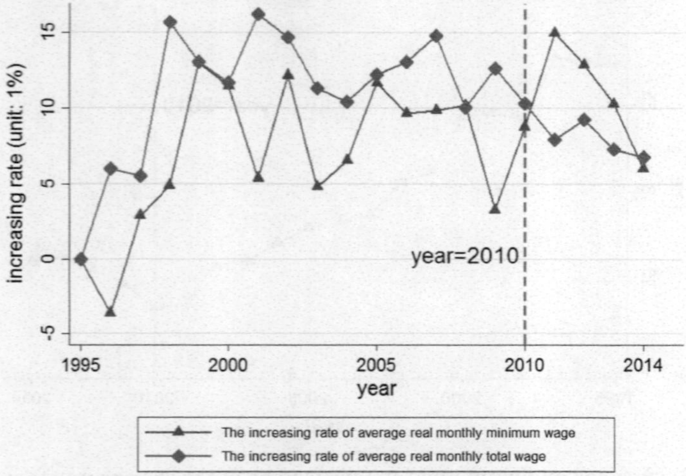

Fig. 9.2 The rate of change in the average real monthly wage and monthly minimum wage (*Note* All wages adjusted by urban CPI, base year = 1995)

Figure 9.2 shows year-to-year rates of change in real average wages and average real minimum wages in China from 1995 to 2015. We can see from Fig. 9.2 that both average wages and minimum wages have been increasing every year since 1996. However, from 1995 to 2010 the increase in average wages is generally greater than the increase in minimum wages, so that the minimum wage to average wage ratio fell. A recession from 2010 to 2014 led to a reduction in the rate of growth of both real average wages and real minimum wages. Unlike prior to 2010, from 2010 to 2014 the rate of growth of minimum wages was higher than the rate of growth of average wages, so that the minimum wage to average wage ratio increased.

Figure 9.3 presents the minimum wage/average wage ratio in China from 1995 to 2014. Consistent with Fig. 9.2, Fig. 9.3 shows that the minimum wage/average wage ratio decreased steadily from 1995 to 2010 and then increased from 2010 to 2015. Overall, the minimum wage-average wage ratio in China is low compared to other countries. As of 2015, this ratio in OECD countries was well above 35%, while in China this ratio was only a little more than 25%. Important for this article, the minimum wage to average wage ratio is similar in the two years for which we have data, 2007 and 2013.

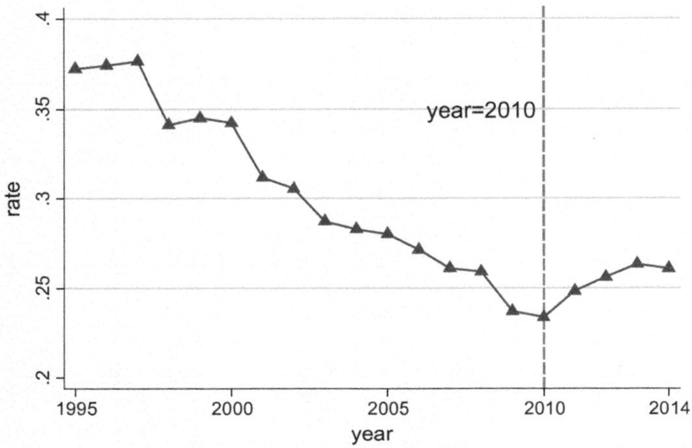

Fig. 9.3 Average minimum wage as a percentage of the average wage

9.3 Literature Review

As noted, official Chinese minimum wages are set in monthly terms for full-time workers. Almost all papers found that there is broad compliance with legal monthly minimum wages in China. Jia and Du (2015) use the Chinese Urban Labour Survey (CULS) data to examine compliance with minimum wage. Three waves of Chinese Urban Labour Survey, CULS2001, CULS2005, and CULS2010. CULS surveyed urban and migrant workers in 5 cities (Shanghai, Wuhan, Shenyang, Fuzhou, and Xian). They found that the proportion of workers whose wages below monthly minimum wage is 9.84% in 2001, 17.26% in 2005, 13.26% in 2010. The wage of female and low education workers is more likely to be below minimum wage. Unlike in 2001 and 2005, there was no difference in compliance with minimum wages between different cities in 2010. Fang and Lin (2013), using the annual Urban Household Survey from 2002 to 2009, find that the proportion of civilian employees (excluding self-employed and students) whose total monthly wage is below the minimum wage was 5.6%. Yang et al. (2014), using a survey of internal migrants from 2011 and 2012, estimate that approximately 5% of migrants earned at or below the monthly minimum wage,

Ma and Li (2015), using Chinese Household Income Survey Data for 1995, 2002, and 2007, find that less than 5% of workers earned less than the monthly minimum wage in any year. Ye et al. (2015) use a matched firm-employee dataset to examine the extent of compliance with minimum wage and overtime pay regulations in Chinese formal sector firms. They find evidence that there is broad compliance with legal minimum wages in China; fewer than 3.5% of full-time workers earn less than the legal monthly minimum wage.

However, many Chinese work more than full-time. Gan and Zhao (2016), using a survey of 528 migrant workers from Quanzhou and Fuzhou enterprises of Fujian Province in 2012, found that 93.3% of the surveyed migrant employees work overtime regularly and 57.8% of them work 10–12 hours a day. Employers arrange for employees work overtime in accordance with the regulation of enterprise in the form of double-shift work. Gu and Lv (2015) use 1% of the national population census data in 2005 to examine the compliance with minimum wage. They found that overtime work is widespread in China; 93.64% of workers work overtime (64.04% of workers whose weekly working hours are between 40 and 48. 29.6% of workers whose weekly working hours are more than 48 hours). According to the relevant laws and regulations, workers who work more than 40 hours per week should be paid at least 1.5 times their regular hourly wage for the overtime hours that they work (2.0 times on weekends and 3.0 times on holidays). In order to consider the long working hours for migrant workers, many papers calculate the imputed hourly minimum wage for full-time workers. When using imputed hourly minimum wage, almost all papers find that there is substantial non-compliance with overtime pay regulations.

Xie (2010) surveys 485 rural migrants in three cities in Jiangsu province in 2009, finding that the proportion of workers whose total monthly wage is below the monthly minimum wage is 3.9%, while over 25% of workers in his sample earn less than the hourly minimum wage when overtime hours are taken into account. Sun and Shu (2011) study rural migrants in 9 cities in Guangdong province in 2006, 2008, 2009, and 2010. They find that the proportion of workers whose monthly wage is less than the monthly minimum wage is 9.0, 7.7, 4.0, and 4.2%, respectively, in these four years, while the proportion of workers whose hourly wage is below the implicit hourly minimum wage for full-time workers was 45.3, 33.3, 28.1, and 23.8%. Du and Wang (2008) use data from five capital cities in Shanghai, Wuhan, Shenyang, Fuzhou, and Xian in 2001 and 2005 and find that the monthly wage is below the monthly minimum wage for 11.2% of workers, but that the hourly wage was below the implicit hourly minimum wage for full-time workers for 52.2% of workers. Ye et al. (2015) use a matched firm-employee dataset to examine the extent of compliance with minimum wage and overtime pay regulations in Chinese formal sector firms. They find evidence that there is broad compliance with legal minimum wages in China; fewer than 3.5% of full-time workers earn less than the legal monthly minimum wage. On the other hand, they find evidence that there is substantial non-compliance with overtime pay regulations; almost 29% of the employees who work overtime are not paid any additional wage for overtime hours and 70% are paid less than the legally required 1.5 times the regular wage.

Ye and Yang (2015) use data on 3451 migrant workers in fifteen cities in nine provinces in 2008 to examine the compliance with minimum wage. They also use the family of violation indices developed by Bhorat et al. (2013) that takes into account the depth of violation. They found that the proportion of workers whose monthly total wage below the monthly minimum wage is 4.26%. The percentage shortfall of the average wage from the minimum wage is 16.51%. When using imputed hourly minimum wage, the proportion of workers whose hourly wage below hourly minimum wage rises to 32.21% and the percentage shortfall of the average wage from the minimum wage rises to 22.87%. When they consider that overtime pay should be at least 1.5 times of the regular salary, the proportion of workers whose wage below hourly minimum wage rises to 43.94% and the percentage shortfall of the average wage from the minimum wage rises to 27.16%. They also examine the difference of compliance with minimum wage between different cities. After controlling the individual characteristics and job characteristics, there are still significant differences between cities in compliance with minimum wage. They found that minimum wage level and enforcement are two main reasons determining the compliance difference of different cities.

All the above papers have found that there is broad compliance with the official monthly legal minimum wage in China. On the other hand, they also find evidence that there is substantial non-compliance with overtime pay regulations.

Almost of all of the papers in the literature use only one year of cross-sectional data to examine the compliance with minimum wage regulations. In particular, there are no papers that use data before the year 2008 and after the year 2008 to examine compliance with minimum wage regulations. As noted, a big change took place in the Chinese labor market regulations in 2008. In this article, we use Chinese household survey data for 2007 and 2013 to examine the new changes of compliance with minimum wage regulations. What is more, this article not only examines the violation rate of the minimum wage but also the depth of violation.

9.4 Data

We use the Chinese Household Income Project (CHIP) survey data for 2007 and 2013 to examine compliance with minimum wage. The CHIP survey data includes three parts: the urban household survey, the rural household survey, and the rural-to-urban migrant household survey. For 2007, the urban survey covered 5000 households containing 14,683 individuals selected from 18 cities in nine provinces, whereas the rural survey covered 8000 households containing 31,791 individuals selected from 69 counties in nine provinces. The migrant survey covered nearly 5000 households containing 8446 individuals selected from 18 cities in nine provinces. For 2013, the urban survey covered 6674 households containing 19,887 individuals selected from 126 cities in fourteen provinces, whereas the rural survey covered 10,490 households containing 39,065 individuals selected from 123 counties in fourteen provinces. The migrant survey covered 726 households containing 2210 individuals selected from 87 cities in fourteen provinces.

For stratified samples such as CHIP, the numbers of urban versus rural respondents and of respondents in different regions and provinces are not proportional to the populations in these different locations. In this case, using weights may be needed when the sample sizes of the strata and sampled groups are not proportional to their population shares. Historically, the CHIP survey sample was stratified on two geographic dimensions, rural/urban and East/Center/West. In the construction of weights, it is possible to disaggregate the sample further among provinces within each of the East/Central/West regions. Weights can be used to adjust for the fact that the provincial sample sizes are not proportional to their populations. The CHIP survey, however, does not cover all of China's provinces, the numbers of provinces differ among the three regions, and the provinces covered have changed across rounds of the survey. Consequently, in the discussion below we mainly use urban/rural/migrant and region (two levels) weights. The three regions

(East/Center/West) are subdivided into their respective urban, rural, and migrant populations, for a total of nine subgroups or strata. Weights are constructed accordingly based on the sample sizes versus population sizes of the nine strata.

Construction of weights requires information on the population of individuals in each of the different subgroups or strata of the survey. The National Bureau of Statistics (NBS) regularly publishes population statistics for China's urban populations by region and by province, but not for migrants. Some NBS publications report statistics on migrants, but different publications give different estimates of the size of the migrant population. Using information from these different publications, we construct alternate sets of weights that reflect lower, upper, and middle estimates of the size of the migrant population. Our weights are based on numbers in the population census and 1% population sample surveys, which yield the smallest estimates of the migrant population.

Shares of migrants in the population for 2007 and 2013 are calculated using data from the 2005 1% population sample survey and 2010 population census, respectively. These shares are applied to national population data for 2007 from the 2008 *Yearbook* and for 2013 from the 2014 *Yearbook*. The migrant population is equal to the share of the migrant population times the national population. Based on the estimates of the national migrant population and using the information on the urban and total population, we calculate the urban/migrant population shares by region in each of 2007 and 2013.

We use the population information discussed above together with information from the CHIP datasets to construct weights which are urban/migrant x region weights for individual-level analysis when using CHIP datasets that have individuals as the unit of observation. To obtain a clear estimate of compliance with minimum wages we need to constrain our data. First, the sample of rural area was dropped as rural areas are not covered by minimum wage policy. Second, because minimum wages apply only to paid employees of firms, we exclude the unemployed, unpaid family workers, self-employed, those with temporary jobs. Third, to be consistent with the official Chinese definition of the labor force, we only keep employees whose age is between 16 and 60. Finally, as the minimum wage schedule for part-time workers is different from that of full-time workers, and few part-time workers exist in the CHIP data, we keep data only on full-time workers. After cleaning the data, in 2007, 6008 urban individuals and 4907 migrant individuals are left.[2]

In 2013, the urban survey covered 6674 households containing 19,887 individuals selected from 126 cities in fourteen provinces. The migrant survey covered 726 households containing 2210 individuals selected from 87 cities in fourteen provinces. Descriptive statistics are presented in the Appendix, Table 9.5.

9.5 Percentage of Workers Earning Below the Minimum Wage, 2007 and 2013

Table 9.1 presents the proportion of workers earning below the monthly and implicit hourly minimum wage for 2007 and 2013 (assuming that workers should be paid the same hourly rate for overtime work as the implicit hourly wage for full-time work). There are important differences between these two measures in the proportion of workers earn less than the minimum wage. First, in both years the proportion of workers whose hourly wage is below the hourly minimum wage (13.64% in 2007) is much greater than the number of workers whose monthly earnings are below the monthly minimum wage (3.91% in 2007). Second, while the proportion earning less than the monthly minimum wage increases significantly from 2007 to 2013 (by 3.72 percentage points), the proportion of workers earning less than the hourly minimum wage decreased significantly (by −1.36 percentage points).

The differences between the proportion earning less than the monthly and hourly minimum wage are explained by differences in overtime hours worked by low-wage workers. Table 9.2 shows that, in both 2007 and 2013, workers in the lowest quintiles of the earnings distribution are

Table 9.1 Estimates of the proportion of workers earning below the minimum wage, 2007 and 2013

	Proportion of workers whose monthly earnings are below the monthly minimum wage			*Proportion of workers whose hourly wage is below the imputed hourly minimum wage*		
	2007	*2013*	*2007–2013 change*	*2007*	*2013*	*2007–2013 change*
All	3.91 [3.54–4.26]	7.32 [6.8–7.86]	3.41	13.64 [13.00–14.28]	12.74 [12.04–13.43]	−0.9

Note 95% confidence intervals in brackets

Table 9.2 Average weekly working hours, 2007–2013

	Average weekly hours		
	2007	*2013*	*2007–2013 change*
All	48.0	48.4	0.4
Ascending sort by workers' total monthly wage			
The first quintile	52.1	49.1	−3.0
The second quintile	50.4	48.8	−1.6
The third quintile	48.4	48.7	0.3
The fourth quintile	45.7	48.3	2.6
The fifth quintile	43.7	47.1	3.4

more likely to work overtime hours than higher-wage workers. In 2007, the average workweek for workers in the first quintile of the wage distribution was 52.1 and for the second quintile was 50.4 (compared to a legal full-time workweek of 40 hours). Ye et al. (2015) present data that shows that employers in China are likely to comply with the monthly minimum wage but that a large proportion of employers do not comply with overtime pay regulations. That is, employers require low-skilled workers to work more than the legal workweek, but do not pay these workers for these overtime hours, or pay less than required. Therefore, low-skilled workers who have monthly earnings near the minimum wage have hourly wages below the hourly minimum.

Figures 9.4 and 9.5 illustrate the differences in the distribution of monthly earnings and hourly wages relative to the monthly and implicit hourly minimum wage. As is clear from these figures, in both 2007 and 2013, while the top of the distributions of both monthly earnings and hourly wages is similar, the bottom of the distribution of hourly wages is quite different from the bottom of the distribution of monthly earnings. Specifically, there are many more workers whose hourly wages are below the hourly minimum wage compared to the monthly minimum wage. These workers tend to be those whose monthly earnings are above the minimum wage but whose hourly wages are below (but near) the minimum wage. It is also clear from these figures that the differences between the distributions of monthly earnings and hourly wages at the bottom of the distribution are much smaller in 2013 than in 2007.

Figure 9.6 shows how the distribution of monthly earnings relative to the monthly minimum wage changed between 2007 and 2013.

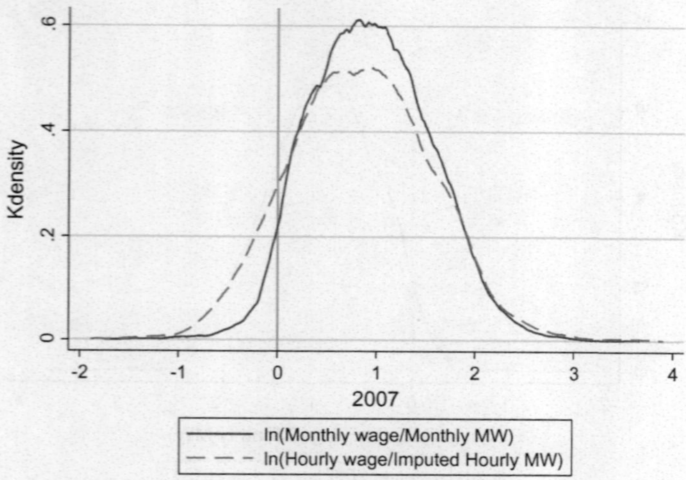

Fig. 9.4 The Kdensity of Ln(Monthly Wage/Monthly MW) and Ln(Hourly Wage/Imputed Hourly MW) in 2007 (bw=0.1)

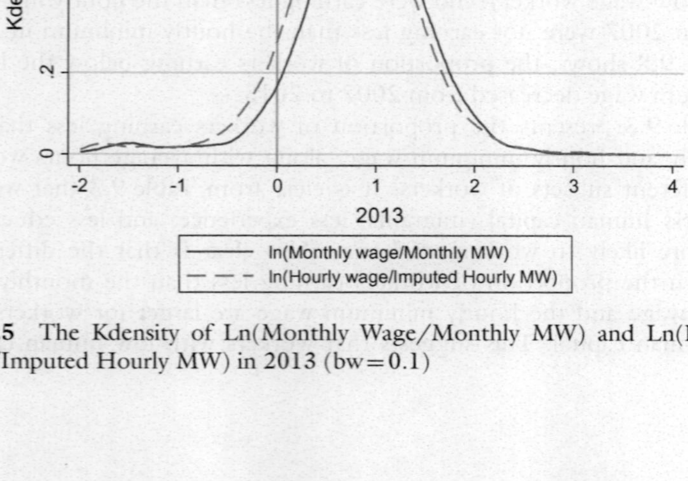

Fig. 9.5 The Kdensity of Ln(Monthly Wage/Monthly MW) and Ln(Hourly Wage/Imputed Hourly MW) in 2013 (bw=0.1)

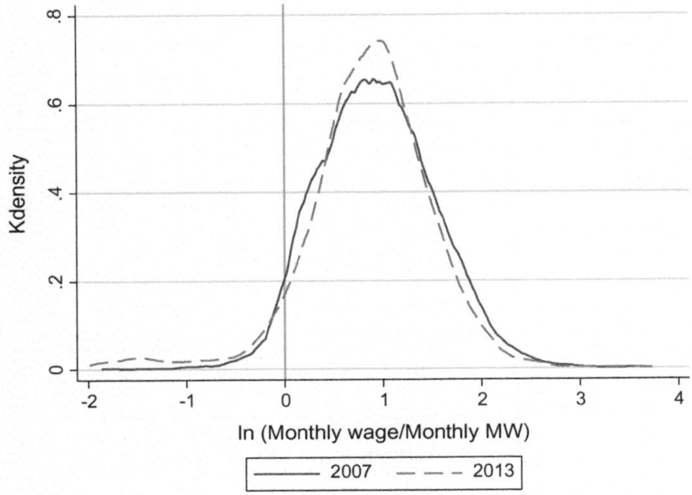

Fig. 9.6 The Kdensity of Ln(Monthly Wage/Monthly MW) (bw=0.1)

From this figure, one can see that the proportion of workers earning below the monthly minimum wage increased between 2007 and 2013. However, as Fig. 9.7 shows, the proportion of sub-minimum wage workers who worked overtime hours decreased substantially between 2007 and 2013.[3] The result is that workers with low monthly wages saw their hourly wages (monthly wage divided by hours worked) increase more rapidly than their monthly wages between 2007 and 2013.[4] Thus, many low-wage workers who were earning less than the hourly minimum wage in 2007 were not earning less than the hourly minimum in 2013. As Fig. 9.8 shows, the proportion of workers earning below the hourly minimum wage decreased from 2007 to 2013.

Table 9.3 presents the proportion of workers earning less than the monthly and hourly minimum wage, along with average hours worked, for different subsets of workers. It is clear from Table 9.3 that workers with less human capital (migrants, less experience, and less education) are more likely to work more hours. Also clear is that the differences between the proportion of workers earning less than the monthly minimum wage and the hourly minimum wage are larger for workers with less human capital. This suggests that workers with low human capital,

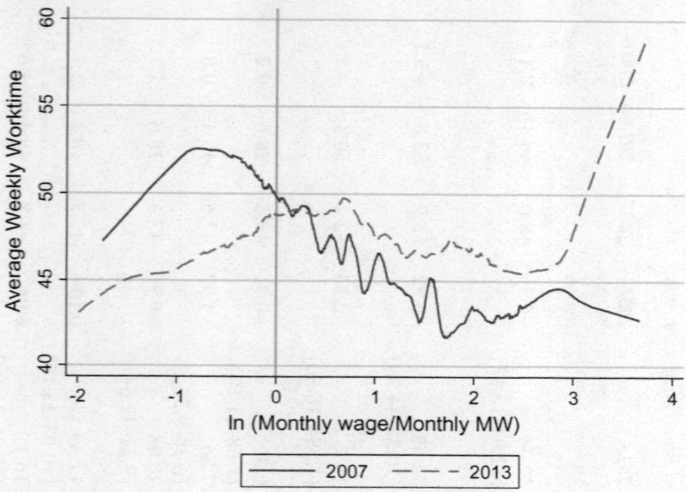

Fig. 9.7 Average weekly working hours for different Ln(Monthly Wage/Monthly MW) (bw=0.1)

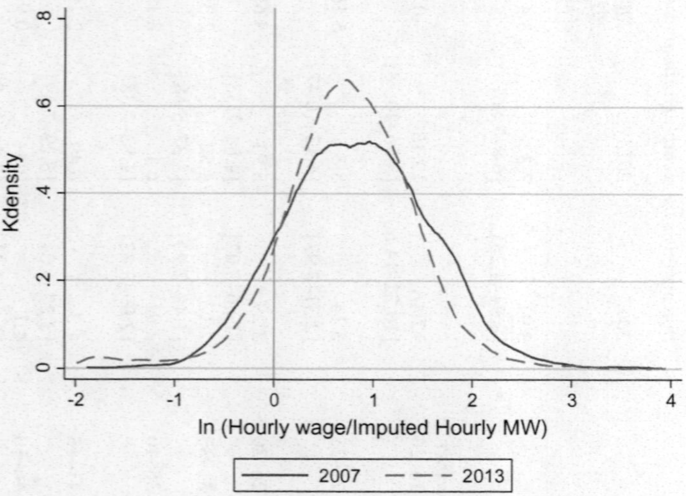

Fig. 9.8 The Kdensity of Ln(Hourly Wage/Imputed Hourly MW) (bw=0.1)

Table 9.3 Estimates of the proportion of workers earning below the minimum wage, 2007 and 2013

	Proportion of workers whose monthly earnings are below the monthly minimum wage			*Proportion of workers whose hourly wage is below the imputed hourly minimum wage*			*Average weekly hours worked*		
	2007	*2013*	*2007–2013 change*	*2007*	*2013*	*2007–2013 change*	*2007*	*2013*	*2007–2013 change*
All	3.91 [3.54–4.26]	7.32 [6.8–7.86]	3.41	13.64 [13.00–14.28]	12.74 [12.04–13.43]	−0.9	48.0	48.4	0.4
Age cohort									
Age 16–20	12.46 [10.32–14.60]	12.15 [3.56–20.73]	−0.31	41.57 [38.38–44.76]	32.65 [20.33–44.98]	−8.92	58.9	53.8	−5.1
Age 21–25	3.14 [2.31–3.97]	8.3 [6.13–10.47]	5.16	18.03 [16.20–19.87]	15.7 [12.84–18.56]	−2.33	52.2	50.1	−2.1
Age 26–30	2.29 [1.56–3.02]	5.94 [4.54–7.33]	3.65	9.7 [8.26–11.14]	9.39 [7.68–11.10]	−0.31	48.4	48.6	0.2
Age 31–35	2.17 [1.43–2.90]	4.52 [3.37–5.68]	2.35	9.78 [8.27–11.28]	7.86 [6.38–9.36]	−1.92	47.6	48.4	0.8
Age 36–40	2.91 [2.09–3.73]	6.1 [4.83–7.38]	3.19	11.94 [10.36–13.52]	10.98 [9.31–12.64]	−0.96	47.4	48.6	1.2
Age 41–45	4.3 [3.27–5.34]	6.49 [5.29–7.69]	2.19	11.41 [9.78–13.04]	11.59 [10.03–13.15]	0.18	45.7	48.4	2.7
Age 46–50	4.1 [2.90–5.31]	9.34 [7.84–10.85]	0.9	10.13 [8.30–11.96]	16.17 [14.26–18.08]	6.04	44.8	48.4	3.6
Age 51–55	4.5 [2.99–6.00]	8.82 [6.99–10.65]	4.32	11.55 [9.23–13.88]	15.11 [12.80–17.42]	3.56	44.5	47.2	2.7

(continued)

Table 9.3 (continued)

	Proportion of workers whose monthly earnings are below the monthly minimum wage			*Proportion of workers whose hourly wage is below the imputed hourly minimum wage*			*Average weekly hours worked*		
	2007	*2013*	*2007–2013 change*	*2007*	*2013*	*2007–2013 change*	*2007*	*2013*	*2007–2013 change*
Age 56–60	6.1 [3.49–8.72]	13.66 [10.77–16.54]	7.56	12.35 [8.76–15.94]	21.5 [18.05–24.95]	9.15	44.4	47.0	2.6
Gender									
Female	5.16 [4.52–5.81]	10.02 [9.08–10.95]	4.86	16.15 [15.07–17.22]	16.99 [15.81–18.16]	0.84	46.9	47.7	0.8
Male	3.01 [2.60–3.43]	5.21 [4.60–5.83]	2.2	11.86 [11.07–12.64]	9.42 [8.61–10.23]	−2.44	48.8	49.1	0.3
Marital status									
Unmarried	5.42 [4.61–6.23]	7.06 [5.53–8.60]	1.64	21.23 [19.82–22.74]	13.32 [11.28–15.36]	−7.91	52.2	48.5	−3.7
Married	3.44 [3.04–3.84]	7.36 [6.78–7.94]	3.92	11.29 [10.60–11.99]	12.49 [11.82–13.39]	1.2	46.8	48.5	1.7
Experience cohort									
Experience 1–2	7.6 [6.72–8.48]	10.01 [8.51–11.50]	2.41	27.4 [25.92–28.88]	20.33 [18.33–22.33]	−7.07	53.3	50.5	−2.8
Experience 05-Mar	3.65 [2.85–4.45]	8.86 [7.50–10.21]	5.21	14.7 [13.19–16.20]	15.7 [13.96–17.44]	−0.93	49.2	50.3	1.1

(continued)

Table 9.3 (continued)

	Proportion of workers whose monthly earnings are below the monthly minimum wage			*Proportion of workers whose hourly wage is below the imputed hourly minimum wage*			*Average weekly hours worked*		
	2007	*2013*	*2007–2013 change*	*2007*	*2013*	*2007–2013 change*	*2007*	*2013*	*2007–2013 change*
Experience 6–10	2 [1.37–2.64]	7.4 [6.14–8.65]	5.4	10.11 [8.76–11.47]	12.58 [11.00–14.16]	−0.93	47.9	48.6	0.7
Experience 11–15	2.03 [1.14–2.93]	6 [4.60–7.39]	3.97	6.46 [4.90–8.02]	9.66 [7.92–11.4]	3.2	46.4	48.0	1.6
Experience 16–20	1.86 [0.90–2.82]	3.62 [2.40–4.84]	1.76	3.85 [2.48–5.22]	5.83 [4.30–7.36]	1.98	43.7	46.6	2.9
Experience 20+	2.67 [1.87–3.47]	5.27 [4.26–6.29]	2.6	3.76 [2.81–4.71]	7.1 [5.93–8.26]	3.34	41.7	45.2	3.5
Educational attainment									
Junior high school or below	6.59 [5.82–7.36]	9.26 [8.16–10.35]	2.67	26.16 [24.79–27.52]	19.62 [18.12–21.12]	−6.54	54.2	52.4	−1.8
High school	3.90 [3.29–4.51]	8.91 [7.82–10]	5.01	12.86 [11.81–13.92]	13.50 [12.2–14.81]	0.64	47.9	47.9	0.0
Junior college	1.85 [1.23–2.47]	5.61 [4.53–6.69]	3.76	3.68 [2.8–4.55]	7.88 [6.62–9.14]	4.20	42.8	45.7	2.9
College or above	0.77 [0.28–1.25]	2.84 [2.08–3.6]	2.08	1.37 [0.72–2.02]	3.14 [2.35–3.94]	1.78	41.9	44.5	2.6
Industry sectors									
Manufacturing	3.03 [2.34–3.72]	5.57 [4.41–6.74]	2.54	9.74 [8.55–10.93]	10.57 [9–12.13]	0.83	47.3	50.5	3.2

(continued)

Table 9.3 (continued)

	Proportion of workers whose monthly earnings are below the monthly minimum wage			*Proportion of workers whose hourly wage is below the imputed hourly minimum wage*			*Average weekly hours worked*		
	2007	*2013*	*2007–2013 change*	*2007*	*2013*	*2007–2013 change*	*2007*	*2013*	*2007–2013 change*
Construction	3.66	4.56	0.90	19.38	7.07	−12.31	56.5	50.5	−6.0
	[2.37–4.96]	[2.72–6.41]		[16.66–22.1]	[4.81–9.34]				
Wholesale and retail trade	5.11	8.63	3.53	20.95	21.10	0.14	51.0	53.0	2.0
	[3.93–6.29]	[5.83–11.43]		[18.78–23.13]	[17.03–25.16]				
Hotels and catering services	9.31	3.40	−5.90	35.41	5.74	−29.67	57.5	46.3	−11.2
	[7.59–11.03]	[1.32–5.49]		[32.57–38.24]	[3.07–8.41]				
Other industry	3.24	8.14	4.91	9.74	13.54	3.79	45.3	47.4	2.1
	[2.76–3.72]	[7.47–8.82]		[8.94–10.55]	[12.69–14.38]				
Firm ownership									
State funded enterprises	2.13	5.72	3.59	4.78	7.82	3.05	42.8	45.2	2.4
	[1.67–2.59]	[5–6.45]		[4.1–5.45]	[6.99–8.66]				
Collective enterprises	3.99	8.25	4.25	10.66	16.75	6.10	46.1	46.7	0.6
	[2.45–5.53]	[5.73–10.77]		[8.23–13.08]	[13.33–20.17]				

(continued)

Table 9.3 (continued)

	Proportion of workers whose monthly earnings are below the monthly minimum wage			*Proportion of workers whose hourly wage is below the imputed hourly minimum wage*			*Average weekly hours worked*		
	2007	*2013*	*2007–2013 change*	*2007*	*2013*	*2007–2013 change*	*2007*	*2013*	*2007–2013 change*
Private enterprise	4.82 [4.13–5.51]	7.39 [6.4–8.39]	2.57	20.72 [19.41–22.03]	14.05 [12.73–15.37]	−6.67	53.0	50.3	−2.7
Foreign funded enterprise	0.58 [−0.01–1.18]	2.45 [0.7–4.19]	1.87	2.77 [1.49–4.05]	4.62 [2.25–6.99]	1.85	44.6	46.9	2.3
Self employed and other	7.47 [6.33–8.62]	11.01 [9.44–12.58]	3.53	27.17 [25.23–29.11]	20.68 [18.65–22.71]	−6.49	53.8	52.5	−1.3
Firm size									
Micro	8.52 [7.16–9.89]	11.66 [10.01–13.3]	3.13	29.16 [26.94–31.38]	22.69 [20.54–24.83]	−6.47	54.6	51.6	−3.0
Small	4.38 [3.79–4.97]	7.57 [6.72–8.41]	3.19	15.26 [14.22–16.3]	12.72 [11.67–13.78]	−2.53	48.2	48.4	0.2
Medium	2.12 [1.62–2.61]	5.21 [4.33–6.1]	3.10	8.28 [7.33–9.23]	8.47 [7.36–9.57]	0.19	45.9	47.1	1.2
Large	1.56 [0.88–2.24]	3.52 [2.4–4.64]	1.96	4.43 [3.31–5.55]	5.46 [4.08–6.84]	1.03	45.5	46.6	1.1

(continued)

Table 9.3 (continued)

	Proportion of workers whose monthly earnings are below the monthly minimum wage			*Proportion of workers whose hourly wage is below the imputed hourly minimum wage*			*Average weekly hours worked*		
	2007	*2013*	*2007–2013 change*	*2007*	*2013*	*2007–2013 change*	*2007*	*2013*	*2007–2013 change*
Region									
East	5.35 [4.73–5.98]	6.00 [5.25–6.75]	0.65	20.04 [18.92–21.15]	11.54 [10.54–12.55]	−8.49	48.7	48.4	−0.3
Middle	2.47 [1.95–2.99]	8.59 [7.6–9.57]	6.12	7.16 [6.3–8.03]	13.79 [12.58–15]	6.63	46.1	48.5	2.4
West	2.71 [2.07–3.35]	9.32 [8.03–10.61]	6.61	8.47 [7.38–9.57]	14.70 [13.14–16.27]	6.23	48.9	48.5	−0.4
Type of workers									
Urban	2.60 [2.2–3]	7.53 [6.96–8.11]	4.94	5.89 [5.3–6.49]	12.40 [11.68–13.11]	6.51	43.1	47.2	4.1
Migrant	6.78 [6.07–7.48]	6.63 [4.92–8.33]	−0.15	30.64 [29.35–31.93]	13.85 [11.48–16.21]	−16.80	58.8	52.5	−6.3

Note 95% confidence intervals in brackets

and therefore low wages, likely are required to work overtime hours without being paid for the additional hours worked.

Table 9.3 also shows that, between 2007 and 2013, the average hours worked fell for those with less human capital and did not change, or even rose, for those with the most human capital. Consistent with this, the proportion of workers earning less than the hourly minimum wage fell only for those workers with low levels of human capital.

By industry sector, average hours worked fell between 2007 and 2013 in only two industry sectors, construction and hotels, and catering service, with the biggest fall in hotels and catering services (which is also the industry sector with the largest proportion of workers earning less than the minimum wage). In addition, only for these two industry sectors does the proportion of workers earning less than the hourly minimum wage falls between 2007 and 2013. By firm size, average hours worked in micro-firms fell between 2007 and 2013, and it is only in these types of firms that the proportion of workers earning below the hourly minimum wage falls significantly (−6.47%) between 2007 and 2013 (even as the proportion of workers earning below the monthly minimum wage increases between 2007 and 2013). Average hours worked in small firms almost did not change between 2007 and 2013, and the proportion of workers earning below the hourly minimum wage falls 2.53%.

By gender, women are more likely to earn less than the minimum wage compared to men. At the same time, men fared better between 2007 and 2013; the proportion of men earning less than the hourly wage fell by more than for women, and the proportion earning less than the monthly minimum wage increased by less for men than for women.

An important focus of minimum wage laws in China is to protect rural immigrants to urban areas.[5] Therefore, it is reasonable to examine how compliance with minimum wages differs for migrants compared to other urban workers. Table 9.3 shows that in 2007, the proportion of migrants earning less than the minimum wage (both monthly and hourly) was significantly higher than that of other urban workers. There were, however, important changes, especially for migrants, between 2007 and 2013. Between 2007 and 2013 the average hours worked (and implicitly the proportion of migrants working overtime) fell, while the average hours worked for other urban workers increased. Along with this, the proportion of migrants earning less than the hourly minimum wage fell from 30.64 to 13.85%, even while the proportion of other urban workers earning less than the hourly minimum wage increased (from 5.89 to 12.40%), and the proportion of migrants earning below the monthly minimum wages almost did not change (from 6.78 to 6.63). By 2013, the proportion earning less than the hourly minimum wage for migrants was not significantly different from that of other urban workers. Consistent with Table 9.3, Figs. 9.9 and 9.10 show how between 2007 and 2013 the distribution of hourly wages relative to the minimum wage for migrant workers became much more similar to that of other urban workers.

In summary, we have developed a set of stylized facts about changes in compliance with minimum wages and overtime pay between 2007 and 2013 in China. These are: (1) In 2007, employers in China generally complied with monthly minimum wage laws but not with overtime pay laws. (2) Low-wage workers with low human capital are more likely than higher-wage workers to be required by employers to work overtime hours without additional pay. (3) Because of this, the proportion of employees with hourly wages below the hourly minimum wage is greater than the proportion of employees with monthly earnings below the monthly minimum wage. (4) Between 2007 and 2013, the proportion of employees with monthly earnings below the monthly minimum wage

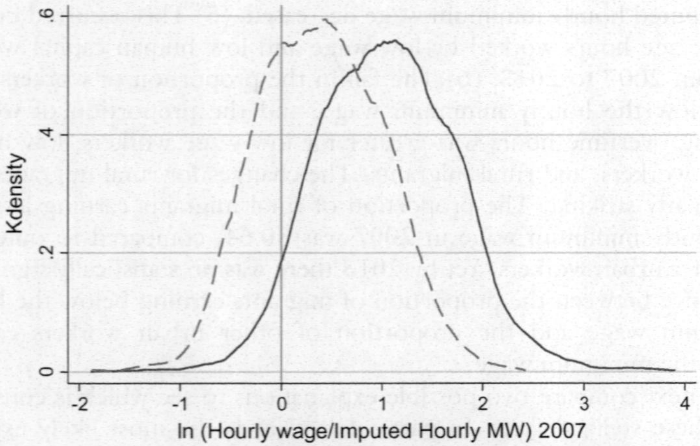

Fig. 9.9 The Kdensity of Ln(Hourly Wage/Imputed Hourly MW) about urban workers and migrant workers in 2007 (bw=0.1)

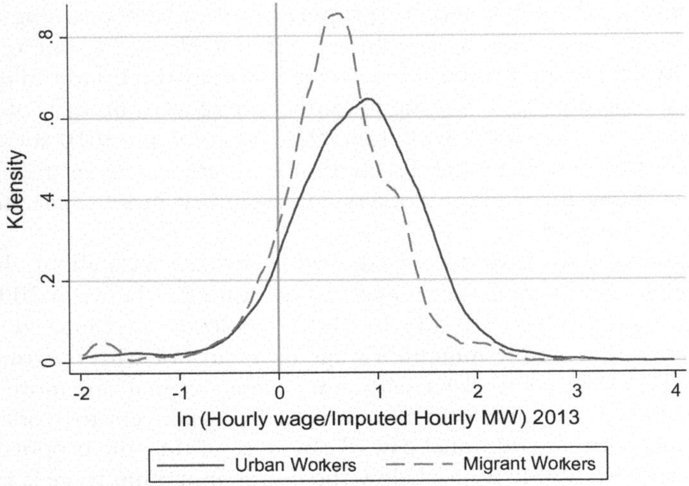

Fig. 9.10 The Kdensity of Ln(Hourly Wage/Imputed Hourly MW) about urban workers and migrant workers in 2013 (bw=0.1)

increased, while the proportion of employees with hourly wages below the imputed hourly minimum wage decreased. (5) This occurred because the average hours worked by low wage and low human capital workers fell from 2007 to 2013. (6) The fall in the proportion of workers earning below the hourly minimum wage, and the proportion of workers working overtime hours was greater for low-wage workers, low human capital workers, and rural migrants. The changes for rural migrants were particularly striking. The proportion of rural migrants earning less than the hourly minimum wage in 2007 was 30.64, compared to only 5.89 for other urban workers. Yet by 2013 there was no statistically significant difference between the proportion of migrants earning below the hourly minimum wage and the proportion of other urban workers earning below the minimum wage.

We next compare two possible explanations to see which is consistent with these stylized facts. In particular, what is the most likely explanation for the increase in the proportion of employees earning less than the monthly minimum wage and the fall in the average hours worked? The first possible explanation is the recession, which may have driven down the demand for labor for all workers, resulting in employers reducing both monthly wages and hours worked. The second is that the 2008 Labor Contract Law, which effectively increased enforcement of minimum wage and overtime laws, led to a reduction in unpaid overtime but a much smaller fall in the monthly earnings of workers earning the minimum wage.

We argue that the increased effective enforcement of minimum wage and overtime laws is more consistent with the stylized facts than the effects of the recession. We would have expected the effects of the recession to have similar effects on different groups of workers: driving down employment, hours worked, and monthly earnings for all workers. However, we find that the effects on hours worked are different for different groups of workers and that this difference is not consistent with the recession explanation, but is consistent with increased compliance with workweek limits and overtime pay for workers earning at or near the monthly minimum wage. For example, real average monthly wages increased fastest between 2007 and 2013 for workers most likely to be affected by minimum wages and most likely to see a decline in their working hours. This is not consistent with the explanation that the fall in demand for labor caused by the recession affected minimum wage workers disproportionately (or even in the same way as other workers). On the other hand, it is consistent with the explanation that minimum wage laws keep the monthly wages of low-wage workers from falling as fast as the wages of high wage workers. The fall in the average hours worked by workers likely to be affected by minimum wages is also consistent with an increase in compliance with the maximum workweek and overtime hours.

The evidence comparing rural migrants to other urban workers is also consistent with the explanation that increased compliance with minimum wage and overtime laws caused the changes in the distribution of earnings. In 2007, the distribution of hourly wages relative to minimum wages was very different for migrants and other urban workers, with rural migrants earning less than other urban workers at all points in the distribution. But then between 2007 and 2013 the distribution of earnings relative to minimum wages did not simply shift left for both migrants and other urban workers, as you might expect if the recession was driving the changes. Rather, the distribution for migrants changed, shifting to the right due to a fall in the number of hours worked, while the distribution for other urban workers barely changed. By 2013 the distribution for rural migrants was similar to the distribution for other urban workers. This suggests that there was an increase in compliance with minimum wage and overtime laws, which disproportionately affected the group that was previously earning below the minimum wage (migrants).

As additional piece of evidence that we use to understand how changes in minimum wage enforcement changed wages across the distribution, we use a newly developed empirical technique to measure not only the number of workers earning less than the minimum wage, but also the degree to which sub-minimum wage workers are earning less than the minimum wage (Bhorat et al. 2013). Using the proportion of workers earning below the minimum wage as a measure of the degree to which minimum wage laws are violated does not distinguish between different degrees of violation. For example, a wage just below the minimum is counted the same as a wage at one-third of the minimum. In this article, we use a family of violation indices developed by Bhorat et al. (2013) that takes into account the depth of violation.

Consider a distribution of actual wages $F(w)$ with density function $f(w)$, and an official minimum wage w^m. If there is full compliance, we should not see any wages at all below w^m. Bhorat et al. (2013) define the measure of violation as:

$$v = v(w^m, w)$$

where v is positive if and only if w is less than w^m, and zero if w is equal to or greater than w^m. Bhorat et al. (2013) use a specific functional form for v:

Table 9.4 Estimates of the index of violation in 2007 and 2013

	v0		*v1*		*v2*		*v1/v0*	
	2007	*2013*	*2007*	*2013*	*2007*	*2013*	*2007*	*2013*
Monthly earnings	3.91	7.32	1.03	3.21	0.50	2.09	26.38	43.82
	[3.54–4.27]	[6.78–7.86]	[0.90–1.16]	[2.92–3.50]	[0.41–0.61]	[1.86–2.31]	[23.99–28.78]	[41.52–46.11]
Hourly wages	13.64	12.74	3.76	4.62	1.57	2.71	27.57	36.28
	[13.00–14.28]	[12.04–13.43]	[3.53–3.98]	[4.29–4.95]	[1.43–1.70]	[2.46–2.96]	[26.60–28.55]	[34.61–37.93]

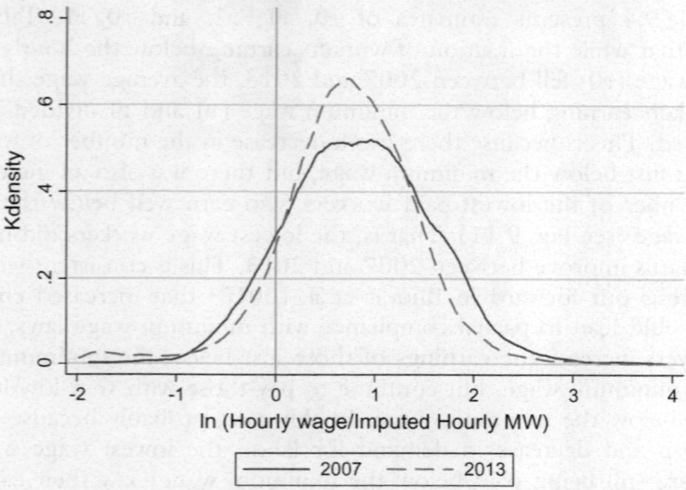

Fig. 9.11 The Kdensity of Ln(Hourly Wage/Imputed Hourly MW) (bw=0.1)

$$v(w^m, w) = \begin{cases} [(w^m - w)/w^m]^\alpha; & w < w^m \\ 0; & w \geq w^m \end{cases}$$

when $\alpha = 0$, v becomes an indicator function, taking on the value 1 when w is less than w^m, and a value of 0 when w is greater than or equal to w^m. When $\alpha = 1$, v is the gap between the actual wage and the minimum wage, expressed as a fraction of the minimum wage. For values of a greater than 1, the violation function emphasizes large gaps more.

Averaging v over the sample results in summary statistics measuring the extent of violation of minimum wage laws. Averaging $v0$ results in the proportion of workers earning below the minimum wage. Averaging $v1$ results in the average the gap between the actual wage and the official minimum wage for minimum wage workers expressed as a fraction of the minimum wage. Dividing $v1$ by $v0$ results in a measure of the percentage shortfall of the average wage from the minimum wage. Bhorat et al. (2013) note that this measure is analogous to the Foster et al. (1984), FGT,' measure of poverty, with the minimum wage acting as the poverty line and the wage as the income. A higher value of α captures greater poverty aversion.

Table 9.4 presents estimates of $v0$, $v1$, $v2$, and $v0/v1$. Table 9.4 shows that while the fraction of workers earning below the hourly minimum wage ($v0$) fell between 2007 and 2013, the average wage shortfall of workers earning below the minimum wage ($v1$ and $v1$ divided by $v0$) increased. This is because there was a decrease in the number of workers earning just below the minimum wage, but there was also an increase in the number of the lowest-paid workers who earn well below the minimum wage (see Fig. 9.11). That is, the lowest wage workers did not see their status improve between 2007 and 2013. This is consistent with the hypothesis put forward in Bhorat et al. (2015) that increased enforcement could lead to partial compliance with minimum wage laws, where employers increase the earnings of those just below the minimum wage to the minimum wage, but continue to pay those with very low human capital below the minimum wage. In this case, probably because of the recession and decrease in demand for labor, the lowest wage workers (who are still being paid below the minimum wage) saw their earnings actually decrease after the increase in enforcement.

9.6 Conclusions

We used CHIPs 2007 and 2013 to examine the extent to which minimum wages are complied within China. We found that 3.91% of employees in 2007 and 7.32% of employees in 2013 were receiving less than the monthly minimum wage. Overall, there are more workers whose wages below the monthly minimum wage in 2013 than in 2007. However, when we consider weekly working hours and calculate how many workers are earning below the hourly minimum wage, the proportion of workers was higher than the proportion earning below the monthly minimum wage (13.64% of employees in 2007 and 12.74% in 2013). The difference between the percent earning below the monthly minimum wage and the hourly minimum wage is explained by the fact that low-wage workers are required to work overtime hours with no additional pay.

When we compare 2007 and 2013, we find that the proportion of workers earning below the monthly minimum wage rose while the proportion earning below the hourly minimum wage fell. This occurred because the working hours of low-skilled workers (and implicitly the number of low-wage workers working overtime) decreased substantially from 2007 to 2013. Overtime work without overtime pay is widespread in the Chinese labor market. Since the Labor Contract Law of the People's Republic of China took effect on May 1, 2008, minimum wage and overtime regulations have become more and more strict. We argue that the evidence is consistent with the explanation that the new Labor Contract Law led to the fall in hours worked by low-wage workers, while their monthly wages did not fall. Therefore, the hourly wages of low-wage workers increased between 2007 and 2013, resulting in a fall in the percent of low-wage workers earning below the hourly minimum wage.

When we also measure both the fraction of workers earning below the minimum wage and the extent by which these workers have wages below the minimum wage, we find that while the fraction of workers earning below the hourly minimum wage fell between 2007 and 2013, the average wage shortfall of workers earning below the minimum wage increased. This is because there was a decrease in the number of workers earning just below the minimum wage, but there was also an increase in the number of the lowest-paid workers who earn well below the minimum wage. This is consistent with the hypothesis put forward in Bhorat et al. (2015) that increased enforcement could lead to partial compliance with minimum wage laws, where employers increase the earnings of those just below the minimum wage to the minimum wage but continue to pay those with very low human capital below the minimum wage.

Appendix

See Table 9.5.

Table 9.5 Statistical description of variables

	Number of obs		*Mean*		*Min*		*Max*	
Variables	*2007*	*2013*	*2007*	*2013*	*2007*	*2013*	*2007*	*2013*
Age	10,915	8935	35	40	16	60	16	60
Gender								
Proportion male	10,915	8935	0.588	0.560	0	0	1	1
Marital								
Proportion married	10,915	8932	0.721	0.876	0	0	1	1
Experience	10,783	8796	9	11	0	0	43	45
Educational attainment								
Junior high school or below	10,915	8935	0.368	0.331	0	0	1	1
High school	10,915	8935	0.354	0.288	0	0	1	1
Junior college	10,915	8935	0.164	0.185	0	0	1	1
College or above	10,915	8935	0.114	0.196	0	0	1	1
Industry sectors								
Manufacturing	10,915	8935	0.219	0.183	0	0	1	1
Construction	10,915	8935	0.075	0.058	0	0	1	1
Wholesale and retail trade	10,915	8935	0.123	0.049	0	0	1	1
Hotels and catering services	10,915	8935	0.101	0.033	0	0	1	1
Other industry	10,915	8935	0.483	0.678	0	0	1	1
Firm ownership								
State funded enterprises	10,801	8919	0.356	0.406	0	0	1	1
Collective enterprises	10,801	8919	0.057	0.052	0	0	1	1
Private enterprise	10,801	8919	0.339	0.321	0	0	1	1
Foreign funded enterprise	10,801	8919	0.060	0.038	0	0	1	1

(continued)

Table 9.5 (continued)

	Number of obs		*Mean*		*Min*		*Max*	
Variables	*2007*	*2013*	*2007*	*2013*	*2007*	*2013*	*2007*	*2013*
Self-employed and other	10,801	8919	0.188	0.183	0	0	1	1
Firm size								
Micro	10,701	8748	0.151	0.178	0	0	1	1
Small	10,701	8748	0.427	0.438	0	0	1	1
Medium	10,701	8748	0.301	0.268	0	0	1	1
Large	10,701	8748	0.120	0.116	0	0	1	1
Region								
East	10,915	8935	0.433	0.536	0	0	1	1
Middle	10,915	8935	0.313	0.294	0	0	1	1
West	10,915	8935	0.254	0.170	0	0	1	1

Notes

1. The monthly minimum wage does not apply to part-time workers. Instead, in 2004 the government mandated a separate hourly minimum wage for part-time workers. Because employers are not required to pay some non-wage benefits for part-time workers, the part-time hourly minimum wage is set above the monthly minimum wage for full-time workers (or, more specifically, the monthly minimum wage divided by the number of hours worked per month by a full-time worker). For clarity and simplicity, we do not consider part-time workers in this paper.
2. The term "migrant" refers to workers in urban areas whose home is in rural areas and who are only in urban areas temporarily for work purposes.
3. The proportion of high wage workers working overtime remained the pretty much the same between 2007 and 2013.
4. Between 2007 and 2013 the real average monthly wages of low-skilled workers (young, less experienced, with less education and migrants) increased by more than the increase in the wages of workers with more human capital. Real hourly wages for low-skilled workers increased even faster (because of falling working hours). At the same time, the increase in the real minimum wage was similar for all groups. This suggests that there was an increase in the relative demand for low-skilled workers between 2007 and 2013.
5. The term "rural migrant" in China refers to workers whose legal residence (citizenship or "hukou") is in rural areas but who are temporary migrants

to urban areas. Under the "hukou" (household registration) system, social services, such as government-subsidized health care, education, and pension, are available to workers only in their legal residence. Rural migrants generally return to their legal residence in rural areas to access these services, for holidays, and when they leave their jobs in urban areas. It is difficult to change your legal residence. Rural migrants tend to earn less than citizens of urban areas, and one key motivation for the introduction of legal minimum wages was to protect rural migrant workers (Ye et al. 2015).

References

Andalon M, Pages C (2008) Minimum Wages in Kenya. IZA Discussion Papers 5:374–376.

Basu A, Hasler, PE (2010) Nullcline-Based Design of a Silicon Neuron. IEEE Transactions on Circuits & Systems Part I Regular Papers 11:2938–2947.

Basu AK, Chau NH, Kanbur R (2010) Turning a Blind Eye: Costly Enforcement, Credible Commitment and Minimum Wage Law. The Economic Journal 120(543):244–269, March.

Bhorat H, Kanbur R, Mayet N (2013) A Note on Measuring the Depth of Minimum Wage Violation. Labour 2(2):192–197.

Bhorat H, Kanbur R, Stanwix B (2015) Partial Minimum Wage Compliance. IZA Journal of Labor and Development 4(18), November.

Du Y, Wang M (2008) The Implementation of Minimum Wage System and Its Effect in China. Journal of Graduate School of Chinese Academy of Social Sciences 6:56–62 (in Chinese).

Fang T, Lin C (2013) Minimum Wages and Employment in China. IZA Discussion Paper No. 7813, December.

Foster JE, Greer J, Thorbecke E (1984) A Class of Decomposable Poverty Indices. Econometrica 52(3):761–766.

Gan M, Zhao D (2016) Problems and Suggestions for Current Minimum Wage Standards in the Process of Execution. Journal of Chongqing Technology and Business University (Social Science Edition) 5:1–6(in Chinese).

Gindling TH, Mossaad N, Trejos JD (2015) The Consequences of Increased Enforcement of Legal Minimum Wages in a Developing Country: An Evaluation of the Impact of the Campaña Nacional de Salarios Mínimos in Costa Rica. Industrial and Labour Relations Review 3:666–707.

Gu H, Lv L (2015) The Relationship Between the Minimum Wage Standard and China Urban Workers' Wage: The Influence of the Implementation of the Minimum Wage System. Yuejiang Academic Journal 3:30–37(in Chinese).

Jia P, Du Y (2015) Minimum Wages in China: Standard and Implementation. Studies in Labor Economics 1:67–95 (in Chinese).

Ma XX, Li S (2015) Impact of Minimum Wage On Gender Wage Gaps in Urban China. IZA Journal of Labor & Development 1:1–22.

Maloney W, Mendez J (2004) Measuring the Impact of Minimum Wages: Evidence from Latin America's in Heckman J. and Pages C. (eds) Law and Employment. Lessons from Latin America and the Caribbean, Chicago, IL: University of Chicago Press: 109–130.

Ronconi L (2010) Enforcement and Compliance with Labor Regulations in Argentina. Industrial and Labor Relations Review 63(4): article 9. Available at: http://digitalcommons.ilr.cornell.edu/ilrreview/vol63/iss4/9.

Strobl E, Walsh F (2003) Minimum Wages, and Compliance: The Case of Trinidad and Tobago. Economic Development and Cultural Change 51:427–450.

Sun ZW, Shu BB (2011) The Standard of the Minimum Wage, and the Wages of Peasant-Workers: A Case Study Based on Zhujiang Delta. Management World 8:45–56 (in Chinese).

Wang J, Gunderson M (2012) Minimum Wage Effects on Employment and Wages: Dif-in-Dif Estimates From Eastern China. International Journal of Manpower 8:644–647 Vol. 1.

Xie Y (2010) The Implementation of Minimum Wage Regulation in Migrant Workers and Its Determinants: Evidence from Jiangsu Province. Economic Management Journal 3:164–170 (in Chinese).

Yang J, Gunderson M, Li S (2014) The Impact of Minimum Wages on Migrant Workers' Wages the Impact of Minimum Wages on Migrant Workers' Wages China Institute for Income Distribution. Working Paper No. 15. http://www.ciidbnu.org/news/201402/20140212192553706.html 2014-08-24.

Ye JY, Yang Y (2015) Minimum Wage Standard and Its Implementation Differences: Violation Rate and Depth. Economic Perspectives 8:51–63 (in Chinese).

Ye LX, Gindling TH, Li S, Xiong L (2015) Compliance with Legal Minimum Wages and Overtime Pay Regulations in China. IZA Journal of Labor & Development 2015(4).

CHAPTER 10

Estimating the Effect of Minimum Wages on Firm Profitability in China

Quheng Deng

10.1 Introduction

The minimum wage policy is a way that government intervenes the labor market by maintaining a minimum wage level for salaried workers. Despite its clear policy target, the real effect of minimum wage policy is highly controversial. The inconclusiveness of the impact of minimum wage policy lies in two aspects. On the one hand, the minimum wage policy has not only direct effects on wage level but also indirect effects on employment, wages, and firm profits. On the other hand, due to the data and methodology issues, even the direct effect on wage level of minimum wage policy is hard to measure with sound precision, not to say the indirect effect, the measurement of which turns out to be more difficult in general.

Although no consensus has yet been reached, there is a voluminous literature examining the impact of minimum wage policy on wage and employment. As minimum wage tends to increase the wage level of the salaried workers whose wage was below the minimum wage standard, it is expected that low-wage workers will benefit most from minimum wage

Q. Deng (✉)
Institute of Economics, Chinese Academy of Social Sciences, Beijing, China

L. Shi and C. Lin (eds.), *Minimum Wages in China*,
https://doi.org/10.1007/978-981-15-2421-9_10

policy. This conjecture has been confirmed in many studies. For instance, using the CPS data spanning from 1979 to 1997, Neumark et al. (2004) find that low-wage workers are most strongly affected, while higher-wage workers are little affected. However, to investigate the overall effect of minimum wage policy on employees, the disemployment effect of minimum wage policy has to be gauged since the increase in wages may decrease labor demand.

As discussed by the competitive labor market model, labor demand plays the key role in determining the quantity of employment in the presence of a binding price floor set by the minimum wage level (Boeri and van Ours 2008; Card and Krueger 1995). It follows naturally that an increase in the minimum wage leads to a decrease in employment. However, the empirical findings of Card and Krueger (1994, 1995) runs counter to the theoretical prediction abovementioned. They find that an increase in the minimum wage does not have a negative but has a small positive effect on employment. The findings of Card and Krueger are consistent with the labor monopsony model, under which firms face an upward-sloping labor supply curve. Thus, it is possible that an increase in the minimum wage results in an increase in employment.

Card and Krueger (1994, 1995) reignited the debate on the effect of minimum wage on wage and employment, joined by numerous later studies. Despite extensive studies on the effects of minimum wage on employees, there is a scanty of literature examining the effect of minimum wage on firms. As wage and employment are the labor market outcomes co-determined by the labor supply side (workers) and the labor demand side (firms), it is vital to analyze how firms respond to changes in minimum wage. Still, there is no consensus on the impact of minimum wage on firm profitability—the focus of this article. Ceteris paribus, an increase in minimum wage leads to higher-wage costs, to which firms may adjust by lowering profits. However, firms may have other alternatives to cope with the increase in minimum wage without suffering from loss of profits. Firstly, firms can simply choose not to comply with the minimum wage policy if the cost of noncompliance is not too high. Secondly, firms can also pass on the higher-wage costs to consumers by increasing prices of their products. Thirdly, higher-wage costs may induce firms to substitute away from labor with capital. Finally, rising wage costs may push firms to enhance efficiency (Card and Krueger 1995, 313, 353).

Empirical studies present mixed evidence on the impact of minimum wage on firm profitability. Card and Krueger (1995) utilized the stock market event study methodology to evaluate the impact of the 1989 minimum wage hike on shareholder wealth. They calculated excess returns as the abnormal returns to stockholders of each firm in the sample, which is the predicted return deducted from the daily return. After examining the changes in excess returns following the news about minimum wage hikes, they found that the evidence was mixed that news about a minimum wage hike induced investors to adjust their valuation of firms downward (Card and Krueger 1995, 347). The same methodology was applied to the data from New Zealand by Pacheco and Naiker (2006), who found that there was an insignificant impact of a significant reform to the youth minimum wage on profit expectations for low-wage employers by investors. Lin (2012) improved the stock market event study methodology by decomposing excess returns. Based on the decomposition results, he found that there was a significant negative impact on firms that was neutralized by positive market performance, yielding a neutral aggregate effect of the 1989 minimum wage hike. Utilizing the introduction of a UK national minimum wage in 1999 as a natural experiment, Draca et al. (2011) examine the effect of minimum wage on firm profitability with a difference-in-differences approach. Their findings show that minimum wages reduce firm profitability significantly.

There are also studies on the effects of minimum wage on firm profitability in developing countries and emerging economies. For instance, Harasztosi and Lindner (2015) exploited the large increase in the minimum wage in Hungary in 2001 and found that the rise minimum wage did not lower profitability among low-wage employers. Cuong (2017) investigated the effect of minimum wage increase in 2005 on profitability in Vietnam using a difference-in-differences with propensity score matching method and found that the increase in the minimum wage had no effect on firm profitability.

Minimum wage standard has increased dramatically in China in recent years. The sharp increase in the minimum wage in China has aroused wide debate on its effects on wage, employment, and income distribution among scholars, policymakers, and the general public. As China is approaching the end of cheap labor force, some argue that increases in minimum wage will induce more labor supply. However, others disagree that increases in minimum wage may raise firms' cost and then reduce labor demand. Both views are supported by empirical studies in China and the impact of minimum wages on employment remains an open question. However, little research has been done to investigate the effect of the minimum wage policy on the employer side. Among exceptions, Sun et al. (2013) examined the effect of minimum wages on firm's export and found that the effect of minimum wages on export exhibited a U shape. Ma and Gan (2013) found that minimum wages tended to decrease firms' tendency of providing on-the-job training. Mayneris et al. (2015) uncovered that minimum wages reduced the survival probability of firms, increased incumbents' productivity, and maintained incumbents' employment and profits.

This article attempts to add to the literature by analyzing the effect of minimum wages on firm profitability. Using the firm-level panel data and the hand-collected county-level minimum wage data, this article estimates the effect of minimum wages on firm profitability. Compared with previous studies applying impact evaluation methods (mainly, difference-in-difference) to very few (usually two) time points, this article examines the effect of minimum wages on profitability over a much longer time horizon and thus makes use of much more information from the data.

Since firms may take time to adjust in response to the changes in the minimum wage, this article estimates a dynamic panel model allowing for lagged effects of minimum wages through the use of the difference GMM method, with further lags of minimum wages as instruments for current and the first lag of profitability. However, as the linear dynamic panel model cannot reveal the heterogeneous effects of the minimum wage on profitability, this article estimates a quantile regression dynamic panel model, which is also less susceptible to outliers.

The estimation results of that quantile regression dynamic panel model suggest that the effect of the minimum wage in the current year is negative across the whole conditional distribution of profitability and it exhibits an inverted-U shape across conditional quantiles. Instead, the effect of the lagged minimum wage is positive at the 5th, 10th, 15th quantiles, negative at the 90th and 95th quantiles, and not significant at other quantiles. Turning to the overall effect of minimum wages, we can find that minimum wages exert significantly negative effect on profitability at the 5th quantile and quantiles higher than 40th and the absolute value of the effect of minimum wages increases with these quantiles. For other quantiles, the overall effect of minimum wages on profitability is negligible.

10.2 Background

From 1994, the minimum wage policy has been implemented in China. Minimum wage standard is set by the provincial governments. Local variations in the minimum wage at the county level are made possible after considering differences in living costs and economic situations across counties. The minimum wage standard of various provinces had increased steadily after the introduction of the minimum wage policy. In 2004, the Regulation on Minimum Wage was issued by Ministry of Labor and Social Security, which promoted the implementation of the minimum wage policy. As a minimum wage standard is more or less consistent with the local living cost and the level of economic development, large variations in minimum wage across counties are not surprised. As shown in Table 10.1, the Gini coefficient of minimum wage at the county level in 2005 was 0.1125 and the Theil index was 0.0233. Table 10.1 also demonstrates decomposition of Theil index by province and by city (at the prefecture level). Between-province and between city variations explain the overwhelming majority of the regional variations in minimum wages.

Minimum wages also vary along the timeline. Figure 10.1 depicts the increase in minimum wage from 1999 to 2009. In nominal terms, the (unweighted) mean of minimum wage increases from 228 RMB in 1999 to 569 RMB in 2009. Variation of minimum wage across counties changes over years. The Gini coefficient of minimum wage at the county level decreases from 0.1350 in 1999 to 0.0839 in 2009, with oscillations

Table 10.1 Variation of minimum wage standards at the county level from 1999 to 2009

Inequality index	*Value*	*Proportion (%)*
Gini coefficient	0.1125	
Theil index	0.0233	100
Within provinces	0.0056	24.03
Between provinces	0.0177	75.97
Theil index	0.0233	100
Within cities	0.0013	5.56
Between cities	0.0221	94.44

Data source Author's own calculation based on minimum wage data of the county level collected by the China Institute for Income Distribution of Beijing Normal University

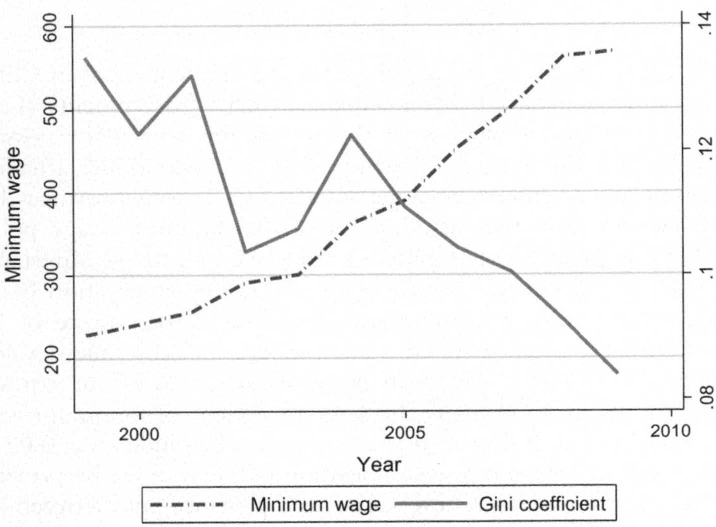

Fig. 10.1 Steady increase in the minimum wage standard (*Data source* Author's own calculation based on county level minimum wage data)

from 2001 to 2004. Substantial variation of minimum wage both across counties and over the sample period provides a precious opportunity to evaluating the effects of minimum wage policy.[1]

10.3 Data and Summary Statistics

The data used in this article comes from two sources. The first one is the firm-level panel data from the annual industrial surveys conducted by the National Bureau of Statistics, which cover all industrial firms that are either state-owned or non-state-owned firms with the sales above 5 million RMB. In the annual industrial surveys, firms are divided into mining, manufacturing, and public utilities. In this article, only firms in the manufacturing industry are included, and our data covers the period from 1999 to 2009. The firm-level panel data provides information about sales, profit, asset, number of workers, industry, ownership, and starting year. This information makes it possible for us to analyze firm profitability.

The firm-level panel data is supplemented with hand-collected minimum wage data at the county level. As stated in the previous section, a minimum wage standard is more or less locally determined to reflect the regional variation in the living cost as well as economic situations. A minimum wage standard has also been increased dramatically in recent years. However, there is no open data documenting the large variation of minimum wage across regions and over years. The research group at China Institute for Income Distribution of Beijing Normal University has made an enormous effort to check local governments' documents and publications for yearly changes in minimum wage standards.

Table 10.2 provides summary statistics of the firm sample. As can be seen from this table, the mean of firm profitability, defined as the ratio of profit to sales, is 0.0306 for firms in our sample. The standard deviation of firm profitability is 0.1039, suggesting that a large variation in profitability across firms. Firm age measures years after the start-up of the business. The mean of firm age is 14.22 years in our sample. On the one hand, some firms may exit from our sample simply due to the shrinkage of their profits thus the mean firm age may be larger in the population than that in the sample. On the other hand, some young

Table 10.2 Summary statistics

	Mean	*Standard deviation*
Profitability	0.0306	0.1039
Age/100	0.1422	0.1249
Asset (10 billion RMB)	0.0081	0.0725
Number of workers (10 thousand persons)	0.0580	0.1910
Share of sales in the industry	0.0044	0.0182
Ownership (%)		
SOEs	8.25	
Collective	0.07	
Foreign	33.28	
Private	32.69	
Joint stock	7.63	
Joint Venture	0.30	
Other	17.77	
No. of observations	202,456	

Data source Author's calculation based on firm-level panel data collected by National Bureau of Statistics of China

firms may not be included in the firm survey since it takes time for them to increase their sales value to the threshold for entering the survey, which had been 5 million RMB from 1998 and was set to 20 million RMB in 2011. Thus, both an upward and downward bias exist for firm age in our sample.

As the information on fixed capital stock at original purchase prices is not available for the 2008 and 2009 firm survey data, it is not possible to calculate capital with the perpetual inventory method. Thus, we use asset as a proxy for capital. The mean of asset is 81 million RMB for firms included in our sample. And the number of workers is 580, on average. We also calculate the share of each firm's sales in the four-digit industry per year as a measure of monopoly power, the mean value of which is 0.0044, shown in Table 10.2. Ownership distribution of firms is also illustrated in Table 10.2. Foreign and private firms in total comprise 2/3 of the sample, while only 8.25% of our sample are state-owned enterprises.

10.4 Econometric Method

The firm profitability function can be written as follows[2]:

$$P_{ijt}=\beta MW_{jt}+\gamma Z_{ijt}+\nu_{ijt} \tag{1}$$

where P_{ijt} is profit margin of firm i in county j in year t. MW_{jt} is the minimum wage standard implemented at county j in year t. Z_{ijt} is a vector of variables measuring firm characteristics, including assets, number of workers, firm age, etc. The error term, ν_{ijt}, is assumed to contain county-level and firm-level fixed effects and time-varying firm-level unobservables.

$$\nu_{ijt} = \alpha_{ij} + \tau_j + \sigma_{jt} + \varepsilon_{ijt} \tag{2}$$

As minimum wage standard is set according to county-level observables and unobservables to some extent, MW_{jt} is correlated with county fixed effect, τ_j, and time-varying county-level unobservables, σ_{jt}. Since τ_j and σ_{jt} also affects firm profitability, P_{ijt}, MW_{jt} is thus an endogenous variable. α_{ij} denotes firm-level fixed effect. ε_{ijt} represents time-varying firm-level unobservables, which is independent across firms.

After first difference or eliminating firm fixed effects, the correlation of MW_{jt} with county fixed effect could be purged out. However, the correlation of MW_{jt} with time-varying county-level unobservables still exists. Thus, first difference or fixed-effects model cannot correct for the endogeneity bias of MW_{jt}. Instrumental variables which correlate with MW_{jt} but not directly correlate with P_{ijt} could be an option. As time-varying county-level economic situations are always considered when setting local minimum wage standard, valid instrumental variables, if any, are difficult to find, however. In this article, lagged MW_{jt} will be used as potential instruments for MW_{jt}.

Firms take time and monetary costs to reallocate their resources (Hamermesh and Pfann 1996). Due to the existence of adjustment costs, firms are unable to change their demand quickly in response to the shocks.[3] If firms cannot make adjustments of their input allocation in a timely fashion, minimum wages in previous period may have lasting effects on firm profitability in the current period. Thus, a finite distributed lag model is needed to capture the possible effect of the lagged information of minimum wages.

Minimum wages in the previous period may also affect firm profitability, calling for a distributed lag model.[4] Meanwhile, lagged firm profitability is included as well to reflect the imperfect adjustment of distributed firms in response to minimum wage changes in a short period, leading to an autoregressive lag model. Thus, the firm profitability function can be modified as:

$$P_{ijt}=\rho P_{ij,t-1}+\beta MW_{j,t-1}+\gamma Z_{ijt}+v_{ijt} \tag{3}$$

Taking first difference, we can get:

$$\Delta P_{ijt} = \rho \Delta P_{ij,t-1} + \beta \Delta MW_{jt} + \delta \Delta MW_{j,t-1} + \gamma \Delta Z_{ijt} + \Delta u_{ijt} \tag{4}$$

It is clear that firm-level and county-level fixed effects are eliminated after first differencing. However, Δu_{ijt} is correlated with ΔMW_{jt}, $\Delta P_{ij,t-1}$, and ΔMW_{jt-1}.[5] To deal with the potential endogeneity of differenced minimum wage and firm profitability, dynamic panel data models are employed in this article, utilizing further lags of endogenous variables as instruments. The basic idea is to use further lags of minimum wage and firm profitability, which is correlated with differenced minimum wage and firm profitability but not correlated with time-varying firm-level unobservables, as instruments (Anderson and Hsiao 1981). If there is no serial correlation in u_{ijt}, then $P_{ij,t-2}$ serves as a valid instrument for $\Delta P_{ij,t-1}$. Similar instruments can be found for ΔMW_{jt} and $\Delta MW_{j,t-1}$. If u_{ijt} is serially distributed as AR(1), then $P_{ij,t-3}$ instead of $P_{ij,t-2}$ becomes a valid instrument for $\Delta P_{ij,t-1}$. The order of autoregressive distribution of u_{ijt} can be tested statistically.

As the Anderson and Hsiao estimator utilizes only one specific lag of endogenous variables as an instrument, it is criticized as being not efficient since the information about further lags is not fully utilized. By contrast, the GMM estimator developed by Holtz-Eakin et al. (1988) and Arellano and Bond (1991) use all lags possible as instruments. For instance, if ε is not serially correlated, $P_{ij,t-2}$ and further lags, $P_{ij,t-2}, \ldots, P_{ij1}$, can serve as instrument for $\Delta P_{ij,t-1}$. Formally, the instrument matrix can be written as[6]:

$$Z_{ijt} = \begin{bmatrix} Z_{ij1} & 0 & \cdots & 0 \\ 0 & [Z_{ij1}, Z_{ij2}] & & 0 \\ \vdots & & \ddots & 0 \\ 0 & \cdots & 0 & [Z_{ij1}, \ldots, Z_{ij,t-2}] \end{bmatrix} \tag{5}$$

However, as the number of instruments increases rapidly with the length of available lags, several problems may arise in the finite sample including possible singularity of the matrix, weakening the Hansen test, and over-fitting endogenous variables (Roodman 2009). As there is no clear guidance on how many instruments are suitable, the number of instruments should not exceed the number of individual units in the panel is treated as a minimally arbitrary rule of thumb. Although this rule of thumb is satisfied in our sample, we 'collapse' the instruments to reduce the number of instruments. After 'collapsing,' the instrument matrix is now:

$$Z_{ijt} = \begin{bmatrix} Z_{ij1} & 0 & \cdots & 0 \\ Z_{ij2} & Z_{ij1} & & 0 \\ \vdots & & \ddots & 0 \\ Z_{ij,t-2} & Z_{ij,t-3} & \cdots & Z_{ij1} \end{bmatrix} \tag{6}$$

Theoretically, the first difference of lagged profitability and minimum wage can also be employed as instruments. However, the instruments added with the first differences of lagged profitability and minimum wage does not pass the Sargan test. Thus, only lagged profitability and minimum wage are used as instruments in this article. Accordingly, difference GMM instead of system GMM is adopted here. With lagged firm profitability and minimum wage as instruments, the GMM method is employed to estimate (4). To correct for the downward bias of standard errors, the Windmeijer (2005) finite-sample correction is employed.

Since the dynamic linear panel model is estimated upon the whole sample, the dynamics of firm profitability, as well as the effect of minimum wage on firm profitability, are restricted to be the same for all firms. In reality, however, firms with different levels of profitability may react differently to minimum wage. It follows that the effect of minimum wage on firm profitability may be different across the distribution of profitability. Thus, the quantile regression dynamic panel model is estimated, following Galvao (2011), to capture the differing effect of minimum wage on firm profitability across the conditional quantile of profitability. The quantile regression dynamic panel model outperforms the dynamic linear panel model as it allows for the variations in coefficients across conditional quantiles and is less sensitive to outliers. Like the dynamic linear panel model, the quantile regression dynamic panel model can correct for the endogeneity bias. In the quantile dynamic panel model with firm-level fixed effects, the τth conditional quantile function of firm profitability can be written as:

$$\begin{aligned} &Q_{P_{ijt}}(\tau|P_{ij,t-1}, MW_{jt}, MW_{j,t-1}, Z_{ijt}) \\ &\quad = \rho(\tau)P_{ij,t-1} + \beta(\tau)MW_{jt} + \delta(\tau)MW_{j,t-1} + \gamma(\tau)Z_{ijt} + \nu_{ijt} \end{aligned} \tag{7}$$

To estimate the quantile dynamic panel model, Galvao (2011) proposes a method which utilizes the instrumental variables quantile regression method of Chernozhukov and Hansen (2006) and uses lagged regressors as instruments. The estimator suggested by Galvao (2011) is actually a combination of the IV method applied to dynamic panel models and the IV quantile regression method.

10.5 Results

Estimates of OLS, static, and dynamic panel models are reported in Table 10.3. Column 1 in Table 10.3 lists the OLS estimates of firm profitability function as specified in (1). The OLS estimates suggest that minimum wage has a negative effect on firm profitability.[7] Both fixed assets and number of workers have positive effects on firm profitability. The share of firms' sales in total sales in the four-digit industry measures the monopoly power of firms, which, not surprisingly, helps to increase firm profitability. Firm ownership also affects profitability. Private enterprises

Table 10.3 Estimation results

	OLS	*Static panel*	*Dynamic panel*	*Dynamic panel*
Lagged profitability			0.4317***	0.4314***
			(0.0379)	(0.0378)
Minimum wage	−0.0264***	−0.0343***	−0.0192***	−0.0159***
	(0.0019)	(0.0052)	(0.0053)	(0.0052)
Lagged minimum wage				0.0158***
				(0.0060)
Age	−0.0402***	−0.0090*	−0.0120	−0.0120
	(0.0022)	(0.0047)	(0.0081)	(0.0081)
Asset	0.0186***	0.0013	−0.0148	−0.0147
	(0.0041)	(0.0096)	(0.0185)	(0.0185)
No. of workers	0.0058***	−0.0034	−0.0364	−0.0364
	(0.0016)	(0.0036)	(0.0435)	(0.0434)
Share of sales	0.3878***	0.2518***	0.1731***	0.1735***
	(0.0132)	(0.0260)	(0.0360)	(0.0359)
Ownership				
SOEs				
Collective	0.0352***	0.0105	0.0067	0.0066
	(0.0089)	(0.0141)	(0.0085)	(0.0085)
Foreign	0.0501***	0.0193***	0.0011	0.0011
	(0.0011)	(0.0033)	(0.0042)	(0.0042)
Private	0.0577***	0.0171***	−0.0000	−0.0000
	(0.0011)	(0.0025)	(0.0034)	(0.0034)
Joint stock	0.0510***	0.0129***	−0.0006	−0.0006
	(0.0012)	(0.0027)	(0.0037)	(0.0037)
Joint Venture	0.0426***	0.0101	0.0019	0.0018
	(0.0042)	(0.0075)	(0.0115)	(0.0115)
Other	0.0453***	0.0127***	−0.0018	−0.0018
	(0.0011)	(0.0024)	(0.0034)	(0.0034)
Industry dummies	Yes	Yes	Yes	Yes
Year dummies	Yes	Yes	Yes	Yes
AR(1)			Pr > z=0.000	Pr > z=0.000
AR(2)			Pr > z=0.000	Pr > z=0.000
AR(3)			Pr > z=0.462	Pr > z=0.469
Sargan test			Pr > Chi^2 = 0.854	Pr > Chi^2 = 0.849
Hansen test			Pr > Chi^2 = 0.956	Pr > Chi^2 = 0.954
Adj. R^2	0.0458			
Overall R^2		0.0072		
No. of observations	202,456	202,456	202,456	202,456

Note Variable definitions are the same as those in Table 10.2. Two-digit industry dummies and year dummies are controlled in all estimations. Standard errors are in parenthesis. ***, **, * denote statistical significance at the 1, 5, 10% level, respectively

Data source Author's own calculation based on county level minimum wage data and firm-level panel data

enjoy the highest profitability while SOEs have the lowest profitability. Two-digit industry dummies and year dummies are also controlled but estimates of these variables are not reported here due to limited length.

As discussed in the previous section, however, the firm-level and local fixed effects may confound the OLS estimates. Column 2 in Table 10.3 reports fixed-effects estimates of a static panel firm profitability model shown in (3). After purging out the firm-level and local fixed effects, the negative effect of minimum wage on firm profitability becomes slightly bigger. Age and share sales of firms still have significant effect on firm profitability, though to a lesser extent. Asset and number of workers do not affect firm profitability. Since some firms may change ownership or enter other industries, ownership, and industry dummies can still be estimated in the fixed-effects model.[8]

Profitability in the previous period may affect profitability in the current period. To analyze state dependence of profitability, a dynamic panel model is estimated. As illustrated in (4), differenced lagged profitability is correlated with differenced error term by construction, we use further lags of profitability as instruments for differenced lagged profitability. The length of lags should be determined by the order of autocorrelation of u_{ijt}. The autocorrelation tests suggest that Δu_{ijt} is serially correlated with order 2. It follows that u_{ijt} is serially correlated with order 1. To be uncorrelated with Δu_{ijt}, lagged levels of profitability dated $t-3$ and earlier are used as instruments. As too many instruments may overfit endogenous variables and long lags may be weak instruments, we just use lagged levels of profitability dated from $t-3$ to $t-5$ as the instruments for differenced profitability. The results of Sargan–Hansen test suggest that our instruments are exogenous and cannot be rejected. The results of the difference GMM estimates of the dynamic panel model are listed in Column 3 of Table 10.3. Obviously, lagged profitability has a positive effect on profitability in the current year. After extending the static panel model to the dynamic panel model, minimum wage still has a negative effect on firm profitability but with a smaller magnitude. Share of sales has positive effect on profitability while firm age, asset, number of workers, and firm ownership do not affect profitability.

As firms may take time to adjust in response to changes in the minimum wage, a lagged minimum wage is introduced into the dynamic panel data model specified in (4), which is also our preferred linear dynamic panel model specification. We focus on the estimates of the minimum wage and the lagged minimum wage since results are rather similar for other variables if comparing Columns 3 and 4. After a lagged minimum wage is included, the minimum wage in the current period remains significantly negative; however, the coefficient of the lagged minimum wage is significantly positive. Moreover, the absolute values of the minimum wage and its lag are almost the same. The overall effect of minimum wages on firm profitability would be −0.0001 and is not statistically different from zero.[9]

The linear dynamic panel model is estimated at the conditional mean of firm profitability, which restricts the effect of minimum wage on profitability is the same for firms at different conditional quantiles of profitability. In reality, it may not be the case. To capture the different effect of minimum wage on profitability, a quantile regression dynamic panel model with the use of instruments is employed following Galvao (2011), the results of which are reported in Table 10.4. As shown in Table 10.4, state dependence of profitability is higher in the middle of the conditional distribution of profitability than both ends of conditional distribution. The minimum wage in the current period has a negative effect on profitability across conditional quantiles of profitability, and the absolute value of this negative effect exhibits a U shape with conditional quantiles. The effect of lagged minimum wage on profitability turns out, however, to have different effect on profitability. At the low end of conditional distribution of profitability, lagged minimum wages have a positive effect on firm profitability. In the middle of conditional distribution of profitability, lagged minimum wage does not affect profitability. At high conditional quantiles of profitability, lagged minimum wage tends to have a negative effect on profitability.[10] It is worth noting that median regression is shown in Table 10.4, and mean regression listed in Table 10.3 yields quite different estimates. For instance, lagged minimum wage has no effect on profitability as suggested by the median regression. However, it affects profitability positively as reflected by the mean regression. The striking difference in the estimates implies that the linear dynamic panel model may suffer from bias due to outliers, lending further support for the use of the quantile regression dynamic panel model. Taking minimum wage and its lag together, minimum wage has no effect on profitability for firms at the 10th and 30th quantiles.[11] However, the overall effect of minimum wage has negative effect on profitability for firms at the 50th, 70th, and 90th quantiles and its effects are statistically significant at the 1% level.

Table 10.4 Regression results of the quantile regression dynamic panel model

	10th quantile	*30th quantile*	*50th quantile*	*70th quantile*	*90th quantile*
Lagged profitability	0.3383***	0.4003***	0.4758***	0.4170***	0.1621***
	(0.0110)	(0.0079)	(0.0075)	(0.0079)	(0.0113)
Minimum wage	−0.0275***	−0.0093*	−0.0163***	−0.0314***	−0.0369***
	(0.0074)	(0.0053)	(0.0050)	(0.0053)	(0.0076)
Lagged minimum wage	0.0226***	0.0077	0.0046	−0.0015	−0.0284***
	(0.0078)	(0.0057)	(0.0053)	(0.0057)	(0.0081)
Age	−0.0430***	−0.0109***	−0.0128***	−0.0207***	−0.0347***
	(0.0033)	(0.0024)	(0.0023)	(0.0024)	(0.0034)
Asset	−0.0051	−0.0008	0.0080*	0.0253***	0.0577***
	(0.0063)	(0.0045)	(0.0042)	(0.0045)	(0.0064)
No. of workers	0.0086***	0.0026	−0.0006	−0.0046***	−0.0136***
	(0.0025)	(0.0018)	(0.0017)	(0.0018)	(0.0025)
Share	0.1701***	0.1188***	0.1172***	0.1776***	0.3398***
	(0.0206)	(0.0149)	(0.0140)	(0.0149)	(0.0212)
Ownership SOEs					
Collective	0.0423***	0.0042	0.0075	0.0094	0.0092
	(0.0137)	(0.0099)	(0.0093)	(0.0099)	(0.0140)
Foreign	0.0614***	0.0090***	0.0073***	0.0131***	0.0275***
	(0.0017)	(0.0012)	(0.0012)	(0.0012)	(0.0018)
Private	0.0933***	0.0150***	0.0095***	0.0102***	0.0126***
	(0.0017)	(0.0012)	(0.0012)	(0.0012)	(0.0018)
Joint stock	0.0749***	0.0111***	0.0064***	0.0090***	0.0180***
	(0.0019)	(0.0014)	(0.0013)	(0.0014)	(0.0020)
Joint Venture	0.0536***	0.0081*	0.0033	0.0068	0.0180***
	(0.0064)	(0.0047)	(0.0044)	(0.0047)	(0.0066)
Other	0.0756***	0.0106***	0.0056***	0.0064***	0.0129***
	(0.0017)	(0.0012)	(0.0012)	(0.0012)	(0.0018)
Industry dummies	Yes	Yes	Yes	Yes	Yes
Year dummies	Yes	Yes	Yes	Yes	Yes
No. of observations	202,456				

Note Standard errors are in parenthesis. ***, **, * denote statistical significance at the 1, 5, 10% level, respectively

Data source Author's own calculation based on county level minimum wage data and firm-level panel data

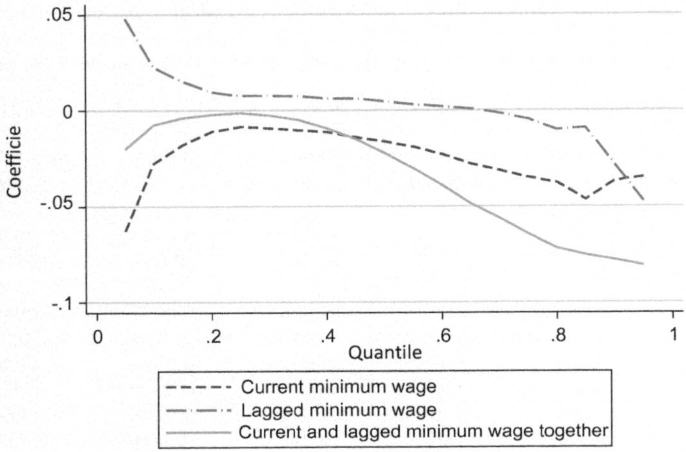

Fig. 10.2 Estimates of current minimum wage across the whole conditional distribution (*Data source* Author's own calculation based on county-level minimum wage data and firm-level panel data)

Table 10.4 reports estimates of the quantile regression dynamic panel model at only 5 conditional quantiles of profitability. Figure 10.2, instead, depicts the estimates of minimum wage and its lag across the whole conditional distribution of profitability. As shown in Fig. 10.2, the effect of the minimum wage in the current period on profitability exhibits an inverted-U shape across the conditional quantiles and its effects are significantly negative.[12] In contrast, the lagged effect of minimum wage on profitability is positive from the 5th quantile to 65th quantile and then becomes negative from the 70th quantile onwards. Lagged minimum wage is significant only at the 5th, 10th, 15th, 90th, and 95th quantiles. The overall effect of minimum wage on profitability is significant at the 5th quantile and quantiles higher than 40th. Turning to the magnitude of the overall effect of minimum wage, we can find that the absolute value of the effect of minimum wage on profitability increases with quantiles starting from the 40th quantiles.

10.6 Concluding Remarks

There is a large body of literature examining the effect of minimum wage on the wage level and employment. However, much less work has been undertaken on the effect of minimum wage on firms' profitability. As the minimum wage standard has been increasing and economic growth has slowed down in China, measuring the effect of minimum wage on firms' profitability is of vital importance. If the minimum wage is proven to have impressed negative effect on firm profitability, an increase in the minimum wage should be exercised with care, as the negative effect on profitability will be transmitted to wage level and employment.

Some previous studies examined the effect of minimum wage on firm profitability through the impact evaluation methods such as difference-in-difference. However, these studies usually focus on limited (most often, two) time scale. In contrast, this article utilizes firm-level panel datasets covering 11 years and thus makes use of much richer information from data. The firm-level panel data is combined with hand-collected data on minimum wage at the county level. Significant variations of minimum wage across counties and over years are, undoubtedly, of great help to accurately identify the effect of minimum wage on profitability.

To shed light on how firm-level and county-level fixed effects may affect the estimation results, an OLS and static panel data model are estimated. Although the static panel model purges fixed effects, the remaining time-varying unobservables, which may correlate with minimum wage, can still bias the estimates. More importantly, firms cannot adjust instantaneously in response to changes in the minimum wage. To this end, this article further estimates a dynamic panel model with lagged minimum wage. However, since the dynamic linear panel model is estimated upon the whole sample, the dynamics of firm profitability, as well as the effect of minimum wage on firm profitability, are restricted to be the same for all firms. In reality, the effect of minimum wage on firm profitability may be different across the distribution of profitability. Thus, the quantile regression dynamic panel model is estimated, following Galvao (2011), to capture the differing effect of minimum wage on firm profitability across the conditional quantile of profitability.

As the quantile regression dynamic panel model not only allows for the heterogeneous effect of the minimum wage but also is less susceptible to outliers, we treat it as our preferred model. Estimation results of that quantile regression dynamic panel model suggest that the effect of minimum wage in the current year is negative across the whole conditional distribution of profitability and it exhibits an inverted-U shape across conditional quantiles. Instead, the effect of lagged minimum wage is positive at the 5th, 10th, 15th quantiles, negative at the 90th and 95th quantiles, and not significant at other quantiles. Turning to the overall effect of minimum wage, minimum wage exerts significantly negative effect on profitability at the 5th quantile and quantiles higher than 40th and the absolute value of the effect of minimum wage increases with these quantiles. For other quantiles, the overall effect of minimum wage on profitability is negligible.

These results imply that firms cannot avoid the negative effect of current-year minimum wage on profitability. However, firms at the low end and middle of conditional distribution of profitability can cope with the negative effect of the lagged minimum wage. Firms with relatively low conditional profitability can even successfully increase their profitability in the second year in response to a minimum wage change in the previous year. As the shock of minimum wage in the current year is so large, the overall effect of minimum wage on profitability is negative for firms at the 5th conditional quantile and at the quantiles higher than 40th.

There are several caveats to be borne in mind and further studied, however, when interpreting the findings of this article. Firstly, as discussed earlier, there are several channels through which firms can cope with the change in the minimum wage. While this article estimates the effect of minimum wage on firm profitability, how firms adjust in response to changes in minimum wage remains unknown. Secondly, the firm sample used in this article is mainly composed of large firms. Since small- and medium-scaled firms are more likely to be affected by changes in minimum wage, more representative firm data is needed to better measure the effect of minimum wage on profitability. Thirdly, the attrition rate of our firm sample is ineligible,[13] which may introduce a selection bias to our estimates of the effect of minimum wage on profitability.

Notes

1. The same argument is made by Baker et al. (1999), who claimed that, compared to the USA, the minimum wage in Canada was under provincial, rather than federal, jurisdiction, providing a better basis for investigating the minimum wage effect.
2. The constant term is omitted here for easy exposition.

3. For studies on the effect of adjustment cost on firms' input reallocation in China, please see Cooper et al. (2013) as an example.
4. Baker et al. (1999) examine carefully the lagged effect of minimum wage on employment.
5. $\Delta u_{ijt} = \Delta \sigma_{jt} + \Delta \varepsilon_{ijt}$
6. Z_{ijt} includes MW_{jt} and P_{ijt}.
7. Similar findings are documented for Indian firms in Majumdar (1997) and for EU food processing firms in Hirsch et al. (2014).
8. Admittedly, measurement errors in ownership and industry may cause false time-varying changes.
9. $\frac{\widehat{\beta}+\widehat{\delta}}{1-\widehat{\rho}} = -0.0001$ with Prob > $Chi^2 = 0.9931$.
10. For brevity, we choose not to comment on estimates of other variables.
11. The corresponding p value is 0.1171 and 0.4702, respectively.
12. Standard errors are not reported here.
13. As reported by Brandt et al. (2012), the annual rate of attrition in the firm data covering the period from 1998 to 2007 was nearly 14%.

References

Anderson, Theodore W., and Cheng Hsiao. 1981. "Estimation of Dynamic Models with Error Components." *Journal of the American Statistical Association* 76 (September): 589–606.

Arellano, Manuel, and Stephen Bond. 1991. "Some Tests of Specification for Panel Data: Monte Carlo Evidence and an Application to Employment Equations." *Review of Economic Studies* 58 (2): 277–297.

Baker, Michael, Dwayne Benjamin, and Shuchita Stanger. 1999. "The Highs and Lows of the Minimum Wage Effect: A Time-Series Cross-Section Study of the Canadian Law." *Journal of labour Economics* 17 (2): 318–350.

Boeri, Tito, and Jan van Ours. 2008. *The Economics of Imperfect Labour Markets.* Princeton, NJ: Princeton University Press.

Brandt, Loren, Johannes van Biesebroeck, and Yifan Zhang. 2012. "Creative Accounting or Creative Destruction? Firm-Level Productivity Growth in Chinese Manufacturing." *Journal of Development Economics* 97 (2): 339–351.

Card, David, and Alan B. Krueger. 1994. "Minimum Wage and Employment: A Case Study of the Fast-Food Industry in New Jersey and Pennsylvania." *American Economic Review* 84: 772–793.

Card, David, and Alan B. Krueger. 1995. *Myth and Measurement: The New Economics of the Minimum Wage*. Princeton, NJ: Princeton University Press.

Chernozhukov, Victor, and Christian Hansen. 2006. "Instrumental Quantile Regression Inference for Structural and Treatment Effects Models." *Journal of Econometrics* 132: 491–525.

Cooper, Russell, Guan Gong, and Ping Yan. 2013. "Costly Labour Adjustment: General Equilibrium Effects of China's Employment Regulations." NBER Working Paper No. 19324.

Cuong, Nguyen Viet. 2017. "Do Minimum Wage Increases Matter to Firm Profitability? The Case of Vietnam." *Journal of International Development* 29 (6): 790–804.

Draca, Mirko, Stephen Machin, and John van Reenen. 2011. "Minimum Wages and Firm Profitability." *American Economic Journal: Applied Economics* 3 (1): 129–151.

Galvao, Antonio F. 2011. "Quantile Regression for Dynamic Panel Data with Fixed Effects." *Journal of Econometrics* 164 (1): 142–157.

Hamermesh, Daniel S., and Gerard A. Pfann. 1996. "Adjustment Costs in Factor Demand." *Journal of Economic Literature* 34 (3): 1264–1292.

Harasztosi, Péter, and Attila Lindner. 2015. "Who Pays for the Minimum Wage?" Working Paper No?

Hirsch, Stefan, Jan Schiefer, Adelina Gschwandtner, and Monika Hartmann. 2014. "The Determinants of Firm Profitability Differences in EU Food Processing." *Journal of Agricultural Economics* 65 (3): 703–721.

Holtz-Eakin, Douglas, Whitney Newey, and Harvey S. Rosen. 1988. "Estimating Vector Autoregressions with Panel Data." *Econometrica* 56 (6): 1371–1395.

Lin, Carl. 2012. "Less Myth, More Measurement: Decomposing Excess Returns from the 1989 Minimum Wage Hike." IZA Discussion Paper No. 6269.

Ma, Shuang, and Li Gan. 2013. "Zuidi Gongzi dui Qiye Zaizhi Peixun de Yingxiang Fenxi" [Minimum Wage and On-the-Job Training]. *Jingjixue Jikan* [*China Economic Quarterly*] 13 (1): 1–26.

Majumdar, Sumit. 1997. "The Impact of Size and Age on Firm-Level Performance: Some Evidence from India." *Review of Industrial Organization* 12: 231–241.

Mayneris, Florian, Sandra Poncet, and Zhang Tao. 2015. "The Cleansing Effect of Minimum Wage: Minimum Wage Rules, Firm Dynamics and Aggregate Productivity in China." Revised Version of IRES DP 2014–15.

Neumark, David, Mark Schweitzer, and William Wascher. 2004. "Minimum Wage Effects Throughout the Wage Distribution." *Journal of Human Resources* 39 (2): 425–450.

Pacheco, Gail, and Vic Naiker. 2006. "Impact of the Minimum Wage on Expected Profits." *International Review of Applied Economics* 20 (4): 469–490.

Roodman, David. 2009. "How to Do xtabond2: An Introduction to Difference and System GMM in Stata." *The Stata Journal* 9 (1): 86–136.

Sun, Churen, Ka Zhang, and Tao Zhang. 2013. "Zuidi Gongzi Yiding hui Jianshao Qiye de Chukou ma" [Does Minimum Wage Decrease Firms' Export]. *Shijie Jingji y* [*World Economy*] 8: 100–124.

Windmeijer, Frank. 2005. "A Finite Sample Correction for the Variance of Linear Efficient Two-Step GMM Estimators." *Journal of Econometrics* 126 (1): 25–51.

CHAPTER 11

How Does the Minimum Wage Affect Firm Investments in Fixed and Human Capital? Evidence from China

Tobias Haepp and Carl Lin

11.1 Introduction

As part of its endeavor to ensure the provision of basic living standards for its workforce, China accepted the ILO Minimum Wage Fixing Convention in 1984 and issued the "Enterprises Minimum Wage Regulations" in 1993. In 2004, the government passed new minimum wage regulations, requiring each province to increase its minimum wage at least biannually and increasing the fines for non-compliant companies. The frequency and scale of minimum wage adjustments across the Chinese economy have subsequently increased significantly. In those parts of the country that had implemented a minimum wage by

T. Haepp (✉)
Institute for Employment Research (IAB), Nuremberg, Germany
e-mail: tobias.haepp@iab.de

C. Lin
Bucknell University, Lewisburg, PA, USA
e-mail: carl.lin@bucknell.edu

L. Shi and C. Lin (eds.), *Minimum Wages in China*,
https://doi.org/10.1007/978-981-15-2421-9_11

1996, nominal minimum wage levels increased by 90.42% until 2004. This was followed by an increase of 178.05% in the subsequent years until 2012. During our study period from 2000 until 2007, the average national nominal minimum wage rose from 252 RMB (about US$ 30) to 496 RMB (about US$ 68).[1] According to data from the Urban Household Survey used in Fang and Lin (2015), 8.91% of urban workers and 57.01% of urban female workers were earning the minimum wage or less between 2004 and 2009. While data on rural migrant workers are scarce, the effect of the minimum wage on this group is estimated to be even larger due to their predominance in low-wage sectors (Wang and Gunderson 2011).

The expansion of the Chinese minimum wage system has been accompanied by an ongoing controversy regarding the suitability of the policy for the Chinese economy. Proponents argue that it is a necessary means to warrant sufficient living standards for vulnerable workers and that it introduces incentives for companies to upgrade excessively labor-intensive production technology, while opponents of the minimum wage policy argue that the policy interferes with the transition to a market economy and that it raises production costs, in turn harming the international competitiveness of Chinese companies (Cooke 2005; Wang and Gunderson 2011). Recent research has investigated the effect of the minimum wage on employment and found adverse effects for parts of the Chinese labor force, including female labor (Wang and Gunderson 2012; Jia 2014), and workers in non-state-owned enterprises and slow-growing regions (Wang and Gunderson 2011) as well as young adults and low-skilled workers (Fang and Lin 2015). The effect of the Chinese minimum wage policy on firm investment behavior, which is a direct determinant of long-term company competitiveness, has not been analyzed thus far and the current work aims to make a contribution to fill this gap in the literature. We first analyze whether the cost burden imposed on companies through an increase in minimum wages has harmed company competitiveness in terms of the ability to invest in fixed capital. We then investigate how minimum wages affect the ability of companies to invest in human capital. Investment in human capital is of particular importance in the Chinese case, since it is a key channel to achieve the envisioned skill upgrading in the industrial sector.

The theoretical predictions regarding the effect of an exogenous change in the price of labor due to an increase in the minimum wage differ between standard neoclassical models and non-competitive models of the labor market. Based on standard neoclassical theory, an increase in the price of labor induces firms to substitute away from affected workers. The effect on capital thus depends on the degree of substitutability or complementarity between the two factors of production. Moreover, the cost burden imposed on companies through minimum wages potentially affects capital investments via a scale effect as product prices rise and the level of output drops. The overall effect of an increase in the minimum wage on capital investment therefore depends on the direction and size of the substitution effect and the size of the scale effect.

For the theoretical effect of minimum wage hikes on company training investments, the standard human capital model with competitive labor markets based on Becker (1993) predicts a negative effect on company training expenditures since workers finance their on-the-job training through lower wages. In this case, the introduction of a minimum wage reduces the level of training because it restricts the pay reductions workers can accept to finance the training (Rosen 1972; Feldstein 1973).

More recently, non-competitive models of the labor market have been developed in which labor market frictions and asymmetric information lead to a wedge between wages and marginal productivity (Acemoglu and Pischke 1999). In these models, it can be profitable for a firm to retain a worker despite the increase in wage costs if it can increase worker productivity through investments in capital or training and claim the resulting rents. Contrary to the results from traditional models, a compression of wages through minimum wages may thus induce an increase in fixed capital investments and firm-sponsored training in non-competitive models (Pischke 2005; Acemoglu and Pischke 2003). Hybrid models of the labor market that relax the assumption of perfect competition generally predict that the incidence of the minimum wage varies with the degree of competition and the amount of rents that can be allocated.

Currently, there is an ongoing debate reinforced by mixed empirical evidence about which model provides a better fit for empirical data. The present work aims to contribute to this debate by jointly analyzing the effect on the two types of investments and by providing the first piece of evidence on the link between the minimum wage and firm-financed training from a developing economy.

To empirically analyze our research question, we employ the Chinese Annual Census of Industrial Firms (CASIF) data set, which covers the introduction of the new minimum wage regulations in 2004.

We include the three years leading up to the reform as well as the four subsequent years during which the magnitude and frequency of minimum wage adjustments across China increased significantly. We then estimate dynamic panel data regressions accounting for the inter-temporal adjustment of fixed capital investments as well as logit and tobit panel data regressions accounting for the incidence of censoring of our dependent variable in the human capital regressions. We find that the minimum wage hikes have caused a decrease in the likelihood of firms to invest in human capital, as well as in the amount of human capital investment per worker.

11.2 Review of the Empirical Literature

A monumental body of literature has analyzed the various adjustment channels through which firms absorb the labor cost increase due to minimum wage hikes. In addition to the employment effect, which has been identified for the case of China at least for parts of the labor force, profit reductions are generally considered a key channel of adjustment. Analyzing this topic for another Asian developing economy, Nguyen (2017) employs a difference-in-difference methodology with propensity score matching and finds no statistically significant effect on firm profits in Vietnam after a minimum wage hike of about 20% in 2005. Draca et al. (2011) adopt a difference-in-difference approach and show that the introduction of the UK minimum wage in 1999 has reduced firm profitability. Metcalf (2008) concludes that the ability of firms to absorb the increase in labor costs through a reduction in company profits is one of the reasons for an absence of a negative employment effect of the policy in the UK. In a detailed survey study jointly analyzing a range of adjustment channels for local US quick-service restaurants, Hirsch et al. (2011) find that companies adjust through a range of channels, including price increases, profit reductions, lower wage growth for high-pay workers and savings on other cost components. While an extensive exposition of the literature analyzing company effects of minimum wages other than those on firm investment is beyond the scope of this article, it is important to bear in mind that the ability of companies to absorb the cost increase resulting from minimum wages through other channels also affects the rates of fixed and human capital investments.

Regarding the company fixed capital investment decision, little research has been conducted on this topic thus far and mixed effects have been found in these studies. Rama (1999, 2001) finds that doubling the minimum wage in Indonesia during the early 1990s has led to a decrease in employment of 2% and a decrease in investment of 5%. Based on a model of labor markets with frictions, Pischke (2005) argues that labor market institutions such as unions and minimum wages, which distribute rents to lower-skilled workers, raise the incentive for firms to invest in their training and the fixed capital that is associated with their jobs. His empirical analysis based on OECD economies and differences in labor market institutions between Europe and the USA roughly supports this theory. A recent report by Riley and Bondibene (2013), however, concludes that the introduction of a national minimum wage in the UK has not affected employment and investment levels.

As explained in the introduction, according to the two different theories on the link between the minimum wage and training, minimum wages could lead to either a reduction in on-the-job training (Rosen 1972; Feldstein 1973) or an increase in training (Acemoglu and Pischke 2003). Interestingly, the empirical evidence on this topic is also mixed which could be due to either the absence of any effect, heterogeneous and potentially offsetting effects or problems related to the measurement of training in the different studies (Neumark and Wascher 2008). After most of the earlier studies on the topic were plagued by methodological problems, Neumark and Wascher (2001) were the first to control for US state variation in minimum wage levels and inter-state differences in training unrelated to the minimum wage. The authors conclude that the minimum wage has led to a reduction in on-the-job training. Acemoglu and Pischke (2003) criticize the methodology in Neumark and Wascher (2001) for using all young workers as treatment group and arriving at unreasonably high estimates for the size of the negative effect. After revising their treatment group to workers with wages below the minimum wage, the authors find no significant effects of the minimum wage. The effect on training expenditures may therefore vary between companies and industries depending on these factors. More recently, Fairris and Pedace (2004) were the first to utilize an employer survey on the incidence of training and found no evidence of a reduction in training hours or the amount of workers covered by staff training.

In the only notable study conducted outside the USA, Arulampalam et al. (2004) find no evidence that the minimum wage has reduced training and some evidence that it has improved training in the UK. The inconsistency of previous results, the scarcity of studies from less advanced economies and a frequent focus on the introduction of a uniform national level minimum wage as single policy shift underline the fact that significant scope exists for future research on the effect of minimum wages on firm investment behavior.

11.3 Methodology

11.3.1 Measuring the Firm-Level Impact of the Minimum Wage

For our empirical analysis of the effect of Chinese minimum wages on the capital investment decision, we construct a panel data set of Chinese firms. Since the new minimum wage regulations were introduced in 2004, we choose the period from 2000 to 2007 as our study period. Including the reform year as well as the pre- and post-reform periods provides significant variation over time in terms of the impact of the minimum wage on individual firms.[2]

A crucial element of our methodology is to identify the firms that are affected by the minimum wage in their county.[3] As in previous work employing firm data (Draca et al. 2011; Riley and Bondibene 2013; Nguyen 2017), we make use of average worker wage cost data to measure the extent to which firms are affected by the local minimum wage level.[4] In particular, we calculate two measures for the exposure to the minimum wage for the firms in our data set: a dichotomous treatment indicator variable and a continuous variable measuring the treatment intensity for those firms whose average wage is below the minimum wage. Using aw_{it} to denote the logarithm of the average wage level of firm i in year t and mw_{jt} to denote the logarithm of the minimum wage level of county j in period t, our treatment dummy variable takes the following values:

$$treatdum_{it} = \begin{cases} 0 & \text{if } aw_{it} \geq mw_{jt} \\ 1 & \text{if } aw_{it} < mw_{jt} \end{cases} \tag{11.1}$$

and our continuous variable measuring the treatment intensity for treated firms is as follows[5]:

$$treatint_{it} = \begin{cases} 0 & \text{if } aw_{it} \geq mw_{jt} \\ mw_{jt} - aw_{it} & \text{if } aw_{it} < mw_{jt} \end{cases} \tag{11.2}$$

Both of our treatment indicators therefore take on the value zero for our control group firms and values greater than zero for treated companies.

A question that arises with these measures of a minimum wage treatment is whether the changes in minimum wages are exogenous. In order to engage with this concern, we provide evidence based on Urban Household Surveys collected by the National Bureau of Statistics of China (NBS) in Table 11.11 in the appendix of this article showing that minimum wages cannot be explained by local labor market conditions.[6]

11.3.2 *Fixed Capital Investments: Estimation Strategy*

After identifying our treatment and control groups, we proceed to the estimation strategy for our fixed capital and human capital regressions. Our empirical specification for our fixed capital estimations is based on an error-correction model of firm investment (Bean 1981; Bond et al. 2003). In this framework, firms face barriers to instant adjustment of their capital stock and the movement of a firm toward its optimal capital stock can be modeled as a dynamic process. Assuming that the optimal capital stock (K^*) of firm i is a function of its output (Υ), unobserved firm-specific effects (θ_i) and unobserved year-specific effects (ζ_t), a second-order autoregressive distributed lag model of the dynamic relationship between the realized (K) and the optimal capital stock can be written in error-correction form as[7]:

$$\Delta k_{it} = \alpha 0 \Delta k_{i,t-1} + \alpha 1 \Delta y_{it} + \alpha 2 \Delta y_{i,t-1} + \alpha 3 \left(k_{i,t-2} - y_{i,t-2}\right) + \theta_i + \zeta_t + \varepsilon_{it} \tag{11.3}$$

where lower-case Latin letters denote the logarithms of upper-case variables. Similar to the empirical implementation in Chen and Zheng (2008), we also include current and lagged firm profits and debt levels as additional explanatory variables to control for the impact of financial factors on the investment decision.[8] As a normalization, we divide both of these variables by the capital stock at the beginning of each period. Using I to denote investment rates, *treat* to denote either our dichotomous or continuous treatment variable and summarizing the above coefficients (α) and variables (x_{it}) in matrix notation, we obtain our fixed capital investment regression equation as:

$$I_{it} = \alpha^0 x_{it} + \beta \, treat_{it-1} + \varepsilon_{it} \tag{11.4}$$

Special attention needs to be given to the appropriate estimation strategy for this equation. In particular, estimating this dynamic process via an OLS estimation of the levels or by estimating the within-group fixed-effect transformation of the above equation would both yield biased estimators due to the positive correlation of regressors with the error term (Nickell 1981). An estimator that yields unbiased and consistent results for such an autoregressive process with possibly endogenous regressors in a situation with a large number of cross-sectional units and few time periods as in our case is the first-difference Generalized Method of Moments (GMM) estimator developed by Arellano and Bond (1991). Their estimation procedure first removes the time-invariant firm-specific effects through first differencing and then derives instruments to be utilized in the estimation from lagged values of the regressors. Since the problem of instrument proliferation is negligible in our case, we adopt the most general specification and employ all available higher-order lagged values of our right-hand side variables in Eq. 11.3 as well as of our financial variables as instruments.[9] The consistency and unbiasedness of our GMM estimator rely on the assumptions that serial correlation in the error term is absent and the instruments are valid.[10] We implement the Sargan/Hansen test for joint instrument validity and autocorrelation tests proposed in Arellano and Bond (1991) to ascertain the validity of both assumptions.

11.3.3 Human Capital Investments: Estimation Strategy

For our analysis of the effect of minimum wage hikes on the human capital investment decision, we estimate the following regression:

$$H_{it} = \gamma^0 z_{it-1} + \delta \, treat_{it-1} + \varepsilon_{it} \tag{11.5}$$

where our dependent variable H is investments in human capital measured as training expenditures per worker, *treat* is either our dichotomous or our continuous treatment variable, z is a vector of control variables and ε is a stochastic error term. As in previous literature analyzing the effect of the minimum wage on firm training expenditures (Arulampalam et al. 2004; Fairris and Pedace 2004), our firm-level controls essentially aim to capture firm-level heterogeneity by including variables such as workforce size, wages and labor productivity. These controls are measured in the previous period to ensure the exogeneity of these variables.[11] We also include dummy variables for state or foreign ownership and exporter status of a firm. These variables take on zero values for non-state-owned companies, local companies and non-exporters, respectively.[12]

Because of the censoring of our human capital investment variable, least squares estimation of human capital models would result in biased estimators (see, e.g., Greene 2003). We therefore first estimate a logit model with a binary dependent variable measuring the presence or absence of human capital investment in order to analyze the impact of the minimum wage on the likelihood of firms to undertake human capital investments for those firms that have invested in human capital in some periods and have not invested in others. Secondly, we then estimate tobit models with human capital investment rates as the dependent variable and analyze the effect of the minimum wage on the level of human capital investment rates of all firms. In our logit regressions for human capital investment, we are able to control for firm-level fixed effects. For the tobit model panel data estimator, no estimator with individual fixed effects exists that allows for conditioning on covariates. In our tobit regressions, we thus control for industry-level fixed effects at the two-digit level and mimic individual effects by including a range of variables reflecting the staff structure of companies. These variables have only been investigated in the 2004 version of the CASIF survey, and we include those values for each firm in all time periods covered. In particular, we include a dummy variable for the presence of a workers' union and calculate the shares of technical staff, staff holding a university degree and the share of female workers.

11.4 Data Set and Statistics of Key Variables

11.4.1 Data Sources and Data Editing

The first type of data used in this section is the minimum wage data that have been collected from the Web sites of local governments across China. In particular, we obtain the precise dates of minimum wage amendments and minimum wage levels for a total of 2606 Chinese counties and calculate the respective weighted annual average minimum wage in each of these geographical units.[13] The development of real minimum wages over time is shown in Table 11.1. As mentioned in the introduction, Chinese minimum wages have increased rapidly, especially after the introduction of the new regulations in 2004. From an empirical

Table 11.1 Chinese provincial minimum wages over time (in RMB per month)

Province	*2000*	*2001*	*2002*	*2003*	*2004*	*2005*	*2006*	*2007*
East Beijing	406.0	410.8	444.5	458.2	507.6	541.2	581.8	638.0
Fujian	259.8	282.6	302.6	313.9	314.6	343.4	406.6	463.0
Guangdong	338.6	350.7	362.7	371.2	365.0	417.4	447.9	488.9
Hainan	277.5	308.6	348.9	348.4	361.2	383.1	415.2	434.9
Hebei	242.5	241.3	283.9	285.9	354.4	426.9	424.8	419.9
Jiangsu	275.8	301.0	319.6	360.8	404.3	426.2	488.5	535.6
Shandong	264.1	287.0	325.4	347.5	335.3	408.9	416.1	430.8
Shanghai	424.8	467.5	510.0	549.4	586.5	638.8	676.2	720.1
Tianjin	347.3	394.1	425.0	449.0	481.2	524.6	600.6	641.1
Zhejiang	372.5	398.6	410.6	423.8	468.8	525.9	578.6	625.5
Northeast Heilongjiang	262.6	260.5	262.4	284.9	274.4	271.2	353.0	377.4
Jilin	231.6	228.6	251.8	278.3	303.0	298.5	369.7	514.6
Liaoning	265.7	268.7	278.4	273.8	276.1	346.1	378.1	424.3
Central Anhui	220.1	272.9	290.7	300.5	293.8	308.3	321.5	361.0
Henan	209.8	208.4	208.2	216.5	238.3	253.3	309.0	325.7
Hubei	203.7	203.1	276.8	270.8	258.1	289.7	293.1	351.8
Hunan	231.3	252.4	280.9	311.6	326.1	345.7	373.2	392.1
Jiangxi	214.1	220.3	220.1	218.4	243.1	300.6	301.7	392.6
Shanxi	225.9	226.3	270.7	265.9	387.1	418.6	417.1	431.6
West Chongqing	246.2	257.5	279.0	287.9	322.9	343.6	373.9	431.1
Gansu	227.6	235.2	235.2	232.7	283.2	278.4	291.0	304.2
Guangxi	172.0	223.7	313.0	309.7	313.4	354.8	359.0	366.9
Guizhou	213.4	209.6	238.8	290.3	291.1	323.4	349.3	430.5
Inner Mongolia	238.1	236.7	251.2	289.9	324.5	358.6	363.2	375.5
Ningxia	264.2	264.0	311.1	306.1	321.3	319.0	362.7	377.4
Qinghai	236.3	230.3	225.1	220.7	238.8	311.2	352.7	374.3
Shaanxi	213.0	225.7	273.3	269.2	262.4	335.4	420.2	413.8
Sichuan	160.9	161.4	211.0	253.4	276.6	318.1	291.4	366.0
Xinjiang	257.7	258.4	292.0	290.8	306.6	316.4	345.1	401.1
Yunnan	233.1	235.2	261.2	283.2	286.5	339.6	367.3	379.0

Note Minimum wages have been calculated as time-weighted and population-weighted average values based on county-level minimum wage data. Values have been deflated to the price level in year 2000

perspective, another interesting feature of the Chinese system of minimum wages is that it has not only developed rapidly over time, but the levels also differ significantly between provinces and within provinces between different counties. For example, at the end of our study period in 2007, the nominal minimum wage in Shanghai was at 840 RMB, approximately 2.6 times the level of 320 RMB in the less developed areas of Gansu Province. At the same time, the minimum wage level in Lanzhou, the capital of Gansu Province, was already at 430 RMB, hence approximately 34% above the lowest level in the same province. Liaoning Province can be credited with the most complex minimum wage system and its nominal minimum wages ranged from 420 to 700 RMB in the final year of our study.

The second data source employed in this section is the CASIF, which has been conducted by the NBS. The survey includes data from all state-owned firms as well as all non-state-owned industrial firms with a revenue of more than 5 million RMB (about US$ 680,000).[14] This firm-level data set enables us to calculate our dependent and explanatory variables as well as a range of control variables including sales volume, employment levels, and industry classifications. In order to construct a panel data set, our main method to match companies over time is to utilize their registration ID. Since some company IDs change over time and a few IDs occur for multiple firms, we adopt the procedure proposed in Brandt et al. (2012) and also utilize other firm information such as the names of legal firm representatives, office phone numbers and addresses to merge firms over time.[15] Disaggregated deflators for the prices of output and capital at the industry and province level have been collected from various editions of the China statistical yearbook (NBS 2008).[16] We deflate all monetary values in our data set to the price level in year 2000, which is the first year included in our data set. We then clean our data set from reporting errors and typos in the construction of the database by deleting all firms with zero or negative values for one of the following variables: capital stock, number of employees, output or sales volume and wage expenditures. As a final logical consistency check, we also exclude observations reporting a depreciation in the current period that is higher than the capital stock in the previous period. As in other work analyzing the effects of policies on company investments, we exclude companies with fixed capital investment rates greater than one from our analysis to prevent outliers from contaminating our results. Our firm data set is then merged with our minimum wage data set through a six-digit administrative division code.

11.4.2 Dependent Variables, Explanatory Variable and Descriptive Statistics

We then proceed to the calculation of our wage variable and our dependent variables. We calculate the average wage per worker in year *t* as firm-level wage expenditures divided by the average number of staff employed throughout the year. For the calculation of our fixed capital investment variable, we employ the perpetual inventory method and calculate firm-level investment rates as the change in the firm capital stock plus depreciation, divided by the capital stock in the previous period. Firm investment rates in human capital are calculated as the amount of training expenditures divided by the number of employees.[17] Our final data set consists of 1,118,675 firm-year observations from the seven-year period between 2001 and 2007.[18]

Table 11.2 presents the key statistical properties of our dependent variables as well as the ratio of the minimum wage to the firm-level average wage for each year in our data set. The steady growth in size and number of Chinese companies results in the successive inclusion of additional firms in our database, and the number of annual observations increases from 101,979 observations in 2001 to 237,363 observations in 2007. The minimum wage level amounts to between approximately 50 and 60% of the company-level average wage in most years covered. In the reform year of 2004 and the first year thereafter, the minimum wage rises to more than 60% of average wages until companies adjust their wage levels and the ratio drops to a level below the pre-reform period. Average training expenditures per worker rise from 58 RMB in the first year to a level of about 88 RMB toward the end of our study period. Differences between firms are large for this variable and firms with high investment expenditures in human capital spend more than 1402 RMB per worker. Moreover, about 58.9% of our company-year observations report zero investment in human capital, hence necessitating the estimation of human capital investment regressions through logit and tobit models. The variable with the highest variation both over time and between firms is our fixed capital investment rate. Starting from 7.4% in 2001, it rises to approximately 12.0% in 2005 before dropping again to a level of 9.9% in the final year of our analysis. All three indicators exhibit significant variation both over time and between firms.

Table 11.2 Summary statistics for key variables over time

	Variable	*Mean*	*Std. Dev.*	*Min.*	*Max.*	*Observations*
2001	Investment rate	0.074	0.274	−0.855	1	93,393
	Training/labor	0.058	0.131	0	1.401	101,979
	Min. wage/avg. wage	0.556	0.324	0.04	3.846	101,979
2002	Investment rate	0.088	0.278	−0.855	1	105,964
	Training/labor	0.066	0.143	0	1.401	117,230
	Min. wage/avg. wage	0.560	0.329	0.039	3.839	117,230
2003	Investment rate	0.083	0.288	−0.855	1	112,142
	Training/labor	0.070	0.149	0	1.401	125,674
	Min. wage/avg. wage	0.547	0.325	0.039	4.39	125,674
2004	Investment rate	0.051	0.313	−0.855	1	115,069
	Training/labor	0.066	0.135	0	1.399	130,211
	Min. wage/avg. wage	0.716	0.364	0.042	4.59	130,211
2005	Investment rate	0.120	0.297	−0.855	1	170,285
	Training/labor	0.079	0.163	0	1.401	195,597
	Min. wage/avg. wage	0.521	0.229	0.039	4.79	195,597
2006	Investment rate	0.117	0.295	−0.855	1	186,230
	Training/labor	0.085	0.171	0	1.401	210,621
	Min. wage/avg. wage	0.507	0.222	0.035	4.809	210,621
2007	Investment rate	0.099	0.293	−0.855	1	211,098
	Training/labor	0.088	0.179	0	1.402	237,363
	Min. wage/avg. wage	0.492	0.223	0.044	4.995	237,363

Note Data have been deflated to the price level in year 2000. The unit of measurement for training expenditures per worker is thousand RMB

11.5 Wage Growth Comparison of Firms in Treated and Control Groups

The key underlying assumption of the theoretical link between minimum wage regulations and company development indicators is that a minimum wage increase drives up company wage expenditures for affected companies. We briefly investigate the link between the two variables by analyzing the difference in subsequent wage growth between treated and non-treated companies. To control for the difference in average wage levels between treated and non-treated companies, we split our companies into fifty quantiles according to their wage level and then compare subsequent changes in the log wage for the two groups

Table 11.3 Change in log wage for treated vs. control group firms

Quantile	*1*	2	3	4	5	6	7	8	9	*10*
Control	0.960	0.377	0.281	0.242	0.221	0.226	0.204	0.197	0.189	0.187
Treatment	1.039	0.633	0.623	0.638	0.611	0.602	0.585	0.575	0.598	0.611

Note The average wage of companies in the *1*st and *10*th wage quantile is 162.84 RMB and 469.69 RMB, respectively

in order to analyze whether they have been affected differently. The results displayed in Table 11.3 show that wage growth of treated companies is more than twice as high as wage growth of the non-treated group in the lowest quantiles. As we move up toward higher quantiles in the wage distribution, wage growth of the treated group amounts to more than four times the wage growth of non-treated companies. Relative to prevailing profit levels, the average wage bill of the affected firms increased by an additional 33.8%. We also regress subsequent average wage growth on minimum wage growth for treated and non-treated companies separately to compare the intensity of the impact of subsequent minimum wage growth on average wage growth. The coefficients of the subsequent wage growth variable are at least twice as high for treated companies compared to non-treated companies across different wage quantiles. The assumption therefore proves valid for our data set, and our instrument is an adequate tool to identify affected companies.

As pointed out by Ye et al. (2015), compliance rates with the minimum wage policy differ between companies depending on the ownership structure of a firm.[19] We therefore also investigate whether the impact of the minimum wage treatment differs between different firm types. In particular, we distinguish between local non-state-owned firms, state-owned firms and firms with investors from Hong Kong, Macao or Taiwan as well as foreign-invested firms. As displayed in Table 11.4, the four company types differ markedly in terms of their wage growth even within the same wage quantile. Foreign firms exhibit the highest wage growth, while wage growth in the state-owned sector is the lowest among the four at approximately one-quarter of foreign firm wage growth. The four company groups, however, hardly differ in terms of the treatment effect on wage growth and wage growth among treated companies is higher in almost all quantiles for all four company types. Despite the differences in policy compliance rates and wage growth, the treatment effect on wage growth therefore occurs for all four company types.

Table 11.4 Change in log wage for treated vs. control group firms by ownership type

	Quantile	*1*	2	3	4	5	6	7	8	9	*10*
LO	Control	0.444	0.299	0.253	0.241	0.224	0.204	0.193	0.193	0.179	0.167
	Treatment	0.753	0.619	0.624	0.599	0.575	0.560	0.570	0.592	0.574	0.589
SO	Control	0.449	0.225	0.245	0.178	0.172	0.163	0.131	0.127	0.144	0.089
	Treatment	0.675	0.480	0.438	0.411	0.334	0.339	0.351	0.344	0.332	0.456
NO	Control	0.518	0.386	0.379	0.310	0.305	0.276	0.244	0.238	0.181	0.188
	Treatment	0.951	0.690	0.639	0.683	0.666	0.653	0.664	0.524	0.726	0.467
FO	Control	0.570	0.382	0.380	0.330	0.317	0.264	0.296	0.231	0.210	0.197
	Treatment	0.946	0.804	0.710	0.728	0.757	0.632	0.810	0.702	0.745	0.751

Note LO refers to local privately or collectively owned firms, SO refers to state-owned enterprises, the nonmainland Chinese-owned enterprises (NO) are those owned by investors from either Hong Kong, Macao or Taiwan and FO refers to foreign-owned enterprises

11.6 Fixed and Human Capital Investment Regression Results

11.6.1 Employment Regression Results

To develop a more detailed account of how the Chinese minimum wage has affected investment levels, we first implement panel data regressions estimating the effect of the minimum wage on firm-level employment levels. To this end, we regress firm-level employment in the current period (L_{it}) on our treatment indicators, as well as on employment and a number of control variables (z_{it-1}) from the previous period. We also include controls for industries, cities and year-effects ($\mu_{c,k}$). The regression specification, which is similar to the prespecified research design adopted in Neumark (2001) and Campolieti et al. (2006), takes the following form:

$$L_{it} = \alpha^0 z_{it-1} + \beta L_{it-1} + \gamma \mu_{c,k} + \delta\, treat_{it-1} + \varepsilon_{it} \tag{11.6}$$

Our employment regression results shown in Table 11.5 indicate that the minimum wage has exerted a negative impact on firm-level employment levels. Huang et al. (2014) also find this negative effect for low-wage firms in the Chinese economy, which is the group of firms most similar to those in our treatment group. The negative effects from our firm-level analysis also reflect the negative employment effects found in studies using individual microdata (Jia 2014; Fang and Lin 2015) and those found based on provincial economic data (Wang and Gunderson 2011, 2012).

11.6.2 Basic Investment Regression Results

We then move on to the investment regressions, which is the main focus of our analysis. The first column in Table 11.6 displays the regression results of our fixed capital investment models with our dummy treatment indicator as explanatory variables, and the second column presents our fixed capital investment results with our treatment intensity indicator as explanatory variables. For both of our explanatory variables, we find no effect of the minimum wage on fixed capital investments.

Regarding the coefficient of our control variables, the change in the logarithm of output correlates positively and significantly with fixed capital investment, hence confirming the predictions of the accelerator model

Table 11.5 Employment regression results

	FE models	
	(1)	*(2)*
Treatment dummy (lag)	−0.075***	
	(0.003)	
Treatment intensity (lag)		−0.170***
		(0.009)
Log workforce size (lag)	0.458***	0.455***
	(0.007)	(0.007)
Average wage (lag)	0.000***	0.000***
	(0.000)	(0.000)
Labor productivity (lag)	0.426***	0.422***
	(0.048)	(0.048)
Export intensity (lag)	0.024***	0.024***
	(0.004)	(0.004)
Profit margin (lag)	0.198***	0.199***
	(0.010)	(0.010)
State owned (lag)	0.014**	0.014**
	(0.006)	(0.006)
Foreign owned (lag)	0.006*	0.006*
	(0.004)	(0.004)
HK/MC/TW owned (lag)	0.003	0.003
	(0.004)	(0.004)
Observations	750,877	750,877
Firms	255,317	255,317
R^2	0.288	0.287

Note Standard errors are clustered at the county level and displayed in parentheses. The respective significance symbols denote: $^*p < 0.10$, $^{**}p < 0.05$, $^{***}p < 0.01$

of investment. The error-correction term is negative and significant, hence confirming error-correction behavior of firms toward their optimal capital stock. The financial variables are insignificant, which was also previously found in Chen and Zheng (2008) for companies in most Chinese regions.

Table 11.7 displays the logit and tobit regression results of our human capital investment regressions with the dummy treatment indicator as explanatory variables (Models 3 and 5) and our treatment intensity indicator as explanatory variables (Models 4 and 6).[20] In our logit estimations, we omit the firms that do not display any variation in the dependent variable, i.e., the ones that either invest in human capital in

Table 11.6 Fixed capital investment regression results

	GMM models	
	(1)	*(2)*
Treatment dummy (lag)	0.001	
	(0.003)	
Treatment intensity (lag)		−0.004
		(0.010)
Investment rate (lag)	−0.390***	−0.393***
	(0.142)	(0.142)
Change in log output	0.470***	0.471***
	(0.062)	(0.062)
Change in log output (lag)	−0.249***	−0.250***
	(0.035)	(0.035)
Debt per capital	0.000	0.000
	(0.000)	(0.000)
Debt per capital (lag)	−0.000	−0.000
	(0.001)	(0.001)
Profit per capital	−0.004	−0.004
	(0.005)	(0.005)
Profit per capital (lag)	0.003	0.003
	(0.009)	(0.009)
Error correction term	−0.256***	−0.256***
	(0.035)	(0.035)
Average wage (lag)	−0.000 –	0.000
	(0.000)	(0.000)
Observations	222,174	222,174
Firms	94,938	94,938
Number of instruments	44	44
Hansen test (*p*-value)	0.482	0.486
AR(1) (*p*-value)	0.011	0.011
AR(2) (*p*-value)	0.290	0.281

Note Standard errors are clustered at the county level and displayed in parentheses. The significance levels investigated and their notations are: $^{*}p < 0.10$, $^{**}p < 0.05$, $^{***}p < 0.01$

every period or never invest in human capital. Our logit results for both explanatory variables indicate that the total effect on the likelihood of firms to invest in human capital is negative and significant. For our tobit regressions, we can retain all firms and all censored and uncensored firm-year observations.[21] Our tobit regressions with two alternative explanatory variables unequivocally demonstrate that the minimum wage has reduced the amount of training expenditures incurred per worker for Chinese companies.

Table 11.7 Human capital investment regression results

	Logit models		*Tobit models*	
	(3)	*(4)*	*(5)*	*(6)*
Treatment dummy (lag)	−0.089***		−0.014***	
	(0.000)		(0.000)	
Treatment intensity (lag)		−0.225***		−0.036***
		(0.000)		(0.000)
Average wage (lag)	0.000***	0.000***	0.000***	0.000***
	(0.000)	(0.000)	(0.000)	(0.000)
Employees (lag)	0.439***	0.435***	0.028***	0.028***
	(0.000)	(0.000)	(0.000)	(0.000)
Labor productivity (lag)	0.557***	0.549***	−0.034***	−0.035***
	(0.000)	(0.000)	(0.000)	(0.000)
State owned	0 013	0.014	−0.004**	−0.004**
	(0.069)	(0.678)	(0.018)	(0.010)
Foreign owned	0 017	0.017	−0.017***	−0.017***
	(0.505)	(0.473)	(0.000)	(0.000)
Exporter dummy	0.142***	0.142***	0.002	0.002
	(0.000)	(0.000)	(0.104)	(0.122)
Union dummy			0.093***	0.093***
			(0.000)	(0.000)
Technical staff (%)			0.114***	0.114***
			(0.000)	(0.000)
University degree (%)			0.356***	0.356***
			(0.000)	(0.000)
Female staff (%)			−0.081***	−0.081***
			(0.000)	(0.000)
Firm fixed effects	Yes	Yes	No	No
Industry fixed effects	No	No	Yes	Yes
Observations	370,591	370,591	756,511	756,511
Log likelihood	−142,146.8	−142,144.9	−217,787.7	−217,783.5
Chi^2	1332.8	1274.0	36,169.8	42,488.2
Prob $Chi^2 > 0$	0.000	0.000	0.000	0.000
σ_u			0.210***	0.210***
σ_e			0.203***	0.203***
ρ			0.517	0.517

Note Standard errors calculated from 100 bootstraps are shown in parentheses. The significance levels investigated and their notations are: $^{*}p < 0.10$, $^{**}p < 0.05$, $^{***}p < 0.01$

Some interesting findings also emerge from the results of our human capital regression covariates. The human capital stock and firm size both correlate positively with human capital investments. Foreign-owned companies in the Chinese market are characterized by lower investment rates than local companies, while exporters are more likely to invest in human capital. The establishment of a workers' union as well as the shares of technical staff and university graduates in total staff all correlates positively with human capital investment rates, whereas the share of female workers correlates negatively with human capital investment rates.

11.6.3 Investment Regression Results for Different Firm Ownership Types

In this subsection, we again split our firms into groups according to the four different ownership types introduced in the previous section and implement our fixed and human capital investment regressions separately for each group.[22] For our fixed capital investment regressions shown in Table 11.8, the results do not differ between company types.[23] Error-correction behavior and the output effect predicted by the accelerator model of investment are confirmed in all regressions except for the state-owned group.

In contrast to the fixed capital investment regression results, Table 11.9 shows the results of our human capital investment regressions which are remarkably homogeneous across local private owned, state-owned and Hong Kong/Macao/Taiwan owned firms and mirror the results of our basic regression results. The logit model treatment variable is negative and significant for all non-foreign firms. The respective coefficient in our tobit model is negative and significant for the four ownership types. The minimum wage policy therefore negatively affects both the likelihood of firms to invest in human capital and human capital investment rates.

11.6.4 Robustness Checks: Evidence Based on an Alternative Treatment Indicator

In this subsection, we employ data on the staff structure of firms that has been uniquely investigated as part of the 2004 CASIF data set and calculate an alternative measure to our initial treatment indicator based on the relationship between average wages at the firm-level and county-level minimum wage standards. Our motivation is that the average wage may correlate insufficiently with the percentage of affected people in a firm due to differences in within-firm wage distributions.

Table 11.8 Fixed capital investment regression results by firm ownership

	GMM models			
	LOEs	*SOEs*	*NOEs*	*FOEs*
Treatment dummy (lag)	0.005	−0.005	−0.004	0.002
	(0.004)	(0.009)	(0.010)	(0.011)
Investment rate (lag)	−0.249	−0.087**	−0.074	−0.485***
	(0.221)	(0.040)	(0.246)	(0.177)
Chang in log output	0.328***	0.105	0.463**	0.525***
	(0.102)	(0.072)	(0.183)	(0.101)
Change in log output (lag)	−0.166***	−0.047	−0.224**	−0.295***
	(0.055)	(0.040)	(0.090)	(0.051)
Error correction term	−0.166***	−0.046	−0.227***	−0.320***
	(0.055)	(0.043)	(0.087)	(0.050)
Average wage (lag)	−0.000	−0.000	0.000	−0.000
	(0.000)	(0.000)	(0.000)	(0.000)
Observations	149,300	18,730	28,452	26,770
Groups	67,860	8827	13,758	12,867
Number of instruments	18	36	24	32
Hansen test (p-value)	0.642	0.251	0.521	0.152
AR(1) (p-value)	0.054	0.000	0.017	0.086
AR(2) (p-value)	0.762	0.175	0.400	0.176

Note Standard errors are clustered at the county level and displayed in parentheses. The significance levels investigated and their notations are: $^{*}p < 0.10$, $^{**}p < 0.05$, $^{***}p < 0.01$. The definitions of LOEs, SOEs, NOEs and FOEs are mentioned in the footnote of Table 11.4

We therefore revise our treatment indicator as follows. According to the previous analysis on Chinese minimum wages conducted by Fang and Lin (2015), female workers are about six times as likely to receive the minimum wage or less as the average worker. Moreover, workers whose highest educational attainment is a middle school degree or less are about seven times as likely to receive the minimum wage as staff with a college degree.[24] In this subsection, we therefore exploit data on the share of female workers with a middle school degree or less calculated for each firm to obtain an alternative measure of firm exposure to the minimum wage. In particular, we use $fms_{i,2004}$ to denote the share of female staff with a middle school degree or less and $fms_{90p,2004}$ to denote the 90th percentile of this ratio in the distribution of all firms. Based on these two variables, we identify our treatment group as:

$$treatdum_{i,2004}\begin{cases} 0 & \text{if} fms_{i,2004} < fms_{90p,2004} \\ 1 & \text{if} fms_{i,2004} \geq fms_{90p,2004} \end{cases} \quad (11.7)$$

Table 11.9 Human capital investment regression results by firm ownership

	Logit models				*Tobit models*			
	LOEs	*SOEs*	*NOEs*	*FOEs*	*LOEs*	*SOEs*	*NOEs*	*FOEs*
Treatment dummy (lag)	−0.060***	−0.197***	−0.143**	−0.067	−0.010***	−0.035**	−0.014**	−0.014**
	(0.006)	(0.004)	(0.021)	(0.365)	(0.000)	(0.018)	(0.031)	(0.034)
Average wage (lag)	0.000***	0.000***	0.000***	0.000***	0.000***	0.000	0.000***	0.000***
	(0.000)	(0.007)	(0.000)	(0.000)	(0.000)	(0.213)	(0.000)	(0.000)
Log workforce size (lag)	0.0483***	0.476***	0.269***	0.302***	0.034***	0.030***	0.023***	0.028***
	(0.000)	(0.000)	(0.000)	(0.000)	(0.000)	(0.000)	(0.000)	(0.000)
Labor productivity (lag)	0.835***	0.170	−0.394	0.311	−0.009	−0.082***	0.050*	−0.032
	(0.000)	(0.581)	(0.389)	(0.392)	(0.326)	(0.001)	(0.099)	(0.192)
Exporter dummy	0.097***	0.301***	0.203***	0.184***	0.017***	0.012***	−0.014***	0.007**
	(0.000)	(0.000)	(0.000)	(0.001)	(0.000)	(0.007)	(0.000)	(0.023)
Union dummy					0.087***	0.073***	0.091***	0.100***
					(0.000)	(0.000)	(0.000)	(0.000)
Technical staff (%)					0.077***	0.076	0.088	0.168***
					(0.000)	(0.160)	(0.187)	(0.003)
University degree (%)					0.337***	0.353***	0.492***	0.318***
					(0.000)	(0.000)	(0.000)	(0.000)

(continued)

Table 11.9 (continued)

	Logit models				*Tobit models*			
	LOEs	*SOEs*	*NOEs*	*FOEs*	*LOEs*	*SOEs*	*NOEs*	*FOEs*
Female staff (%)					−0.043***	−0.045*	−0.117***	−0.186***
					(0.000)		(0.000)	(0.000)
Firm fixed effects	Yes	Yes	Yes	Yes	No	No	No	No
Industry fixed effects	No	No	No	No	Yes	Yes	Yes	Yes
Observations	252,000	22,680	35,182	35,016	530,453	59,325	87,953	82,416
Log likelihood	−96,320.4	−8462.9	−13,409.2	−13,308.8	−164,120.5	−2922.0	−23,950.3	−26,153.5
Chi^2	652.7	83.5	64.2	72.7	34781.4	5393.8	4226.3	4515.9
Prob $Chi^2 > 0$	0.000	0.000	0.000	0.000	0.000	0.000	0.000	0.000
σ_u					0.208***	0.163***	0.206***	0.218***
σ_e					0.210***	0.144***	0.191***	0.212***
ρ					0.497	0.560	0.537	0.513

Note Standard errors calculated from 100 bootstraps are shown in parentheses. The significance levels investigated and their notations are: $^{*}p < 0.10$, $^{**}p < 0.05$, $^{***}p < 0.01$. The significant constant term has been omitted to save space. The definitions of LOEs, SOEs, NOEs and FOEs are mentioned in the footnote of Table 11.4

We also calculate a measure for the minimum wage treatment intensity as follows:

$$treatint_{i,2004} = \begin{cases} 0 & \text{if } fms_{i,2004} < fms_{90p,2004} \\ \Delta mw_{j,2005-2003} \times treat_{i,2004} & \text{if } fms_{i,2004} < fms_{90p,2004} \end{cases} \quad (11.8)$$

For this cross-sectional specification, we calculate our dependent variables as the two-period average difference in our outcome variables ($\Delta \Upsilon_{i,2005-2003}$). We control for a range of firm characteristics measured in the initial year included in this part of the analysis ($z_{i,2003}$), such as the average wage, labor productivity, staff size and dummy variables for state ownership, foreign ownership, exporter status, as well as for industry and city dummy variables ($\mu_{c,k}$). This model, which is analogous to the model implemented in Mayneris et al. (2014), can be summarized as follows:

$$\Delta Y_{i,2005-2003} = \alpha\, treat_{i,2004} + \beta' z_{i,2003} + \gamma \mu_{c,k} + \varepsilon_{i,2005} \quad (11.9)$$

The results from these regressions are displayed in Table 11.10 and confirm our previous findings that firms have not altered their fixed capital investment behavior, but have decreased their human capital investments in response to the minimum wage.

Table 11.10 Robustness checks: alternative treatment measure

	Fixed capital		*Human capital*	
	(1)		*(2)*	
Treatment dummy (lag)	0.004		−0.002**	
	(0.003)		(0.001)	
Treatment intensity (lag)		0.019		−0.023**
		(0.029)		(0.010)
Observations	62,922	62,922	84,929	84,929
R^2	0.017	0.017	0.011	0.011

Note Standard errors are clustered at the county level and displayed in parentheses. The significance levels investigated and their notations are: $^{*}p < 0.10$, $^{**}p < 0.05$, $^{***}p < 0.01$. The control variables included are wages, labor productivity, employment, profit margins, dummy variables for state-ownership, foreign-ownership and ownership by entities from Hong Kong, Macao or Taiwan, as well as dummy variables for cities and industries

11.7 Conclusions and Discussion

During the past two decades, China has implemented a complex system of minimum wages across the country. Consequently, minimum wages have risen sharply, especially since the introduction of the new minimum wage regulations in 2004. In this article, we focus on the potential adverse effects on firm behavior due to the Chinese minimum wage policy by empirically analyzing the effect on the firm investment decision in a panel data set of all state-owned and all above-scale non-state-owned Chinese firms. According to standard economic theory, an increase in labor costs through minimum wage adjustments imposes a negative scale effect on companies, in turn leading to a reduction in fixed capital investment. Standard models of human capital theory also predict a negative effect on human capital investment since a wage floor reduces the ability of employees to accept wage reductions in order to enable companies to finance worker training. On the other hand, models of non-competitive labor markets generally predict that company fixed and human capital investments associated with affected labor groups will rise in the face of an exogenous increase in labor costs.

Our empirical results indicate that the Chinese minimum wage policy has indeed reduced firm investment in human capital, while it has not led to a change in fixed capital investment rates. In addition, we find a negative effect on firm-level employment levels, thus a twofold negative overall effect on the factor labor that is in line with the predictions of neoclassical models of the labor market. An important detail of our analysis is the finding that the ownership structure of firm matters as the likelihood that foreign firms engage in human capital investments has not decreased in response to the policy. A limitation of our study is that the panel data set of Chinese firms employed in our study does not cover small firms. Minimum wages may affect these firms differently and may also impact the dynamic evolution of the firms that survive in an industry.

Overall, the negative effect on human capital investments is an important consequence of the minimum wage policy, and the competitiveness of Chinese companies may suffer as a consequence of the minimum wage regulations. The decrease in human capital investment rates is likely to reduce labor productivity growth, and further adverse effects on the labor market may occur in the long term.

Appendix

See Appendix Table 11.11.

Table 11.11 Effects of labor market conditions on the minimum wage, 2004–2009

Panel A: Normalized minimum wage						
Dependent variable						
Minimum-to-average-wage ratio						
Independent variables	*(1)*	*(2)*	*(3)*	*(4)*	*(5)*	*(6)*
GDP per capita	.047	.049	.035	.168***	.175***	.162**
	(.055)	(.063)	(.057)	(.062)	(.063)	(.065)
Youth unemployment rate	−.007	−.007	−.008			
	(.021)	(.021)	(.022)			
CPI		1.168	1.230		.661	.936
		(.864)	(.900)		(.682)	(.715)
FDI			−.014			−.008
			(.010)			(.010)
Unemployment				−.002	−.002	−.005
				(.015)	(.015)	(.017)
R^2	.120	.121	.133	.101	.103	.107
Observations	1640	1640	1640	1640	1640	1640
Panel B: Non-normalized minimum wage						
Dependent variable						
Minimum wage level						
Independent variables	*(1)*	*(2)*	*(3)*	*(4)*	*(5)*	*(6)*
GDP per capita	.177	.153	.262	.115**	.116**	.099*
	(.255)	(.248)	(.287)	(.047)	(.048)	(.051)
Youth unemployment rate	−.113	−.111	−.099			
	(.527)	(.534)	(.543)			
CPI		−.572	−.350		−.109	−.257
		(.422)	(.324)		(.420)	(.435)
FDI			−.168			−.019
			(.295)			(.018)
Average wage	.225	.225	.239	.266*	.267*	.245
	(.150)	(.145)	(.148)	(.149)	(.149)	(.150)
Unemployment				−.009	−.009	−.010
				(.013)	(.013)	(.015)
R^2	.323	.334	.339	.270	.290	.292
Observations	1640	1640	1640	1640	1640	1640

Note All regressions are estimated with year and county fixed effects. Dependent and independent variables are in log form. Cluster-robust standard errors at the county level are in parentheses. The respective significance symbols denote: *$p < 0.10$, **$p < 0.05$, ***$p < 0.01$

Notes

1. The increase between 2000 and 2007 raised the Chinese minimum wage level from merely 2.4 times to 4.3 times the international poverty line of US$ 1.25 a day (at PPP exchange rates). The increases were also significant relative to the development of local subsistence levels for urban residents. For instance, the subsistence level in Shanghai rose from 280 RMB to 350 RMB, while the minimum wage rose from 435 RMB to 840 RMB during the same time period.
2. Since we need to take first differences for the calculation of our investment variable, our study period includes three pre-policy years and the year when the new minimum wage regulations were implemented (2004) as well as three post-policy years.
3. Compliance with minimum wage regulations is generally problematic in developing countries (see, e.g., Rani et al. 2013). However, Ye et al. (2015) conclude that Chinese firms broadly comply with minimum wage laws. The authors link this to the strict enforcement of labor regulations conducted annually around the Chinese New Year. The positive effect of enforcement on compliance in other economies was also found in Gindling et al. (2015) for the case of Costa Rica and Ronconi (2010) for the case of Argentina, whereas the effect was insignificant in a study on South Africa by Bhorat et al. (2012).
4. Because of regional differences in the Chinese minimum wage regulations, the minimum wage level in five jurisdictions also includes social security contributions in addition to wage expenditures. For the calculation of the explanatory variables calculated in this subsection, we, therefore, add the contributions for labor and health insurance and pensions incurred by firms located in Beijing, Henan, Jiangsu, Jiangxi and Shanghai to their wage expenditures.
5. An alternative variable measuring the intensity of the minimum wage treatment effect on companies has been proposed by Mayneris et al. (2014). Implementing our regressions with their explanatory variable does not qualitatively alter our treatment intensity results, and we do not report the alternative results.
6. In particular, we use a panel regression model with year and county fixed effects and define the dependent variable as the normalized minimum-to-average wage ratio or non-normalized minimum wages, and include GDP per capita, the youth unemployment rate, CPI and FDI as the independent variables. We also replace the youth unemployment rate with the general unemployment level (in log form) to see if the results change. We report these results in Appendix Table 11.11. In specifications (1) to (3) of Table 11.11, the results show that all estimates are

statistically insignificant which suggests that labor market conditions cannot predict minimum wage changes. In addition, specifications (4) to (6) use the general unemployment level instead of the youth unemployment rate. The results also show that all estimates, except for GDP per capita, are statistically insignificant.

7. We also implemented a third-order autoregressive model to check the robustness of our results. This did not affect the significance of our error-correction terms and our explanatory variables.
8. A difference to the implementations in Bond et al. (2003) and Chen and Zheng (2008) is that we resort to operating profits because cash flow data have only been included in the CASIF data set since 2003.
9. Roodman (2009) provides a detailed analysis of the problems arising from employing too many instruments in GMM estimation. The rule of thumb in empirical GMM estimations is that the number of instruments should be less than the number of cross-sectional units. In our case, we employ a maximum of 44 instruments, and the minimum number of cross-sectional units included in the GMM regressions for the smallest subset of firms is 8827.
10. Note that first-order autocorrelation of the differenced error terms is expected because of the common element of first-differenced error terms in adjacent periods.
11. Larger firms are generally more able to provide workforce training, for example, due to economies of scale. Labor productivity and wages reflect the initial skill level of the workforce and affect the returns to human capital investments.
12. Our definition of state-owned companies includes all state-owned and state-holding companies, i.e., all companies in which the state holds a majority. This is the broad definition adopted by the Chinese National Bureau of Statistics. Local non-state-owned companies include collectively owned and private companies. For foreign ownership, we also adopt the Chinese definition and consider companies with a foreign capital share of at least 25% as foreign invested.
13. In this article, we collectively refer to counties and prefecture-level cities as "counties." These administrative units included in our analysis are located across all of the Chinese provincial-level administrative divisions, i.e., the 22 provinces, five autonomous regions and four municipalities, to which we collectively refer as "provinces."
14. The China national economic census conducted by the NBS in 2004 allows for a comparison with the 2004 CASIF data set. The firms included in the 2004 CASIF survey constitute approximately 20.3% of all Chinese firms included in the economic census. They contribute approximately 90.7% of Chinese industrial output, hence covering almost all of Chinese industrial activity.

15. Among the observations that could be matched to the previous year, we were able to match 95.93% based on company IDs, and the remaining 4.07% were matched using other firm information.
16. Upward et al. (2013) have collected the deflators from NBS and make them available on their Web site. Since we also need deflators from 1999, we supplement their data set with deflators obtained directly from national yearbooks.
17. The training expenditures variable refers to a range of expenditures related to staff training, including training in new technologies, continuing staff education and the purchase of teaching equipment.
18. Observations from the years 1999 and 2000 are only used as lagged values in our GMM estimations.
19. According to Ye et al. (2015), compliance rates are lowest for Hong Kong, Macao and Taiwan invested companies, and 9.4% of workers for this company type earn below the minimum wage. Compliance rates for non-state-owned domestic companies and state-owned companies are 2.9 and 2.8%, respectively. Foreign-owned companies are the most compliant, and only 2.3% of their workers earn less than the minimum wage.
20. We also conduct a robustness check by using training per log output as an alternative dependent variable measuring training intensity, and our results did not change qualitatively.
21. The sample for these regressions includes 419,487 censored and 337,024 uncensored observations.
22. To make the exposition more concise, we only report the results of our dummy treatment variable regressions in this subsection. The results for our treatment intensity variable are in line with the results for the treatment dummy variable, i.e., both either insignificant or significant with the same sign.
23. To simplify the search for the optimal set of instruments, we drop the insignificant financial variables and implement the basic error-correction model shown in Eq. 11.3. Our strategy for selecting the optimal number of instruments is to start from the specification implemented for our complete sample. If this specification fails the Hansen test or the second-order autocorrelation test for any of our sub-samples, we move on toward deeper lags; see Guariglia et al. (2011). The number of instruments employed therefore differs between different sub-samples of firms.
24. The precise percentages of workers earning no more than the minimum wage calculated based on the Urban Household Survey employed in the study are: 67.01% of female workers compared to 8.91% for all workers, 25.16% of workers with no more than an elementary school degree, and 15.43% of workers with a middle school degree compared to, for example, only 2.99% of workers with a college degree; see Table 3 in Fang and Lin (2015).

References

Acemoglu, Daron and Jörn-Steffen Pischke, "The Structure of Wages and Investment in General Training," *Journal of Political Economy* 107 (1999):539–572.

———, "Minimum Wages and On-the-Job Training," *Research in Labor Economics* 22 (2003):159–202.

Arellano, Manuel and Stephen Bond, "Some Tests of Specification for Panel Data: Monte Carlo Evidence and an Application to Employment Equations," *The Review of Economic Studies* 58 (1991):277–297.

Arulampalam, Wiji, Alison L. Booth, and Mark L. Bryan, "Training and the New Minimum Wage," *The Economic Journal* 114 (2004):C87–C94.

Bean, Charles, "An Econometric Model of Manufacturing Investment in the UK," *Economic Journal* 91 (1981):106–121.

Becker, Gary, *Human Capital: A Theoretical and Empirical Analysis, with Special Reference to Education*, Chicago: The University of Chicago Press (1993).

Bhorat, Haroon, Ravi Kanbur, and Natasha Mayet, "Estimating the Causal Effect of Enforcement on Minimum Wage Compliance: The Case of South Africa," *Review of Development Economics* 16 (2012):608–623.

Bond, Stephen, Julie Ann Elston, Jacques Mairesse, and Benoît Mulkay, "Financial Factors and Investment in Belgium, France, Germany, and the United Kingdom: A Comparison Using Company Panel Data," *The Review of Economics and Statistics* 85 (2003):153–165.

Brandt, Loren, Johannes Van Biesebroeck, and Yifan Zhang, "Creative Accounting or Creative Destruction? Firm-Level Productivity Growth in Chinese Manufacturing," *Journal of Development Economics* 97 (2012):339–351.

Campolieti, Michele, Morley Gunderson, and Chris Riddell, "Minimum Wage Impacts from a Prespecified Research Design: Canada 1981â-1997," *Industrial Relations: A Journal of Economy and Society* 45 (2006):195–216.

Chen, Minjia and Yongnian Zheng, "China's Regional Disparity and Its Policy Responses," *China & World Economy* 16 (2008):16–32.

Cooke, Fang Lee, *HRM, Work and Employment in China*, London: Routledge (2005).

Draca, Mirko, Stephen Machin, and John Van Reenen, "Minimum Wages and Firm Profitability," *American Economic Journal: Applied Economics* 3 (2011):129–151.

Fairris, David and Roberto Pedace, "The Impact of Minimum Wages on Job Training: An Empirical Exploration with Establishment Data," *Southern Economic Journal* 70 (2004):566–583.

Fang, Tony and Carl Lin, "Minimum Wages and Employment in China," *IZA Journal of Labor Policy* 4 (2015):1–30.

Feldstein, Martin, "The Economics of the New Unemployment," *Public Interest* 33 (1973):3–42.

Gindling, T. H., Nadwa Mossaad, and Juan Diego Trejos, "The Consequences of Increased Enforcement of Legal Minimum Wages in a Developing Country—An Evaluation of the Impact of the Campaña Nacional de Salarios Mínimos in Costa Rica," *Industrial and Labor Relations Review* 68 (2015):666–707.

Greene, William, *Econometric Analysis*, Englewood Cliffs, NJ: Prentice Hall (2003).

Guariglia, Alessandra, Xiaoxuan Liu, and Lina Song, "Internal Finance and Growth: Microeconometric Evidence on Chinese Firms," *Journal of Development Economics* 96 (2011):79–94.

Hirsch, Barry T., Bruce E. Kaufman, and Yetyana Zelenska, "Minimum Wage Channels of Adjustment," IZA Discussion Paper No. 6132 (2011).

Huang, Yi, Prakash Loungani, and Gewei Wang, "Minimum Wages and Firm Employment: Evidence from China," Federal Reserve Bank of Dallas. Globalization and Monetary Policy Institute Working Paper No. 173 (2014).

Jia, Peng, "Employment and Working Hour Effects of Minimum Wage Increase: Evidence from China," *China & World Economy* 22 (2014):61–80.

Mayneris, Florian, Sandra Poncet, and Tao Zhang, "The Cleansing Effect of Minimum Wage," Paper presented at the Conference on Industrial Upgrading and Urbanization, Stockholm China Economic Research Institute, Stockholm (2014).

Metcalf, David, "Why Has the British National Minimum Wage Had Little or No Impact on Employment?" *Journal of Industrial Relations* 50 (2008):489–512.

National Bureau of Statistics of China, *China Statistical Yearbook*, Beijing: China Statistics Press (2008).

Neumark, David, "The Employment Effects of Minimum Wages: Evidence from a Prespecified Research Design," *Industrial Relations: A Journal of Economy and Society* 40 (2001):121–144.

Neumark, David and William L. Wascher, "Minimum Wages and Training Revisited," *Journal of Labor Economics* 19 (2001):563–595.

———, *Minimum Wages*, Cambridge, MA: MIT Press (2008).

Nguyen, Viet Cuong, "Do Minimum Wage Increases Matter to Firm Profitability? The Case of Vietnam," *Journal of International Development* 29 (2017):790–804.

Nickell, Stephen, "Biases in Dynamic Models with Fixed Effects," *Econometrica* 49 (1981):1417–1426.

Pischke, Jörn-Steffen, "Labor Market Institutions, Wages, and Investment: Review and Implications," *CESifo Economic Studies* 51 (2005):47–75.

Rama, Martin, "The Consequences of Doubling the Minimum Wage: The Case of Indonesia," Policy Research Working Paper 1643, The World Bank (1999).

———, "The Consequences of Doubling the Minimum Wage: The Case of Indonesia," *Industrial and Labor Relations Review* 54 (2001):864–881.

Rani, Uma, Patrick Belser, Martin Oelz, and Setareh Ranjbar, "Minimum Wage Coverage and Compliance in Developing Countries," *International Labour Review* 152 (2013):381–410.

Riley, Rebecca and Chiara Rosazza Bondibene, "The Impact of the National Minimum Wage on Firm Behaviour During Recession," Research Report for the Low Pay Commission, Unpublished (2013).

Ronconi, Lucas, "Enforcement and Compliance with Labor Regulations in Argentina," *Industrial and Labor Relations Review* 63 (2010):719–736.

Roodman, David, "A Note on the Theme of Too Many Instruments," *Oxford Bulletin of Economics and Statistics* 71 (2009):135–158.

Rosen, Sherwin, "Learning and Experience in the Labor Market," *The Journal of Human Resources* 7 (1972):326–342.

Upward, Richard, Zheng Wang, and Jinghai Zheng, "Weighing China's Export Basket: The Domestic Content and Technology Intensity of Chinese Exports," *Journal of Comparative Economics* 41 (2013):527–543.

Wang, Jing and Morley Gunderson, "Minimum Wage Impacts in China: Estimates from a Prespecified Research Design, 2000–2007," *Contemporary Economic Policy* 29 (2011):392–406.

———, "Minimum Wage Effects on Employment and Wages: Dif-in-Dif Estimates from Eastern China," *International Journal of Manpower* 33 (2012):860–876.

Ye, Linxiang, TH Gindling, and Shi Li, "Compliance with Legal Minimum Wages and Overtime Pay Regulations in China," *IZA Journal of Labor & Development* 4 (2015):16.

CHAPTER 12

Regional Variation of the Minimum Wages in China

Chunbing Xing and Jianwei Xu

12.1 Introduction

Wages in China were set by the authority in the earlier economic regime of central planning, and no labor market existed. With the establishment of a socialist market economy, the labor market has become to function (Chi et al. 2012). Employers have the autonomy to hire and fire workers, and the workers have more freedom to choose employers. The wages are mainly determined by the labor market conditions. Meanwhile, wage inequality increases. In particular, the low wages of those disadvantaged workers (less educated, young workers, laid-off workers, rural-to-urban migrants) constitute a major contributor to the rising wage inequality (Xing and Li 2012).

The minimum wage policy was supposed to serve several purposes including increasing the income of low-paid workers, guaranteeing the living standard of their families, and reducing income inequality. The complication of the minimum wage policy varies considerably across countries (Rani et al. 2013). Some countries set a uniform minimum

C. Xing (✉) · J. Xu
Beijing Normal University, Beijing, China
e-mail: xingchb@bnu.edu.cn

L. Shi and C. Lin (eds.), *Minimum Wages in China*,
https://doi.org/10.1007/978-981-15-2421-9_12

wage for the whole country, while others set minimum wages for different regions, industries, or employment of different characteristics such as age, gender, and education levels. In China, the minimum wages vary across regions, and existing studies use variations of this dimension (as well as temporal variations) to identify the effect of the minimum wage policy on wages, employment, inequality, etc. (See Fang and Lin 2014; Yang and Gunderson 2014). However, little is known about the factors that influence the regional variation of the minimum wages. This article aims to describe the institutional background for the determination of regional minimum wages and to explore mechanisms behind this variation.

We first describe the procedure for the adjustment of local minimum wages, emphasizing China's decentralized feature and the incentives of local government. Then we describe the regional variations of the minimum wage using detailed minimum wage data. We find a large regional variation during the period studied. Meanwhile, most inequality measures we use suggest a decline in the regional variation especially after 2004. Third, we explain the regional variation in the minimum wages using city-level variables collected from the city statistical yearbook. Economic development factors, including GDP, economic structure, and consumption level, are the main driving force for the large regional variation in minimum wages. Finally, there also is weak evidence suggesting that the regional variation is influenced by political factors, such as competition between officials of different locations.

12.2 Literature Review

Conceptually, the minimum wage should be determined according to its goals, which vary considerably over time and across countries with different institutions. Such goals include poverty reduction (Stigler 1946; Sobel 1999), increasing the total income of minimum wage workers (Sobel 1999), reducing inequality (Johnson and Browning 1983), and even industry upgrading, that is forcing firms to adopt more advanced labor-saving techniques (Stigler 1946). Textbook economics show that unemployment increases if the minimum wage is set above the market equilibrium level. An optimal minimum wage policy is determined by the trade-off between those goals and the adverse employment effect. That is why a considerable amount of effort has been spent to estimate the unemployment effect of the minimum wage. Unfortunately, the literature has not reached a consensus regarding the employment effect of the policy (Card and Krueger 1995; Neumark and Wascher 2008).

In this context, minimum wages should be determined by factors related to living standard, labor cost, income distribution, and employment situations. Importantly, the minimum wage should be related to some economic parameters. For example, Sobel (1999) points out that the minimum wage should be set where the labor demand elasticity is unitary to maximize the total income of minimum wage workers.

However, most research shows that the minimum wage is heavily influenced by political factors. Such factors include voting, interest group pressure, and partisan ideology. Flinn (2011, p. 10), for example, documents the fierce political conflicts regarding whether the federal government should set minimum wages for each state. Sobel (1999) asks whether the adjustment of the minimum wage is influenced by political factors other than economic factors, and he finds that unions play an important role. Many other studies show that the passage of the minimum wage legislation and its subsequent increases are mainly driven by interest group pressures (Silberman and Durden 1976; Kau and Rubin 1978; Bloch 1980, 1993; Seltzer 1995). Empirically, researchers looked at the relative power of some interest groups (the union vs. business ratio, for example, Sobel 1999; Johnson 2002), voting in congress elections, and ideological factors (Kau and Rubin 1978). But these variables do not readily apply in China.

When minimum wages vary across regions as in China, the process is often decentralized, and the local governments play an important role. First, they have more autonomy to set the minimum wages according to local economic conditions. Second, minimum wages could be an instrument for them to manage the local economy and to compete with other regions. On the one hand, higher minimum wage might be a signal of better economic performance that not only attracts quality workers but also enhances the promotion probability of local officials. On the other hand, a higher minimum wage increases labor cost and deter capital investment. When labor and capital are mobile across regions, this will be a real concern for local governments. They are forced to consider each other's behavior.

Political consideration influences not only the level of the minimum wage but also the effective date of the changes and the number and timing of the series of steps (Sobel 1999). In this article, we will discuss how the timing of the minimum adjustment is related to the magnitude of its changes.

Thus, the article is related to a growing literature that studies the promotion competition between local officials (Li and Zhou 2005). Existing studies show that this competition (like a tournament model) plays an important role in China's economic growth. The basic story is as follows: Officials who are more capable of producing high GDP growth have a higher probability of being promoted. This provides a strong incentive for local officials to take measures to boost the local economy. Guo et al. (2013) indicate that personal characteristics of the local officials have a significant effect on the local policies such as the supply of land for different uses. As the minimum wage policy might influence the local economy in many ways (firm profits, firm's location choice, employment), it serves as a potential instrument of this competition.

12.3 Institutional Background of the Minimum Wage Policy in China

China's minimum wage policy came into shape in the early 1990s. In late 1993, the former Ministry of Labor issued Provisions of Minimum Wage, the first document on the minimum wage policy. This policy did not have a substantive effect because it is poorly implemented. In 2004, the Provisions of Minimum Wage was amended substantially by the Ministry of Human Resources and Social Security. The new provisions are different from the old version in the following aspects: (1) Minimum wages are applicable to all enterprises including the town and village enterprises (TVEs), privately or individually owned enterprises, and non-profit organizations like schools and hospitals. (2) Hourly minimum wages were introduced into the system, which is applied to part-time employment. (3) The new regulation requires local governments to adjust the minimum wage at least once every two years. (4) It requires the local government to publicize the minimum wages through public media. (5) The enforcement of the minimum wage policy is strengthened.

Under the new regulation, employers are more likely to abide the regulations as the punishment for the violation of this provision has increased significantly (it could be as high as five times of the wages detained). Meanwhile, the department of human resource and social security of the local government has the authority to inspect the enforcement of the minimum wage regulations within its jurisdiction. Unions of different levels can monitor the implementation of the minimum wage, and they can demand enforcement and penalty if the violation of the minimum wage provisions was found.

Local governments play a dominant role in the process of adjusting minimum wages. The basic procedure is as follows: The department of human resources and social security at the provincial level (including province, autonomous regions, and municipalities administered directly by the central government) works out a minimum wage schedule for negotiation. This schedule is made according to the guidance of the central government (the Ministry of Human Resource and Social Security), which is usually a guideline for calculating minimum wages taking into consideration of various factors. These firstly include factors influencing the living standard of people in poverty such as urban consumer price index and the subsistence expenditure of the urban residents. As minimum wages above the equilibrium market wages will increase the labor cost of the employers and therefore reduce employment, the employment situation should also be considered. Finally, the minimum wage should be adjusted according to whether it includes the social security fees and housing funds paid by the employees.

Economic development level varies a lot within a province, and the provincial government usually applies several minimum wages according to the economic development level of different regions. Usually, the provincial capital city has the highest minimum wage, while remote poor regions apply the lowest. Even for the provincial capital city, it may include some relatively poor counties in suburban areas, which may choose lower minimum wages.

This adjustment plan will then be negotiated between several parties, including the provincial government, provincial-level unions, associations of entrepreneurs/enterprises, and chamber of commerce. The local government of the lower level can also influence the minimum wage schedule. For example, a prefecture-level city may negotiate a lower level minimum wage (or simply choose a lower level of minimum wage) due to the concern that high minimum wages are harmful to local governments to attract investment and to create employment.

After reaching an agreement, the plan will often be submitted to the provincial executive meetings for discussion. The provincial executive meeting is usually convened by the governor or the vice governor of a province. Thus provincial leaders can also influence the minimum wage policies, the influence depending on the relative power and preference of the leaders. In particular, local officials need to compete for higher positions. The minimum wage policy might be an instrument in the competition. First, the minimum wage could be a direct measure for the welfare of the local residents, with higher minimum wages representing a higher economic development level and higher living standard. Thus the local officials tend to set a higher minimum wage, a so-called keep-up-with-the-Joneses effect. On the other hand, a high minimum wage might be harmful to the economy by deterring investments and reducing employment, because, from the perspective of the employers, a region with lower minimum wage seems more attractive due to lower labor cost. But, there also are some local governments, who believe that higher minimum wage will help them attract skilled workers.[1] Whether these incentives (mechanisms) exist and the extents they matter are subject to empirical investigation.

The minimum wage policy determined by the provincial government will then be submitted to the Ministry of Human Resources and Social Security for approval. It should be ratified by the All China Federation of Trade Unions and All China Federation of Industry and Commerce. This minimum wage adjustment policy should be publicized through the government gazette and at least one local newspaper within seven days of approval.

The Minimum Wage Provisions issued in 2004 requires the local (provincial) government to adjust the minimum wages at least once in every two years but does not mandate the exact date of the adjustment. Local governments often choose different dates to announce the newly adjusted minimum wage policy.

12.4 Regional Variation of Minimum Wage and Its Evolution

We use several data sets in the following analysis. The minimum wage data is collected from various Web sites as every province publishes them once new minimum wages are determined. When a province publishes the minimum wage policy, it declares the minimum wage levels applicable to various regions or it allows local government to choose appropriate levels. Different from other studies, we use the most detailed (disaggregated) minimum wage data. Second, we collect city-level information from the China City Statistical Yearbook, including the average wages for the urban workers, GDP growth rate, GDP per capita, employment, unemployment, actually utilized foreign direct investment (FDI). We use this information to construct explanatory variables to explain regional minimum wages (see below in Sect. 12.5).

As the effective date of the new minimum wage is not necessarily at the beginning of a year, we average the minimum wage according to the months applicable within a year. In addition, in order to match our minimum wage data with the city-level variables, we also calculated the weighted average of the minimum wages using the employment of the region where the minimum wages are applicable, and the formula is as follows:

$$MW_{ct} = \frac{\sum_{j \in c} MW_{jct} * employ_{jct}}{\sum_{j \in c} employ_{jct}}$$

Among which, MW_{jct} is the minimum wage in county j of city c at time t, $employ_{jct}$ is the employment of the same region at time t. Using a similar formula, we are able to calculate the minimum wage at the provincial level. Having detailed minimum wage information has the advantage that we cannot only have different measures of the regional minimum wage (highest level and the lowest level of the minimum wages, in addition to the weighted average of the minimum wage), but also can describe the regional variation more fully. For example, we can calculate the regional variation of the minimum wage within a city or within a province.

Finally, in addition to the absolute value of the minimum wages, we also investigate the relative minimum wage levels, which is the minimum wage divided by the average wage of all the workers in the region. The formula is as follows:

$$MW_{ct} = \frac{\sum_{j \in c} MW_{jct} * employ_{jct} \Big/ \sum_{j \in c} employ_{jct}}{AW_c}$$

AW_{ct} is the average wage in city c at time t, which can be obtained from the Chinese City Statistical Yearbook. MW_{jct} and $employ_{jct}$ are as previously defined.

Before describing the regional variation of the minimum wage, we investigate the trend of minimum wages at the national level. Figure 12.1 shows that the average minimum wage for the whole nation increased significantly between 2004 and 2010. However, the increase

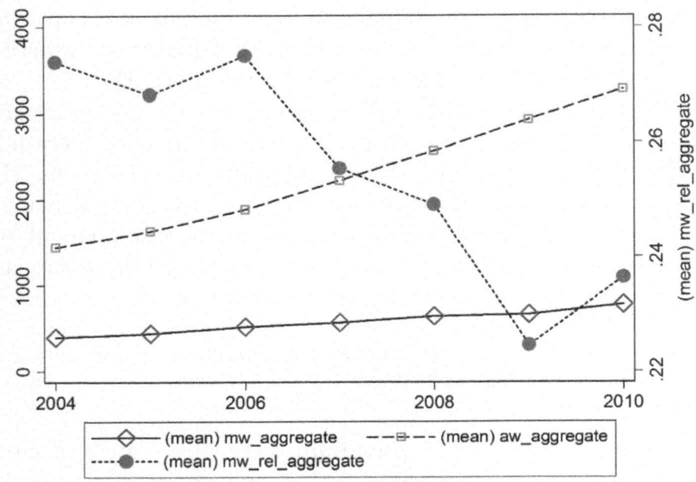

Fig. 12.1 Minimum wages and average wages for China, 2004–2010

is slower than that of the wages for urban workers, and the ratio of the minimum wage over average wages decreased significantly during this period.

To see the regional variation, Fig. 12.2a reports the average number of minimum wages applied within a province and such a number for the whole China in each year. The solid line in the figure shows that the number of minimum wages for a representative province decreased significantly. In 2004, an average province applied over five minimum wages, and by 2012 it has decreased to less than four. If we count the minimum wages of different levels for China as a whole, the number increased in recent years. This seemingly contradictory phenomenon is caused by the fact that different provinces become less likely to have minimum wages of the same level than before.

Figure 12.2b further reports another dimension of the regional variation for the minimum wages, namely the ratio of the highest over the lowest minimum wages (high-to-low or HL ratio) for each province and for China. Again, the regional gap appears to have decreased from the late 1990s. In around 2000, the ratio was 1.5 for an average province and it decreased to 1.3 by 2012. The same pattern is also observed for the whole country, with the ratio decreasing from 3.5 in around 2000 to 2.5 in 2012.

Fig. 12.2 Regional variation of minimum wages within province and within China

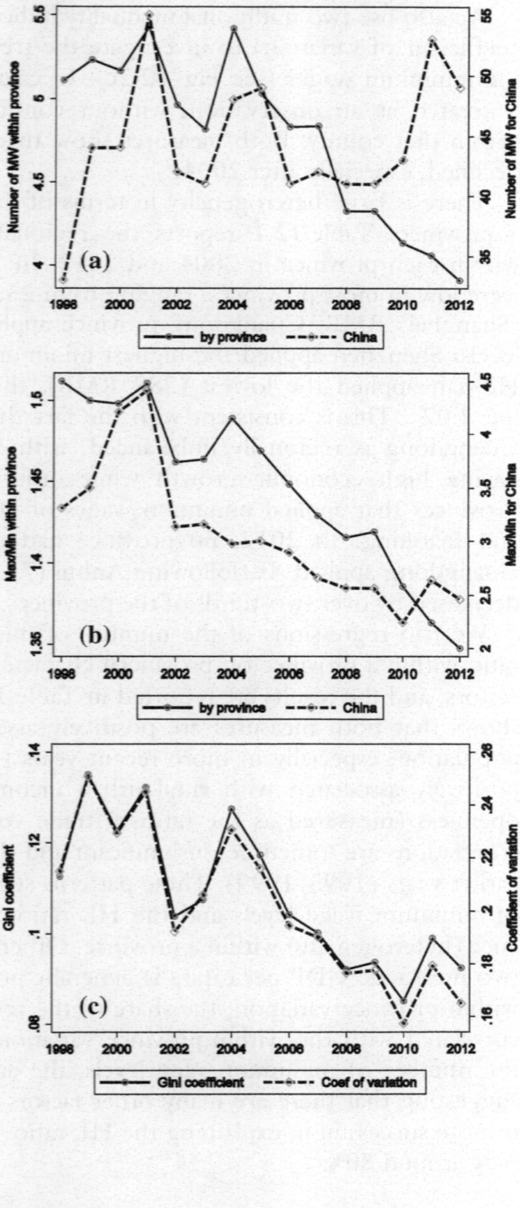

We also use two traditional inequality indices (Gini coefficient and the coefficient of variation) to investigate the trend in regional variation of the minimum wages (see Fig. 12.2c). In calculating them, each county is treated as an observation, without considering relevant population within that county. Both measures show that the regional variation has declined, especially after 2004.[2]

There is large heterogeneity in terms of the regional variation within a province. Table 12.1 reports the regional gap of minimum wages within each province in 2004 and 2012. In 2004, the minimum wages were low in most provinces, ranging from 253 (Jiangxi province) to 603 (Shanghai) RMB. Guangdong province applied minimum wages of 14 levels: Shenzhen applied the highest minimum wage (607 RMB), while Heyuan applied the lowest (288 RMB), the high-to-low ratio reaching 2.07.[3] This is consistent with the fact that the development within Guangdong is regionally unbalanced, with Shenzhen and Guangzhou having high economic growth while other inner cities grew slower. Provinces that applied minimum wages of 10 levels also include Anhui and Liaoning. In 2012, no province had over ten minimum wages. Guangdong applied six, following Anhui (7). The high-to-low ratio also decreased by over two-thirds of the provinces.

We run regressions of the number of minimum wages and the HL ratio within a province on provincial characteristics to explore associated factors, and the results are reported in Table 12.2. Panel A of Table 12.2 shows that both measures are positively associated with the provincial population, especially in more recent years (2000–2007); they are also positively associated with rural–urban income gap and the degree of openness (measured as the ratio of trade volume over GDP), but the correlations are sometimes insignificant and the correlation is stronger in earlier years (1995–1999). These patterns suggest that both the number of minimum wage levels and the HL ratios reflect the regional imbalance (heterogeneity) within a province. Other factors also influence these two measures: GDP per capita is generally positively correlated with the within-province variation; the share of the tertiary industry is negatively correlated with the within-province variation. In the model explaining the number of minimum wage levels, the adjusted R2 is around 15%, suggesting that there are many other factors in play as well. The model is more successful in explaining the HL ratio, but still, the adjusted R2 is only around 30%.

Table 12.1 Minimum wages by province, 2004 and 2012

Province	*2004*					*2012*				
	Average	*Max*	*Min*	*# of mw*	*Max/min*	*Average*	*Max*	*Min*	*# of mw*	*Max/min*
Anhui	312	410	290	10	1.52	712	1010	680	7	1.49
Beijing	495	495	495	1	1.00	1260	1260	1260	1	1.00
Fujian	324	480	280	7	1.71	897	1200	830	4	1.45
Gansu	304	340	300	3	1.13	839	980	860	4	1.14
Guangdong	369	684	330	14	2.07	925	1500	850	6	1.76
Guangxi	330	460	320	4	1.44	819	1000	690	4	1.45
Guizhou	309	400	320	3	1.25	801	930	740	3	1.26
Hainan	358	500	350	3	1.43	788	1050	900	3	1.17
Hebei	376	520	420	3	1.24	1058	1320	1040	4	1.27
Henan	257	380	240	3	1.58	913	1080	820	3	1.32
Heilongjiang	288	390	235	7	1.66	677	1160	850	4	1.36
Hubei	277	400	240	5	1.67	827	1100	750	3	1.47
Hunan	346	460	320	7	1.44	885	1160	870	4	1.33
Jilin	323	360	300	3	1.20	919	1150	950	3	1.21
Jiangsu	425	620	360	4	1.72	997	1320	950	3	1.39
Jiangxi	253	360	270	4	1.33	715	870	610	5	1.43
Liaoning	288	440	230	11	1.91	891	1100	780	5	1.41
Inner Mongolia	344	420	380	3	1.11	962	1200	900	4	1.33
Ningxia	342	380	320	3	1.19	960	1100	950	3	1.16
Qinghai	264	370	330	4	1.12	924	1070	1050	3	1.02
Shandong	356	410	290	5	1.41	1044	1240	950	3	1.31
Shanxi	355	520	400	4	1.30	906	1125	855	4	1.32
Shaanxi	275	320	245	4	1.31	881	1000	790	4	1.27

(continued)

Table 12.1 (continued)

Province	*2004*					*2012*				
	Average	*Max*	*Min*	*# of mw*	*Max/min*	*Average*	*Max*	*Min*	*# of mw*	*Max/min*
Shanghai	603	635	635	1	1.00	1408	1450	1450	1	1.00
Sichuan	270	450	230	7	1.96	891	1050	800	4	1.31
Tianjin	501	530	510	2	1.04	1273	1310	1310	1	1.00
Tibet	306	495	445	3	1.11	1171	1200	1150	2	1.04
Xinjiang	325	480	300	9	1.60	949	1340	980	4	1.37
Yunnan	304	470	350	3	1.34	949	1100	830	3	1.33
Zhejiang	491	620	440	4	1.41	1170	1310	950	4	1.38
Chongqing	342	400	330	4	1.21	931	1050	950	2	1.11
Average				4.81	1.40				3.48	1.28

Table 12.2 Explaining the number of minimum wage levels and the high/low ratio within province

	Number of MW			*Max/min*		
	(1)	*(2)*	*(3)*	*(4)*	*(5)*	*(6)*
	1995–2007	*1995–1999*	*2000–2007*	*1995–2007*	*1995–1999*	*2000–2007*
Ln(population)	0.810***	0.226	1.043***	0.121***	0.0587	0.150***
	(0.223)	(0.396)	(0.310)	(0.0229)	(0.0422)	(0.0295)
Ln(GDP per capita)	1.276*	2.231*	0.783	0.0782	0.169	−0.00300
	(0.712)	(1.158)	(0.966)	(0.0730)	(0.124)	(0.0917)
Tertiary sector share in GDP	−5.765*	−3.995	−6.981*	−0.291	0.471	−0.817**
	(2.995)	(5.997)	(3.678)	(0.307)	(0.640)	(0.349)
Urban–rural income gap	0.759**	1.574***	0.369	0.0574*	0.145**	0.000945
	(0.327)	(0.546)	(0.426)	(0.0335)	(0.0583)	(0.0405)
Ln(average wage)	−2.437*	−3.066	−1.463	−0.419***	−0.743***	−0.121
	(1.292)	(2.114)	(1.752)	(0.132)	(0.226)	(0.166)
Trade share in GDP	1.218*	2.159	0.986	0.327***	0.719***	0.202***
	(0.656)	(1.335)	(0.769)	(0.0673)	(0.143)	(0.0730)
Fiscal expenditure in GDP	2.618	−1.328	3.573	0.503*	0.689	0.496
	(2.526)	(6.004)	(3.171)	(0.259)	(0.641)	(0.301)
Fixed investment/GDP	−1.542	−8.145**	−0.750	−0.215	−0.988**	−0.203
	(1.511)	(3.564)	(1.951)	(0.155)	(0.381)	(0.185)
N	365	141	224	365	141	224
Adj-R2	0.146	0.136	0.153	0.284	0.299	0.349

Note (1) Standard errors in parentheses; (2) *, **, and *** represent significance levels of 10%, 5%, and 1%, respectively

Table 12.3 Minimum wages relative to average wages by province, 2004 and 2010

	2004					*2010*				
	Min	*Max*	*Mean*	*Media*	*S.D.*	*Min*	*Max*	*Mean*	*Media*	*S.D.*
Anhui	0.195	0.368	0.292	0.292	0.044	0.161	0.264	0.207	0.207	0.028
Beijing	0.198	0.198	0.198	0.198	0.000	0.173	0.173	0.173	0.173	0.000
Fujian	0.208	0.311	0.245	0.245	0.032	0.212	0.335	0.259	0.259	0.042
Gansu	0.183	0.459	0.303	0.303	0.077	0.184	0.370	0.283	0.283	0.067
Guangdong	0.197	0.420	0.286	0.286	0.067	0.205	0.344	0.260	0.260	0.040
Guangxi	0.261	0.373	0.320	0.320	0.038	0.216	0.502	0.274	0.274	0.073
Guizhou	0.307	0.342	0.324	0.324	0.016	0.263	0.303	0.280	0.280	0.017
Hainan	0.341	0.411	0.376	0.376	0.050	0.291	0.298	0.295	0.295	0.005
Hebei	0.310	0.439	0.375	0.375	0.037	0.234	0.298	0.262	0.262	0.022
Henan	0.184	0.378	0.269	0.269	0.056	0.226	0.378	0.295	0.295	0.039
Heilongjiang	0.186	0.529	0.314	0.314	0.091	0.215	0.458	0.289	0.289	0.078
Hubei	0.171	0.589	0.310	0.310	0.100	0.244	0.651	0.332	0.332	0.109
Hunan	0.257	0.473	0.315	0.315	0.058	0.201	0.331	0.268	0.268	0.039
Jilin	0.204	0.441	0.326	0.326	0.082	0.253	0.411	0.319	0.319	0.057
Jiangsu	0.220	0.359	0.299	0.299	0.040	0.199	0.245	0.222	0.222	0.015
Jiangxi	0.228	0.433	0.303	0.303	0.053	0.213	0.303	0.255	0.255	0.030
Liaoning	0.177	0.351	0.234	0.234	0.047	0.172	0.335	0.261	0.261	0.040
Inner Mongolia	0.268	0.422	0.347	0.347	0.058	0.196	0.350	0.268	0.268	0.045
Ningxia	0.239	0.329	0.293	0.293	0.036	0.177	0.250	0.222	0.222	0.029
Qinghai	0.238	0.238	0.238	0.238	0.000	0.269	0.269	0.269	0.269	0.000
Shandong	0.158	0.365	0.289	0.289	0.048	0.217	0.350	0.256	0.256	0.031
Shanxi	0.344	0.554	0.412	0.412	0.063	0.184	0.355	0.272	0.272	0.049
Shaanxi	0.220	0.300	0.272	0.272	0.024	0.196	0.294	0.238	0.238	0.027
Shanghai	0.254	0.254	0.254	0.254	0.000	0.187	0.187	0.187	0.187	0.000

(continued)

Table 12.3 (continued)

	2004					2010				
	Min	*Max*	*Mean*	*Media*	*S.D.*	*Min*	*Max*	*Mean*	*Media*	*S.D.*
Sichuan	0.185	0.338	0.244	0.244	0.039	0.195	0.358	0.281	0.281	0.038
Tianjin	0.283	0.283	0.283	0.283	0.000	0.208	0.208	0.208	0.208	0.000
Xinjiang	0.249	0.281	0.265	0.265	0.023	0.233	0.299	0.266	0.266	0.046
Yunnan	0.210	0.437	0.307	0.307	0.068	0.203	0.355	0.256	0.256	0.051
Zhejiang	0.221	0.320	0.275	0.275	0.032	0.220	0.355	0.279	0.279	0.039
Chongqing	0.277	0.277	0.277	0.277	0.000	0.186	0.186	0.186	0.186	0.000

Table 12.4 Decomposing the regional variation of minimum wages

	Variation across province	*City variation within province*	*Country variation within city*
Minimum Wage (%)	60.40	30.75	8.86
Average Wage (%)	39.23	60.77	0.00

It is also important to keep in mind that we are trying to explain within-province variation, which is only a portion of the overall regional variation. In Table 12.4, we decompose the variance in the minimum wage into three parts: variance due to provincial differences, city-level differences within a province, and county-level differences within a city. If we look at the minimum wage in absolute terms, over 60% of the variation comes from provincial-level difference, and 31% from city-level difference. Variation within a city is less important, accounting for less than 10%. This is consistent with the fact that the minimum wages are determined at the provincial level.

We next consider the relative level of minimum wages, which is the ratio of the minimum wage to the average wage of this region. The ratio is calculated at the city level: We first calculate the average minimum wage for each city and divided it by the average wage of the same city. We calculate the statistics of the relative minimum wage distributions for each province, which are reported in Table 12.3. The mean relative minimum wage varies a lot across provinces, ranging from 40% (like in Shanxi, Hebei) to 20% (Beijing) in 2004. The range is around 18–33% in 2010.

Similar to the statistics for the absolute value, there is large variation for the relative minimum wage within a province. Take Anhui province for example. In 2004, the minimum wage was only 19.5% of the average wage in the region with the lowest relative minimum wage, while the highest ratio was 37%. The within-province variations of relative minimum wages also vary considerably across provinces. The province with the largest standard deviation of the relative minimum wage was Hubei in 2004, which is 0.10. Beijing, Tianjin, Shanghai, and Chongqing had the lowest standard deviation, zero. Around two-thirds of the provinces experienced decreases in the regional variation between 2004 and 2010.

12.5 The Determinants of Minimum Wages

What determines the minimum wages of different regions? This section explores this question by running regressions of the minimum wages on candidate explanatory variables. Our goal is to explain the regional variation rather than to identify the causal relationship. Therefore, we do not use panel data models. However, we control for city fixed effects in some regressions later.

In a decentralized system, local economic conditions play an important role in determining minimum wages. We use GDP per capita (in log) to capture the local economic development level and use the GDP growth rate to capture the dynamics of the economy. Although the GDP level is expected to be positively correlated with the minimum wage, its growth rate is not. For example, a growth-rate-seeking leader may purposely set a low minimum wage to attract investment. The share of tertiary sector in GDP reflects the structure of the local economy, and a more advanced economy usually has a higher share of the tertiary sector and also has a higher minimum wage. However, the tertiary sector includes many sub-sectors that are of quite different nature. Therefore, we also control for the share of the service sector in GDP. As the tertiary share and the service share contain different information, we consider both in the regression.

Because the unemployment effect is the main concern of the minimum wage setting, we consider the employment rate, which is calculated as the share of the employed in the total working-age population. As both working-age population and the employment could be endogenously determined, the minimum wage is not necessarily positively correlated with employment rate. For example, the population may become larger in a high minimum wage region while the employment remains unchanged (or even decline), causing a negative relationship between the employment rate and minimum wages (Harris and Todaro 1970). Another measure we consider is the number of enterprises per capita, which is more related to employment opportunities.

Private employment share captures the importance of the private sector, which may reflect the relative power of the employees/employers in the private sector. FDI share reflects the importance of foreign investment in the economy. Fiscal expenditure reflects the relative size of the government and it is related to the employment of employees in the public service sector. Finally, while the local GDP reflects more of the general economic development, the local consumption level is more related to the living standard of workers. We consider consumption per capita in both rural and urban areas because the minimum wage often varies considerably within a city. In regions with the lowest minimum wage, rural consumption level may be more appropriate for calculating the minimum wage. In richer regions, however, urban consumption may be more appropriate.

As we are mainly using the variables of the city-level characteristics from the city statistical yearbook, we have several choices for the dependent variables to be used in the regression. First, we use the log of the highest minimum wage within a city, and the results are reported in columns 1–4 in Table 12.5.

Economic development seems to be the major factor that influences the minimum wage. In particular, GDP per capita, economic structure (share of the tertiary industry in GDP), and the per capita number of enterprises are strong predictors for the city-level minimum wages, and these variables are positively correlated with the minimum wage at the significance level of 1%. The amount of FDI (relative to GDP) is also positively correlated with the minimum wage, but only marginally significant at the 10% level. In the second column, we control for the consumption level in both rural and urban areas within the city. This decreases the number of observations of city-year from 2042 to 1866, but the pattern remains unchanged. The urban consumption level is highly significant. Column 3 controls for provincial dummies, which reduces the magnitude and the significance level of most variables. One major change is that the coefficient on the share of employment in private sectors becomes positive and insignificant rather than being significantly negative. Column 4 further controls for city dummies. Unsurprisingly, most of the coefficients become insignificant.

In columns 5–8, we consider another measure: log of the lowest minimum wage within a city. Without controlling for province dummies, the results are similar to those in columns 1–2, but the effects of those proxy variables for economic development are smaller in magnitude. Another difference is that the lowest minimum wage within a city is positively correlated with the consumption level of the rural areas.

The adjusted R2 in Table 12.5 suggests that the OLS regressions are fairly successful in explaining the variation of the minimum wages. The explanatory power of the model is 80–85% without controlling for regional dummies, and it reaches over 90% when provincial dummies are controlled for. The marginal gain in the explanatory power is low if we substitute provincial dummies with city dummies, consistent with the fact that province-level difference constitutes the major proportion of the regional variation.

Table 12.5 The determinants of the minimum wages at the city level, OLS

	Dep var.=							
	Log (highest minimum wage within a city)				*Log (lowest minimum wage within a city)*			
	(1)	*(2)*	*(3)*	*(4)*	*(5)*	*(6)*	*(7)*	*(8)*
Ln(GDP per capita)	0.138***	0.103***	0.0389***	0.00738	0.128***	0.0711**	0.0147	−0.00956
	(0.0239)	(0.0328)	(0.0138)	(0.0216)	(0.0229)	(0.0311)	(0.0205)	(0.0298)
Employment rate	−0.120	−0.152	0.0292	0.0314	−0.212	−0.234	0.0365	0.0433
	(0.162)	(0.191)	(0.0879)	(0.174)	(0.138)	(0.168)	(0.116)	(0.229)
GDP growth rate	−0.221*	−0.272**	−0.118*	−0.00639	−0.0390	−0.174	−0.0834	0.0120
	(0.113)	(0.115)	(0.0675)	(0.0832)	(0.145)	(0.163)	(0.0950)	(0.0920)
Tertiary sector share	0.280***	0.225***	0.0680**	−0.136	0.262***	0.181*	−0.0252	−0.102
	(0.0672)	(0.0731)	(0.0287)	(0.0897)	(0.0919)	(0.0941)	(0.0551)	(0.117)
Private employment share	−0.137	−0.244**	0.0378	−0.0249	−0.105	−0.196	0.0150	0.0259
	(0.0934)	(0.0922)	(0.0459)	(0.0580)	(0.127)	(0.120)	(0.0629)	(0.0535)
FDI share in GDP	0.515*	0.394	0.401*	0.166	0.429	0.173	0.361	0.299
	(0.276)	(0.316)	(0.198)	(0.124)	(0.384)	(0.400)	(0.265)	(0.190)
Fiscal expenditure/GDP	−0.138	−0.0891	−0.119*	−0.0815	0.164	0.191	0.114*	−0.0433
	(0.161)	(0.154)	(0.0656)	(0.111)	(0.174)	(0.159)	(0.0604)	(0.133)
Service sector/GDP	0.867	0.663	0.0892	−0.203	0.327	0.675	−0.0169	0.178
	(1.184)	(1.073)	(0.586)	(0.684)	(1.361)	(1.334)	(0.538)	(0.844)
Per capita number of enterprises	0.0159***	0.00916***	0.00186*	−0.00475	0.0200***	0.00944***	0.00323	−0.00573
	(0.00360)	(0.00303)	(0.00102)	(0.00400)	(0.00437)	(0.00336)	(0.00208)	(0.00546)
Ln(consumption per capita)_rural		0.00858	0.0323	0.00291		0.110**	0.0993***	0.0643
		(0.0434)	(0.0194)	(0.0370)		(0.0468)	(0.0292)	(0.0519)

(continued)

Table 12.5 (continued)

	Dep var:=							
	Log (highest minimum wage within a city)				*Log (lowest minimum wage within a city)*			
	(1)	*(2)*	*(3)*	*(4)*	*(5)*	*(6)*	*(7)*	*(8)*
Ln(consumption per capita)_urban		0.258***	0.217***	0.0491		0.252***	0.151***	0.0407
		(0.0712)	(0.0394)	(0.0682)		(0.0796)	(0.0361)	(0.0773)
Province dummies	No	No	Yes	No	No	No	Yes	No
City dummies	No	No	No	Yes	No	No	No	Yes
Year dummies	Yes	Yes	Yes	Yes	Yes	Yes	Yes	Yes
N	2042	1866	1866	1866	2042	1866	1866	1866
Adj. R-sq	0.846	0.858	0.933	0.951	0.791	0.819	0.909	0.940

Note (1) Standard errors in parentheses; (2) *, **, and *** represent significance levels of 10%, 5%, and 1%, respectively

As we include year dummies in our regressions and the minimum wage increases significantly, it is possible that the year dummies play a major role in explaining the minimum wage. We next run regressions for each year, and without losing important information, we report the results for 2003 and 2009 in Table 12.6. Column 1 reports the results for 2003. The listed variables altogether can explain half of the variation across cities. However, only two variables (GDP per capita and consumption per capita for urban residents) are significant at the 5% level. Controlling for provincial dummies increases the explanatory power by nearly 40% from 0.513 to 0.881 (see column 2). If we use the lowest minimum wage within the city as the dependent variable (columns 3–4), GDP per capita becomes less important in both the magnitude and the significance level of its coefficient. The consumption in rural areas becomes significant, regardless of whether we control for provincial dummies. Again, city-level characteristics are not enough to capture relevant differences at the province level.

In 2009, the explaining power of these variables reaches 60% when the highest minimum wage within the city is used as a dependent variable. Controlling for province dummies increases the R-squared to 0.853. It suggests that province-level differences become less important, or the differences are highly correlated with the city-level characteristics.

Some new patterns emerge as we run regressions for each year. For example, the GDP growth rate turns out to be negatively associated with the minimum wage. One explanation for this correlation is that a lower minimum wage is beneficial for GDP growth conditional on the economic development level.

Next, we consider the relative minimum wage. We have two alternative dependent variables: the ratio of the highest and the lowest minimum wage within a city to the average wage of that city. The results of using these two measures are similar to each other (See Table 12.7). Several factors that are positively correlated with the absolute value of the minimum wage turn to be negatively correlated with the relative minimum wage, including the GDP per capita and the per capita consumption of the urban residents. This suggests that the high GDP region have a higher average wage, which might be influenced more by high-income individuals. The fiscal expenditure share in GDP is insignificant in explaining the absolute minimum wage (see Tables 12.5 and 12.6), but it turns negatively correlated with the relative minimum wage in Table 12.7. The relative number of scaled enterprises and the share of

Table 12.6 The determinants of minimum wages in 2003 and 2009, OLS

	2003				*2009*			
	Max	*Max*	*Min*	*Min*	*Max*	*Max*	*Min*	*Min*
	(1)	*(2)*	*(3)*	*(4)*	*(5)*	*(6)*	*(7)*	*(8)*
Ln(GDP per capita)	0.109**	0.0494**	0.0818*	0.0230	0.115***	0.0502**	0.0802**	0.0307
	(0.0409)	(0.0209)	(0.0479)	(0.0239)	(0.0287)	(0.0183)	(0.0297)	(0.0217)
Employment rate	−0.484*	−0.203	−0.612*	−0.141	0.0778	0.140	0.193	0.167
	(0.274)	(0.169)	(0.318)	(0.124)	(0.177)	(0.0876)	(0.199)	(0.142)
GDP growth rate	−0.448	−0.232*	−0.260	−0.00420	−0.666***	−0.221***	−0.570**	−0.318*
	(0.322)	(0.129)	(0.352)	(0.133)	(0.197)	(0.0708)	(0.220)	(0.183)
Tertiary sector share	0.0458	−0.00792	0.0403	−0.0464	0.367***	0.155***	0.324**	0.0729
	(0.0981)	(0.0582)	(0.135)	(0.0486)	(0.0948)	(0.0558)	(0.126)	(0.105)
Private employment share	−0.104	0.0834	−0.260	−0.209**	−0.278**	−0.0547	−0.134	0.0402
	(0.272)	(0.132)	(0.341)	(0.0867)	(0.109)	(0.0688)	(0.135)	(0.0923)
FDI share in GDP	0.524	0.656***	0.330	0.700***	−0.266	0.113	−0.818*	−0.0560
	(0.387)	(0.206)	(0.415)	(0.234)	(0.383)	(0.205)	(0.415)	(0.327)
Fiscal expenditure/GDP	−0.197	−0.154	0.349	0.133	−0.0715	−0.0678	0.130	0.0892
	(0.314)	(0.144)	(0.313)	(0.114)	(0.104)	(0.0940)	(0.0990)	(0.0873)
Service sector/GDP	0.612	0.811	−0.500	0.737	0.599	−0.362	−0.501	−0.768
	(2.133)	(0.809)	(2.090)	(0.597)	(0.806)	(0.799)	(1.350)	(1.056)
Per capita number of enterprises	0.0109	0.00512	0.00890	0.00940**	0.0101***	0.00331**	0.0108***	0.00490*
	(0.00869)	(0.00405)	(0.00884)	(0.00454)	(0.00345)	(0.00142)	(0.00391)	(0.00264)
Ln(consumption per capita)_rural	0.0135	−0.00786	0.119**	0.103**	0.00467	0.0415	0.100*	0.0944**
	(0.0429)	(0.0303)	(0.0519)	(0.0437)	(0.0428)	(0.0248)	(0.0529)	(0.0381)
Ln(consumption per capita)_urban	0.245**	0.192***	0.293**	0.0563	0.110	0.157***	0.0690	0.0572
	(0.109)	(0.0602)	(0.124)	(0.0607)	(0.0736)	(0.0381)	(0.0869)	(0.0488)
Province dummies	No	Yes	No	Yes	No	Yes	No	Yes
N	240	240	240	240	262	262	262	262
Adj. R-sq	0.513	0.881	0.479	0.899	0.591	0.853	0.460	0.763

Note (1) Standard errors in parentheses; (2) *, **, and *** represent significance levels of 10%, 5%, and 1%, respectively

Table 12.7 The determinants of the *relative* minimum wages, OLS

	Dep var.=							
	Log (highest minimum wage within a city/average wage)				*Log (highest minimum wage within a city/average wage)*			
	(1)	*(2)*	*(3)*	*(4)*	*(5)*	*(6)*	*(7)*	*(8)*
Ln(GDP per capita)	−0.00458***	−0.00126	−0.00324***	−0.000811	−0.00447***	−0.00168*	−0.00336***	−0.00111
	(0.000465)	(0.000787)	(0.000687)	(0.000875)	(0.000421)	(0.000944)	(0.000606)	(0.000941)
Employment rate	0.00127	0.0118	−0.00278	0.00690	0.00106	0.0143*	−0.00144	0.00712
	(0.00485)	(0.00890)	(0.00605)	(0.0115)	(0.00396)	(0.00805)	(0.00523)	(0.0109)
GDP growth rate	−0.00330	−0.00552	−0.00269	−0.00405	−0.00269	−0.00489	−0.00189	−0.00362
	(0.00449)	(0.00359)	(0.00446)	(0.00378)	(0.00414)	(0.00329)	(0.00405)	(0.00342)
Tertiary sector share	−0.00146	−0.00446	−0.00133	−0.00368	−0.00274	−0.00268	−0.00268	−0.00202
	(0.00193)	(0.00322)	(0.00196)	(0.00342)	(0.00195)	(0.00350)	(0.00194)	(0.00356)
Private employment share	−0.00199	−0.00185	−0.000602	−0.00271	−0.00303*	−0.00114	−0.00124	−0.00163
	(0.00178)	(0.00280)	(0.00187)	(0.00362)	(0.00169)	(0.00240)	(0.00195)	(0.00298)
FDI share in GDP	0.00755	0.00387	0.00944*	−0.000662	0.00763	0.00721	0.00874	0.00220
	(0.00470)	(0.00523)	(0.00513)	(0.00547)	(0.00516)	(0.00553)	(0.00567)	(0.00585)
Fiscal expenditure/GDP	−0.0124***	−0.0113***	−0.0123***	−0.00783**	−0.00697*	−0.00885***	−0.00652*	−0.00629*
	(0.00377)	(0.00326)	(0.00338)	(0.00357)	(0.00379)	(0.00310)	(0.00325)	(0.00338)
Service sector/GDP	0.0181	0.00900	0.0442	0.0190	0.0124	0.0000916	0.0342	0.0197
	(0.0308)	(0.0508)	(0.0358)	(0.0556)	(0.0228)	(0.0459)	(0.0279)	(0.0501)
Per capita number of enterprises	0.000289***	0.000206	0.000334***	0.000194	0.000303***	0.000162	0.000325***	0.000142
	(0.0000956)	(0.000146)	(0.000105)	(0.000177)	(0.0000655)	(0.000134)	(0.0000677)	(0.000170)
Ln(consumption per capita)_rural			−0.000166	−0.000602			0.00122	0.000700
			(0.000949)	(0.00203)			(0.00101)	(0.00215)
Ln(consumption per capita)_urban			−0.00456**	−0.00631**			−0.00531***	−0.00552*
			(0.00206)	(0.00305)			(0.00159)	(0.00297)
Province dummies	No	Yes	No	Yes	No	Yes	No	Yes
N	2033	2033	1862	1862	2033	2033	1862	1862
Adj. R-sq	0.260	0.432	0.263	0.390	0.273	0.459	0.247	0.396

Note (1) Standard errors in parentheses; (2) *, **, and *** represent significance levels of 10%, 5%, and 1%, respectively

Table 12.8 The determinants of the relative minimum wages in 2003 and 2009, OLS

	2003				*2009*			
	Max	*Max*	*Min*	*Min*	*Max*	*Max*	*Min*	*Min*
	(1)	*(2)*	*(3)*	*(4)*	*(5)*	*(6)*	*(7)*	*(8)*
Ln(GDP per capita)	−0.0000853	−0.00216**	−0.000730	−0.00257***	−0.00241**	−0.00374***	−0.00280***	−0.00368***
	(0.00131)	(0.00101)	(0.000992)	(0.000732)	(0.000877)	(0.000869)	(0.000723)	(0.000792)
Employment rate	−0.0242**	−0.0163**	−0.0224**	−0.0111*	0.00448	0.000359	0.00641	0.00170
	(0.0104)	(0.00744)	(0.00847)	(0.00561)	(0.00517)	(0.00615)	(0.00518)	(0.00531)
GDP growth rate	−0.0109	−0.00231	−0.00476	0.00356	0.000781	0.00807	0.00361	0.00534
	(0.0118)	(0.00807)	(0.0103)	(0.00706)	(0.00827)	(0.00748)	(0.00852)	(0.00719)
Tertiary sector share	−0.00402	−0.00193	−0.00290	−0.00164	−0.00279	−0.00529*	−0.00296	−0.00583**
	(0.00317)	(0.00319)	(0.00297)	(0.00247)	(0.00453)	(0.00293)	(0.00369)	(0.00263)
Private employment share	0.00403	0.000513	−0.000623	−0.00600**	−0.00886***	−0.00528*	−0.00493*	−0.00291
	(0.00745)	(0.00348)	(0.00717)	(0.00288)	(0.00245)	(0.00259)	(0.00274)	(0.00272)
FDI share in GDP	0.0223	0.0104	0.0162	0.0101	0.00870	0.00822	−0.00162	0.00441
	(0.0135)	(0.00958)	(0.0118)	(0.00717)	(0.0123)	(0.0113)	(0.0101)	(0.00866)
Fiscal expenditure/GDP	−0.0260***	−0.0218***	−0.0123*	−0.0140**	−0.00689	−0.00537	−0.00301	−0.00215
	(0.00821)	(0.00748)	(0.00671)	(0.00554)	(0.00467)	(0.00417)	(0.00411)	(0.00436)
Service sector/GDP	0.0935	0.0833*	0.0534	0.0675*	0.0998*	0.106***	0.0595	0.0810**
	(0.0574)	(0.0415)	(0.0433)	(0.0336)	(0.0516)	(0.0358)	(0.0471)	(0.0331)
Per capita number of enterprises	0.000392	0.000558*	0.000312*	0.000602***	0.000330***	0.000270***	0.000295***	0.000272***
	(0.000238)	(0.000287)	(0.000168)	(0.000175)	(0.0000752)	(0.0000770)	(0.0000761)	(0.0000682)
Ln(consumption per capita)_rural	−0.000874	−0.000248	0.00172	0.00235	−0.00288**	−0.00153	−0.000929	−0.000476
	(0.00180)	(0.00187)	(0.00173)	(0.00181)	(0.00115)	(0.00116)	(0.00129)	(0.00129)
Ln(consumption per capita)_urban	−0.0125***	−0.0102**	−0.0104***	−0.0123***	−0.00152	0.000929	−0.00160	−0.000933
	(0.00336)	(0.00381)	(0.00313)	(0.00299)	(0.00175)	(0.00240)	(0.00202)	(0.00212)
Province dummies	No	Yes	No	Yes	No	Yes	No	Yes
N	240	240	240	240	258	258	258	258
Adj. R-sq	0.251	0.488	0.234	0.529	0.135	0.450	0.095	0.401

Note (1) Standard errors in parentheses; (2) *, **, and *** represent significance levels of 10%, 5%, and 1%, respectively

the service sector in GDP are positively correlated with the relative minimum wage. These patterns largely remain when we run regressions for separate years (see Table 12.8).

It is worth mentioning that we are less successful in explaining the relative minimum wage than in explaining the absolute value of the minimum wage in terms of the adjusted R-squared in the OLS regressions. For example, the adjusted R-squared is only around 10% in the regression for 2009 when the province dummies are not controlled for. Even with the province dummies being controlled for, the explaining power is only around 40–45%. However, although many studies focus on the relative levels of the minimum wages, it is the absolute values that are determined by the tripartite negotiation process.

12.6 The Time to Adjust the Minimum Wages

The new provisions issued in 2004 require the local governments to adjust the minimum wage at least once in every two years. The local governments decide when to do so. It is interesting to see whether the timing of the minimum wage adjustment is related to regional characteristics and more importantly to minimum wage levels. Two alternative stories can be told.

The first is the race-to-the-bottom story. The local officials compete in GDP growth performance to gain a better chance of promotions. If they believe that higher minimum wage drove up labor costs, deterred potential investors, and eventually harmed growth, they have incentives to set minimum wage levels lower than competing regions. A province that adjusts its minimum wage later would choose lower levels than a similar province that adjusts the minimum wage earlier. The second story, which we heard of often in conversation with officials and scholars, is the keep-up-with-the-Joneses one. Local officials do not want to have minimum wages lower than competing provinces, for several reasons, justified or unjustified. First, a higher minimum wage is itself an indicator of better economic performance, which might be valued in official promotions. Second, while seeming unfriendly to employers, it may help a region attract quality workers, which seems to be truly believed by some local officials.[4] If the keep-up-with-the-Joneses hypothesis is true, provinces adjusting their minimum wages later should choose higher minimum wages.

In both theories, announcing the new minimum wage policy later allows the local government to observe the new policy of other local governments. Therefore, we hypothesize that the local government tends to adjust the minimum wage policy later, which leads to the procrastination of the minimum wage adjustment within a year.[5]

Table 12.9 reports the number of provinces that implement new minimum wages in each month from 1995 to 2007. There is considerable variation in the time chosen for new minimum wages and also the variation changed from 1995 to 2007. In earlier years, most local governments chose January and July, the starting point of a year or the half year. From around 2003, more provinces choose the last two-quarters in a natural year to implement their new minimum wages. A regression of the month of adjustment on year gives a coefficient of 0.25, and the standard error is 0.04. This might be due to the fact that local governments compete on minimum wage levels, and waiting allows them to observe the action of other provinces.

Is there any relationship between the month of minimum wage adjustments and minimum wage levels?[6] Announcing the minimum wage later allows the local government to observe the behavior of his peer local governments. If the race-to-the-bottom story dominates, the local government would like to set a lower minimum wage than his competitors. On the other hand, if the keep-up-with-the-Joneses story dominates, local governments will set a higher minimum wage than his competitors. Which story dominates, in reality, is subject to empirical test.

Table 12.10 provides a rigorous empirical study, where we regress the level of minimum wages on the month of minimum wage adjustments and a set of other control variables. These control variables are important as they allow us to compare regions with similar economic development levels. In the first row, we use the highest level of minimum wage within a city as the dependent variable. The results suggest that regions adjusting their minimum wages later tend to have slightly higher minimum wages. In the second row, we use the natural log of the highest minimum wage within a city as the dependent variable. Again, the coefficients on the month of the minimum wage adjustment are significantly positive, but small in magnitude, none of them greater than 1%. In panel C, we use relative minimum wage (the ratio of the highest minimum wage within a city to the average wage of the city) as the dependent variable, and we get similar results. Using the lowest minimum wage within

Table 12.9 Month when the new minimum wage implemented

	1995	*1996*	*1997*	*1998*	*1999*	*2000*	*2001*	*2002*	*2003*	*2004*	*2005*	*2006*	*2007*
January	12	7	8	8	4	4	3	5	6	6	5	1	3
February	1	1	0	0	0	0	0	0	0	1	1	0	0
March	0	0	1	1	1	3	4	3	3	0	1	2	1
April	2	2	1	1	0	0	1	2	0	0	0	1	1
May	4	5	4	3	3	2	3	3	1	3	2	3	2
June	1	1	1	0	0	0	0	0	0	0	0	0	0
July	7	10	9	11	15	15	14	11	11	10	10	7	5
August	0	0	0	0	0	0	0	0	0	0	0	2	2
September	0	2	4	4	4	2	0	2	3	2	3	6	4
October	1	1	2	2	3	3	4	4	6	8	6	7	7
November	0	0	0	0	0	0	0	0	0	1	2	1	3
December	0	0	0	0	0	1	1	1	1	0	1	1	3
Total	28	29	30	30	30	30	30	31	31	31	31	31	31

Table 12.10 Time adjusted and the level of minimum wages (coefficients on the month of adjustment)

	(1)	*(2)*	*(3)*
Dependent var. =			
A: the highest level of mw within a city	2.811*	1.957*	1.543
	(1.602)	(1.106)	(1.203)
B: Ln (the highest level of mw within a city)	0.00761**	0.00734***	0.00621**
	(0.00323)	(0.00258)	(0.00291)
C: The highest level of mw within a city relative to average wage	0.0000794	0.000218***	0.000224**
	(0.0000767)	(0.0000791)	(0.0000890)
D: the lowest level of mw within a city	1.187	1.952*	1.712*
	(1.751)	(0.999)	(0.996)
E: Ln (the lowest level of mw within a city)	0.00431	0.00767***	0.00688**
	(0.00428)	(0.00249)	(0.00279)
F: The lowest level of mw within a city relative to average wage	−0.00000654	0.000195***	0.000205**
	(0.0000705)	(0.0000699)	(0.0000761)
Year dummies	Yes	Yes	Yes
Province dummies	No	Yes	No
City dummies	No	No	Yes

Note (1) The controls that are not reported are the same as those in Table 13.8. (2) Standard errors in parentheses; (3) *, **, and *** represent significance levels of 10%, 5%, and 1%, respectively

a city (panels D to E) produces similar results. These results indicate that local government wants to keep-up-with-the-Joneses, but at the same time, they do not want to raise minimum wages too much higher than other provinces with the risk of damaging growth.

12.7 Discussion and Conclusions

The emerging literature on the minimum wage policy in China reflects a growing demand for redefining the labor relations in the Chinese labor market. Minimum wage policies, along with unions, and collective bargaining, are discussed more often than ever in both academia and public policies. Although there are many studies showing the impact of China's minimum wage policy on wages, employment, and inequality, large or small, significant or insignificant, expected or unexpected, results in this article suggest that the significant increase in the minimum wage is mainly a reflection rather than a cause of the rapid growth of the Chinese economy.

China is a large country with economic development level varying substantially across regions (Kanbur and Zhang 2005). It decentralizes the implementation of the minimum wage policy, leading to large regional variation in minimum wages. Our findings have a major implication in making predictions about the regional variation in minimum wages in the future. The basic pattern we observe is that the regional variation has been declining. A question then emerges: Will the regional variation continue to decrease? The answer seems to be yes, for the following reasons. First, the simple extrapolation of the existing trend predicts fewer levels of minimum wages within a province and declining HL ratios both within a province and within the whole country. If we assume a linear trend in the number of the minimum wages within a province, the number will decrease to around 3 by 2020, and the HL ratio will decrease to around 1.2. Second, this prediction is supported by our regression results as well (see Table 12.2). For the HL ratio results, in particular, the share of the tertiary sector in GDP is negatively correlated with the HL ratio, and the trade share and the rural–urban income gap (the latter not being significant for the period 2000–2007) are positively correlated with the HL ratio. The most possible changing direction of these factors points to a decreased regional variation: The share of the tertiary sector will increase continuously; China will become less dependent on export to boost its economy, and the rural–urban income gap has shown a declining trend. All suggest lower within-province HL ratio in the future.

What about the regional difference in the minimum wage for the whole country? Although the number of minimum wage levels shows no consistent trend, the HL ratio, the Gini coefficient, and the coefficient of variation decrease significantly. This is consistent with the fact that the regional wage gaps for unskilled workers decreased in recent years. Whalley and Xing (2014) show that while the wage gaps across the province for skilled workers increased significantly between 2002 and 2007, those of the unskilled workers decreased. As the unskilled workers constitute a major part of the population targeted by the minimum wage policy, the convergence of regional wages for them suggests a convergence in the minimum wage levels across regions.

Notes

1. Shenzhen for example: http://www.cnr.cn/2004news/internal/200505310023.html.
2. We also calculate the standard deviation of the regional minimum wages. Because this measure depends on the level of minimum wages, it increases. Once we use the natural of minimum wages, the standard deviation also decline, which is consistent with the results we report in the article.
3. In the end of 2004, the minimum wages applied in Guangzhou and Shenzhen were 684 and 610 RMB, respectively. The new minimum wage in Guangzhou is only applicable after December 1. It was 510 RMB before that date.
4. Among the five reasons to raise minimum wage in 2008, local officials in Shenzhen point out that raising minimum wage will help them attract skilled workers (http://sztqb.sznews.com/html/2008-06/03/content_199567.htm accessed on 2014-12-17).
5. Although the new regulation in 2004 mandates the local government to adjust the minimum wages at least once in every two years, most of the provinces adjustment the minimum wages once a year.
6. This question was partly inspired by a conversation to a government official in Shenzhen. He said Shenzhen raised its minimum wage to 1600 RMB/month in February 2013, which was overtaken by Shanghai in April. But the differential is only 20 RMB, which is symbolic rather than substantive.

References

Bloch, Farrell E. (1980). "Political Support for Minimum Wage Legislation." *Journal of Labor Research*, 1(Fall 1980): 245–253.

Bloch, Farrell E. (1993). "Political Support for Minimum Wage Legislation: 1989." *Journal of Labor Research*, 14(Spring 1993): 187–190.

Card, David, and Krueger Alan. (1995). *Myth and Measurement: The New Economics of the Minimum Wage*. Princeton, NJ: Princeton University Press.

Chi, Wei, Richard B. Freeman, and Hongbin Li. (2012). "Adjusting to Really Big Changes: The Labor Market in China, 1989–2009." NBER Working Papers 17721.

Fang, Tony, and Carl Lin. (2014). "Minimum Wages and Employment Transitions: Longitudinal Evidence from China." Working Paper.

Flinn, Christopher J. (2011). *The Minimum Wage and Labor Market Outcomes*. Cambridge, MA: MIT Press.

Guo, Ji, Jianwei Xu, and Muyang Zhang. (2013). "Political Tournament, Land Supply and Housing Price: Evidence from Chinese Cities." Working Paper.

Harris, John R., and Michael P. Todaro. (1970). "Migration, Unemployment and Development: A Two-Sector Analysis." *American Economic Review*, 60(1): 126–142.

Johnson, Colleen F. (2002). "The Politics of Minimum Wage Legislation in the Western United States: Lessons in Policy and Power." *Journal of Economic Issues*, 36(2): 331–337.

Johnson, William R., and Edgar K. Browning. (1983). "The Distributional and Efficiency Effects of Increasing the Minimum Wages: A Simulation," *American Economic Review*, 73(1): 204–211.

Kanbur, Ravi, and Xiaobo Zhang, 2005. "Fifty Years of Regional Inequality in China: A Journey Through Central Planning, Reform, and Openness." *Review of Development Economics*, 9(1): 87–106, 02.

Kau, James B., and Paul H. Rubin. (April 1978). "Voting on Minimum Wages: A Time-Series Analysis." *Journal of Political Economy*, 86(2), pt. 1: 337–342.

Li, Hongbin, and Li-an Zhou. 2005. "Political Turnover and Economic Performance: The Incentive Role of Personnel Control in China." *Journal of Public Economics*, 89: 1743–1762.

Neumark, David, and William Wascher. (2008). *Minimum Wages*. Cambridge, MA: MIT Press.

Rani, Uma, Patrick Belser, Martin Oelz, and Setareh Ranjbar. (2013). "Minimum Wage Coverage and Compliance in Developing Countries." *International Labour Review*, 153(3–4): 381–410.

Silberman, Jonathan I., and Garey C. Durden. (April 1976). "Determining Legislative Preferences on the Minimum Wage: An Economic Approach." *Journal of Political Economy*, 84: 317–329.

Seltzer, Andrew J. (December 1995). "The Political Economy of the Fair Labor Standards Act of 1938." *Journal of Political Economy*, 103: 1302–1342.

Sobel, Russell S. (1999). "Theory and Evidence on the Political Economy of the Minimum Wage." *Journal of Political Economy*, 107(4): 761–785.

Stigler, George J. (1946). "The Economics of Minimum Wage Legislation." *The American Economic Review*, 36(3): 358–365.

Whalley, John, and Chunbing Xing. (2014). "The Regional Distribution of the Skill Premia in Urban China and its Implications for Growth and Inequality." *International Labour Review*, 153(3): 395–420.

Xing, Chunbing, and Li Shi. (2012). "Residual Wage Inequality in Urban China, 1995–2007." *China Economic Review*, 23(2): 205–222.

Yang, Juan, and Morley Gunderson. (2014). "The Impact of Minimum Wages on Migrant Workers' Wages." Working Paper.

CHAPTER 13

Minimum Wage Competition Between Local Governments in China

Ravi Kanbur, Yanan Li and Carl Lin

13.1 Introduction

Strategic interactions of fiscal policies among governments have been well discussed in both theoretical and empirical studies. Early examples of theory papers on tax competition include Kanbur and Keen (1993), Edwards and Keen (1996), Altshuler and Goodspeed (2003) and Wilson and Wildasin (2004).[1] Compared to tax competition and environmental policy competition, however, jurisdictional interactions between labor

Another version of this paper was published in the Journal of Development Studies.

R. Kanbur
Cornell University, Ithaca, NY, USA
e-mail: sk145@cornell.edu

Y. Li (✉)
Beijing Normal University, Beijing, China
e-mail: yananli@bnu.edu.cn

C. Lin
Bucknell University, Lewisburg, PA, USA
e-mail: carl.lin@bucknell.edu

L. Shi and C. Lin (eds.), *Minimum Wages in China*,
https://doi.org/10.1007/978-981-15-2421-9_13

standards and regulatory policies have not been studied as intensively (some examples include Duanmu 2014).

A conventional wisdom is that there is a potential "race to the bottom" in labor standards across countries—governments undercut each other's labor standards in order to attract foreign capital (e.g., Chau and Kanbur 2006; DeSombre 2006; Davies and Vadlamannati 2013; Olney 2013). On the other hand, there are also studies concluding the opposite to be true, i.e., "race to the top"—FDI inflows are positively correlated with workers' rights as firms are competing for labor (e.g., Mosley and Uno 2007). The key point is whether policies in one country are influenced by those in others. While most of these studies provide evidence for international interactions in labor standards, there is little evidence so far on within-country competition, especially in developing countries, which is surprising given the importance of this issue. This article fills the gap by providing evidence for strategic interactions on minimum wage standards in China.

Minimum wage standards across local jurisdictions could be interdependent for several reasons, in general and specifically in China. First, the mobility of multinational companies and foreign capital produces incentives for local governments to engage in a "race to the bottom" on minimum wages (Drezner 2001). Secondly, a tightening labor market in an era of high growth gives workers stronger wage bargaining power. This situation motivates manufacturing firms to improve labor rights in recruitment. Thirdly, from the behavioral point of view, the interdependencies of labor standards may merely come from status-seeking incentives. Government officials may not want to "lose face" when they see neighboring governments taking active action on labor protection. For these types of reasons, in theory a change in labor standards by other jurisdictions provides incentives for a given jurisdiction to make adjustments. But what is the evidence on such interactions?

This article focuses on minimum wages as a leading example of a labor standard. First, minimum wage standards are visible to investors, and increasing minimum wages leads to a rightward shift of the wage distribution (Neumark 2004), both of which are generally viewed as negative factors for capital inflow. Thus, the visibility of minimum wage standards plus the spillover wage effects provide governments with incentives to undercut minimum wages relative to competing jurisdictions. Second, there has been a major shift in policy in China in the 2000s. Before the year 2000, a minimum wage standard was close to nonexistent, in terms of statutory levels and the enforcement of minimum wage laws. From the mid-2000s onwards, however, rising concerns on inequality led to considerable strengthening of regulation and enforcement. A relatively decentralized decision-making system on minimum wages, leading to frequent adjustments in the recent period, makes China an ideal setting for studying minimum wage interactions across local jurisdictions within a country. We manually collect a panel data set of city-level minimum wage standards for 326 prefecture cities from China's government Web sites.

Although some studies have started using natural experiments to study interjurisdictional competition (e.g., Lyytikäinen 2012; Baskaran 2014), we cannot use such methods in the Chinese case. We rely therefore on a route followed by most of the literature, which of a spatial lag framework combined with exogenous covariates to study this issue.[2] We use spatial lag methodology and maximum likelihood (ML) estimation to study city-level strategic interactions in setting minimum wage standards during 2002–2012 in China. The results support the story of a race to the bottom. If other cities decrease minimum wage standards by 1 RMB, the city in question will decrease its standard by 0.7 RMB.

Besides competition on minimum wage standards, jurisdictions can also compete on enforcement of those standards. Bhorat et al. (2012) are an example of a recent literature documenting noncompliance with minimum wage regulation in developing countries. Ronconi (2012) finds that governments react to the competitive pressures produced by FDI inflow by turning a blind eye to noncompliance. Cremer and Gahvari (2000) also states that enforcement policies are sometimes used as instruments for fiscal competition, when competition in tax rates are banned. Despite data limitations, this article also makes a first attempt to assess competition on the enforcement of minimum wage standards. We find that if the violation rate in other cities increases by 1 percentage point, the city in question will respond by an increase of roughly 0.3 percentage points.

13.2 Institutional Background and Data

13.2.1 Minimum Wage Setting in China

Minimum wage regulations have existed in China dating back to the mid-1990s, but the standards were low and enforcement was poor. In the 2000s, rising income inequality became of increasing concern to Chinese policymakers. In 2004, the Ministry of Labor and Social Security issued a "Minimum Wage Regulations" law and the next decade saw rising minimum wage standards coupled with substantial improvements in compliance (see Appendix Table 13.8). This law established two types of the minimum wage: A monthly minimum wage applied to full-time workers and an hourly minimum wage applied to non-full-time employees. For full-time workers, minimum wage regulation only relies on monthly wage, not including subsidy or overtime bonus. This article focuses on the monthly wages that full-time workers receive at their primary occupations.

China's administrative structure goes from province to prefecture-level city to other sub-divisions. A prefecture-level city comprises a main central urban area (a city in the usual sense, and normally with the same name as the prefecture city), and its surrounding rural areas containing many smaller cities and counties. We define "city" in this article as the central urban area in any prefectural-level city, and "counties" as the above-mentioned surrounding smaller cities and counties.

Minimum wage standard setting begins at the province level. Typically, the provincial government issues three or four levels of minimum wage standards which are calculated based on local living standards, average wages, and economic development. Then each prefecture-level city issues a more detailed law, specifying minimum wage adjustments in the central city and its surrounding counties. Finally, each of these areas takes the level that fits their economic development. Some counties may make adjustments according to their specific condition, though most of them do not.

The possibility of jurisdictional interactions on minimum wage standards comes from the flexibility of local governments in setting and enforcing minimum wage standards at different stages of the process. A provincial government tends to involve prefecture cities to obtain information on their social and economic development, which begins the chain of possible inter-city competition. Second, even if cities and counties are not directly involved in the first stage, they still have the flexibility of adjustments based on their own economic situation after minimum wage adjustment laws are announced. In addition to the hierarchical characteristics, regional difference is also an interesting angle. Within a province, cities have greater influence than their surrounding counties in setting minimum wages. Then, when it comes to enforcing minimum wage laws, city-level governments have almost full control of local compliance levels of minimum wages. In addition to regional variation of minimum wage levels, adjustment dates also differ across provinces. Since 2004, minimum wage standards have been adjusted almost every year. Frequent adjustments provide a good source of time variation in the data.

13.2.2 Data Sources and Basic Trends

We use a number of complementary data sources for the analysis. Data on city-level minimum wages are manually collected from local government Web sites over 2002–2012. Data on city characteristics and boundary shapefiles are compiled from China Data Online. Finally, for the enforcement question we merged the 2002–2009 Urban Household Survey (UHS hereafter) so as to construct city-level noncompliance variables.

In the final data for minimum wage competition, there are 252 prefecture cities across our study period 2002–2012. The data set covers 25 provinces in China, all provinces other than Gansu, Qinghai, Xinjiang, Guizhou, Hainan, Guizhou, Tibet, Hongkong, and Macao.[3] When merging city demographic data to minimum wage data, where there are multiple levels of minimum wage levels in one prefecture city we keep the highest one as that city's standard. Table 13.1 shows the trend of minimum wage standards in our sample. For almost all years in the study period, real minimum wages grew more slowly than GDP and per capita GDP. In 2009, no provinces adjusted minimum wages due to the financial crisis, hence the growth rate of nominal minimum wages is zero. However, the growth rate of *real* minimum wages is positive in 2009

Table 13.1 Trend of minimum wage standards, 2002–2012

Year	*Min. wage*	*Growth of min. wage (%)*	*GDP growth rate (%)*	*Per capita GDP growth (%)*	*% of jurisdictions adjusting min. wage (%)*
2002	283.83				
2003	289.23	2.0	13.0	6.5	22
2004	330.66	15.1	17.0	10.3	66
2005	350.82	7.6	16.7	10.4	35
2006	404.76	16.8	15.4	9.5	88
2007	427.61	6.5	15.8	9.4	62
2008	452.70	6.7	14.3	9.4	64
2009	455.54	0.6	14.0	11.7	0
2010	553.00	22.2	16.7	11.6	99
2011	613.75	11.0	15.9	14.7	78
2012	675.90	10.7	11.7	12.0	68
Total	439.80	9.9	15.0	10.6	58

Note All values are deflated by the provincial level CPI

because of a decrease of CPI. Then 2010 saw a big percentage increase compared to 2008 minimum wages. The last column of Table 13.1 shows that, on average, 60% of counties and cities made minimum wage adjustments in each study year. In cases of two upward adjustments in 2007, i.e., Hebei Province and Beijing city, we take the second (and higher) one as that year's minimum wage standard.

UHS is a continuous, large-scale social-economic survey conducted by the National Bureau of Statistics of China aiming to study the conditions and living standards of urban households, which include local urban households, non-local urban households who have lived in the city for at least six months, and some rural-urban migrant households. The survey data covers 16 representative provinces out of 31 provinces in China. It includes demographic information such as gender, marriage status, and age as well as yearly wage data and employment information.[4]

By comparing individual monthly wage (derived by annual income/the number of months worked in the year) to the minimum wage standard in this city, we obtain a binary indicator of whether this person received a sub-minimum wage or not. Then we aggregate individual level to city level and calculate various measures of violation. The trends of the average monthly wage, minimum wages, and compliance levels are provided in Table 13.8. Descriptive statistics of city characteristics are provided in Table 13.9.

We need UHS data to quantify noncompliance, but UHS only covers 2002–2009 and 16 provinces. Thus, in merging UHS to city-level data, we have only 66 cities left in each year.[5] However, the relatively small sample size should not bias our estimates of the spillover effect of minimum wage enforcement, given the randomness of UHS sampling.

13.3 Empirical Specification and Identification

We use the spatial lag framework to estimate city-level strategic interactions of setting minimum wage standards (e.g., Brueckner 2003; Davies and Vadlamannati 2013; Ollé 2003). Expressed mathematically, the specification for the Spatial Autoregression Regression (SAR) is as follows:

$$\begin{aligned} MW_{i,t} &= \beta_i + \rho \sum_{j \neq i} \omega_{j,i} MW_{j,t} + \alpha \cdot MW_{i,t-1} \\ &\quad + \beta \cdot X_{i,t-2} + \eta_i + \delta_t + \varepsilon_{i,t} \qquad \text{(SAR)} \end{aligned} \tag{1}$$

where $MW_{i,t}$ is the minimum wage standard in city i in year t; $\sum_{j\neq i}\omega_{j,i}MW_{j,t}$ is the weighted average of minimum wage standards in other jurisdictional areas, or Spatial Lag; η_i controls for city fixed effects, and δ_t controls for year fixed effects; ρ captures the spatial dependence of minimum wages. $\omega_{j,i}$ is a distance-based weight, explained in greater detail below. City-level economic characteristics $X_{i,t-2}$ are taken with a 2-year lag to enhance the case for exogeneity. $X=\{$GDP, per capita GDP, industry share in total GDP, labor force participation rate,[6] the proportion of employees in primary industry, student enrollment in secondary schools, student enrollment in primary schools, the number of enterprises, the number of beds in hospitals$\}$. All values such as GDP and minimum wages are deflated by the provincial level Consumer Price Index. For key descriptive statistics, see Table 13.9.

The baseline weighting matrix is constructed by simple contiguity, i.e., for each city i, neighbors are defined as prefecture cities that share borders with it. The weighting matrix is normalized so that row sum equals to unity. If city i has n_i neighbors, then weights are defined as,

$$\omega_{j,i}=\begin{cases}\frac{1}{n_i}, & \text{if city } i \text{ is a neighbor of } j,\\ 0, & \text{otherwise}\end{cases} \tag{W1}$$

Alternatively, considering the fact that closer neighbors may have a stronger impact on city i than cities farther away, we multiply above contiguity matrix by the inverse distance between the centroids of two cities, $1/d_{ij}$. Distance matrices in this article are all generated from boundary shapefiles using GIS software. The neighborhood-inverse distance matrix is as follows.

$$\omega_{j,i}=\begin{cases}\frac{1}{d_i}, & \text{if city } i \text{ is a neighbor of } j,\\ 0 & \text{otherwise}\end{cases} \tag{W2}$$

Economic characteristics of neighboring cities may also influence minimum wage settings. One hypothesis is that, among all neighboring cities, city i is more likely to reference minimum wage standards in more affluent cities than in poor cities. Thus, we multiply the contiguity matrix by economic characteristics, and then standardize row sum to one. We use economic characteristics in the initial year 2003 to calculate weights, so that weighting matrix is arguably exogenous. In the case of per capita GDP,

$$\omega_{j,i} = \begin{cases} \frac{1}{n_i} * \text{Per Capita GDP}_{j,t=2003}, & \text{if city } i \text{ is a neighbor of } j, \\ 0, & \text{otherwise} \end{cases} \quad \text{(W3)}$$

Other weighting matrices are used in our robustness checks, reported in Sect. 13.5.

In terms of identification, the first and fundamental assumption underlying these empirical models is that at year t cities reference other cities' minimum wage decisions in the current year, rather than in year $t-1$ or $t+1$. This idea is reflected in the spatial lag term $\sum_{j\neq i} \omega_{j,i} MW_{j,t}$ in Eq. (1), where we use contemporaneous minimum wage levels rather than lags or leads. Admittedly, minimum wage standards in different cities are not announced in the same day in a given year. However, it's not unreasonable to assume that the *process* of making decisions is a simultaneous game, considering the fact that the usually long decision-making period gives cities enough time to look at their neighbors. Even if city A announces minimum wage on May 1 and city B on September 1, it's still plausible that city A has made a guess about city B's adjustment level and taken that into account prior to announcing its own minimum wage level.

To study jurisdictional areas' interactions over enforcement, we modify model (1) by changing $MW_{i,t}$ to $E_{i,t}$, where $E_{i,t}$ is the enforcement level in city *i*. Ideally, enforcement intensity could be measured by the amount of resources (e.g., inspectors) that government invests to regulate minimum wage laws. Because of the lack of data on this variable and considering the fact that a stronger enforcement intensity will help reduce minimum wage noncompliance (Bhorat et al. 2012), we use minimum wage violation as a proxy variable of enforcement. The measurement of violation is simply the headcount ratio of violation, i.e., the number of workers receiving below minimum wages divided by the total number of the working population.[7] The model is as follows,

$$\begin{aligned} E_{i,t} = \beta_i + \rho \sum_{j\neq i} \omega_{j,i} E_{j,t} + \alpha \cdot E_{i,t-1} \\ + \beta \cdot X_{i,t-2} + \text{Kaitz}_{i,t} + \eta_i + \delta_t + \varepsilon_{i,t} \end{aligned} \quad \begin{matrix} (2) \\ \text{(SAR)} \end{matrix}$$

Note that the weighting matrix slightly differs from that in model (1), because the relatively small number of cities in the enforcement analysis. Many cities are "islands" with no contiguous neighbors, so we cannot construct the contiguity matrix as in model (1). Rather, we directly use the inverse distance between the centroids of two cities, $1/d_i$. Essentially,

$\omega_{j,i} = \frac{1}{d_i}$, where d_{ij} is the distance between the centroids of city i and city j.

Similarly, if taking economic distance into account, an alternative weighting matrix is as follows:

$$\omega_{j,i} = \frac{1}{d_i} * \text{Per Capita GDP}_{j,t=2003}$$

Another difference of the model is the extra control variable, Kaitz ratio, the ratio of the minimum wage to the median wage, calculated for each city. We add it as a control variable because cities with higher minimum wage standards tend to have lower enforcement. Because there are two minimum wage levels in a year, i.e., pre-adjustment and post-adjustment minimum wages, in order to control for the average minimum wage level within a year, we use month-weighted average in the model. Further, we assume that the host city i references current (rather than past) enforcement levels in other cities.

A central econometric issue is the endogeneity of covariates. In our minimum wage setting, the causality could be in both directions because of the interdependencies of minimum wage decisions among neighboring jurisdictions. Two common approaches in the literature of obtaining consistent estimates are using ML, and instrumental variables (IV) (Brueckner 2003). We use ML estimation, because one disadvantage of IV/GMM estimators in spatial lag models is that they ignore the Jacobian term, hence the possibility of ending up with a coefficient estimate for ρ outside its parameter space $(-1, 1)$ (Elhorst 2009; Allers and Elhorst 2005).[8] In addition to the assumption of independently and identically distributed error term $\varepsilon_{i,t}$, ML estimator also relies on the assumption of normality of the errors. We plotted the residuals for main regressions of the model. We also conducted the one-sample Kolmogorov-Smirnov test. The results are available upon request. Both residual plots and test statistics indicate that residuals cannot be distinguished from normally distributed data.

13.4 Results

Tables 13.2 and 13.3 present estimates from models (1) and (2), respectively. That is, Table 13.2 presents results for jurisdictional interdependence on minimum wage standards and Table 13.3 shows the results on enforcement.

Table 13.2 Results of race on minimum wage standards, 2004–2012

	(1)	(2)	(3)	(4)
	Baseline	*Contiguous*	*Contiguous and distance*	*Contiguous and per capita GDP*
Main				
Lag min. wage	0.27***	0.18***	0.18***	0.20***
	(0.02)	(0.02)	(0.02)	(0.02)
Per capita GDP (log)	8.78	3.22	3.70	5.11
	(7.09)	(5.86)	(5.75)	(5.62)
GDP (log)	−11.09	−4.02	−4.49	−5.17
	(8.45)	(6.65)	(6.58)	(6.39)
Industry share	−69.55***	−17.24	−16.01	−27.25
	(23.95)	(21.28)	(21.05)	(21.96)
Labor force participation rate	13.25	21.26	24.39	21.39
	(34.65)	(25.09)	(26.29)	(26.48)
# of enterprises	7.46**	7.20**	7.24**	5.21*
	(3.05)	(2.95)	(3.03)	(3.02)
# of beds in hospitals	12.56*	16.76**	16.25**	17.62**
	(7.35)	(6.85)	(6.77)	(6.91)
Spatial dependence				
ρ		0.72***	0.71***	0.68***
		(0.02)	(0.02)	(0.02)
Observations	2072	2016	2016	2016

Note Model 1 shows baseline results using fixed effect model without adding spatial lags. Models 2–4 differ in the weighting matrix. Column 2 uses simple contiguity matrix (shown in Eq. W1); column 3 uses neighborhood-inverse distance matrix (shown in Eq. W2); column 4 multiplies contiguity matrix by per capita GDP in 2003 to capture the effect of economic distance (shown in Eq. W3). All specifications include a full set of city and year fixed effects. Control variables are taken with a 2-year lag. Robust standard errors in parentheses are clustered at the city level. ***$p < 0.01$, **$p < 0.05$, *$p < 0.1$

13.4.1 Race on Minimum Wage Standards

The first column in Table 13.2 shows the baseline results using a fixed-effect model without adding spatial lags. It gives a positive coefficient on the minimum wage, meaning that if a city has a higher minimum wage last year, then it is very likely that it also has a relatively high minimum wage this year. The number of enterprises also gives a positive sign. It means that with more enterprises in the economy, the city tends to have higher minimum wages. The number of beds in hospitals acts as a proxy variable for city health infrastructure and city economic development. Our estimates show infrastructure positively affects minimum wage standards.

Columns 2–4 add spatial lags of dependent variables, but they differ in the weighting matrix used. Column 2 uses simple contiguity matrix (shown in Eq. W1); column 3 uses a neighborhood-inverse distance matrix (shown in Eq. W2); column 4 multiplies contiguity matrix by per capita GDP in 2003 to capture the effect of economic distance (shown in Eq. W3).

These models give consistent estimates of spatial dependence ρ, presented in the second to the last row. The magnitude of spatial dependence is about 0.7, meaning that if other areas increase their minimum wage by 1 RMB, the city in question will increase its minimum wage by 0.7 RMB. This magnitude is comparable to estimates by other studies, e.g., Davies and Vadlamannati (2013). This magnitude also makes sense from a theoretical point of view, because a larger-than-one estimate of spatial dependence is not a stable Nash equilibrium.

13.5 Race on Enforcement

Table 13.3 presents estimates from model (2) by using the head-count ratio of violation as the proxy variable for enforcement rates. The results show evidence of a race on enforcement. The first column shows baseline results using a fixed-effect model without adding spatial lags. The positive coefficient on the lag violation rate supports the interdependence of violation rates between cities. If a city has higher violation rate last year, it is very likely that it has a higher violation rate in the current year as well. Industry share also shows a positive sign. The greater role secondary industry plays in the economy, the higher violation rate of the minimum wage law in the city. In addition, the positive estimates of Kaitz ratio indicate that with a higher minimum-to-median wage ratio, the city is more likely to violate the minimum wage law.

Columns 2 and 3 additionally include spatial lags of the dependent variables, in which they differ in the weighting matrix. That is, column 2 uses inverse distance weighting matrix, whereas column 3 multiplies the inverse distance matrix by per capita GDP in 2003. The results show that the magnitude of the spatial dependence ranges between 0.3 and 0.4. For instance, column 3 shows that if the weighted violation rate in other cities increases by 1 percentage point, the violation rate in the host city will increase by 0.35 percentage points.

Table 13.3 Results of race on minimum wage enforcement, 2002–2009

	(1)	(2)	(3)
	Baseline	*Distance*	*Distance and per capita GDP*
Main			
Lag violation rate	0.14***	0.12***	0.13***
	(0.04)	(0.04)	(0.04)
Per capita GDP (log)	0.01	0.01	0.01
	(0.01)	(0.01)	(0.01)
GDP (log)	−0.01	−0.01	−0.01
	(0.01)	(0.01)	(0.01)
Industry share	0.10**	0.11*	0.11*
	(0.05)	(0.06)	(0.06)
Labor force participation rate	0.06	0.05	0.04
	(0.08)	(0.08)	(0.08)
# of enterprises	−0.00	−0.00	−0.00
	(0.01)	(0.00)	(0.00)
# of beds in hospitals	−0.00	−0.01	−0.01
	(0.02)	(0.02)	(0.02)
Kaitz ratio	0.41***	0.39***	0.39***
	(0.03)	(0.05)	(0.05)
Spatial dependence			
ρ		0.31*	0.35**
		(0.18)	(0.16)
Observations	396	396	396

Note All specifications include a full set of city and year fixed effects. Control variables are taken with a 2-year lag. Robust standard errors in parentheses are clustered at the city level. ***$p < 0.01$, **$p < 0.05$, *$p < 0.1$

13.6 Robustness Checks

13.6.1 Weighting Matrix

In our main results of race on minimum wage standards, we use per capita GDP to measure economic distance. In this section, we replace per capita GDP by other economic indicators to construct five new weighting matrices. Essentially,

$$\omega_{j,i} = \begin{cases} \frac{1}{n_i} * X_{j,t=2003}, & \text{if city } i \text{ is a neighbor of } j, \\ 0, & \text{otherwise} \end{cases}$$

Table 13.4 Results of race on minimum wage standards by different weighting matrices

	(1)	(2)	(3)	(4)	(5)
	Labor force part. rate	*Population*	*# of enterprise*	*GDP 2003*	*Mean GDP*
Main					
Lag min.	0.19***	0.20***	0.20***	0.20***	0.19***
wage	(0.02)	(0.02)	(0.02)	(0.02)	(0.02)
Per capita	4.26	5.11	5.11	5.11	4.11
GDP (log)	(6.11)	(5.62)	(5.62)	(5.62)	(6.22)
GDP (log)	−5.23	−5.17	−5.17	−5.17	−7.23
	(7.05)	(6.39)	(6.39)	(6.39)	(6.93)
Industry share	−14.59	−27.25	−27.25	−27.25	−20.80
	(21.34)	(21.96)	(21.96)	(21.96)	(21.96)
Labor partici-	22.34	21.39	21.39	21.39	26.10
pation rate	(27.85)	(26.48)	(26.48)	(26.48)	(28.13)
# of	6.67**	5.21*	5.21*	5.21*	6.17**
enterprises	(3.09)	(3.02)	(3.02)	(3.02)	(3.01)
# of beds in	17.45**	17.62**	17.62**	17.62**	21.57***
hospitals	(6.84)	(6.91)	(6.91)	(6.91)	(6.70)
Spatial dependence					
ρ	0.69***	0.68***	0.68***	0.68***	0.63***
	(0.02)	(0.02)	(0.02)	(0.02)	(0.02)
Observations	2016	2016	2016	2016	2016

Note All specifications include a full set of city and year fixed effects. Control variables are taken with a 2-year lag. All weighting matrices are multiplied by a contiguity matrix. Robust standard errors in parentheses are clustered at the city level. ***$p < 0.01$, **$p < 0.05$, *$p < 0.1$

where n_i is the number of cities in this province, $X=\{$labor force participation rate, population, the number of enterprises, GDP in 2003, mean GDP over 2003–2012$\}$.

Similarly, we construct new weighting matrices for enforcement results to see if our results are sensitive to the choice of different weighting matrices. Essentially,

$\omega_{j,i} = \frac{1}{d_i} * X_{j,t=2003}$, where d_{ij} is distance between the centroids of city i and city j, and X is same as above.

Table 13.4 presents the estimates of model (1) with each column using a different weighting matrix. It shows similar results to Table 13.2, in terms of the magnitude of spatial dependence in minimum wage standards. Thus, our results are not sensitive to the choice of different

Table 13.5 Results of race on minimum wage enforcement by different weighting matrices

	(1)	*(2)*	*(3)*	*(4)*	*(5)*
	Labor force part. rate	*Population*	*# of enterprise*	*2003 GDP*	*Mean GDP*
Main					
Lag violation	0.12***	0.13***	0.13***	0.13***	0.12***
rate	(0.04)	(0.04)	(0.04)	(0.04)	(0.04)
Per capita	0.01	0.01	0.01	0.01	0.01
GDP (log)	(0.01)	(0.01)	(0.01)	(0.01)	(0.01)
GDP (log)	−0.01	−0.01	−0.01	−0.01	−0.01
	(0.01)	(0.01)	(0.01)	(0.01)	(0.01)
Industry share	0.10*	0.10	0.10	0.10	0.10*
	(0.06)	(0.06)	(0.06)	(0.06)	(0.06)
Labor partici-	0.04	0.05	0.05	0.04	0.04
pation rate	(0.08)	(0.08)	(0.08)	(0.08)	(0.08)
# of	−0.00	−0.00	−0.00	−0.00	−0.00
enterprises	(0.00)	(0.00)	(0.00)	(0.00)	(0.00)
# of beds in	−0.01	−0.01	−0.01	−0.01	−0.01
hospitals	(0.02)	(0.02)	(0.02)	(0.02)	(0.02)
Kaitz ratio	0.39***	0.39***	0.40***	0.39***	0.39***
	(0.05)	(0.05)	(0.05)	(0.05)	(0.05)
Spatial dependence					
ρ	0.35**	0.28*	0.22	0.28**	0.35**
	(0.16)	(0.17)	(0.15)	(0.14)	(0.16)
Observations	396	396	396	396	396

Note All specifications include a full set of city and year fixed effects. Control variables are taken a 2-year lag. All weighting matrices are multiplied by inverse distance. Robust standard errors in parentheses are clustered at the city level. ***$p < 0.01$, **$p < 0.05$, *$p < 0.1$

weighting matrices. In addition, Table 13.5 shows similar results to Table 13.3 which supports our story of a race on enforcement.

13.6.2 *Spatial Durbin Model*

The Spatial Durbin Model (SDM) is similar to Spatial Autoregressive Model except that it includes spatial lags of covariates. Tables 13.6 and 13.7 present estimates from SDM (1′) and (2′), corresponding to model (1) and (2), respectively.

Table 13.6 Results of race on minimum wage standards from SDM

	(1)	*(2)*	*(3)*	*(4)*
	Baseline	*Contiguous*	*Contiguous and distance*	*Contiguous and per capita GDP*
Main				
Lag min. wage	0.27***	0.18***	0.18***	0.19***
	(0.02)	(0.02)	(0.02)	(0.02)
Per capita GDP (log)	8.78	1.67	1.45	2.81
	(7.09)	(5.80)	(5.65)	(5.58)
GDP (log)	−11.09	−5.71	−6.61	−8.18
	(8.45)	(6.83)	(6.69)	(6.51)
Industry share	−69.55***	−2.88	−3.54	−6.57
	(23.95)	(21.41)	(20.92)	(22.36)
Labor force participation rate	13.25	54.40**	59.18**	66.52**
	(34.65)	(27.54)	(28.55)	(29.78)
# of enterprises	7.46**	10.10***	10.66***	9.84***
	(3.05)	(3.02)	(3.01)	(3.06)
# of beds in hospitals	12.56*	16.10**	15.14**	16.63**
	(7.35)	(6.75)	(6.71)	(6.87)
Wx				
Per capita GDP (log)		9.28	12.70	22.17**
		(11.57)	(11.40)	(10.81)
GDP (log)		2.38	3.18	−2.28
		(14.71)	(14.33)	(12.08)
Industry share		−59.25*	−54.62	−99.37***
		(35.67)	(35.23)	(35.93)
Labor participation rate		−111.27**	−112.50**	−161.78***
		(44.73)	(44.94)	(50.09)
# of enterprises		−5.59	−7.10	−7.07
		(6.95)	(6.67)	(6.29)
# of beds in hospitals		−4.32	1.40	4.25
		(10.52)	(10.92)	(13.03)
Spatial dependence				
ρ		0.72***	0.71***	0.68***
		(0.02)	(0.02)	(0.02)
Observations	2072	2016	2016	2016

Note All specifications include a full set of city and year fixed effects. Control variables are taken with a 2-year lag. *Wx* panel presents the estimates on the weighted covariates in Eq. (1′). Robust standard errors in parentheses are clustered at the city level. ***$p < 0.01$, **$p < 0.05$, *$p < 0.1$

Table 13.7 Results of race on minimum wage enforcement from SDM

	(1)	*(2)*	*(3)*
	Baseline	*Distance*	*Distance and per capita GDP*
Main			
Lag violation rate	0.14***	0.11***	0.12***
	(0.04)	(0.04)	(0.04)
Per capita GDP (log)	0.01	0.01	0.01
	(0.01)	(0.01)	(0.01)
GDP (log)	−0.01	−0.01	−0.00
	(0.01)	(0.01)	(0.01)
Industry share	0.10**	0.09	0.09
	(0.05)	(0.06)	(0.06)
Labor force participation rate	0.06	0.02	0.03
	(0.08)	(0.07)	(0.08)
# of enterprises	−0.00	−0.00	−0.00
	(0.01)	(0.00)	(0.00)
# of beds in hospitals	−0.00	0.01	0.00
	(0.02)	(0.02)	(0.02)
Kaitz ratio	0.41***	0.39***	0.38***
	(0.03)	(0.05)	(0.05)
Wx			
per capita GDP (log)		0.05	−0.06
		(0.13)	(0.11)
GDP (log)		0.05	0.05
		(0.12)	(0.13)
Industry share		−1.38***	−1.22***
		(0.40)	(0.44)
Labor force participation rate		0.19	−0.05
		(0.60)	(0.38)
# of enterprises		−0.10*	−0.02
		(0.05)	(0.03)
# of beds in hospitals		0.34**	0.09
		(0.17)	(0.08)
Spatial dependence			
ρ		0.19	0.17
		(0.16)	(0.14)
Observations	396	396	396

Note All specifications include a full set of city and year fixed effects. Control variables are taken with a 2-year lag. *Wx* panel presents the estimates on the weighted covariates in Eq. (2′). Robust standard errors in parentheses are clustered at the city level. $^{***}p < 0.01$, $^{**}p < 0.05$, $^{*}p < 0.1$

$$MW_{i,t} = \beta_i + \rho \sum_{j \neq i} \omega_{j,i} MW_{j,t} + \alpha \cdot MW_{i,t-1} + \beta \cdot X_{i,t-2} + \gamma \sum_{j \neq i} \omega_{j,i} X_{j,t-2} + \eta_i + \delta_t + \varepsilon_{i,t} \quad \text{(SDM)} \tag{1'}$$

$$E_{i,t} = \beta_i + \rho \sum_{j \neq i} \omega_{j,i} E_{j,t} + \alpha \cdot E_{i,t-1} + \beta \cdot X_{i,t-2} + \gamma \sum_{j \neq i} \omega_{j,i} X_{j,t-2} + \text{Kaitz}_{i,t} + \eta_i + \delta_t + \varepsilon_{i,t} \quad \text{(SDM)} \tag{2'}$$

where all variables have the same meanings as in models (1) and (2).

The sign and magnitude of the spatial dependence given by Table 13.6 are similar to that in Table 13.2, which support our findings of a race on minimum wage standards documented in Sect. 13.4. The second portion of Table 13.6 shows that SDM cannot be rejected, which means spatial lags of covariates do directly affect the dependent variable, hence justifying our choice of ML estimation over the IV method.

On the enforcement side, however, SDM does not show similar results to SAR model. In Table 13.7, the estimates of the race on enforcement variable turn out to be insignificant under SDM. This might be due to the small sample size which consists of only 66 cities each year. When including more explanatory variables in the estimation, both the degree of freedom and the precision decrease.

13.7 Conclusions

The theory of fiscal and regulatory competition between jurisdictions is more advanced than its empirical testing. This is particularly true of labor regulation in general, and minimum wage regulation in particular, and especially so for developing countries. Olney (2013) finds evidence of a race to the bottom in employment protection among OECD countries, with the reaction coefficient of 1.0–2.8. Davies and Vadlamannati (2013) find labor rights in one country are positively correlated with those elsewhere, i.e., a cut in labor rights in other countries reduces labor rights in the country in question, with reaction coefficient about 0.55–0.88. They also argue that international competition lies more in enforcement than in labor laws.

This article focuses on within-country competition on labor standards and takes up the case of China, which introduced a vigorous minimum wage regime from the mid-2000s onwards. The analysis utilizes spatial lag methodology and ML estimation to study city-level strategic interactions in setting and enforcing minimum wage standards during 2002–2012 in China. We manually collect a panel data set of city-level minimum wage standards from China's government Web sites. The analysis finds strong evidence of spatial correlation in minimum wage standards and enforcement among main cities in China. If other cities decrease minimum wage standards by 1 RMB, the city in question will decrease its standard by about 0.7 RMB. We also find evidence of enforcement competition, although the finding is not as robust because of data limitations. If the violation rate in other cities increases by 1 percentage point, the city in question will respond by an increase of roughly 0.3 percentage points.

The Chinese government has expanded minimum wage intervention greatly, in response to concerns about rising inequality. Our results show that there is significant interjurisdictional competition on the level of the minimum wage and in enforcement among local governments. Such competition could be wasteful, and lead to a race to the bottom, undermining the government's objectives. The interactions identified in this article thus suggest the need for policy coordination on labor regulation in China.

Our analysis has broader significance given the resurgence of interest in minimum wages in developing countries as an instrument for addressing rising inequality. Thus, Bhorat et al. (2015) provide a review of minimum wages in Africa. They find that "Most countries in Sub-Saharan Africa (SSA) have adopted minimum wage regulation" and that "SSA as whole reflects a bias towards a more aggressive minimum wage policy compared to the rest of the world." In South Africa, for example, the current government has proposed a national minimum wage to replace the collection of sector and region-specific minimum wages. The question of whether to allow local setting of minimum wages to take account of local conditions is an area of open debate. In Asia, the decentralization reforms in Indonesia were accompanied by a decree allowing local governments to set minimum wages. As countries like Myanmar start a new era of labor regulation, the questions of minimum wages and local flexibility in implementation are at the forefront. In Russia, minimum wage setting was decentralized in 2007. Around the world, therefore, interjurisdictional competition in minimum wages is a live issue. Our analysis provides an initial framework in which competing perspectives on these debates can be assessed quantitatively.

Our evidence on jurisdictional interdependence in minimum wage setting within a country also raises a set of interesting further research questions. What we have shown is that local government react to each other in setting minimum wages, and in the enforcement of minimum wages. A natural interpretation is that of a possible "race to the bottom," as jurisdictions lower labor standards to attract investment. But could there also be a "race to the top" in other dimensions? Rather than lower labor standards, a local government could improve infrastructure, or improve the quality of local governance, to make investment more attractive. This could set in motion a chain of reactions through which other localities respond by improving their infrastructure and business environment so that there is an upward virtuous cycle of overall improvement in labor productivity rather than a downward vicious spiral of lowering labor costs through lowering labor standards. This raises the empirical question—do we see such a virtuous race to the top in practice? And the policy question—what can the government do to trigger the virtuous spiral?

Appendix

See Tables 13.8 and 13.9.

Table 13.8 Trend of minimum wage standards and violation in 2002–2009

Year	*Monthly wage*	*Min. wage*	*Violation rate (%)*	*Growth of monthly wage (%)*	*Growth of min. wage (%)*
2002	831.08	292.10	11.59		
2003	905.79	308.77	10.43	9.26	5.70
2004	965.85	335.65	9.95	6.99	9.45
2005	1078.23	370.52	10.07	12.22	11.92
2006	1220.25	450.07	9.44	13.33	23.23
2007	1389.79	487.92	9.24	11.52	8.75
2008	1535.95	533.23	9.30	10.91	9.74
2009	1770.82	559.04	7.32	16.72	5.05
Total	1291.60	442.04	9.43	12.02	10.06

Note Average monthly wages and minimum wages are discounted by provincial level CPI. Violation rate is calculated at the city level, i.e., the number of individuals paid below according minimum wages divided by the number of observations in the sampling city

Table 13.9 Descriptive statistics, 2002–2009

Variable	*Mean*	*Std. dev.*
Monthly wage (RMB)	1195.11	491.65
GDP (log)	5.36	1.43
Per capita GDP (log)	9.02	0.93
Labor force participation rate	0.10	0.09
GDP industry Share	0.48	0.12
Kaitz ratio	0.39	0.26
Min. wage standards	412.96	123.49
Spatial lag (min. wage standards)	484.84	91.38
Violation rate (V0)	0.10	0.10
Spatial lag (V0)	0.08	0.02

Note Kaitz ratio is calculated at the city level, i.e., Kaitz = minimum wage/median wage

Notes

1. Examples of other papers on tax competition, environmental regulation competition, welfare competition, and competition on education spending include: Allers and Elhorst (2005), Brueckner and Saavedra (2001), Edmark and Ågren (2008), Wilson and Wildasin (2004), Redoano (2014), Fredriksson et al. (2004), Plümper et al. (2009), Saavedra (2000), Markusen et al. (1995), Kennedy (1994), Swire (1996), Fredriksson and Millimet (2002), Konisky (2007), Bailey et al. (2004).
2. See, for example, Plümper et al. (2009), Edmark and Ågren (2008), Redoano (2014); Fredriksson et al. (2004), Konisky (2007), Levinson (2003), Brueckner (2003), Davies and Vadlamannati (2013), Ollé (2003).
3. We initially had 259 cities distributed in 28 provinces. However, there are 7 cities in Gansu, Qinghai, Xinjiang with no neighboring cities, thus we drop these "islands" in constructing the contiguity weighting matrix.
4. Note: The surveyed households are coded and ordered only within a county in a given year, thus we use the following as unique identifier of households—year, county code, and household code. In a household, the variable "household member" is not a unique identifier, hence we use individual characteristics to identify a person in a household—household member, relation to household head, gender, and date of birth.
5. Here are some details about how we modified and merged the data. On the one hand, many prefecture cities are coded as detailed sub-areas ("区" in Chinese, pronounced as "Qu") in UHS, such as Beijing, whereas its minimum wage standards do not vary within this city regardless of urban or suburban areas, and city characteristics information is also at city level

rather than at sub-area level. Therefore, we aggregate the first 10 sub-areas (i.e., the last two digits of city area code is between 1 and 10) into the prefecture city. The implicit assumption is that all these sub-areas (or "Qu") have the same level of minimum wages, which is very likely to true. On the other hand, there are some prefecture cities that have multiple levels of minimum wages in different sub-areas ("Qu"). Since we are looking at the very central part of a city, we use the maximum one among them (usually at most 4 levels) as the minimum wage standard for this city. Examples are Taiyuan city and Datong city.

6. Industry share in total GDP = Secondary industry GDP/total GDP. Labor force participation = the number of employees/population.
7. In their original paper, they have depth and severity measures in addition to level measure, i.e., $V_\alpha = E\{\left[\frac{w^m - w}{w^m}\right]^\alpha$ *if* $w^m > w$; 0 otherwise}, where w denotes wage, w^m denotes the relevant minimum wage, α is an index that emphasizes concern on the depth of violation, and E is the expectation operator with respect to the wage distribution in the sector to which w^m applies. In our article, we set $\alpha = 0$.
8. Empirically, we use Stata command xsmle programmed by Belotti et al. (2014).

References

Allers, Maarten A., and J. Paul Elhorst. "Tax mimicking and yardstick competition among local governments in the Netherlands." *International Tax and Public Finance* 12.4 (2005): 493–513.

Altshuler, R., and T.J. Goodspeed. *Follow the leader? Evidence on European and US tax competition* (No. 2002, 26). Working Papers, Department of Economics, Rutgers, The State University of New Jersey, 2003.

Bailey, Michael A., Mark Carl Rom, and Matthew M. Taylor. "State competition in higher education: A race to the top, or a race to the bottom?" *Economics of Governance* 5.1 (2004): 53–75.

Baskaran, Thushyanthan. "Identifying local tax mimicking with administrative borders and a policy reform." *Journal of Public Economics* 118 (2014): 41–51.

Belotti, Federico, Gordon Hughes, and Andrea Piano Mortari. "XSMLE: Stata module for spatial panel data models estimation." *Statistical Software Components*, 2014.

Bhorat, Haroon, Ravi Kanbur, and Benjamin Stanwix. *Minimum wages in Sub-Saharan Africa: A primer*. CEPR Working Paper no. 10760, 2015.

Bhorat, Haroon, Ravi Kanbur, and Natasha Mayet. "Estimating the causal effect of enforcement on minimum wage compliance: The case of South Africa." *Review of Development Economics* 16.4 (2012): 608–623.

Brueckner, Jan K. "Strategic interaction among governments: An overview of empirical studies." *International Regional Science Review* 26.2 (2003): 175–188.

Brueckner, Jan K., and Luz A. Saavedra. "Do local governments engage in strategic property—Tax competition?" *National Tax Journal* 54 (2001): 203–229.

Chau, Nancy H., and Ravi Kanbur. "The race to the bottom, from the bottom." *Economica* 73.290 (2006): 193–228.

Cremer, Helmuth, and Firouz Gahvari. "Tax evasion, fiscal competition and economic integration." *European Economic Review* 44.9 (2000): 1633–1657.

Davies, Ronald B., and Krishna Chaitanya Vadlamannati. "A race to the bottom in labor standards? An empirical investigation." *Journal of Development Economics* 103 (2013): 1–14.

DeSombre, Elizabeth R. *Flagging Standards: Globalization and Environmental, Safety, and Labor Regulations at Sea*, vol. 1. Cambridge, MA: MIT Press Books, 2006.

Drezner, Daniel W. "Globalization and policy convergence." *International Studies Review* 3.1 (2001): 53–78.

Duanmu, J.L. "A race to lower standards? Labor standards and location choice of outward FDI from the BRIC countries." *International Business Review* 23.3 (2014): 620–634.

Edmark, Karin, and Hanna Ågren. "Identifying strategic interactions in Swedish local income tax policies." *Journal of Urban Economics* 63.3 (2008): 849–857.

Edwards, Jeremy, and Michael Keen. "Tax competition and Leviathan." *European Economic Review* 40.1 (1996): 113–134.

Elhorst, J.P. "Spatial panel data models." In M.M. Fischer and A. Getis (Eds.), *Handbook of Applied Spatial Analysis*, pp. 377–407. London and New York: Springer, 2009.

Fredriksson, Per G., and Daniel L. Millimet. "Strategic interaction and the determination of environmental policy across US states." *Journal of Urban Economics* 51.1 (2002): 101–122.

Fredriksson, Per G., John A. List, and Daniel L. Millimet. "Chasing the smokestack: Strategic policymaking with multiple instruments." *Regional Science and Urban Economics* 34.4 (2004): 387–410.

Kanbur, Ravi, and Michael Keen. "Jeux Sans Frontières: Tax competition and tax coordination when countries differ in size." *The American Economic Review* 83.4 (1993): 877–892.

Kennedy, Peter W. "Equilibrium pollution taxes in open economies with imperfect competition." *Journal of Environmental Economics and Management* 27.1 (1994): 49–63.

Konisky, David M. "Regulatory competition and environmental enforcement: Is there a race to the bottom?" *American Journal of Political Science* 51.4 (2007): 853–872.

Levinson, Arik. "Environmental regulatory competition: A status report and some new evidence." *National Tax Journal* 56.1 (2003): 91–106.

Lyytikäinen, Teemu. "Tax competition among local governments: Evidence from a property tax reform in Finland." *Journal of Public Economics* 96.7 (2012): 584–595.

Markusen, James R., Edward R. Morey, and Nancy Olewiler. "Competition in regional environmental policies when plant locations are endogenous." *Journal of Public Economics* 56.1 (1995): 55–77.

Mosley, Layna, and Saika Uno. "Racing to the bottom or climbing to the top? Economic globalization and collective labor rights." *Comparative Political Studies* 40.8 (2007): 923–948.

Neumark, David. "Minimum wage effects throughout the wage distribution." *Journal of Human Resources* 39.2 (2004): 425–450.

Ollé, Albert Solé. "Electoral accountability and tax mimicking: The effects of electoral margins, coalition government, and ideology." *European Journal of Political Economy* 19.4 (2003): 685–713.

Olney, William W. "A race to the bottom? Employment protection and foreign direct investment." *Journal of International Economics* 91.2 (2013): 191–203.

Plümper, Thomas, Vera E. Troeger, and Hannes Winner. "Why is there no race to the bottom in capital taxation?" *International Studies Quarterly* 53.3 (2009): 761–786.

Redoano, Michela. "Tax competition among European countries. Does the EU matter?" *European Journal of Political Economy* 34 (2014): 353–371.

Ronconi, Lucas. "Globalization, domestic institutions, and enforcement of labor law: Evidence from Latin America." *Industrial Relations: A Journal of Economy and Society* 51.1 (2012): 89–105.

Saavedra, Luz Amparo. "A model of welfare competition with evidence from AFDC." *Journal of Urban Economics* 47.2 (2000): 248–279.

Swire, Peter P. "The race to laxity and the race to undesirability: Explaining failures in competition among jurisdictions in environmental law." *Yale Law & Policy Review* 14.2 (1996): 67–110.

Wilson, John Douglas, and David E. Wildasin. "Capital tax competition: Bane or boon." *Journal of Public Economics* 88.6 (2004): 1065–1091.

CHAPTER 14

Minimum Wage Effects on Employment and Working Time of Chinese Workers

Wenkai Sun, Xianghong Wang and Xiaoxi Zhang

14.1 Introduction and Policy Background

The minimum wage policy has been used in many countries as an instrument to regulate the labor market. China started to try to implement such a policy since joining ILO's "Minimum Wage-Fixing Machinery Convention" in 1984. In November of 1993, China issued a formal government executive order that first set minimum wage regulations. Since then, the minimum wage was first tested in some developed regions such as Shenzhen and Zhuhai. Some new legislatures have set the earlier framework for minimum wage policies, including "Regulations on Minimum Wages in Enterprises" and "Labor Law of the People's Republic of China." In March of 2004, when the new "Minimum Wage Regulations" was issued, minimum wages started to be formally and widely implemented in China, covering all types of enterprises. Many provinces set up new minimum wage standards since that year. In 2004

W. Sun · X. Wang (✉) · X. Zhang
Renmin University of China, Beijing, China
e-mail: shwang06@ruc.edu.cn

L. Shi and C. Lin (eds.), *Minimum Wages in China*,
https://doi.org/10.1007/978-981-15-2421-9_14

alone, 24 provincial-level governments raised their minimum wage levels, with an average increase of 20%. In the "Labor Contract Law" of 2008, the addition of minimum wage provision further strengthened the power of the minimum wage policy. After one year's pause of minimum wage adjustments during the financial crisis of 2008, the second wage of frequent changes appeared since 2009.

There are a few features worth noticing about minimum wage policies in China. First, the level of the minimum wage is relatively low to the workers' average wage, about 32% of the average level, while the international ratio of the minimum wage to the average is about 40–60% (Han and Wei 2006). Second, the growth rate of the minimum wage is lower than that of the average wage, with their relative ratio reduced from 0.44 in 1995 to 0.31 in 2011 (Du and Pan 2009). This might affect the effectiveness of the minimum wage policy if the minimum wage standard were too low compared with the equilibrium market wages. Third, minimum wage standards are set by provincial governments. The level, frequency, and timing of minimum wage adjustments may vary between regions. Therefore, studying the minimum wage effects at the country level is not likely to obtain reliable results.

Minimum wage policies have been long debated among scholars. Some are concerned that minimum wages will distort the resource distribution, reduce efficiency, leading to an increase in poverty (e.g., Stigler 1946). Others contend that minimum wages may actually increase employment and income (e.g., Card and Krueger 1994). Opinions about minimum wage policies in China are also divided. Zhang (2004) criticizes the minimum wage policy as a way of price control, reducing China's industrial competitiveness. Tong (2006), however, argues that labor cost only accounts for a small part, 3–4%, of firms' production cost in China, so the minimum wage will not significantly affect the competitiveness of Chinese firms.

Empirical findings from studies of minimum wage effects in China are not all consistent. Wang and Gunderson (2011, 2012) study the employment effect of minimum wages using provincial data. They find a negative effect of minimum wages on employment in low-growth regions, especially in firms that not stately owned. Luo (2007) and Luo and Cong (2009) find that the minimum wage reduces the employment of migrant workers and slightly increases wages for all occupations. Xiao and Xiang (2009) study the minimum wage spillover effect using panel data from six large cities between 1995 and 2006. They find that minimum wages can narrow the wage gap for employees.

To further facilitate the debate about minimum wage policies, this article investigates the minimum wage effects using individual-level data from multiple aspects including employment, income, and with special attention to working time. The existing literature in China seems to have focused much on the direct effects of minimum wages on employment, wages, and firm profits, but rarely on working time of workers except in Jia (2014). Working time can be used by firms as an instrument to respond to the minimum wage policies (Couch and Wittenburg 2001; Linneman 1982). When the hourly minimum wage level is raised, firms can reduce costs by reducing working hours and increasing work intensity. If the minimum wage standard is set for a month, firms can dilute hourly pay through increasing monthly working hours. It is worth to investigate whether the minimum wage effect on working time is significant and whether it has a spillover effect on the higher-income group.

We combine microdata from China Health and Nutrition Survey (CHNS, 2004, 2006, 2009, and 2011), provincial minimum wages, macroeconomic, and population statistics to form pooled cross-sectional empirical analysis based on the methodological framework used by Neumark (2001) and Neumark et al. (2004) for minimum wage effects on income distribution. In the study of spillover effect on working time, we extend the method of Neumark et al. (2004) that is originally used for the study of the spillover effect of minimum wages on the distribution of workers' wage income. The channels of wage spillover effects may come from internal substitutions between workers within a firm and employer's incentives that may have changed workers' reservation wages (Neumark et al. 2004; Flinn 2006; Wang 2012). The same logic also applies to the possible spillover effect on employee's working time. This article contributes to the existing literature mainly in three aspects. First, while existing studies in China mostly depend on macrodata or very short panels, our household data observed in four years between 2004 and 2011 cover a longer time span, contain more detailed information, and contain more frequent provincial minimum wage changes. Second, compared with the simple difference-in-difference method traditionally used in minimum wage studies, using the method of pooled cross-sectional analysis makes it possible to analyze the effects of multiple minimum wage changes over time. Third, we fill the gap of minimum wage effects on working time in the existing literature, especially its spillover effects to higher-income groups.

14.2 Data

The data sets used in this article are drawn from three sources. The microdata for employment, wages, and working hour are from CHNS. The data for provincial minimum wages are compiled by the authors from various policy outlets provided by provincial governments. The macroeconomic data and population statistics are drawn from China's statistical yearbooks. The three groups of data are described as follows.

14.2.1 Microdata for Workers

The micro-household data for workers are from CHNS. The survey is jointly conducted by the Carolina Population Center at UNC-Chapel Hill and the Chinese Center for Disease Control and Prevention. Nine surveys have been carried out since the first one in 1989, covering nine representative provinces of China including Liaoning, Shandong, and Jiangsu in eastern China; Heilongjiang, Henan, Hubei, and Hunan in the central region; and Guizhou and Guangxi in the western region. The survey contains information on demographic characteristics, job, and employment, consumption and expenditure, diet and nutrition, health and leisure time activities, etc., designed for households and individuals. While CHNS has been used mainly for studies of health-related topics, it contains rich information that has allowed for studies of labor issues (Chen et al. 2014), children's education (Chyi and Zhou 2014), income inequality (Ward 2014), and many others. This study makes use of its information on working time. To better investigate the effects of China's minimum wage policies, we select the CHNS data from four years, 2004, 2006, 2009, and 2011, covering two waves of minimum wage adjustments since 2004, with a sample of 15,159 individuals in total.

14.2.2 Minimum Wage Data

The data for provincial MW are collected from issued regulations and documents on adjustments of minimum wages published at the provincial government Web sites and news media. These include monthly minimum wage standards, hourly minimum wage standards, and specific implementation time of the new standards. Some provinces have multiple minimum wage levels set for different areas within the province. Based on the method of Neumark and Wascher (1991), we use the highest level as the minimum wage standard for that province. Divided by 2008 and 2009, the later period witnessed a dramatic increase in adjustment frequency, adjustment magnitude, and the gap between the eastern, central, and western regions of China compared with the earlier period.

The actual implementation date of minimum wage adjustments varies between provinces because provincial governments have the discretionary power for implementation decisions. In order to obtain annual minimum wage standards in one year to make it comparable between provinces, we follow the method of Rama (2001) and adjust it by working out the average of the actual monthly minimum wage weighted by the number of months covered by that standard during the twelve months of that year. Over the seven years' period, the minimum wage level in different regions increased by nearly three times. Across regions, the absolute value of the annual minimum wage in the east is noticeably higher than that in the central and western regions. The central region has a slightly higher minimum wage level than the western region.

14.2.3 Provincial Macrodata

The provincial macroeconomic data and population statistics are compiled from national or regional statistical yearbooks, including major indicators such as per capita GDP, agricultural share in the economy, and population of the labor force. The differences in macroeconomic indicators among provinces should be controlled for in analyzing minimum wage effects. By compiling the above three sources of data, we form a panel data set that includes micro-household survey and macro-socioeconomic statistics in 9 provinces of China in 2004, 2006, 2009, and 2011.

We mainly analyze three dependent variables: employment, wage income, and weekly working hours. Working time is reflected both by whether a person is employed or not and by weekly working hours. We define "employment" (*employment*=1) as being engaged in a job under the minimum wage system and being at a working age. Specifically, respondents are supposed to be non-students between 16 and 65 years old, with a job and a positive wage income. They should not be re-employed after retirement. Excluded observations include farmers, military officers, soldiers, and other unspecified occupations; self-employed, household helpers and those with unspecified jobs; and workers under the household contract responsibility system and other unspecified sectors. The data show that the labor force population has been declining at an average annual rate of 42.27%. Male labors outnumber female labors, and rural labor force outnumbers the urban one. The highest proportion of the labor force is the group aged between 30 and 49, followed by young adults aged between 16 and 29. In terms of education level, those with a college degree or higher accounts the highest proportion. In contrast, only 38% of those with a primary school diploma are employed.

Monthly wage income is our second variable of interest. Within the sample range, the monthly wage income has experienced an increase, reaching 2109.5 RMB in 2011. The wage of males is higher than that of females, and the wage of urban employees is higher than that of rural employees. Young adults aged between 16 and 29 who have just started their career and middle-aged people aged between 40 and 59 who have reached the peak of their career receive the highest income. Those with a college degree or higher receive higher wages than others. The wage income in eastern and central regions of China is considerably higher than that in the western regions. Wage income is also higher for permanent employees than for contract and temporary workers and higher for state-owned public institutions, research institutions, and government agencies than for collective and privately owned enterprises.

The third dependent variable of our focus is weekly working hours. Considering the whole sample, the average working hour per week is 43.5, which is higher than the statutory length of working time, 40 hours per week.[1] There is no significant difference between males and females. Yet a significant difference is observed between urban and rural areas, with urban employees working shorter hours than rural employees. Working hours reduce with age.

The core independent variable in this article is the ratio of the minimum wage (adjusted for coverage time) to the average wage. For the whole sample, the ratio is 32.33% on average (see Note 1). Contrary to the absolute value of the minimum wage, the relative minimum wage (minimum wage/average wage) has witnessed a decline, despite a slight recovery in 2011.

Another key issue in this article is the spillover effect of minimum wage adjustments. In order to investigate possible spillover effect on different income groups, we divide the workers into seven groups of different income levels according to the ratio of their wages relative to minimum wages, with 20% as the range within each group. These six income groups are: less than 90% of the minimum wage (minimum-income group), 90–110% of the minimum wage, 110–130%, 130–150%, 150–170%, 170–190%, and more than 190% of the minimum wage. The minimum-income group accounts for 13% of the sample; high-risk group (whose monthly wages are between the old and new minimum wage standards) accounts for 8.49%. Among the minimum-income group and high-risk group, there are twice female workers as male workers, and twice rural employees as urban employees. Education level is negatively related to the probability of falling into the low-income groups. Those with the education of lower than primary school are 12 times more likely to belong to the minimum or high-risk group than those with a college degree or higher. In addition, contract workers, temporary workers, and family workers are more likely to receive a lower wage than permanent employees.

14.3 Methodology

14.3.1 *Overall Effect of Minimum Wages*

The typical method scholars have used in analyzing minimum wage effects is to estimate the following time series model (Neumark 2001):

$$E_t = \alpha_0 + \alpha_1 MW_t + X_t\beta + \varepsilon_t \tag{14.1}$$

where E_t is a dummy for employment status; MW_t is the minimum wage adjusted for coverage time; X is a set of control variables to control economic cycles and effects of demographic changes, and the subscript t indicates different time periods.

Due to China's large size, it features uneven socioeconomic development and uneven minimum wage standards across the country. Using national data undoubtedly conceals large differences in the minimum wage effects of various regions, which gets in the way of identifying the real impact of minimum wage adjustment. By integrating both microdata and macrodata at the provincial level, we adopt the method of pooled cross-sectional analysis as seen in Neumark (2001) and Wang and Gunderson (2011). Specifically, we estimate the following model:

$$Y_{i,t} = \alpha_0 + \alpha_1 MW_{i,t} + \alpha_2 MW_{i,t-1} + S_{i,t}\beta + Year_t\delta + Province_{i,t}\lambda + \varepsilon_{i,t} \tag{14.2}$$

where $Y_{i,t}$ is the dependent variable; $MW_{i,t}$ is the minimum wage adjusted for coverage time; $MW_{i,t-1}$ is the minimum wage adjusted for coverage time in the prior period; $s_{i,t}$ is a set of variables to control for economic cycles and demographic changes; *Year*$_t$ and *Province*$_i$ are year fixed effects.

The dependent variables include whether a person has a job (employment), the logarithm of monthly wage (lnwage), and the logarithm of weekly working hours (lnhour). For the first dependent variable, we estimate a Logit model adjusted for heterogeneity in variances. For the latter two dependent variables, we use the robust ordinary least squares (OLS) method to estimate for the subsample of workers with a job (employment=1). In all three estimates, we control for the same regional variables including logarithm of per capita GDP, the share of agriculture in the economy, and the logarithm of the employed population.

14.3.2 Minimum Wage Spillover Effects on Working Hours

Based on the empirical research frame proposed by Neumark et al. (2004), we study the different impacts of minimum wage changes on working hours of employees in different income levels and analyze the time spillover effect of the minimum wage. While their method is originally used for estimating the effect of minimum wages on changes of the income distribution, the same framework can be used to analyze its possible effect on working time for different income groups. The estimated model is as follows:

$$\begin{aligned}\frac{H_{ist} - H_{ist-1}}{H_{ist-1}} &= \alpha + \sum_k \beta_k \frac{mw_{st} - mw_{st-1}}{mw_{st-1}} D_k(w_{ist-1}; m_{st-1}) \\ &+ \sum_k \gamma_k \frac{mw_{st-1} - mw_{st-2}}{mw_{st-2}} D_k(w_{ist-1}; m_{st-1}) \\ &+ \sum_k \delta_k D_k(w_{ist-1}; m_{st-1}) \\ &+ \sum_k \theta_k D_k(w_{ist-1}; m_{st-1}) \frac{w_{st-1}}{mw_{st-1}} \\ &+ X_{ist} \times \pi + Province_{is} \times \tau \\ &+ Year_{it} \times Province_{is} \times \varphi + \varepsilon_{ist}\end{aligned} \tag{14.3}$$

where subscript *i* represents individual, *s* stands for the provinces, and *t* is the time. The dependent variable is the change rate of working hours, with H_{ist} and H_{ist-1} referring to the employees' weekly working hours in currents and prior period, respectively. The key dependent variables of this model are the change rate of the minimum wage in the current period compared with that in the prior period, and the lagged change rate of the minimum wage in the last period. Particularly, mw_{st}, mw_{st-1}, and mw_{st-2} represent the provincial minimum wage standards in the current period, the prior period, and the one before the prior period. W_{st-1} is the wage income of the prior period, and the ratio of W_{st-1} to mw_{st-1} reflects the ratio of wage relative to the minimum wage in the prior period. $D_k(w_{ist-1}; m_{st-1})$ is a set of dummy variables. The whole sample is divided into seven groups according to the ratio of wage to the minimum wage in the prior period as we have explained earlier. According to Neumark et al. (2004), since the highest-income group is least influenced by minimum wages, and its impact of labor supply and demand for this group is rather indirect, the group with a rate above 170% is chosen as the reference group, with the other 5 groups' dummy variables added into the model. In addition, $X\text{-}_{ist}$ is a group of controlled variables for individual characteristics including gender, households, age, age squared, and education level; $Year_{it}$ and $Province_{is}$ are dummy variables for year and province, respectively.

In the above model, we pay special attention to the following parameters: β_k, γ_k, δ_k, and θ_k; β_k refers to the impact of increasing minimum wages in the current period on the income group defined by $D_k(w_{ist-1}; m_{st-1})$; γ_{kr} refers to the impact of increasing minimum wages in the prior period on the income group defined by $D_k(w_{ist-1}; m_{st-1})$; δ_k refers to the fixed effect of different income groups, measuring the change of working hours of other groups compared to the highest-income group, or the inter-group inequality of working hours for all employees; θ_k refers to the inter-group distribution of working hours of employees with different income levels measured by the ratio of wages to minimum wages, across all income groups defined by $D_k(w_{ist-1}; m_{st-1})$.

To analyze how the minimum wage adjustment affects working hours and income, we mainly consider how firms respond to such policy adjustment strategically. In a recent working paper, Maynerisy et al. (2014) find that China's minimum wage policies have increased firms' efficiency, making them adequately respond to its negative impacts on outputs and employment. The increased efficiency comes from the substitution of low-efficiency firms for high-efficiency firms. When faced with the shock of the minimum wage increase, firms may use multiple management strategies including layoffs, increase or reduction of working hours, cutting benefits, and enhancing technologies, etc. As our study is at the individual level, our focus is on the MW effect on workers' working hours and income.

An important methodology issue in this study is measurement errors in our dependent variables. Income and working time are measured by average values in a year while minimum wage adjustments do not always fall at the end of the year. Therefore, using annual average values do not accurately reflect changes before or after minimum wage adjustments. We solve this issue in two ways. First, we adjust the minimum wage standard by weights according to the number of months it covered in a year. Second, we use robust standard errors in our regression analyses to correct the effects of measurement errors of dependent variables.

14.4 Results

14.4.1 *Minimum Wage Effects on Employment*

We first examine the effect of minimum wages on workers' employment status. Table 14.1 reports regression results for the effect of the minimum wage on employment. The main explanatory variables are the ratio of the minimum wage to average income level and its lag. Column (1) lists the result for the whole sample, while columns (2) and (3) compare the results for eastern and other regions, and columns (4) and

Table 14.1 Minimum wage effects on employment (by region)

	(1)	*(2)*	*(3)*	*(4)*	*(5)*
	Whole	*Eastern*	*Central/western*	*Coastal*	*Inland*
mw_avg	−2.134	0.317	0.778	1.362	−0.0264
	(2.241)	(2.971)	(1.441)	(1.832)	(1.531)
mw_avg_{-1}	Y	Y	Y	Y	Y
Individual characteristics	Y	Y	Y	Y	Y
Macro-economic variables, province dummy, year dummy	Y	Y	Y	Y	Y
N	12,861	3081	4358	3935	3504
R^2	0.13	0.140	0.208	0.163	0.187

Note mw_avg and mw_avg_{-1} represent the ratio of the minimum to the average wage and its lag. Robust standard errors are in parentheses

(5) report the result for coastal and inland regions. It shows that the minimum wage has made non-significant negative effects on employment both regionally and nationally. As mentioned above, one of the explanations may be that the minimum wage level is lower than the average wage and even the equilibrium wage, thus producing little effect on equilibrium employment.

Another possible explanation for the non-significant effect of the minimum wage could be due to the mobile rural migrant workers in cities included in the sample. Once unemployed, they may leave for another place or return home, hence unable to be reflected on the impact of the minimum wage on employment. In addition, as shown by Jia (2014), an increase of minimum wages may reduce employment more for female workers. Therefore, we test the minimum wage effects in urban and rural areas separately, and for male and female workers separately. The results are reported in Table 14.2. The effects of the minimum wage are not significant on employment for any of the subgroups, even though for those with rural hukou, employment seems to be reduced more for females in magnitude.

Characterized by different forms of ownership, firm in China may adopt very different management policies in recruiting, firing, and wage setups. This may cause the minimum wage effect to be different for these different types of firms. Table 14.3 presents the different minimum wage effects on employment in different types of enterprises, which indicates that only employees in private and individual enterprises are affected significantly and negatively.

Table 14.2 Minimum wage effects on employment (by gender and hukou)

	Urban hukou		*Rural hukou*	
	Male	*Female*	*Male*	*Female*
mw_avg	−5.316 (3.676)	−4.770 (4.110)	−0.730 (3.312)	−4.598 (4.080)
mw_avg_{-1}	Y	Y	Y	Y
Individual characteristics	Y	Y	Y	Y
Macro-economic variables, province dummy, year dummy	Y	Y	Y	Y
N	4083	3170	8777	7131
Pseudo R^2	0.021	0.020	0.046	0.065

Note Robust standard errors are in parentheses

Table 14.3 Minimum wage effects on employment (by enterprise type)

	Government agency	*Shiye unit*	*SOE*	*Collective firms*	*Private enterprises*	*Foreign companies*
mw_avg	19.03 (13.76)	−16.55 (15.24)	28.02 (18.20)	−19.26 (12.62)	−7.616** (3.139)	−8.731 (37.79)
mw_avg_{-1}	Y	Y	Y	Y	Y	Y
Individual characteristics	Y	Y	Y	Y	Y	Y
Macro-economic variables, province dummy, year dummy	Y	Y	Y	Y	Y	Y
N	501	1632	853	797	5883	216
Pseudo R^2	0.038	0.050	0.069	0.071	0.027	0.132

Note Robust standard errors are in parentheses. **denotes $p<0.05$

Minimum wage policies may affect employment through firms' reactions by adjusting labor costs. With a fixed number of employees, a rise in the minimum wage leads to an increase of the long-run cost. Being aware of that, firms may replace regular employees with temporary workers, which can reduce the loss caused by regular employees with the unsaturated workload and in the meantime offset the effect of the minimum wage regulation. Nevertheless, the cost of adjusting employees may limit the impact of the minimum wage on firms' behavior. As seen in the regression results in Table 14.4, the employment effect of the minimum wage is not significant for the three types of workers.

14.4.2 *Minimum Wage Effects on Employees' Income*

The minimum wage effect on income is not easy to predict. While it can increase the income of employees who use to earn lower than the minimum wage level, it can also reduce income for those who use to earn higher than the minimum wage level due to the firm's intention to offset increased labor cost in the lower end. We examine the effects first for the whole sample and then by regions and other demographic groups.

As shown in column (1) of Table 14.5, the minimum wage variables do not have a significant effect on average income for the whole sample.

Table 14.4 Minimum wage effects on employment (by employment type)

	Regular employment	*Contract employment*	*Temporary worker*
mw_avg	−5.898	−1.244	8.987
	(6.874)	(9.940)	(7.385)
mw_avg_{-1}	Y	Y	Y
Individual characteristics	Y	Y	Y
Macro-economic variables, province dummy, year dummy	Y	Y	Y
N	3746	1526	2019
Pseudo R^2	0.023	0.033	0.017

Note Robust standard errors are in parentheses

Table 14.5 Minimum wage effects on income (by region)

	(1)	*(2)*	*(3)*	*(4)*	*(5)*
	Whole	*Eastern*	*Central/western*	*Costal*	*Inland*
mw_avg	1.433	0.317	0.778	1.362	−0.0264
	(1.126)	(2.971)	(1.441)	(1.832)	(1.531)
mw_avg_{-1}	Y	Y	Y	Y	Y
Individual characteristics	Y	Y	Y	Y	Y
Macro-economic variables, province dummy, year dummy	Y	Y	Y	Y	Y
N	4498	6126	12,485	8637	9974
R^2	0.187	0.046	0.010	0.041	0.014

Note Robust standard errors are in parentheses

We also perform the same analysis for different regions and find no significant effects as shown in other columns of Table 14.5.

We next examine the minimum wage effect on lower-income employees, with the results reported in Table 14.6. A rise in the minimum wage increases income for the lowest-income group and the high-risk group, which is in line with the results obtained by Grossman (1983) and Ma et al. (2012) from different data in China. Compare these results

Table 14.6 Minimum wage effects on income (by income level)

	People with lowest income	*People at risk*
mw_avg	5.665***	2.874***
	(1.502)	(0.275)
mw_avg_{-1}	Y	Y
Individual characteristics	Y	Y
Macro-economic variables, province dummy, year dummy	Y	Y
N	953	647
R^2	0.283	0.951

Note The lowest income group refers to those within the 90% of the minimum wage level. Robust standard errors are in parentheses. ***denotes $p<0.01$

with those in Table 14.5, the non-significant effect for the whole sample could be because the minimum effect is not significant for high-income groups.

Table 14.7 reports the results for the gender difference in minimum wage effects. Females with the lowest income or with high risk respond strongly to the increase of minimum wages. The income of lower-paid females with rural hukou increases significantly with minimum wage adjustments ($p<0.01$), with a magnitude twice as much as that of males. In urban areas, the minimum wage effect on income is not significant for males or females, which is probably because the income level is relatively high already.

14.4.3 Minimum Wage Effects on Working Hours

The above analyses indicate that while higher minimum wages do not result in more job losses, they increase the earnings of low-income workers. If the minimum wage increases firms' labor cost, how do they respond to it? Since staff turnover can lead to higher costs, the employer may find it more desirable to cut working hours to offset the rise of minimum wages instead of cutting the number of staff. The minimum wage effect on working hours can be of crucial importance and may exist for two reasons. First, due to weak enforcement and loopholes in laws and regulations, some employers may increase working hours in one way or another in order to make up the cost increase resulted from higher pays meeting the minimum standard. Second, since the government has set definite minimum hourly wages since 2007, some employers

Table 14.7 Minimum wage effects on income (by gender and hukou)

	Whole		*Urban hukou*		*Rural hukou*	
	Male	*Female*	*Male*	*Female*	*Male*	*Female*
mw_avg	1.433 (1.126)	2.242* (1.285)	1.225 (1.356)	0.269 (1.549)	2.501 (1.922)	5.683*** (2.132)
mw_avg_{-1}	Y	Y	Y	Y	Y	Y
Individual characteristics	Y	Y	Y	Y	Y	Y
Macro-economic variables, province dummy, year dummy	Y	Y	Y	Y	Y	Y
N	4498	2940	2615	1861	1882	1079
R^2	0.187	0.184	0.195	0.225	0.198	0.204

Note Robust standard errors are in parentheses. *denotes $p<0.10$, ***denotes $p<0.01$

may reconsider their policies on staffing size, working hours, and types of employment (permanent staff, contract workers, temporary workers, etc.) and cut down high-cost working hours in order to reduce labor cost.

The report of the results of our analysis for working time in Table 14.8. The results seem to support the second point above: an increased minimum wage leads to a general decline of working hours for Chinese workers, which is consistent with the findings of Machin et al. (2003) and Stewart and Swaffield (2008).

We next compare the minimum wage effect on working time for urban and rural labor force. Table 14.9 shows that the decline in working hours of the rural labor force is greater than that of the urban one, and that working hours are reduced more for rural female workers than for their male counterparts. These may suggest that setting the minimum wage has caused the employers to alter their working arrangements and has led to better pays, fewer working hours, and higher living standards for low-income workers.

Table 14.8 Minimum wage effects on work time (by region)

	(1)	*(2)*	*(3)*
	Whole	*Eastern*	*Central/western*
mw_avg	−2.073**	−7.102***	−1.758*
	(0.834)	(2.533)	(1.011)
mw_avg_{-1}	Y	Y	Y
Individual characteristics	Y	Y	Y
Macro-economic variables, province dummy, year dummy	Y	Y	Y
N	10,500	3081	4358
R^2	0.020	0.140	0.208

Note Robust standard errors are in parentheses. *denotes $p<0.10$, **denotes $p<0.05$, ***denotes $p<0.01$

Table 14.9 Minimum wage effects on work time (by gender and hukou)

	Whole		*Urban hukou*		*Rural hukou*	
	Male	*Female*	*Male*	*Female*	*Male*	*Female*
mw_avg	−2.073**	−3.425***	−1.834**	−1.885*	−2.064*	−3.648***
	(0.834)	(1.013)	(0.932)	(1.129)	(1.164)	(1.351)
mw_avg_{-1}	Y	Y	Y	Y	Y	Y
Individual characteristics	Y	Y	Y	Y	Y	Y
Macro-economic variables, province dummy, year dummy	Y	Y	Y	Y	Y	Y
N	10,500	8110	3271	2385	7228	5725
R^2	0.020	0.027	0.014	0.021	0.021	0.033

Note Robust standard errors are in parentheses. *denotes $p<0.10$, **denotes $p<0.05$, ***denotes $p<0.01$

14.4.4 *Spillover Effects on Working Hours*

The above analysis shows that increases in minimum wages shorten average working hours. In this section, we investigate whether the minimum wage also has a distribution or spillover effect on working hours as it does to workers' income (Stewart 2012). It is possible that when the minimum wage is increased, due to management's adjustment, working loads or hours of certain income groups are significantly increased while other groups are not significantly affected.

We use the same method of Neumark et al. (2004) as we used in Sect. 14.3.2 when analyzing the minimum wage effect on income. The dependent variable is now the working hours of a worker. The target sample contains only employed workers. We perform the analysis for the whole sample and for different groups. For group analysis, we divide the whole sample according to worker's gender, hukou status, type of firm a worker is employed for, type of employment contract, and the region of residence.

Our main estimation interest is the interaction of minimum wage changes and the dummy of a worker's income group. Our estimation results indicate the following: Minimum wage adjustments do not have a significant effect on the relative working hours for different income groups; the results are similar when the analysis is conducted by gender, hukou, contract type, and regions. Two explanations are possible for this finding. First, while an increase of the minimum wage directly increases the labor cost for the employment of low wage workers, it could have indirectly increased the labor cost for the whole labor force, thus reduced average working hours. Second, the reference effect between workers can lead to the reduction of average working hours for the whole labor force when workers compare themselves with others. In the analysis by firm type, we find that only in collective business firms, working hours of low wage workers are significantly lowered by minimum wage adjustments. Other firm types include government agencies, state-owned public units, state-owned business, private business, and other firms. The income of workers is lowest in collective business compared with those in other firms. Since collective businesses have the most flexible employment institution, the minimum wage may affect working hours of the low wage workers the strongest in these firms.

There are many possible ways of dividing a target group into different income groups. Considering that dividing into too many groups may

Table 14.10 Spillover effects of minimum wages on working hours (by firm type)

	(1)	(2)	(3)	(4)	(5)	(6)
<110% MW	8.234	−1.225	1.135	−1.961*	1.672	−6.162
	(9.749)	(0.944)	(1.149)	(1.133)	(1.665)	(6.030)
110–170% MW	41.34	−0.393	−0.612	1.272	0.567	1.222
	(37.94)	(0.462)	(0.465)	(1.659)	(1.442)	(2.258)
Control variables	Y	Y	Y	Y	Y	Y
_cons	−18.61	−1.446***	−0.116	−1.408*	−1.093	−5.185
	(15.12)	(0.413)	(0.717)	(0.820)	(1.985)	(4.540)
N	164	654	252	220	601	61
R^2	0.195	0.058	0.147	0.156	0.093	0.326

Note Columns (1)–(6): (1) government agency; (2) state non-business; (3) state corporate business; (4) collective business; (5) individually owned business; and (6) joint-ventures and others. Robust standard errors are in parentheses. * $p<0.10$, *** $p<0.01$

reduce the sample size in each group, we eventually choose to report the results of dividing the sample into three income groups: lower than 110% of the minimum wage, between 110 and 170% of the minimum wage, and higher than 170% of the minimum wage. Table 14.10 shows the results for this division of income and by firm type. Other estimations for the whole sample, and for other group analyses are omitted as we have summarized the main findings and do not find a significant minimum wage distribution effect on working hours.

14.5 Robustness Check

In the above analyses on the minimum wage effect on employment, wages, and working hours, we have followed previous literature and used minimum wage standards adjusted by coverage months as the explanatory variables. However, the boundary of such adjustments is not clear cut. We check the robustness of the results by substituting the logarithms of the absolute values of the current and previous minimum wages for the two explanatory variables. We report only the results by genders in Table 14.11.[2]

The results for employment show that, with previous minimum wages controlled for, the minimum wage adjustment does not affect employment significantly, but increases wage significantly, slightly more so for females than for males. The last two columns show that minimum wage

Table 14.11 Robustness check

	Employment		*Income*		*Working hours*	
	Male	*Female*	*Male*	*Female*	*Male*	*Female*
Lnmw	−0.201	−0.822	0.604**	0.816***	−0.293	−0.473*
	(0.543)	(0.626)	(0.280)	(0.304)	(0.209)	(0.253)
lnmw_{-1}	Y	Y	Y	Y	Y	Y
Individual characteristics	Y	Y	Y	Y	Y	Y
Macro-economic variables, province dummy, year dummy	Y	Y	Y	Y	Y	Y
N	12,861	10,301	4498	2940	10,500	8110
R^2	0.027	0.027	0.188	0.185	0.019	0.026

Note Robust standard errors are in parentheses. *denotes $p<0.10$, **denotes $p<0.05$, ***denotes $p<0.01$

changes significantly reduce working hours for females by 4.7%, but does not affect male workers' hours significantly. Thus, the result of the robustness check is largely consistent with our earlier analyses and supports similar conclusions.

14.6 Conclusions

This chapter investigates the minimum wage effect on employment, wages, and working hours using a pre-specified model controlling minimum wage of the previous period, individual characteristics, provincial characteristics, and fixed effects of provinces and years. We find that minimum wages have little impact on employment, but have contributions to wage increases, especially for low-income workers, such as female workers and those with rural hukou. Minimum wage adjustments have also significantly reduced working hours, especially for women. This implies that, without significant impact on total production, minimum wages have the potential of increasing the welfare for the low-income workers.

Notes

1. There are few existing surveys that contain information about working hours. Another survey with such information is Rural-Urban Migration in China (RUMIC) with which we have obtained an average of 59 weekly working hours. Since RUMIC focuses on migrant workers, the difference between the two data sets implies that migrant workers work longer hours than the average of those workers in CHNS that include both migrant workers and urban workers. Workers in both data sets work longer than the legal cap 40 hours probably because they contain migrant workers.
2. All the analyses for different subgroups we performed earlier stood the robustness check. Given the limited space, only regression results classified by gender are listed in the table.

References

Card, D., and Krueger, Alan B. 1994. Minimum wages and employment: A case study of the fast-food industry in New Jersey and Pennsylvania. *The American Economic Review*, 84(4): 772–793.

Chen, Jianxian, Shao, Xiaokuai, Murtaza, Ghulam, and Zhao, Zhongxiu. 2014. Factors that influence female labor force supply in China. *Economic Modelling*, 37: 485–491.

Chyi, Hau, and Zhou, Bo. 2014. The effects of tuition reforms on school enrollment in rural China. *Economics of Education Review*, 38: 104–123.

Couch, Kenneth, and Wittenburg, David. 2001. The response of hours of work to increases in the minimum wage. *Southern Economic Journal*, 68(1): 171–177.

Du, Yang, and Pan, Weiguang. 2009. Minimum wage regulation in China and its applications to migrant workers in the urban labor market. *China & World Economy*, 17(2): 79–93.

Flinn, Christopher J. 2006. Minimum wage effects on labor market outcomes under search, matching, and endogenous contact Rates. *Econometrica*, 74(4): 1013–1062.

Grossman, Jean Baldwin. 1983. The impact of the minimum wage on other wages. *Journal of Human Resources*, 18(3): 359–378.

Han, Zhaozhou, and Wei, Zhangjin. 2006. The empirical research on China's minimum wage standard. *Statistical Research*, 1: 35–38 (in Chinese).

Jia, P. 2014. Employment and working hour effects of minimum wage increase: Evidence from China. *China & World Economy*, 22: 61–80.

Linneman, Peter. 1982. The economic impacts of minimum wage laws: A new look at an old question. *Journal of Political Economy*, 90(3): 443–469.

Luo, Xiaolan. 2007. An analysis on the minimum wage's employment effect over the rural-workers in China. *Journal of Finance and Economics*, 11: 114–123 + 143 (in Chinese).

Luo, Xiaolan, and Cong, Shuhai. 2009. Impact of Chinese minimum wage on other wages based on the effect of catching up with wage. *Statistical Research*, 6: 60–65 (in Chinese).

Ma, Shuang, Zhang, Zhe, and Zhu, Xi. 2012. The effect of minimum wage on average wage and employment. *Economic Research*, 5132–5146 (in Chinese).

Machin, Stephen, Manning, Alan, and Rahman, Lupin. 2003. Where the minimum wage bites hard: Introduction of minimum wages to a low wage sector. *Journal of the European Economic Association*, 1(1): 154–180.

Maynerisy, Florian, Poncet, Sandra, and Zhang, Tao. 2014. The cleansing effect of minimum wage minimum wage rules, firm dynamics and aggregate productivity in China. Working Paper. Available at https://www.wto.org/english/res_e/reser_e/gtdw_e/wkshop14_e/florian_mayneris_e.pdf.

Neumark, David. 2001. The employment effects of minimum wages: Evidence from a prespecified research design the employment effects of minimum wages. *Industrial Relations: A Journal of Economy and Society*, 40(1): 121–144.

Neumark, David, Schweitzer, Mark, and Wascher, William. 2004. Minimum wage effects throughout the wage distribution. *The Journal of Human Resources*, 204(2): 425–450.

Neumark, David, and Wascher, William. 1991. Evidence on employment effects of minimum wages and subminimum wage provisions from panel data on state minimum wage laws. NBER Working Papers No.3859, National Bureau of Economic Research.

Rama, Martin. 2001. The consequences of doubling the minimum wage: The case of Indonesia. *Industrial and Labor Relations Review*, 54 (4): 864–881.

Stewart, Mark B. 2012. Wage inequality, minimum wage effects, and spillovers. *Oxford Economic Papers*, 64(4): 616–634.

Stewart, Mark B., and Joanna K. Swaffield. 2008. The other margin: Do minimum wages cause working hours adjustments for low-wage workers? *Economica*, 75(297): 148–167.

Stigler, George J. 1946. The economics of minimum wage legislation. *The American Economic Review*, 36(3): 358–365.

Tong, Dahuan. Does minimum wage standard reduces competition? Xinhua Net, May 2006. Available at http://news.xinhuanet.com/comments/2006-05/10/content_4527876.htm.

Wang, Jing, and Morley Gunderson. 2011. Minimum wage impacts in China: Estimates from a prespecified research design, 2000–2007. *Contemporary Economic Policy*, 29(3): 392–406.

Wang, Jing, and Morley Gunderson. 2012. Minimum wage effects on employment and wages: Dif-in-dif estimates from eastern China. *International Journal of Manpower*, 33(8): 860–876.

Wang, Xianghong. 2012. When workers do not know—The behavioral effects of minimum wage laws revisited. *The Journal of Economic Psychology*, 33: 951–962.

Ward, Patrick S. 2014. Measuring the level and inequality of wealth: An application to China. *Review of Income and Wealth*, 60(4): 613–635.

Xiao, Xiao-Yong, and Bao-Lin Xiang. 2009. The impact of minimum wage policy on wages and employment in China. Information management, innovation management and industrial engineering, International Conference on. Vol. 2. IEEE.

Zhang, Wuchang. The curse of minimum wage. *Southern Weekly*, April 2004. Available at http://view.news.qq.com/a/20070422/000006.htm.

The manufacturer's authorised representative in the EU is Springer Nature Customer Service Centre GmbH, Europaplatz 3, 69115 Heidelberg, Germany. If you have any concerns regarding our products, please contact ProductSafety@springernature.com

Printed and bound by CPI Group (UK) Ltd, Croydon, CR0 4YY

25/09/2026

02222881-0004